WITHDRAWN

MEDIÆVAL ROMANCE IN ENGLAND

MEDIÆVAL ROMANCE IN ENGLAND

A STUDY OF THE SOURCES
AND ANALOGUES OF THE NON-CYCLIC
METRICAL ROMANCES

By

LAURA A. HIBBARD
(MRS. LAURA HIBBARD LOOMIS)

Formerly Professor of English Literature,
Wellesley College

New Edition with Supplementary
Bibliographical Index
(1926-1959)

Burt Franklin Bibliographical and Reference Series # XVII

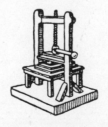

BURT FRANKLIN
New York 25, N. Y.

1960

Published by
BURT FRANKLIN
514 West 113th Street
New York 25, N. Y.

Printed in the United States of America by

NOBLE OFFSET PRINTERS, INC.

TO

THE MEMORY OF

GERTRUDE SCHOEPPERLE LOOMIS

"Truth lies hid in the trappings of a tale."

PREFACE

At the end of the twelfth century there were, according to Jean Bodel, but the three " matières," of France, of Britain, and of " Rome la grant," of which men wished to hear. This observation was as remarkably wrong as are most of the generalizations offered by critics concerning the literary tastes of their own time. For court circles, for the literary elect, the famous cycles of Carolingian, of Arthurian, and of pseudo-classical tales, were certainly the fashion, but so, likewise, and for a much longer period, if we may judge from the number of surviving manuscripts and allusions to stories of wholly different provenance, were what may be called the non-cyclic romances. These were the *romans d'aventure:* the local legends, the traditional tales, which poets could transform into romantic guise. Men who used materials such as these ranged free in them as life and language and taste itself; they drew at will on the great storehouse of folk lore, of local legend, of religious and patriotic tradition, — to say nothing of individual invention. They imitated the style, epic or romantic, of the traditional cycles, and they developed to the full the formulas of speech and theme, of incident and character, in short, the stock materials of mediæval fiction.

Investigation in this great body of miscellaneous romance is no new thing. Single legends and special themes have long been studied with scrupulous care. In the case of certain legends such as those of *Crescentia* (*Florence of Rome*), or of *Constance,* the number of versions discovered has been so large that scholars have sometimes referred to the group itself as a saga or a cycle. But versions of these stories are always essentially the same; they have none of that continuity of character and of incident which is found in a series of romances connected with a favorite hero like Gawain or with a court like Charlemagne's. They are not cyclic in any true sense of the word, but they do afford, in the very multiplicity of their texts, irrefutable proof of their mediæval popularity. Of group study of these non-cyclic romances, there has been, however, comparatively little. Langlois recognized that their value for the social historian was superior to that of the cyclic romances and he, accordingly, based his study of *La Société Française au XIIIe Siècle* (3rd ed., 1911) on ten *romans d'aventure,* on *Joufroi, Guillaume de Dôle, L'Escoufle,* on the *Châtelain de Couci,* and others. In her study of *Le Roman Idyllique dans le Moyen Age* (1913), Madame Lot-Borodine made use of *Floire et Blancheflor* and *Guillaume de Palerme* for illustration of a literary type, of a certain style and spirit, that can hardly be paralleled among the more standardized cycles of romantic literature. Deutschbein in his *Sagengeschichte Englands* (1906) emphasized the historical aspects of legends that culminated in such romances as *Horn, Havelok,* and *Guy of Warwick.*

The amount of intensive work that has been done on the individual non-cyclic romances and the lack of any comprehensive effort to summarize the results have led almost equally to the present undertaking. For the purpose of selection the Middle English romances of this type offered a convenient and somewhat neglected group with which to begin. Though a few of them are relatively unimportant, others are versions of some of the most famous European stories of the Middle Ages, and for the sake of convenient reference it has seemed well to include the less with the more important. Each romance is treated individually in a section, one part of which deals with *Versions,* and one with the *Origins* of the tale. Under *Versions* I have attempted to give something of a life history of each legend by listing all of the literary versions which were composed before 1500, and by indicating so far as possible their relationship. In the section on *Origins* I have recorded the opinions of scholars on the historical and legendary elements that gave rise to the story and have tried to set forth the most important *motifs* which characterize the different versions. The *Index of Matters and Literature* at the close of the book is designed to co-ordinate this material and to reveal for these romances, as the similar index in Volume V of Professor Child's monumental edition of *The English and Scottish Ballads* revealed for the ballads, the recurrent themes, the stock situations, characters, incidents, properties, the dominating conceptions, which mark the favorite patterns of mediæval story-tellers as diverse in purpose and ability as the authors of these romances.

The plan and scope of this book obviously differentiate it from earlier studies on Middle English romance. Dr. Billings's *Guide to the Middle English Metrical Romances*, 1901, 1905, the plan of which was in part suggested by Körting's *Grundriss der Geschichte der engl. Literatur* (3rd ed., 1899), took up only seven of the romances treated here. Professor Wells's invaluable *Manual of the Writings in Middle English* (1916) treated all but two. The fact, however, that he was surveying the whole of Middle English literature naturally limited his discussion of each romance to the briefest possible statement. Especially is this true of his reference to its sources and history, the two aspects which are chiefly developed here. Between his book and this there is a certain necessary duplication of information concerning the manuscripts, dates, and dialects, of the Middle English texts, but in each case the work is of wholly independent character. In the present instance all this material was presented as a doctoral dissertation to the University of Chicago in 1916, shortly before the publication of the *Manual*. Since then the text has been amplified, as has the whole bibliography, by the inclusion of references extending through January, 1923.

A word must be said concerning a departure here in bibliographical method, the wisdom of which remains to be proved. In general the bibliographies appended to each romance have been confined to studies published since 1900. The amazing volume and progress of investigations in this field is thus made plain, and the overweighting of these lists with much that is now discredited, is avoided. On the other hand, it is hoped that no earlier study of enduring worth has been neglected, for to such works full reference is made in the course of the appropriate discussion or in supplementary bibliographical lists. In these discussions a citation with the author's name and page reference only, indicates a work published since 1900 for which complete information is given in the final, alphabetically arranged bibliography at the end of each section. Works of general reference, cited by the author's name and a brief title, are fully described in the Table of Abbreviations.

" The fruit of every tale is for to seye " one's thanks. My own go most warmly to the librarians of the British Museum, of Harvard University, of Wellesley, and of the University of Chicago, who courteously facilitated my work; to Professor Manly and to Professor Nitze of the University of Chicago who gave valuable counsel on my dissertation; to my colleagues, Professor Martha Hale Shackford and Miss Anne K. Tuell; and to my friend and comrade, Gertrude Schoepperle Loomis, who followed this study through all but its latest stages. To the memory of her who was as distinguished an Arthurian scholar as she was keen a lover of all romance, the book is now dedicated.

In conclusion I wish to express my grateful appreciation for the honor of having this volume included in the Wellesley College Semi-Centennial Series.

Laura A. Hibbard

CONTENTS

MEDIÆVAL ROMANCE IN ENGLAND

I. ROMANCES OF TRIAL AND FAITH

SIR ISUMBRAS

VERSIONS. The mediæval mind was not often free from some preoccupation with spiritual destiny. The problem of salvation was immediate and terrible, and the nature of extremest sin and extremest virtue was frequently a subject for frightened speculation. Out of such meditations, which had in them much that was akin to Eastern habits of thought, grew the legend of the Man Tried by Fate. Its hero was Job-like; he was suddenly bereft of home and wealth and family, but he lived with uncomplaining patience until he was at last repossessed of all that he had lost. The theme made an obvious appeal to the pious and to the fatalistic, and its development almost inevitably suggested romantic possibilities. Gerould (pp. 354–72) has listed eight mediæval literary versions belonging to western Europe, and of these all but two, the various texts of the famous legend of Saint Eustache, and the exemplum in the *Gesta Romanorum* (*EETSES*, xxxIII, 87), are highly developed romances. They include the long twelfth-century French romance *Guillaume d'Angleterre* (ed. Foerster, Roman Bibliothek, xx, Halle, 1911); a Middle High German romance, *Wilhelm von Wenden* (Toischer, Prague, 1876), by Ulrich von Eschenbach, who wrote between 1287 and 1297, a thirteenth-century Swabian romance, *Die Gute Frau* (Sommer, *Zts. f. deut. Alterthum*, II, 385 ff.); the early fourteenth-century Spanish romance, *El Cavallero Cifar* (Michelant, Tübingen, 1872), the Middle English romance of *Sir Isumbras*, and a German poem of the fifteenth century, *Der Graf von Savoien* (Eschenburg, Denkmäler, 1799, p. 347). To the same group

3

belong the folk versions, the Danish ballad of Sakarias (Grundtvig, II, 605), the Breton ballads of the King of Romani (Luzel, *Chants populaires*, 1868, I, 179 ff.), and the less truly popular German folk-song about St. Hubert (Simrock, *Deut. Sagen*, p. 46).

In comparison with many of these versions *Isumbras* occupies a modest place. It contains 804 lines, written in the twelve-line tail-rime stanza and in well-worn minstrel phrases. Schleich (p. 97) believed it must have originated in the northeastern Midland district, and as it is mentioned in the *Cursor Mundi* it must have attained some popularity before 1320. It survives in one late fourteenth-century manuscript, that of Caius College, in five manuscripts of the fifteenth and one of the sixteenth century, as well as in William Copland's undated edition and two fragmentary prints.

Though the condensation of the story emphasizes some " preposterous " elements in the original ecclesiastical romance, and though the humble minstrel author of *Isumbras* makes no pretenses at originality of diction, the poem is not without redeeming touches. There is occasionally a blunt realism about it. Thus we are told, after the hero's troubles begin, of the dreary " hirdemen " who accost Isumbras with the news that there is not left " a stotte unto youre plowghe "; we hear that the wretched family of the once proud nobleman suffer in the wood where they see nothing that " come of corn " but only, on " the holtes hare," " the floures of the thorns." In many versions of the original legend, the hero performs manual labor during the period of his humiliation, but it is only the North Midland poet of *Isumbras* who makes his hero labor in a quarry as a " smethyman " carrying out " irynstone," and blowing the bellows at a yeoman's hire until at last he himself becomes a " smethyman " able to forge his own " grymly growndyn gare " and a complete suit of armor. With typical English delight in physical prowess the poet describes how Isumbras can put the stone and how, when some jesters at court, thinking him only a poor palmer, mount him on " ane crokede stede " and send him to a tournament, he does so mightily that the queen laughs out, " My palmere es styffe enoghe, — he is worthi to fede! "

ORIGIN. It is with the earliest western literary version, i.e. the legend of St. Eustache, that the study of origins must begin. Placidus, according to the story, is a Roman general who in the time of Trajan is converted by the sight of a crucifix which appears between the horns of a stag which he is hunting. He is told by the stag that he must be tried by sufferings. Misfortunes immediately overtake him; he loses his servants and cattle through pestilence, and his wife and children through robbery, sailors taking his wife and wild animals his children. For fifteen years he works as a laborer and then again becomes a commander and is served by his own two sons who are ignorant of their parentage. Their mother, happening to lodge the two boys, overhears their talk; she recognizes them and the three return to Rome where they are reunited to Placidus, or Eustathius, according to the name he receives at baptism. Later, under Hadrian, the entire family suffers martyrdom.

In this story Delehaye (p. 182) distinguished three sections, the miraculous conversion, the adventures of the separated family, and the martyrdom. Though Eustache has been considered a Roman saint, there seems no historical basis even for the concluding " passion," and Delehaye (p. 209) was probably right in calling the legend simply a literary composition in hagiographical form. W. Meyer (1915) contended that the oldest version of this legend is the Latin text printed by him from manuscripts dating from the ninth century. He believed (1916, p. 766) that the original Latin version was composed in the fifth or sixth century, was translated after 700 A.D. into Greek and so passed into the East where the story, bereft of the conversion and martyrdom episodes, entered upon an independent life. This view was in flat contradiction to the one held by Gerould, Monteverdi, and Bousset, who thought that the original Eastern story of the Man Tried by Fate was translated into Greek, was known to John of Damascus in the eighth century as the legend of St. Eustache, and was translated from Greek into Latin. Gerould (pp. 344–53) listed some sixteen eastern versions of the story of the Man Tried by Fate. These were in Sanskrit, Singhalese, Arabic, Persian, Hebrew, Turkish, and Armenian, and to them others have been added (Lüdtke, 1917; Meyer, 1917, p. 81). Certain correspondences between some of the latest forms of these tales and the Greek *Placidas* furnished Hilka and Meyer (1917, pp. 92–93) with an argument for their view of the Latin-Greek-Oriental origin of the story, but it does not appear that they considered the possible retroactive influence of the saint legend itself, which Gerould (p. 385) suggested in connection with an Armenian tale narrated in the nineteenth century. Nor did they consider the story which may well have been the kernel of the saint legend, the tale of the future Buddha who appeared in the form of a golden stag to a king over-fond of hunting (Garbe, pp. 538–46).[1] The pre-Christian story offers the earliest instance known of this type of Miraculous Conversion, and predicates an Eastern origin for part of the Eustache legend. Bousset's recent studies of the second part of the legend, the " Wiedererkennungs Märchen," strengthen previous arguments for its Oriental origin.

Whatever its earlier history, by the tenth century the legend of St. Eustache was well known in western Europe. The Latin versions were translated into most of the vernacular languages.[2] In England the history of the legend may be traced from Ælfric's Anglo-Saxon version, written about 996, to the play of Placidus acted at Braintree, Essex, in 1534 (Chambers, *Med. Stage*, II,

---

[1] Cf. *Jataka* XII of the collection in Pali of the stories of the former existences of Buddha (trans. Cambridge, 1895–1907). Three scenes from this conversion story were represented on the great stūpa of Bharhut in India as early as 200 B.C. The citation of this story does away with the difficulty noted by Gerould (p. 386) in explaining the stag incident in the Eustache legend. In later times it was connected with SS. Hubert, Julian, Felix of Valois and others (Garbe, pp. 538–46). Cf. Pschmadt, *Die Sage von der verfolgten Hind*, Greifswald, 1911; Ogle, " The Stag Messenger," *Amer. Jour. Phil.* XXXVII, 411 ff. (1916). Delehaye (pp. 193–210) rejected the idea of any direct connection of the western legend with the eastern tales, although acknowledging their astonishing similarity. But his explanation of them as unrelated folk-tales is not convincing.

[2] Cf. Gerould, p. 354; Meyer, pp. 227 ff.; Delehaye, 1919, p. 176. Monteverdi, *Studi Med.* 1910, pp. 392 ff., gave the fullest account of the Greek and Latin texts; see also p. 418 for notes on the relics of St. Eustache, and App. III for some account of the legend in art. For the versions in French, Italian, Spanish, English, German, Irish, see Monteverdi, II, 27–105 (Bergamo). Fisher, 1917, p. 2, recorded eleven versions in French verse (13th–15th centuries) and four in French prose. In *Rom.* XXXVI, Meyer printed the text of a short thirteenth-century French monorimed poem (Egerton 1066) which shows the influence of the *chansons de geste*. The French poem of 1572 verses in quatrains printed by Ott (Bibl. Nat. Paris, MS. 1374), is more closely related to the Latin versions.

342), or to Henry Chettle's in 1599 (Gerould, *Saints Legends,* Index). With such widespread diffusion both in England and on the Continent as the extant texts reveal, it is not surprising that the legend became the source of many romances, or at least a dominating influence upon them. In the case of the Spanish romance, *El Cavallero Cifar,* the dependence of the romance on the legend is shown not only by the order and nature of identical incidents, but by direct reference to the legend itself (Wagner, pp. 13-29). The romances, like the Eastern tales, in general parallel only the second part of the Eustache legend, the story of the separation and reunion of the family.

In *Isumbras* the hero is pictured as " kynge of curtasye," rich and generous, but over-proud. To him divine warning comes through a bird, as it does also to the hero in the *Gesta* version and in the Breton ballad. The fact that these three versions are alike in having the Bird Warning, and also agree in many subsequent details, suggests some possible relationship between them (Gerould, p. 416). The Choice of Woe, of poverty and woe in youth or in age in *Isumbras,* eternal sorrow or ten years of misery in *Der Graf von Savoien,* woe on earth or in the hereafter in the Danish ballad, *Sakarias,* is found only in the later versions of the Eustache legend, such as that given by Vincent of Beauvais, *Speculum Historiale,* x, cap. 58-61, or in the *Legenda Aurea.* Since this *motif* appears in at least seven independent tales in which the choice is presented to a woman by the Virgin, Gerould (pp. 355, 384, 424-36) believed that it was an originally separate story which was later absorbed by the St. Eustache legend.

The most characteristic incidents linking the legend and the romances are those which tell of the separation of the family. In *Isumbras* the knight carries one son across the water but when he returns a lion carries the first child away, a leopard the second, and ultimately a unicorn takes the third. In the Breton ballad also three children are mentioned; in other versions there are but two. In *Guillaume, Wilhelm,* and *Gute Frau* the children (twins) are born after their parents' departure from home, and this feature connects the *motif* of the Loss of the Children with such romances as *Octavian, Valentine and Orson, La belle Hélène de Constantinople, Beves of Hampton,*

Ogier, Eglamour, and *Torrent of Portyngale.* In these tales a young wife, after she has been driven from her home, gives birth to two children who are stolen from her by wild animals. The vogue of this wildly improbable episode in all these European variants contrasts oddly with the more sober Oriental versions in which the children are usually separated from their parents by robbers, by shipwreck, or by the father's act of penance in deliberately giving them away. In every case the loss of the children seems an integral and natural part of the story of the Man (or Woman) Tried by Fate.³ The Loss of the Wife takes place in *Isumbras, Cifar,* and *Wilhelm* after the loss of the children; in the Eustache legend, the *Gesta, Sakarias,* and the Breton ballad before the children are stolen. The Sale of the Wife (Verkauf der Frau) to which the unfortunate husband is forced by violence in *Isumbras, Guillaume,* and *Graf* is, perhaps, as Jordan (p. 365) surmised, a concession to European taste, for in certain Oriental tales and in even *Die Gute Frau,* the wife herself advises this extreme measure. Likewise the preservation of the heroine's chastity when she is in the hands of her captors is on the whole a distinctive Occidental trait (Gerould, p. 372). But it is not possible, as Monteverdi (*Studi Med.,* III, 227 ff.) pointed out, to accept Jordan's belief that this *motif* (Scheinehe) can determine the relationship of the versions.⁴

The European stories are distinguished by a characteristic subsidiary theme which in *Guillaume, Wilhelm, Die Gute Frau, Isumbras,* and *Graf,* was grafted on the legend of the Man Tried by Fate. *Eustache* has no trace of it. In several stories, *Camaralzaman* in the *Arabian Nights* (Chauvin, *Bibliographie des*

³ In general, stories of the Woman Tried by Fate belong to the type best known as the Calumniated Wife. Gerould (p. 441) noted the danger of deriving these diverse stories from *Eustache* with which they often have, in common, only the incident of the Loss of the Children. *Hélène* alone seems clearly to have borrowed from the legend. In the others the use of the incident is due to the influence of the romances themselves. See *Octavian* here.

⁴ Jordan argued from the fact that in one group of versions the Pretended Marriage is contracted by the wife, and in *Cifar,* in the Arab tale of the "king who lost all" (Chauvin, *Bibl. des Ouvrages Arabes,* VI, p. 164), and in *Beves,* by the husband, who marries the ruler of a country but who, in the hope of recovering his wife, puts off the consummation of his marriage with the princess of the land. Since these three versions have hardly anything more than this one trait in common, no argument can be based upon them. The suggested derivation of the Civile episode in *Beves* from the lost source of *Cifar* is altogether fictitious.

Ouvrages Arabes, IV, 204–12, 1900), and other Eastern variants, in the old French romance, *L'Escoufle,* c. 1204 (ed. Meyer, SATF, 1894), in the various versions of *Pierre de Provence et la belle Maguelonne* (ed. A. Biedermann, Paris, Halle, 1915), one important theme is that of a Lost Treasure. In *Isumbras* it is the gold given to the hero for his wife by the heathens who had carried her off. Isumbras wraps it in his " mantill of skarlet rede," and this an eagle carries away. In the stories just listed, though the circumstances of the hero and heroine are differently motivated from those in the Man Tried by Fate, they are alike in telling of the separation of the lovers, and of their loss through a bird's theft of some object of value. Gerould (p. 412) believed that the Lost Treasure story must have come independently from Asia to Europe, and that at least as early as the twelfth century, it had been incorporated in the Eustache story as represented by *Guillaume d'Engleterre.*

The adventures of the separated family are told with considerable variation. In *Isumbras,* after serving as a smith for seven years the hero fights victoriously in his self-made arms against the Saracens. After many wanderings he comes as a palmer to the land where his wife reigns as queen. Unrecognized, he serves humbly in her court until he is identified by the gold wrapped in his red mantle. This Lost Treasure, in a fashion peculiar to such stories, he had recovered from a bird's nest. He is crowned king and later, in a great battle against the heathen, is aided by his sons who ride on animals like those which had stolen them. The youths announce their parentage and the long severed family is at last reunited. In *Isumbras, Guillaume, Wilhelm, Gute Frau, Graf,* and *Sakarias,* the heroine, when she is separated from her husband, suffers no hardship but through a Marriage in Name or by popular election speedily rises to great place. In this detail the romances differ notably from the St. Eustache legend in which the heroine's humble life of self-support suggests the influence of the legendary story of Helen, the mother of Constantine.[5] The scene in *Isumbras* in which the husband, unrecognized, re-

[5] See *Emare* here. In the *Gesta* tale and the Breton ballad the wife serves as a beggar and a servant. It is a realistic detail in *Isumbras* that she is pictured as going into battle clad " in armour, als scho were a knyghte " (l. 746).

ceives the bounty of his wife may be paralleled by similar ones
in *Beves of Hampton, Guy of Warwick* and *Die Gute Frau*.
The Treasure serves as a Recognition Token in *Isumbras*, and
various other tokens appear in the different versions; in *Guillaume*, for instance, a horn and ring are mentioned. In the
Eustache legend the recognition is accomplished through the
wife's overhearing her two sons tell how they were stolen by
animals, and then through her going to Placidus, their commanding general, to ask for help.

Despite all the romantic and fabulous elements in *Isumbras*,
its structural likeness to the legend of St. Eustache remains
apparent. In spirit too it keeps the insistent note of piety, of
joy " Goddes werkkes for to wyrke."

BIBLIOGRAPHY

TEXTS: (1) C, Caius College, Cam. 175 (A, IX) summarized by Ellis,
Specimens, pp. 479–91 (1848); MS. described, J. Zupitza, *Eng. Stud.*
XIV, 321; (2) T, Thornton MS. Lincoln Cathedral, ed. Halliwell,
Thornton Romances, pp. 88–120, Camden Soc., 1844; see also p.
268 for selection from C; reëd. F. S. Ellis, Kelmscott Press, 1897; (3)
L, Cott. Cal. A II, Brit. Mus., cf. Ward, *Cat. of Romances*, I, 180, 760;
(4) A, Ashmole 61, Oxf. cf. Halliwell, p. 268; (5) E, Advocates Lib. 19,
3, 1, Edin., cf. Halliwell, p. 267; (6) N, Royal Library, Naples, XIII, B.
29, (dated 1457), ed. Kölbing, *Eng. Stud.* III, 200; (7) G, Gray's Inn,
Lond. Early Editions: (8) c, Copland, undated, repr. Utterson, I, 77
ff.; (9) d, Douce fragment 78, Oxf.; (10) D, Douce 261; (11) M,
Malone 941, Bodleian, Oxf., a few lines; cf. *Percy Folio*, ed. Hales and
Furnivall, I, 532; Zupitza, *Archiv.* 88, 72. A critical edition was published by Zupitza and G. Schleich in *Palaestra* xv, 128 pp., Berlin, 1901,
Stammbaum, p. 87. Rev. *Literaturbl.* XXIII, p. 18 (1903).

STUDIES: Cf. Wells, *Manual*, p. 781.
Bousset, W. " Die Geschichte eines Wiedererkennungsmärchens." *Nachrichten von der König. Gesellschaft — -zu Göttingen*, Philol. hist.
Kl. pp. 469–551 (1916): pp. 703–45 (1917).
Delehaye, H. " La Légende de Saint Eustache." *Bull. de la classe des
lettres, Acad. roy. de Belgique*, IV, 175–210 (1919). Bibliog. p. 176.
Esposito, M. " La vie de S. Eustache " (Anglo-Norman, Dublin MS.).
Florence, 1921.
Fisher, J. R. " La Vie de St. Eustache par Pierre de Beauvais." *Rom.
Rev.* VIII, 1–67 (1917).
Garbe, R. " Contributions of Buddhism to Christianity " (St. Eusta-

chius, pp. 538–50). *The Monist*, XXI, Chicago, 1911. Trans. from *Deutsche Rundschau*, 1910–11.

Gerould, G. H. "The Eustache Legend, Forerunners, Congeners, and Derivatives." . . . *PMLA*. XIX, 335–448 (1904).

Hilka, A. u. W. Meyer. "Ueber die neu-aramäische Placidas-Wandergeschichte." *Nachrichten . . . zu Göttingen*, pp. 80–95 (1917).

Jordan, L. "Die Eustachiuslegende, Christians Wilhelmsleben, Boeve de Hanstone u. ihre orientalischen Verwandten." *Archiv*, CXXI, 341–67 (1908).

Lüdtke, W. "Neue Texte zur Geschichte eines Wiedererkennungsmärchens u. zum Text der Placidas-Legende." *Nachrichten . . . zu Göttingen*, pp. 746–760 (1917).

Meyer, P. "Fragment d'une Vie de S. Eustache." *Rom.* XXXVI, 12–28 (1907).

Meyer, W. "Der Rythmus über den h. Placidas-Eustasius." *Nachrichten . . . zu Göttingen*, pp. 226–87 (1915); 1916, pp. 745–799. See Hilka.

Monteverdi, A. *I testi della Leggenda di S. Eustachio*, Bergamo, 1909–10 (2 vols.); *Studi Medievali*, III, 169–226, 392–498.

Ogden, P. *A Comparative Study of the Poem Guillaume d'Angleterre*. Diss. Baltimore, 1900.

Ott, A. C. "Das altfrz. Eustachiusleben." *Rom. Forsch.*, XXXII, 481–607 (1912).

Schleich. See Texts.

Speyer, G. S. "Buddhistische elementen in eenige episoden uit de Legenden van St. Hubertus en St. Eustachius." *Theologisch Tijdschrift*, XL, 427–53. Rev. Delehaye, *Le Muséon*, N.S. XIII, 91–100, Louvain, 1912.

Wagner, C. P. "The Sources of El Cavallero Cifar." *Revue Hispanique*, X, 5–104 (1903).

FLORENCE OF ROME

VERSIONS. Among the mediæval stories of innocent women who suffer a succession of trials and misfortunes, the *Crescentia* story, to which the various versions of *Florence of Rome* belong, is made distinctive by two traits: (1) in the absence of the heroine's husband it is always his own brother who first approaches her with offers of love (*Le conte de la femme chaste convoitée par son beau-frère*); and (2) it is the lady's fame as a healer which ultimately brings together those who have wronged her and who then confess their crimes against her (Wallensköld, 2, p. 105). The story enjoyed a popularity which makes difficult the classification or even the enumeration of the various versions. Of these more than one hundred, dating from the twelfth to the nineteenth century, have been listed by various scholars (Stefanović, p. 467). Karl (p. 164), indeed, referred to two hundred and sixty versions but it is probable that such a list would involve a large amount of repetition. Here only the most important groups of texts can be noted.

The type name for the story comes from what is commonly believed to be the oldest European text, the story of *Crescentia* in the Old High German *Kaiserchronik*, v. 11,352 ff. (ed. E. Schroeder, 1892). This was written about 1150, and other versions in verse and prose of the same text appeared in the thirteenth and fourteenth centuries. The episode was incorporated in practically the same form as that in the *Kaiserchronik* in the *Sächsische Weltchronik*, 1237–1251 (ed. L. Weiland, *Mon. Germ. Hist.*, 1877, p. 139), and in later times had a long history in Volksbuch form. In Wallensköld's opinion (1, p. 60) the *Crescentia* story itself was but a variant of an anonymous *Miracle de Vierge* which other scholars have been inclined to think represented a second and separate group of stories.

The earliest text of the *Miracle* is a twelfth-century prose account (ed. Wallensköld, 1, p. 116 ff.), but in all some thirty-eight texts are known. These include not only versions of the *Miracle* proper, but also the abbreviated account of it given in *Les Vies des Pères* (Le Grand d'Aussy, *Fabliaux*, 1829, v, 125) and in the legend of St. Guglielma (Stefanović, pp. 552-54). The anony- mous *Miracle* itself, according to Wallensköld's enumeration (1, pp. 32-36), exists in four forms, in Latin, in French, in Dutch, and in Icelandic. To these Hilka (p. 136) added three other Latin texts of the fourteenth and the fifteenth centuries. The *Miracle* was introduced into the *Speculum Historiale*, 1244- 54, Bk. VII, cap. 90-92, of Vincent of Beauvais, and so into the many later translations in French, Dutch, and Italian of Vin- cent's work. It was also used as an exemplum by Étienne de Bourbon (1261) in his *Liber de Septem Donis;* by Humbert de Romans (d. 1277) in his *Liber de abundantia exemplorum;* by the author of the *Alphabetum Narrationum*, a book subsequently translated into Spanish and English; by Jean de Garlande in his *Stella Maris* (1288); by Johannes Junior in the *Scala Celi* in the early part of the fourteenth century; by Johannes Herold in his *Promptuarium de Miraculis*, 1435-40; and by the Italian, Gabriel Bareleta (before 1480), in his *Sermones*. As an exem- plum the story was usually given under the heading *Castitas*. In French verse the *Miracle* was retold before 1222 by Gautier de Coincy (Méon, *Nouv. Recueil*, 1823, II, 1-128) in the famous *Miracles de Notre Dame* of which so many manuscripts survive (Wallensköld, 1, p. 37; 2, pp. 118-123). A fourteenth-century Spanish prose translation of Gautier's version of *L'Impératrice de Rome* is known (Mussafia, *Sitz. d. kais. Akad. Ph. hist. Cl.* Vienna, LIII, 508 ff.). In the fourteenth century the *Miracle* was dramatized in France (*Miracles*, 1879, *SATF.*, IV, 234), and again in the fifteenth century turned into French prose by Jean Miélot. In Germany the story appeared in *Der Seelen Trost* (Pfeiffer, *Die deut. Mundarten*, 1856, II, 7-9), a religious book of exempla which was translated into Dutch, Swedish, and Danish; in a fifteenth-century poem of Hans Rosenblüt of Nuremberg; in a " comédie," *Die Unschuldig Keyserin von Rom* of Hans Sachs, 1551; and in a poem of the meistersinger of the sixteenth cen- tury, Albrecht Baumholtz (Wallensköld, 1, pp. 57-59; App. M). In Italy the content of the Latin miracle was well known in popular and dramatic form in the sixteenth and seventeenth centuries, but the earliest extant version of the story is the four-

teenth-century *Istoria di Santa Guglielma,* which differs considerably from the older *Miracle.* In the fifteenth century the
dramatization of this *Istoria* by Antonia Pulci gave a new im-
petus to this particular form of the story (Wallensköld, 1, pp.
46–54; 2, pp. 120–21).

The third group of stories includes the various redactions to
which the heroine gives her name, Florence of Rome. Of a
French *chanson d'aventure* of 6410 lines (ed. Wallensköld, Paris,
1909), composed in the first quarter [1] of the thirteenth century,
there are extant two thirteenth-century manuscripts (PM) and
a late thirteenth-century fragment (L; cf. Ward, *Cat. of Romances,* 1, 711). Besides this there are four versions of approximately the same type: an early fourteenth-century *Dit de Florence* (D) in quatrains (ed. Jubinal, *Nouv. Recueil,* 1839); a
long fifteenth-century version of 4562 alexandrine verses (Q, ed.
Wallensköld, *Florence,* 1909, pp. 130 ff.); the fifteenth-century
Middle English poem (R); and a prose version in Spanish (S)
(ed. Amador de los Ríos, *Historia crítica,* 1864, v, 391–468) of
the late fourteenth or early fifteenth century. The relations of
these versions have been studied with varying results by Wenzel
(p. 62), Knobbe, and Wallensköld. The last (*Flor.,* p. 14; 26)
agreed with Knobbe in finding that the texts LMPS (D?) form
one group which may be distinguished from R and L, the two
texts which apparently represent independent derivatives of the
lost original.

The single Middle English version, *Le Bone Florence,* which
is written in the North-Midland dialect (Knobbe, p. 49), is
what Ritson terms " an excellent old romance." It contains 2187
lines in the twelve-line, tail-rime stanza; and a comparison with
the extant French texts, three of which extend to over four
thousand lines, shows a resolute shortening of the original. To
this the English version often refers as the " boke " (ll. 84, 491,

---

[1] Wallensköld, 2, pp. 99 ff., noted that the earliest French text of *Florence*
contains a reference to *Guillaume de Dole* or the *Roman de la Rose,* c. 1200,
and that the *Roman de la Violette,* c. 1225–30, refers to *Florence.* These dates
serve to place the *chanson d'aventure* between 1200 and 1230. The earliest
reference to the story of *Florence* is found in *La Naissance de la Chevalier
au Cygne* (ed. Todd, *PMLA.* 1889, l. 3098), which is ascribed to the end of
the twelfth or the beginning of the thirteenth century. Wallensköld, p. 104,
thought the reference was not to an extant text of *Florence,* but to the lost
original of the extant versions.

869), the " romance " (ll. 643, 1164, 1539), etc. The author even
suggests that he had consulted more than one version of the story
(l. 84), and in l. 2173 states that the story was written down by
" Pope Symonde " in the " cronykyls of Rome," a pseudonym,
perhaps, for that mysterious " boke of Rome " of which some
scholars are now inclined to think the *Gesta Romanorum* is in
some sort an imitation (Rickert, *Emaré, EETSES* 99, p. 48, n.
2). The Middle English poet seems to have taken something
from Benoit's *Roman de Troie* (Knobbe, p. 7), but the large
number of fantastically spelled classical names which he introduces, he may well have derived from his French original. A
reference in l. 1888 to Sir Lucius Ibarnyus as the founder of
" Beverfayre," in the French versions Beau-Repaire, — a convent said to have been founded by Julius Caesar, — has been
taken as an indication that the author had in mind the Lucius
Iberius of the alliterative *Morte Arthure*, l. 86 (Knobbe, p. 9).
More convincing is the evidence that he was familiar with another Middle English poem, the *King of Tars*, which, like *Florence*, sets forth the grief of a Christian princess who mourns
when a heathen suitor attacks her father's land that so many
men should die for her sake (Siefkin, p. 43). It is possible,
however, that this passage in the *King of Tars* or its original
" geste," was itself influenced by the French original of *Florence*.

The Middle English redactor of *Florence* was of a strongly
religious cast of mind and he tells his story not for the sake of
diversion, but for the picture it gives of Christian fortitude.
The chastity of his heroine, for instance, is not saved by a magic
brooch as in the French versions,[2] but simply by the heroine's
prayer to the Virgin, who makes the persecutor forget his passion. Similarly, prophetic dreams, weird portents, fantastic episodes, such as the successive attacks of wild animals on the
wicked brother-in-law, Miles, which are found in the eminently
pious but far more romantic French texts, are omitted.[3] Even

[2] Wallensköld, 2, p. 37, n. 1, referred to other instances of the jewel (*Aye
d'Avignon*, p. 62, *Charles le Chauve*, l. 10620) or some other object (girdle,
Boeve de Haumtone; herb, *Orson de Beauvais*) which is similarly protective
of chastity.

[3] Wallensköld, 2, ch. III, Caractère de la Chanson, found that the romance
falls into two parts: (1) that which tells of the attack on Rome led by
Garcy, the old king of the Greeks and the brutal suitor of Florence, of its
failure, and of her marriage to Esmeré who, with his wicked older brother

though the English version keeps the essential miraculous elements of the older story, such as the successive escapes of the heroine from her persecutors on sea or on land, and the marvelous ringing of the bells of the convent when the holy heroine draws near, a trait, as Wallensköld pointed out,[4] peculiarly dear to the hagiographical literature of the Middle Ages, still in general it is clear that the author was trying to make his narrative as sober and unromantically moral as possible. On the whole his restraint achieves a more readable result than the too long-winded *chanson d'aventure.*

Three groups of versions of the *Crescentia* saga remain to be noted, two of them European, and one, Oriental. In the early fourteenth century, if not before, a condensed version of the story, derived from the same source as *Florence of Rome,* was incorporated into the *Gesta Romanorum* and from that time it appeared in the Continental, the Anglo-Latin, and Late Middle English redactions. About 1421 it was turned into English rime-royal verse by Hoccleve (ed. Furnivall, 1892, 1, pp. 140 ff.). In the fifteenth century a Bavarian schoolmaster, Johannes Birck, introduced the story, again told at some length, into his chronicle of the Abbey of Kempten. He attributed the founding of the Abbey to Hildegard, reputed the second or third wife of Charlemagne, and made her the heroine of a story frequently resembling Crescentia's.[5] Twenty-eight later texts, chiefly of the sixteenth or seventeenth century, make the same identification, and to this group, therefore, the name of the Hildegard saga is given. Its chronological relations are a matter of grave dispute. One

---

Miles, had come to her aid; (2) that which relates her adventures after she had been separated from her husband by Miles. In attempting to make the story a *chanson de geste,* the French author has described great battles and terrific single combats; given much detail in regard to houses and armor; boldly contrasted his good and evil characters; and infused the whole with fervent piety in the manner of the literary type he imitates.

[4] Wallensköld, 2, p. 39, n. 2. Cf. also Child, *Ballads,* Index, Bells; J. Tatlock, "Bells rung without Hands," *MLN.* xxix, 98 (1914), and P. Barry, *MLN.* xxx, 28 (1915). Church bells are first mentioned by Gregory of Tours. The first reference to their miraculous ringing comes in the *Vita Bonifatii.* By the middle of the tenth century the literary tradition seems to have been established, and in the eleventh century the *motif* passed from religious legend into the *chansons de geste* (Barry).

[5] Cf. G. Paris, *Hist. Poetique de Charlemagne,* 2d. ed., 1905, p. 395; Birck's *Chronik,* ed. K. Reiser, 1899, 1, 442.

point of view is represented by Wallensköld (2, p. 127; 3, p. 72) who held that Birck's version was simply an unhistoric adaptation of the *Miracle de la Vierge*. This view was opposed by Stefanović, who argued (pp. 500–11) that the later versions of Hildegard's story differ too greatly from Birck's work not to have been derived from an independent and presumably much earlier tradition.

The Oriental versions of the story fall into three groups (Wallensköld, 1, p. 9; 2, pp. 109–22). The first and earliest of those now extant is found in a fourteenth-century Persian collection of tales called the *Touti-Nameh* (German trans. by R. Schmidt, Stuttgart, 1899) which in part at least goes back to a very ancient Sanskrit original now imperfectly represented by the *Soukasaptati* (or the *Sixty-Six Tales of a Parrot*). A fifteenth-century Turkish version of the tale of the chaste Merhuma in the *Touti-Nameh* is extant (G. Rosen, 1858, 1, 89–108). In the famous Arabian collection of the *Thousand and One Nights*, there are three versions of the story of the Chaste Wife, and in the *Thousand and One Days* (1710–12), of which the earliest known manuscript is a Turkish redaction written in 1450, occurs the tale of the chaste Repsima.

ORIGIN. In this highly romantic and supernatural fiction concerning a saintly heroine, there is little that seems of local or racial character. In general when attempting to discover the origin of the story, one must depend primarily on a consideration of the nine principal incidents in the different versions: (1) the wooing of the heroine by her brother-in-law;[6] (2) the accusation of adultery brought against her by him;[7] (3) her

[6] In the *Florence of Rome* versions two young nobles, dispossessed by their stepfather, come as soldiers of fortune to aid the Emperor of Rome against the attack of his daughter's barbarous suitor. The brothers become rival suitors for the daughter and ultimately the younger brother Esmeré wins the lady and thereby becomes Emperor of Rome. As Florence will be his wife in name only until he has destroyed her enemy, Esmeré goes at once in pursuit of the routed suitor, leaving his wife in his brother's care. The wicked Miles practises various stratagems to deceive her, once even attempting to pass off a mutilated dead body as Esmeré's. For this deed she has Miles shut up in a tower from which, in her joyous anticipation of Esmeré's return, she later releases him, thereby giving him the opportunity to bring her new suffering.

[7] In other versions than *Florence* the husband commonly believes this

condemnation to death or exile; (4) her flight; (5) her refuge in a household where she is again wooed by a rejected suitor who in revenge murders the child of her protectors and accuses her of the crime; [8] (6) her second flight; (7) her adventure with a debtor whom she frees from debt but who sells her to a ship's captain; (8) her escape from the captain through a storm that wrecks the boat or causes the captain to put her ashore; (9) her life as a holy woman whose fame as a healer brings to her ultimately all her stricken persecutors; her restoration when by their confession her innocence is finally established.

There are four theories in regard to the original narrative embodying all or part of these episodes.[9] Grundtvig (*Danmarks gamle folkeviser*, 1853, I, 195; III, 782; IV, 730) thought that it was of Germanic origin and that the Oriental versions were but importations from the west. His hypothesis rested on an inadequate classification of the extant versions, and a consequent confusion of our story with the type represented by the Danish ballad of *Ravengaard og Memering* (No. 13),[10] which is cousin to the English ballad of *Sir Aldingar*. The first part of his conclusion may, on this ground, be disregarded. In 1865 Mussafia,[11] convinced despite the lateness of the extant Oriental texts, of their actual priority, set forth the theory that the story was of eastern origin, and that it was introduced into the west in the abbreviated form now found in the *Kaiserchronik* and in the *Miracle* group. In this form the seventh and eighth episodes are omitted. Later, he thought, there was a second importation of the story from the East from which the complete versions were derived. This theory was in part discredited by Wallensköld, although in general he believed in the Oriental origin of

---

unsupported accusation, and incidents 3 and 4 follow directly. In *Florence* the falsity of the accusation is known almost at once, but Miles gets the lady into his power by pretending that he has been sent as an escort to bring her to Esmeré. After new attempts to force his love upon her he abandons her in a forest.

[8] See here *Emare*, n. 5.

[9] The history of the discussion of the origins of *Florence* is summarized to 1909 by Wallensköld, *Florence*, pp. 106 ff.

[10] Cf. Child, *Ballads*, II, 34 ff., and *Erle of Tolous*, here.

[11] "Über eine italienische metrische Darstellung der Crescentia Sage." *Sitzungsberichte der phil. hist. Classe der Kais. Akad. der Wiss.*, Vienna, LI, pp. 589 ff.

the story. He argued that since the European versions have an incident, the imprisonment of the brother-in-law in a tower, which is lacking in all the Eastern tales, it is improbable that in two successive western adaptations of the Eastern tale, the same invention should have been made. This episode and the fact that the husband of the heroine is invariably in the western versions a person of exalted rank, an emperor or king, indicate that they had a common source which Wallensköld believed was an Oriental tale introduced into Europe about the end of the eleventh century. In his opinion this tale was represented by the longer western versions and the shorter forms were simplifications of it that were due to oral tradition.

Wallensköld's theory was stoutly opposed by Stefanović who returned to the idea of a Germanic origin, though on different grounds from those proposed by Grundtvig. He asserted, very much as Bédier did in connection with the fabliaux, the lateness of the extant Oriental texts, and the difficulty of finding actual evidence of their transmission to Europe. To him the fact that both the longer European versions and the Oriental texts contained the episodes (7 and 8) of the Man Freed from the Gallows [12] and the Ship's Captain, suggested not a common Oriental source, such as Wallensköld conjectured, but rather the probability that these episodes were added to a European original of the type represented by the *Kaiserchronik,* and that it was this expanded version which passed to the East. This theory adheres at any rate to the chronology of the extant texts and offers a fairer interpretation of the relation of the *Crescentia-Miracle* versions than that suggested by Wallensköld (*Florence,* 123–24). The latter argued that the *Crescentia* story, in which St. Peter rescues the heroine after she has been thrown into the Tiber, was in fact simply a variant of the true *Miracle* type in which it was the Virgin herself who saved the heroine and endowed her with healing power, or gave her a magic healing herb. Yet stories of such miracles were current long before the Mary-

[12] Cf. Köhler, *Kleinere Schriften,* 11, 284–86 (1900), who cited numerous proverbs showing how widespread was the popular belief that anyone who freed a criminal justly condemned to the gallows, thereby made an enemy. Stefanović, p. 490, urged that the episode of the Man Freed came from this belief. In this episode and that of the Ship's Captain, he admitted the possibility in the *Florence* story of Oriental influence, but thought that influence improbable.

cult of the twelfth century drew them round her name. Stefanović (p. 572) referred to legends told by Gregory of Tours (chs. LXIX, CLXX) in which the heroine, who is accused of adultery, is thrown into the river and is saved by St. Genesius or by Christ. It is also important to notice in regard to the chronology of the *Crescentia* and the *Kaiserchronik* stories, that the Tower episode, already noted as a distinctive feature of the Western versions and appearing, of course, in the *Kaiserchronik,* could not have been an original element in the original *Miracle* version since it is lacking in several derivative texts. This fact also favors the priority of the *Crescentia* tale. Stefanović (p. 541) found no evidence of any connection between the nameless Tower in that story and the actual tower of the Roman Crescentius (*c.* 985). The many details in the versions of *Florence* which describe the building and somewhat fantastic appearance of the Tower, do not conceal that it was originally conceived, as in the *Kaiserchronik,* simply as a prison.

In further refutation of the Oriental hypothesis, Stefanović (p. 535) pointed to some minor traits differentiating the two types. The punishment to which the heroine is subjected differs somewhat in each group: it is attempted assassination, drowning, burning, in the European tales; stoning, burning or hanging in the Eastern. So also is the manner of her delivery different. In the oldest European texts she is saved by supernatural intervention; in the Eastern tales she escapes by natural means. The torture which the heroine's first cruel lover inflicts upon her when he hangs her up by the hair, is an incident found only in the western versions and is suggestive of the fate of the holy Juliana. These characteristic differences, like the details which are unique in the western versions, prove little in themselves, but when parallels can be drawn between them and the themes and incidents in European story which precede by two centuries or more the possibility of Oriental influence — granting that this did not become effective in fiction until the end of the eleventh century — the possibility of European origin becomes more convincing. In Stefanović's opinion the terrible severity of the old Germanic laws for the punishment of adultery brought into existence numerous folk-tales, which were made all the more dramatic by the innocence of the accused. From these developed such tales as those related in the stories of Hildegard or Crescentia, or suggested in the Old English poem, the *Wife's Complaint*.[13]

The last theory in regard to the development of the *Florence* legend is that of Karl. He noted that three of the five groups into which the European versions of the story may be divided, the *Gesta*, the long French poem *Florence*, and the *Miracle*, make mention of Hungary. In the first the heroine is a princess of Hungary; in the second her husband is a prince of that land, though by his marriage he becomes Emperor of Rome; and in the third he is a king of Hungary. These local references Karl explained as being due to the influence of the story of St. Elizabeth (d. 1231) of Hungary whose actual experiences were easily adapted to those in the type story of the Innocent Persecuted Woman. After the death of her husband on his way to a Crusade, Elizabeth endured calumny and persecution; she was exiled from her home, and for some years devoted herself to the care of the sick. After a life of signal piety, she was canonized in 1238. Before 1236, however, the influence of her story is perceptible in the *Miracle* of Gautier de Coincy. In large outline at least St. Elizabeth's life accords with the story told of Florence's persecutions, her saintliness, and healing powers. Whether the romantic story was influenced, as Karl (p. 176) also urged, by the legend of Aimeri, another saint (canonized in 1083) of the royal house of Arpad, in whose name and piety Karl would recognize the prototype of Florence's husband Esmeré, is more problematical.

BIBLIOGRAPHY

TEXTS: (1) Cam. Univ. Lib. Ff. II, 38 (Bishop More's Coll., No. 690), ed. Ritson, 1802, III, 1–92; W. Vietor, Marburg, 1893.

STUDIES: Cf. Edwardes, *Summary*, p. 252; Gautier, *Bibliographie*, p. 103; Wallensköld (see below), pp. 81–95; Stefanović, pp. 552–56; Wells, *Manual*, p. 782.
Hilka, A. " Zum Crescentiastoff," *Archiv.*, CXXXIII, 135–41 (1915).
Karl, L. "Florence de Rome et la Vie de deux saints de Hongrie." *Revue des Langues Romanes*, LII, 163–80 (1909).

---

[13] Stefanović, *Anglia*, XXXII, 398–433 (1909). See here, *Emare*, note 2.

Knobbe, A. *Ueber die mittelengl. Dichtung " Le Bone Florence."* Diss. 59 pp. Marburg, 1899.

Siefken, O. *Das gedüldige Weib,* pp. 34–47.

Stefanović, S. " Die Crescentia-Florence Sage, eine kritische Studie ueber ihren Ursprung u. ihre Entwicklung." *Rom. Forsch.* xxix, 461–556 (1911).

Teubert, S. *Crescentia-Studien.* Diss. Halle, 1906.

Wallensköld, A. (1) Le Conte de la Femme Chaste convoitée par son beau-frére. Étude de littérature Comparée. *Acta Societatis Scientiarium Fennicae,* xxxiv, 1–172. Helsingfors, 1907.
(2) " Florence de Rome, Chanson d'Aventure." *SATF.* (Introd., pp. 1–130, Text). Paris, 1909.
(3) " L'Origine et Evolution du Conte de la Femme Chaste." *Neuphilol. Mitteilungen,* pp. 67–78. Helsingfors, 1912.

Wenzel, R. *Die Fassungen der Sage von Florence de Rome u. ihr gegenseitiges Verhältnis.* Diss. Marburg, 1890.

EMARE

VERSIONS. The romance of *Emare* is one of the many branches of that widespread "Constance Saga" of which twenty-three literary and more than forty popular versions have been listed.[1] In these tales an innocent maiden flees from or is banished by an unnatural father; she reaches a foreign land and is there married to a prince. Accused in her husband's absence of bearing monstrous offspring, she is banished, usually through the machinations of her wicked mother-in-law. Letters are forged and the young wife, instead of being kindly treated, as her husband has commanded, is exposed in a forest or set adrift in a rudderless boat. In the one case the Outcast Wife and her two sons are saved by a hermit; in the other, the mother and her one son drift across the sea and when they arrive at last in Rome, find refuge in the house of a noble senator or merchant (Suchier, *Beaumanoir*, 1, pp. xxiv–lv). In all versions the heroine is ultimately reunited with her husband and in some cases with her father also.

To England belong three notable versions of this story. The earliest text[2] is that found in the *Vitae Duorum Offarum* (Cotton Nero D I, Brit. Mus.). This Latin chronicle emanated from St. Albans and may be ascribed to the abbacy, if not to the actual authorship of the learned, pious, and somewhat credulous John de Cella, 1195–1214 (Rickert, 2, 30–39). The *Vita Offae*

[1] See note 8.

[2] Occasional attempts have been made to relate the Old English poem, *The Wife's Complaint* (ed. W. Sedgefield, *Anglo-Saxon Verse Book*, Manchester, 1922, p. 35) to the Offa Saga (Wülker, *Grund. d. ags. Literaturgesch.*, pp. 224–27; E. Rickert, "The OE. Offa Saga," *Mod. Ph.* 11, 29 ff.) The poem alludes to the exile of a wife, to her sorrow for her husband, to the treacherous kinsmen who have separated them, to her own life in what seems to be a forest cave. Wm. Lawrence, "The Banished Wife's Lament," *Mod. Ph.* v, 401 (1908), thought it "equally impossible to prove that the *Lament* is or is not based on the Offa-saga." Stefanović, *Anglia*, xxxii, 431, argued that the *Complaint* was connected not with the *Constance*, but with the original of the *Crescentia* or *Hildegard* legend.

23

Primi[3] (*Originals and Analogues,* Chaucer Society, Lond., 1872) relates that the king of York loves his own daughter, that her executioners abandon her in the forest, that she is found by Offa and that she becomes his wife. After the birth of her children and the lapse of many years, Offa goes to aid the vassal king of Northumbria against the Scots. For Offa's message of victory his son-in-law substitutes a letter commanding that the queen and her children should be left to die in the woods. The hands and feet of the children are cut off but are later miraculously restored by a pious hermit. The mother and children stay with him until they are found by the despairing Offa. The hermit suggests that in gratitude Offa should erect an abbey by the hermitage, but this is not accomplished until the time of one of Offa's descendants, who at last begins the building of St. Albans.

A century or so after this inspired account, a second version of the story was introduced by Nicholas Trivet, a learned Dominican friar, into his *Chronique Anglo-Normande,* 1334–1347 (*Originals and Analogues,* pp. 3 ff.). From this prose text, in which the gentle heroine is called Constance, comes the generic name of the legend. Trivet's account is important in itself and as the source of both Gower's story in the *Confessio Amantis,* Liber II, 587 ff. (ed. G. Macaulay, Oxford, 1901), and of Chaucer's *Man of Law's Tale,*[4] a beautiful version in which all the art of the poet is lavished on the tender pathos, the devoutness, and spiritual fortitude of the heroine's character. In Trivet's account and its derivatives, the Incestuous Father episode is omitted. Constance, the daughter of Emperor Tiberius of Rome, leaves her maiden home in order to wed and convert a heathen Sultan. At the wedding feast there is a massacre of the Christian guests, a crime instigated by the first of the two incredibly similar and wicked mothers-in-law in the story. The young bride is set adrift on the sea. She reaches Northumbria

[3] The first Offa, it is thought, reigned in Schleswig in the fourth century. Allusions to him are found in *Widsith,* v. 335–45, and in *Beowulf,* v. 1931–62. See F. Klaeber, *Beowulf,* N. Y., 1922, pp. 187–91; E. Rickert, 2, pp. 53 ff.; below, note 13.

[4] Cf. E. P. Hammond, *Chaucer, A Bibliographical Manual,* N. Y., 1908, p. 282; Wells, *Manual,* p. 877; Lücke, "Das Leben der Constanze bei Trivet, Gower u. Chaucer," *Anglia,* xiv, 77 ff.

and after enduring various misadventures,[5] she is at last happily married to Alle, the King. At this point the type story begins. When Constance's child is born, her mother-in-law prepares a letter for Constance's husband in which the girl is accused of being a witch and of bearing evil offspring, and another letter, purporting to come from him, in which the exposure of the queen and her child is commanded. They are set adrift and come at last to Rome. There the long separated family is at last reunited. Trivet's story is somewhat dull but edifying, and is of course written in conventional chronicle fashion with many pseudo-historic details. Both in material and style the text might easily be turned into an exemplum on the virtue of resignation to the will of God, or, with the addition of a martyrdom episode, into a saint legend.

What it became in romance is shown in the third version of the story that arose in England, namely, the romance of *Emare*, a poem of 1033 lines. This was written in the last half of the fourteenth century, or possibly as late as 1400, since it is notably lacking in archaic forms (Rickert, 1, p. xxviii). Its popular style, its twelve-line, tail-rime metre, its familiar allusions to minstrels (l. 13 ff.), its North-East Midland dialect, suggest that its author was a minstrel belonging to the Mid-Yorkshire district in which Trivet localized his version (Rickert, 1, pp. xviii, xxviii). The single extant manuscript of the poem was written between 1446 and 1460 (*ibid.*, p. x). The story curiously combines the *motifs* of the two earlier versions. It begins with the episode of the Incestuous Father.[6] He presently orders

---

[5] Notable among these is the episode of the Cruel Lover who, when his love is rejected by the heroine, kills the wife of her kind protector, puts the bloody knife beside the maiden, and accuses her of the crime. This episode is practically identical with one in *Florence of Rome*. In the various versions of this romance, it is the child of the heroine's protector who is killed. The episode is found in the mid-twelfth century *Kaiserchronik* and must have been borrowed from some subsequent version of the story by Trivet. The accusation of an innocent person by the true assassin is a *motif* frequently found in popular tales (Wallensköld, *La Femme Chaste*, p. 10, n. 2; see *Florence of Rome* bibliography).

[6] The Incestuous Father appears in many versions of the *Constance* story. In *Manekine* the king has promised to wed no one save a woman like his dead wife; he is reluctant when his nobles wish to make him marry his daughter. In the Catalan tale, *Historia del rey de Hungrie*, the father loves the daughter because of the beauty of her white hands, and for this reason she cuts them off (Suchier, *Beaumanoir*, 1, p. xlii). For folk tales embodying the theme

that his recalcitrant daughter should be set adrift on the sea. Arrived in " Galys," she is kindly received by the royal steward, Sir Kadore, and is promptly wedded by the king. The episode of the cruel Mother-in-law and the two Forged Letters is the same as in Trivet, and similar also is the account of the heroine's second Exposure on the Sea, her arrival in Rome, and reunion with her husband. Much in this version is made of Emare's beauty, which equalled that of her dead mother. The pseudo-historic details and the accusation that the heroine has murdered the child or wife of a protector are omitted, and the supernatural element is reduced to the two voyages in which the heroine is marvellously preserved. There are no references in *Emare* to any mutilation of the heroine, or to the heavenly vengeance on her murderous lover, such as occur in so many versions of *Constance*. To a large extent the story has been rationalized and its earlier barbarity softened.[7]

The varied development and popularity of the *Constance* legend is best shown by its history on the Continent. Suchier (*Beaumanoir*, 1, xxv ff.) analyzed some seventeen literary versions, and these have been added to and differently classified by later scholars; chronologically, by Gough (2, pp. 2 ff.) and by Däumling (pp. 17 ff.); geographically, and by types, by Dr. Rickert (1, pp. xxxiii ff.).[8] On this basis it appears that five

---

of the Father Who Wishes to Marry his Daughter, see C. M. Cox, *Cinderella* (Catskin). In Sophie Jewett's *Folk Ballads of Southern Europe*, N. Y., 1913, p. 23, is translated the Roumanian ballad of the Sun and Moon, in which the Sun wishes to marry his sister, " Helen of the long gold hair." The Incest *motif* was familiar enough in mediæval story. Cf. *Apollonius*, the legend of Arthur, *La Fille du roi de Hongrie* (Petit de Julleville, *Les Mystères*, II, 300–03), etc. Rickert, 2, p. 357, suggested that Charlemagne's inordinate pride in refusing suitors for his daughters may have caused legends of this type to be associated with him.

[7] *Offa I* tells of the barbarous mutilation of the children and their mother; Trivet of how Alle hacked his mother to pieces in vengeance for her crime against his wife. In this last chronicle, the heroine, when she is assailed by a wicked suitor, pushes him overboard with her own hands. Chaucer's version, like *Emare*, minimizes these elements of horror.

[8] As full bibliographical details have been given by the scholars mentioned above, they are here omitted except in cases of editions later than 1908. For folk versions see Suchier, *Beaumanoir*, 1, lviii–lxxii, forty-two tales; *Rom.* xxx, xxxix; Klapper, *Mitteilungen*, for two Latin exempla, one from a fifteenth-century manuscript in Breslau and one from the *Scala Celi*, *cir.* 1300; Popovic for a Slavic märchen which he believed was derived from Beaumanoir's *Manekine*. See also Hudepöhl, mentioned here under *Amadas*, note 2.

versions were written in France between the thirteenth and fifteenth centuries: *La Manekine, c.* 1270, a French metrical romance by Philippe de Remi, Sire de Beaumanoir, which was dramatized in the Parisian *Miracles de Nostre Dame* (No. 29, *SATF*, 1880); a *dit* (1313–16) by Jehan Maillart (Alart) called *La Contesse d'Anjou* (ed. B. Schumacher & E. Zubke, *Romanisches Mus.* I, Greifswald, 1920); a romance, *La belle Hélène de Constantinople*,[9] presumably of the late thirteenth century, though no known manuscript antedates the fifteenth; an inedited fifteenth-century Latin play, *Columpnarium*, which makes unique combination of the tale of the Persecuted Wife with that of Orestes and Clytemnestra (Rickert, 1, p. xlix); the story, *De Alixandre, Roy de Hongrie, qui voulut espouser sa fille*, which is found in a fifteenth-century manuscript (Langlois, *Nouvelles franç.*, Paris, 1908, pp. 61 ff.). To Germany belong three versions dating from the thirteenth to the fifteenth century: a German metrical romance, *Mai und Beaflor* (*c.* 1260); the versified tale by Jansen Eninkel in his *Weltbuch* (*c.* 1277–1300), *Die Königstochter von Reussen*, which is also known in a prose version (Däumling, p. 18); and another German metrical romance, *Die Königslochter von Frankreich* by Hans von Bühel (*c.* 1401). Three versions belong to Spain: a late fourteenth-century Catalan tale, *Historia del Rey de Hungria;* a tale in the prose chronicle, *Le Victorial*, by Guitierre Diez de Games (*cir.*

9 New edition announced by E. Rickert, *Emare*, p. xxxiii. For a detailed analysis of the long fifteenth-century poetic version in monorimed laisses see Albert Leon, *Une Pastorale Basque, Étude historique et critique*, Paris, 1909, pp. 118–77; for an account of the fifteenth-century prose romance see pp. 179–94. Cf. H. Bussmann, *Grammatische Studien über den Roman de la belle Helaine*, Diss. Greifswald, 1907; W. Söderhjelm, "St. Martin et le roman de la belle Helene," *Memoires de la Soc. neophilologique à Helsingfors*, 1893; R. Ruths, *Die franz. Fassungen des Roman de la belle Hélène*, Diss., Greifswald, 1897. For reproductions of the illuminations of the prose romance by Jean Wauquelin see J. van den Gheyn, *L'Histoire de Helayne*, Brussels, 1913. Suchier, *Beaumanoir*, 1, xxvii–xxxii, dated the original romance in the thirteenth century; he noted the doubtful attribution of the romance to Alexander de Bernay; the evident familiarity of the author with Tours and certain localities in Flanders, and with such legends as those of St. Alexis, of St. Eustache, and of *la reine Sibille*. In this version Hélène bears two sons. They are stolen from her by animals, are saved by a hermit, and are named by him Lyon and Bras, — the last, because the boy carries always with him his mother's severed arm, and the first, because the lad had been stolen by a lion. When they are baptized they receive the names Martin and Brice. Martin subsequently becomes the famous saint of Tours.

1400), and another fifteenth-century Catalan version, *La Istoria de la Filla de l'Emperador Contasti* (ed. Suchier, *Rom.* xxx, 519). To Italy belong seven versions dating from the fourteenth to the seventeenth century: the *Ystoria Regis Franchorum et Filie in qua Adulterium Comitere Voluit* (Rickert, *Emare*, p. xxxiv), a Latin prose tale written in 1370 (ed. Suchier, *Rom.* xxxix, 61); an Italian *novella, Dionigia*, in *Il Pecorone*, x, 1, by Fiorentino (1378); the late fourteenth-century *Novella della Figlia del Re di Dacia;* an Italian romance in *ottava rima, Historia de la Regina Oliva* (*cir.* 1400), on which was based an early Italian drama, *La Rappresentazione di Santa Uliva* (Gough, *Constance*, p. 5); a prose tale in the *Miraculi de la Gloriosa Verzene Maria*, cap. xi, printed in Venice, 1475, and later dramatized (Däumling, p. 20); a Latin prose version in chronicle style, *De Origine inter Gallos et Britannos Belli Historia*, written before 1457 by Bartolomeo Fazio; and a *novella, La Penta Manomozza*, in Basile's *Pentamerone* (n. 22), written before 1637.

These versions, as Dr. Rickert (1, p. xxxiv) noted, show clearly the progress of the legend. "Spreading from England, by the end of the thirteenth century it had passed through France and Germany, during the fourteenth century it reached Italy and Spain, died out in Spain in the fifteenth, but continued in Italy until the seventeenth; in the fourteenth also it was revived in England in English, but is not known to have persisted long after 1400."

ORIGIN. The direct source of *Emare* must have been a French lay, which may or may not have been of Breton origin, but was very probably called, as our poem asserts, *L'Egarée* (1. 1032). In *Emare* are preserved many common words of French origin, besides numerous proper names. Among these the two names of the heroine, Emare, which comes either from *esmarie* (afflicted, troubled) or from *esmaree* (in the sense of one of rare worth), and Egare from *esgarée* (outcast) [10] indicate a French source.

[10] For the derivations, see Rickert, 1, p. xxix. Dr. Rickert, p. xxxi, suggested that the marvelous robe embroidered with the stories of lovers, of Amadas and Ydoyne, of Trystram and Isowde, of Florys and Blawncheflour, which in *Emare* is said to have been given to Emare's father by a king of Sicily, may have been inspired in the original French version of the poem by the wonder felt over the *pannis sericis* which were presented in 1191 to Richard Coeur de Lion by Tancred of Sicily.

This, it is believed, must have antedated the late thirteenth-century French and German versions, but was not earlier than 1200.

In its extant form *Emare* shows the influence of *motifs* popular in romantic story from the middle of the twelfth century. By the end of the century, in the *Vita Offæ Primi*, the central theme of *Emare*, the Innocent Persecuted Wife, had been combined with that of the Incestuous Father. This last was known not only through such a romance as *Apollonius of Tyre*, but also, in all probability, through folk-tales of the type represented by *Catskin* (*Peau d'âne*, or *Allerleirauh*). To this combination of the Persecuted Wife and the *Catskin* type of story, Suchier (1, p. lxxix) ascribed the origin of the *Constance* legend. The emphasis in *Emare* on the unearthly beauty of the heroine, her strange reluctance to explain herself even to her rescuers, — a trait true of practically all the versions, — the accusation brought by her mother-in-law that the young queen has given birth to monstrous offspring, indicate that the type story of *Constance* had also to some extent become confused with that of the Swan-Maiden legend.[11]

The earliest known instance of the device of the Forged Letters in the *Constance* legend, is in the *Vita Offæ I* where, following the king's absence from home, it was a natural enough invention and probably owed nothing to the Uriasbrief and the Substituted Letters which appear in *Li Dis de l'Empereur Coustant* and *Beves of Hampton*. The details of Constance's life in Rome, where she is said to support herself by beautiful needlework, seem reminiscent of the legend of Helena, the mother of Constantine. By the end of the eighth century, genuine romantic coloring had been given to this legend (Rickert, 1, p. xxxix). It told of the laborious, humble life of Helena and her child, of the winning of the father's attention by the boy's grace and charm, of the revelation of the lad's identity, and of the reunion of the humbly situated mother with the royal father. The influence of this legend is especially perceptible in the various versions of the *Constance* saga (with the exception of the *Vita Offæ I*) through the use of the recurrent names, Helena, Constantine or Constans.

[11] See below, note 14. Also here, *Chevalere Assigne*.

The attempt to find out the original nature of the *Constance* legend must be based chiefly on the considerations which follow. The more important early versions localize the story in England, Scotland, or Wales, and commonly in the ancient kingdoms of Northumbria and Mercia. The hero of Trivet's version, which professes to be based on ancient Anglo-Saxon chronicles and actually does contain a number of typically Old English names, is Alle (Aella), the first king of Deira, 559–88 (Gough, 2, pp. 21, 51). This ascription of the legend to an historic personage is of interest, but the historical facts which might explain it are exceedingly meagre.[12] In the *Vita Offæ I*, the story is associated with an Offa who is said to be king of the West Angles. The two Offas of whom legend and history know are the fourth-century Offa, king of the continental Angles, and the historic Offa of Mercia (757–94). With each one was associated a curious marriage legend of a strange woman who came to the king after her exposure on the sea. But the Valkyrie-like Thryth, the woman who is mentioned in *Beowulf* (l. 1950) as having come " ofer fealone flōd " to Offa of the Angles, and the energetic Cynethryth,[13] the actual wife of Offa of Mercia, and the violent legendary Drida who, according to the *Vita Offæ II*, suffered exposure on the sea before she became his wife, were women whose traditional characters do not in the least suggest that of the patient and holy Constance.

Yet a comparison of these facts and legends suggests certain possibilities of important connections. It is evident that by the twelfth century the stories of the two Offas had been confused; the marriage legend of the first Offa had been more or less completely transferred to Offa II, and the latter's character and rule had in turn been confused with that of his supposed ancestor.

[12] In his attempt to prove that there was an Alle-Eadwine saga, Gough, *Constance* (pp. 37 ff.), had to rely chiefly on the *Vita Offæ I*. The available facts seem to be simply that Ælla warred with the Scots, that his famous son Eadwine was born during these wars, and that the latter endured a long exile. This did not begin, however, until after Ælla's death.

[13] Gough's study of this personage brought together much interesting historical material. Dr. Rickert, 2, pp. 327–47, argued that the lady's actual history was confused with the legend of Thryth, with that of Offa's infamous daughter, Eadburga, of whom Asser tells, and with the crimes of Queen Quoenthryth, the slayer of St. Kenelm (819). Cf. R. W. Chambers, *Six thirteenth-century drawings illustrating the story of Offa and Thryth* (Drida), Lond., 1912.

A Carolingian legend may also have been introduced into this complex tradition. Offa II was the actual contemporary of Charlemagne and there was at least raised between them the question of the marriage of Charlemagne's daughter Bertha to Offa's son (Rickert, 2, p. 348). This may account, in the inextricable legendary confusion of the two Offas and their wives, for the possible association with the wife of Offa I of the famous Carolingian legend concerning *Berte aus grans piés,* the mother of Charlemagne. She was falsely accused and was condemned to death in a forest. Her executioners were to bring back as evidence of her death her heart or tongue.[14] They, however, had pity upon her and she was at last, after many trials, reunited with her husband. Though this story of an Innocent Persecuted Wife may have been partly instrumental in suggesting a similar tale for the Offa tradition, and though the influence of the *Berte* legend, especially in those elements suggestive of its Swan-Maiden origin, is evident in various versions of the *Constance* legend, it is improbable that the latter was in any ultimate sense derived from the other. Their essential features are too different.

The fact that the *Constance* story in its earliest version, the *Vita Offæ I,* in Trivet's version and its derivatives, and to a less extent in *Hélène de Constantinople,* in Beaumanoir's *Manekine,* in von Bühel's poem, *Die Königstochter,* is so definitely localized in England, emphasizes the possibility that there was an ancient local tale of this general type. The extant Anglo-Saxon poem, the *Wife's Complaint,*[15] is too fragmentary, too blindly allusive to the facts which would explain the wife's presence in the forest and her grief for her husband, to be mentioned as more than an interesting possibility. At best it could serve only to suggest Anglo-Saxon prototypes for the local and romantic aspects of the *Constance* story, but in no way could it account for the religious element which in the character of the heroine and

[14] The thirteenth-century romance, *Berte aus grans piés* (ed. Scheler, 1874) by Adenes le Roi, was confessedly based on much older versions. Cf. Gaston Paris, *Hist. Poet. de Charlemagne,* 1905, pp. 166, 526; Reinhold, " Berte aus grans piés dans la litteratures germaniques et romanes et Berte dans la mythologie," *Memoires de l'Academie des Sciences de Cracovie,* 3ᵉ Ser., 1910, pp. 1–194; also *Zts. f. rom. Phil.* XXXV. The story of the Hired Murderers and the Evidence of Death which they fabricate, is current in many forms. See Schoepperle, *Tristan,* 1, 208; Cox, *Cinderella,* p. 475.

[15] See above, note 2.

the incidents of her life is so strongly marked a feature of her story.

This religious bias is usually given to the legend by the episodes in which the heroine suffers mutilation and miraculous restoration. Such episodes belong with a large group of folk-tales known as *La Fille sans mains*.[16] This *motif* appears but confusedly in the *Vita Offæ I*, where it is said that only the hands and feet of the heroine's children are cut off and not her own. But the miraculous restoration of the children's limbs and the heroine's association with a holy man and a holy place, are strongly emphasized. Likewise in the other versions in which the Severed Hand *motif* is missing, in *Mai und Beaflor*, in *La Contesse d'Anjou*, in Trivet's chronicle and its derivatives, in *Pecorone*, in von Bühel's romance, in *Emare*, in Fazio's *novelle*, its absence may be explained by the relationship of these versions to each other, or by surviving traits in them which suggest that something has been lost. Däumling (p. 21) noted that in twenty-three European versions of *Constance*, the *motif* appears ten times; in these instances the heroine cuts off her hand[s] in order to avoid a criminal marriage.[17] He believed that Beaumanoir, who was the first to make plain use of the theme, probably borrowed it from some version of the story told in the *Legenda Aurea* (No. lxxxiii) concerning Pope Leo, or possibly from such a tale as that of Jacques de Vitry in his *Exempla* (ed. Crane, 1890, pp. 22, 158). In the first there is literal fulfillment of the command, " Si manus tua scandalizat te, abscinde eam," for the Pope cuts off the hand that has aroused passion through a woman's kiss; and in the second tale, a beautiful nun whose eyes have excited the desire of a prince, plucks them out and casts them before him. In *La Manekine* the legalistic Beaumanoir does not state that the girl sacrificed her hands because their beauty has aroused her father's love,

---

16 For the modern folk versions see Suchier, i, lviii ff., and his articles in *Romania*; J. Bolte und G. Polivka, *Anmerkungen zu den Kinder- und Hausmärchen der Brüder Grimm*, Leipzig, 1913, i, 297; for bibliography of texts and studies to 1912, Däumling, pp. 14–17. For a Philippine version of *Constance*, see *Amer. Jour. Folk-Lore*, xxix, p. 222 (1916).

17 In *La Manekine* and the *Lion de Bourges* the severed hand of the heroine is swallowed by a fish and miraculously preserved, a detail which seems to have been borrowed from the Polykrates legend (Däumling, p. 28).

but because she knows he cannot take for queen a woman " Qui n'ait tous ses membres " (l. 798). In effect, however, the pietistic intention is the same, for the final Divine restoration of the severed hand is, in the *exempla* and the romance, a reward for chastity and religious zeal. The miraculous element, if we are to judge from the romance versions of the *Constance* legend and the many folk-tales of *La Fille sans Mains* and the representations of the story in art,[18] made the greatest appeal to the mind of the Middle Ages and may thus be held to account for the popularity of the legend and the saintly character of its heroine.

BIBLIOGRAPHY

TEXTS: (1) Cotton Caligula A, II, Brit. Mus., ed. Ritson, II, 204–47 (1802); A. B. Gough, *Old and Middle Eng. Texts*, II, Lond., N. Y., Heidelberg, 1901; E. Rickert, *EETSES*, XCIX, Lond., 1908 (rev. *Eng. Stud.*, XL, 413).

STUDIES: Cf. Wells, *Manual*, p. 783; see note 8.

Däumling, H. *Studie über den Typus des Mädchens ohne Hände innerhalb des Konstanzezyklus*. Diss. München, 1912.

Gough, A. B. (1) *On the Middle English Romance of Emare, A Study of the Metrical and Grammatical Aspects of the Texts*. Diss. I, Kiel, 1900. (2) *The Constance Saga, A Study of the Literary Versions of the Saga and of Its Occurrence in English Historical Traditions*. Diss. II, Berlin, 1902; Palæstra, XXIII.

Holthausen, F. "Zu Emare, v. 49 ff.," *Anglia Beiblatt*, 1902, XIII, 46.

Huet, G. "Les Sources de *La Manekine* de Philippe de Beaumanoir." *Rom.*, XLV, 94–99 (1918–19).

Klapper, J. "Das Märchen von dem Mädchen ohne Hände als Predigtexempel." *Mitteilungen der Schlessischen Gesell. f. Volkskunde*, Heft, XIX, 29–75, Breslau, 1908; "Sagen u. Märchen des Mittelalters." Heft XX, 1–29.

Popovic, P. "Die Manekine in der Südslav Lit.," *Zts. f. rom. Phil.*, XXXII, 312–22 (1908).

Rickert, E. (1) *Emare*, see Texts. (2) "The Old English Offa Saga." *Mod. Ph.*, II, 29–76; 321–76 (1904–05).

---

[18] Suchier, I, p. xv, referred not only to the illuminations in the single extant manuscript of Beaumanoir's poetic works, but also (p. liii) to the ivory carvings at St. Germain-des-Prés which represent scenes from the *Fille sans Main* story and from *Florence-Crescentia*, for illustration of scenes of women's goodness in contrast to those of women's wickedness as represented in the stories of Aristotle ridden by a woman and of Virgil in his basket.

Stefanovic, S. "Das angelsächsische Gedicht, *Die Klage der Frau.*" *Anglia,* XXXII, 399–433 (1909).

Suchier, H. (1) Les Œuvres Poétiques de Philippe de Remi, Sire de Beaumanoir. *SATF.* Paris, 1884–85. (2) "La Fille sans Mains." *Rom.,* XXX, 519–38 (1901); XXXIX, 61–76 (1910).

THE ERLE OF TOLOUS

VERSIONS. The story of the *Erle of Tolous* turns on the theme of the Innocent Persecuted Wife. Left by her husband in the charge of two false knights, the Empress of Almayne is traitorously wooed by them. When she rejects their advances, they in vengeance introduce a youth into her room, kill him in the presence of various nobles, and accuse her of infidelity to her lord. She is condemned to death, her husband concurring in the judgment, but is saved at the last moment by a champion who kills in judicial combat one of her accusers and forces the other to confess. The Emperor richly rewards the rescuer of his wife and only then discovers him to be his own former enemy, the chivalrous Earl of Toulouse.

In his study of the versions of this most characteristically mediæval tale, Lüdtke distinguished four main groups or types.[1] To the oldest, the Catalan, belong three Catalan chronicle versions, the first written at the end of the thirteenth century by Bernat Desclot (Buchon, Paris, 1840), the second at the end of the fifteenth century by Pere Miguel Carbonell (Barcelona, 1547), the third in the sixteenth century by Pedro Anton Beuter (Valencia, 1556). With these may be grouped a fifteenth-century Spanish romance, *El Conde de Barcelona* (Duran, *Romancero General*, 11, 210), and two French chronicles written in Provence in the seventeenth century, the first by César de Nostredame (Lyon, 1614), and the second, *La Royalle Couronne des Roys d'Arles*, 1641 (Lüdtke, pp. 78 ff.).

The representative of the second group is our Middle English Lay, a poem of 1224 verses in twelve-line stanzas. Of this there

---

[1] To Lüdtke's list of versions several others must be added. Paris, p. 8, n. 3, cited the fifteenth-century Catalan romance, *Curial y Guelfa* (ed. A. Rubió y Lluch, 1901), as one of the Catalan group of the *Erle of Tolous* stories. Thomas added the story of Gaufier de las Tors, and Stefanović, that of Philopertus (see below, n. 6). Bolte (pp. viii–lx) added a number of versions of Bandello's story dating from the sixteenth to the eighteenth century.

are four texts. The oldest and best is the early fifteenth-century manuscript (A) now in the University Library, Cambridge; the next oldest (C) is in Lincoln Cathedral; and the two Ashmolean manuscripts (BD) are both of the sixteenth century. These four texts seem to be independent derivatives (AB and CD) of two versions (xy) which had a common source. In Lüdtke's opinion (p. 41) the original version was composed about 1400 in the North-East Midland district, or, according to Sarrazin (p. 136), who did not credit Lüdtke's contention that the poem showed signs of Chaucerian influence, about a half century earlier. The " Lay " purports to be derived from a " romance," " a Lay of Bretayne," [2] a " geste — cronyclyd in Rome." Its source was probably a French poem written in the last part of the twelfth, or the early thirteenth century. In the *Erle of Tolous*, the heroine's name, Dame Beulybon, is a translation of the phrase *dame belle et bonne* from this lost original (Lot, p. 152).

Of about the same period as the English version but very different in characterization and detail and in its introduction of scenes of divine intervention in which the Virgin, Gabriel, and Michael appear, is the representative of another group, the *Miracle de la Marquise de la Gaudine*. This is a typical miracle play, a characteristic instance of the transformation for religious purposes of romantic themes. It is found in the famous Parisian repertoire of the *Miracles de Nostre Dame* in the Cange manuscript (Paris and Robert, *SATF*. 1877, 11, 121).

The fourth group of versions seems to have been derived, though indirectly, from the same source as the English poem. It includes a Danish poem of the fifteenth century, *Den Kydske Dronning* by Jeppe Jensen (Brandt, *Romantisk Digtning*, 1870, 11, 89 ff.); a Latin prose narrative, *Philopertus et Eugenia*, 1470 (ed. Schüddekopf, 1891, *Zts. f. vergl. littgesch.* iv, 342); the sixteenth-century French prose romance *L'Histoire de Palanus, Comte de Lyon* (ed. A. de Trebasse, 1833), which was composed before 1539; a German Volksbuch, *Eine schöne . . . History vom edlen . . . Ritter Galmien, c.* 1539, which is now ascribed

---

[2] Paris, p. 7, n. 2, discounted this reference which was probably taken over from the lost French original. Lüdtke, p. 89, believing in the historic fidelity of the Breton lays, was inclined to credit it.

to Georg Wickram (Bolte, p. v) and had long popularity (*ibid.*, pp. xvi–xxvi); and a tale of Bandello's, *Amore di Don Giovanni di Mendozza e della Duchessa di Savoia,* printed in 1554. This last was translated in Painter's *Palace of Pleasure,* 1, no. 45 (1566) and also into Spanish and Dutch (Bolte, p. viii). On Wickram's version Hans Sachs founded his play, *Der Ritter Galmi mit der Hertzogin auss Britanien,* 1552 (Keller, VIII, 261).

ORIGIN. There are many versions of the Innocent Persecuted Wife story in which an accusation similar to that brought against the Empress of Almayne forces upon the heroine either submission to an ordeal or endurance of many hard adventures.[3] Among such stories the *Erle of Tolous* has a special place because it contains the distinctive episode, the Judicial Combat, in which Gaston Paris recognized the true kernel of the story.

The earliest instance in western literature of a story concerning a falsely accused queen and her champion is the legend of Gundeberg, wife of the Lombard king Arioald (*cir.* 630), whose story was recorded by Fredegarius, Paul the Deacon, and Aimoinus.[4] The source was probably a lost Frankish or Lombard poem. In this tale the champion is called Pitto or Carellus and the significance of the diminutive is made clear in the legend attached to the name of Gunhild, daughter of Canute, and wife of him who became the Emperor Henry III (1036). In this legend, according to William of Malmesbury (*De Gestis,* II, c. 12), the champion of the falsely accused queen is a mere boy whom she has brought with her from her English home. In the late English ballad *Sir Aldingar* (Child, no. 59), the champion has become a mysterious unknown little creature of supernatural character. In several of the allied Scandinavian ballads

---

[3] Cf. the story of Richarda, 887, told by Regino of Prum, etc.; of St. Cundegund, 1024; of Emma, wife of Canute (cf. *Athelstan* here); of Gunhild, told by William of Malmesbury and others; of Olif, sister of Charlemagne in the *Karlamagnus* Saga and of Pepin in the Spanish prose romance *Oliva,* 1498 (Child, vol. II, 37–39). In *Tristan* (Béroul, 3032 ff.) to the interest of the Ordeal is added that of the Ambiguous Oath. Cf. Schoepperle, Tristan, 1, 223–26; II, 446–55, Unlawful Love in O. F. Literature. Child (II, 43, n.) cited also *Le Lai du Corn,* l. 325, in which Arthur's queen is willing to submit to the ordeal by fire.

[4] For bibliographical details, cf. Potthast, *Bibliotheca historica medii ævi,* 2d ed., 1896. Rajna, *Le Origini dell 'Epopea francese,* p. 191, and Paris, p. 27, both accepted the authenticity of the Gundeberg story.

the champion is of diminutive size, but not supernatural (Child, vol. II, 34). Though the *Erle of Tolous* lacks this slightly ludicrous aspect of the David-Goliath-like combat,[5] it is nevertheless of the same familiar story type which had from the seventh century down thus associated together the false accusation of a wife's adultery, a terrorizing accuser, and a combat won by an unexpected champion. Within this type of narrative minor variations are of small consequence: whether the accusers are one,[6] as in all the stories just noted and in the *Miracle de la Marquise,* or two, as in the versions belonging to the first, second, and third groups; or what is the size of the champion; or whether he does or does not conceal his identity. Lüdtke, however, on the basis of these differences, would not grant that there is more than a general resemblance between the Gunhild-Gundeberg legend and that which he conceived to be the primitive version of the *Erle of Tolous* as it developed in legendary form from certain historical personages and events.

The heroine of the story, an Empress in the Catalan and English groups, was identified by Lüdtke (pp. 98 ff., 209 ff.) with the Empress Judith, daughter of Wolf I, Count of Bavaria, and the second wife of Louis the Pious (778–840). She was a brilliant, beautiful, and masterful woman, whose exertions to secure a kingdom for her son (Charles the Bald) led to strange chances and changes of fortune. Twice at least Judith was exiled from the imperial court, charged with illicit relations with Bernard, Count of Barcelona, son of that famous William of Toulouse who is known in romance as William of Orange and in religious legends as St. Guillaume de Gellone.[7] She main-

---

[5] The champion story was not infrequently associated with men of notable prowess but of ordinary shape and size. Cf. Bernard of Septimania, Gaufier de Lastours, Ramon Berenger III, the hero of Carbonell's account, etc.

[6] Cf. the story of Philopertus, who champions the Duchess Eugenia of Burgundy against her accuser, Medardus, a Latin tale which is found in a German student notebook of the fifteenth century. Ward, *Cat. of Romances,* I, 713, wrongly ascribed this to the Chaste Duchess type of story. Stefanović, *Rom. Forsch.* xxxix, 464, pointed out that the combat scene makes it one of the *Erle of Tolous* group.

[7] Cf. Paris, p. 15; Bédier, *Les Legendes Epiques,* 2d ed. (1914), ch. iv, St. Guillaume de Gellone; ch. v, Guillaume, Comte de Toulouse; J. Calmette, La Famille de St. Guilhem, *Annales du Midi,* xviii, 145–65 (1906). Calmette showed that Bernard was the youngest son of Guillaume by his second wife,

tained her innocence before an Assembly of the States at Aix in 831; and Bernard himself, though exonerated by her oath, later challenged any one to maintain in battle the accusation against him. When no one accepted his offer, he withdrew to Barcelona. The identity of this Bernard with the Bernard, Count of Toulouse, of the English poem and of its Old French prototype is not to be doubted.

It is evident that the historical situation was dramatic enough to have appealed to the popular imagination and that it was peculiarly capable of romantic transformations. History tells of two political enemies of the Empress, Hugo, Count of Tours, and Matfrid, Count of Orleans, partisans of her stepson Lothair; the legend describes two accusers fired by guilty love and fear. History records Bernard's militant offer; legend tells of bloody accomplishment. In neither case is the change other than what might well be expected in a romance-loving age, and especially in a story as obviously made up of romantic accretions as the *Erle of Tolous*. Notable among these is the change from the unsupported accusation, which it seems probable belonged to the original story, to the rather elaborate conspiracy in which the evidence against the heroine is fabricated. This " stratagème à la fois infame et naïf " by which a pretended lover is discovered in the bed of the Chaste Wife is widely recurrent.[8] In-

---

Witburge; that Bernard himself was married in 824 to a lady named Dhuoda and was condemned and executed in 844. Lot, in his valuable review of Calmette's book, *De Bernardo*, found ch. vii, *De Bernardo in fabulis*, most open to criticism. Calmette believed that the legend of the Empress's exoneration was derived from two independent sources, one in Catalan, and one from the South of France. It is a matter of unnoted interest that the first wife of St. William was named Cunégonde (Calmette, *Annales*, xii, 147). If, as Child (ii, 38) suspected, the exoneration story was told of Gunhild, 1036, daughter of Canute, because after her marriage she was called Cunigund and so was confused with St. Cunigund (1002–24), it may be that the same name, borne by the first wife of Bernard's father, brought the story into association with the great Frankish family.

[8] Paris, p. 12, n. 1, thought this stratagem drawn from the *Chansons de Geste*. It occurs in the French, Italian, and English forms of *Octavian;* in the various versions of *La Reine Sibille* (Köhler, *Kleinere Shriften*, ii, 276). See *Triamour* here. Together with the stratagem *motif* may also be noted the Prophetic Dream of the Emperor. He dreams his wife is attacked by wild beasts and so hastens home, only to be met there by the false accusation of her infidelity. Cf. Mentz, *Die Träume*, p. 53; Benezé, *Das Traummotiv*, p. 30.

deed it is one of the regular devices of that favorite villain of
mediæval romance, the False Seneschal. The luckless dupe in
the different versions of the *Erle of Tolous* story is variously
described as a dwarf (*Miracle*), a scullion (Volksbuch), a servitor (Danish), and in Bandello's tale and the Middle English
poem as a young gentleman.

A second important addition to the original story, according
to Gaston Paris (p. 11), was the introduction of the love element
between the heroine and her champion. Lüdtke thought this a
part of the primitive story because there was some suggestion
for it in the historic tradition. But the idea of an amorous
relation was conveyed, it must be remembered, only in an accusation that was in the eyes of mediæval law adequately disproved.[9] Moreover, if the romantic element were thus early
made an essential part of the story, how account for its insignificance in the French prose romance of Palanus and the
German story of Galmi? It is not strange that the love theme
should not be found in the pietistic *Miracle* but its absence from
the important version discovered since Lüdtke and Paris wrote,
goes far to confirm the latter's opinion. This version explains
that the right to bear the royal fleur-de-lys was granted to the
Provençal, Goufier de Lastours, because, under the same circumstances as those described in the *Erle of Tolous,* he had saved
the life of the Queen of France (Thomas, p. 59). This legend
is now found only in an eighteenth-century manuscript copy of
a lost text dating from the end of the fifteenth or early sixteenth
century, but there is no reason to doubt that the association of it
with Goufier is of much older antiquity. Goufier himself was a
warrior of the First Crusade; he was made famous by his contemporary, Béchada, and was the hero of numerous stories,
among them a Knight of the Lion episode.[10] In the story of
his championship of the Queen, there is but one accuser, and
his service, performed after hearing the Queen's confession, is

---

[9] Calmette (p. 106) agreed with Lüdtke that the love element was an
original part of the story. Paris (pp. 17, 29) and Lot (p. 151) pointed out
that the love *motif* is absent from the oldest, the Catalan versions of the
story, and that historical references to Bernard's supposed passion for the
Empress came only from his enemies.

[10] Cf. Paris, *Rom.*, XXII, 358, n. 1; Thomas, *Rom.*, XXXIV, 56; F. Blondeux,
" La Légende du Chevalier du Lyon, 1, Les Débuts de la Légende," *Revue de
Belgique,* 2d Ser., XXXVIII, XXXIX. See *Guy of Warwick* here.

purely chivalric and not performed for love's sake. M. Thomas
has raised pertinent questions as to when and where this legend
was thus ascribed to Goufier, and has suggested that it may
have been derived from a Provençal version of the *Erle of
Tolous* which preceded the French original of the English poem.
Its simplicity at any rate points to a fairly early date.

We may also note indications in other versions that the relation between the heroine and her champion was originally
Platonic and not romantic. In the *Miracle* the knight Anthenor
performs his service simply out of gratitude to the Marquise;[11]
in the version by Desclot, the Count of Barcelona has never
seen the Empress but is aroused by a minstrel's story of her sad
fate; in no version does the lady grant a greater favor than a
ring or a kiss. In short, the story does seem to represent
" l'incarnation du plus noble ideal chevaleresque," of generosity,
justice, and feudal loyalty (Paris, p. 9). Even in the *Erle of
Tolous*, the most romantic of all the versions, this disinterested
service of chivalry dominates the situation. The Earl, who has
fallen in love with the Empress from the account of her given
by a captive, Sir Tralabas, risks his life in the enemy's country
for the sake of one glimpse of the lady, and is then content to
dream of her from afar. When danger threatens her, unlike
more passionate lovers for whom it is a principle of courtly love
to make no question of right or wrong in regard to the Beloved,
he pauses to assure himself of her innocence before attempting
her defense.[12] Having saved her, he withdraws, his identity
still concealed;[13] and it is evident that in this version the convenient death of the Emperor and the marriage of his wife to
the Earl are but happy after-thoughts. The poet brings them

[11] By kissing Anthenor in the king's presence, the queen allows the latter
to suspect she is Anthenor's love.

[12] In monk's disguise he hears her confession of innocence. Paris, p. 17,
n. 2, referred to *Baudouin de Sebourc;* to *Comte Claros* (Lüdtke, p. 86),
and *La tradition d'Eginhard et d'Emma, MLN.* vii, 450 ff. (1892). Cf. with
the devout and idealistic use of the *motif* of the Lover's Confession in the
Erle of Tolous, its scornful and satiric use in the fabliau, *L'Homme qui fist
sa femme confesse* (see Bédier, *Les Fabliaux*, pp. 253; 409), or in such ballads
as *Queen Eleanor's Confession*. For a comparative study of the last two
types see Hart, " *The Fabliau and Popular Literature,*" *PMLA.* xxiii, 330 ff.

[13] The concealment of the champion's identity is necessitated in the
Erle of Tolous by the mortal enmity between himself and the Emperor.
Paris, p. 9, believed that this was an original element in the story.

in almost incidentally; his real concern and achievement is to make lifelike and touching the stock character of the Chaste Wife, which in other stories, like those of *Constance* or *Florence of Rome,* inclines to saintliness rather than credibility (Siefken, p. 66). Memorable in truth in the *Erle of Tolous* is this un-named Empress of Almayne for the vigor of her scorn against her false guardians and the treacherous Trylabas, and for the grave and beautiful dignity with which she requites the reckless gallantry of the Earl's attempt to see her. In no version, per-haps, is she a finer or purer or more vitalized character than in this, but none the less her nobility is not conceived here more than elsewhere for romantic purposes.

The allusion in the *Erle of Tolous* to an original Breton lay as its source must, obviously, be taken as a conventional refer-ence, for there is nothing in the poem characteristically Celtic. The widespread diffusion of stories of the same type led Child (vol. II, 34) to believe that to seek a single source for them all, too much emphasizes " the poverty of human invention." But there is, it must be admitted, a certain persistent resemblance in the stories associated not only with Gundeberg and her de-fender Pitto and with the Empress Judith and Bernard, but with other ladies such as the wife of Sancho the Great, King of Navarre (1001),[14] with Gunhild (1036), daughter of Canute, and in later times with Marie de Brabant, second wife of Philippe III of France (1276).[15] Fact and fiction are always strangely mingled in mediæval tradition, and in some cases the one influences the other. In Paris's opinion (p. 28), the authen-ticated seventh-century history of Gundeberg, itself perhaps in-fluenced by some earlier imaginary poem of a queen delivered by a champion in a judicial combat, passed into France as a poem which was in its turn to influence the authentic story of Judith and Bernard when their fortunes delivered them into the mouths of story-tellers. In England there is hardly any doubt that the earlier history of Gundeberg was substantially the base of the story told of Gunhild and her dwarf defender, Mimecan (*Lives of Edward the Confessor,* ed. Luard, ll. 506–31). In

[14] Milá y Fontanals, *Poesía heróico — popular castellana,* 1874, p. 200. Paris, p. 22, thought it probable that this is the oldest extant trace of the legend.

[15] See Paris, p. 31.

Spain the story of Sancho's wife keeps clearly the outlines of the romanticized Judith narrative. Here the champion has to fight against two enemies; here a monk and a confession, though differently introduced, play, as in the romantic version, an important part (Paris, p. 22, n. 1). In England again, the *Erle of Tolous*, which alone of all the extant versions of the story keeps the name *Bernard*, shows the survival of this bit of fact in all the changes which fiction imposed on the actual story of Judith and Bernard.

The original form of the story of Judith was supposed by Lüdtke to have been a ninth-century Latin account, written, perhaps, by a partisan of Bernard's. Paris (p. 19) agreed with this conjecture and suggested that the name *Palanus* in the French prose version may well go back to some form of this Latin story in which the hero may have been styled " Comes quidam palatinus." Lot (p. 153) accepted the explanation, thinking that the word *palatinus* may have been introduced as a gloss into the text. He also reëmphasized the necessary anonymity of the characters in any contemporary story in which Bernard of Septimania played his part.

BIBLIOGRAPHY

TEXTS: (1) A, Cambridge·Univ. Lib. Ff. 11, 38, ed. Ritson, 111, 93–144; from l. 895 to end, by O. F. Emerson, *Middle English Reader*, N. Y., 1908, 1915; (2) B, Oxford, Ashmole 45; (3) D, Ashmole 61; (4) C, Lincoln Cathedral, Thornton MS. A. 5. A critical edition of all the texts was made by G. Lüdtke, Berlin, 1881, *Sammlung englischer Dankmaeler in kritischer Ausgaben*, vol. 111; rev. Sarrazin, *Eng. Stud.*, VII, 136–40; Anglia V, Anz., pp. 4–6 (1882). Trans. E. Rickert, *Romances of Love*, pp. 80 ff.

STUDIES: Cf. Körting, Grundriss, § 125; Wells, *Manual*, pp. 137, 784.
Bolte, J. "Georg Wickrams Werke, *Galmy.*" *Bibliothek des litterarischen Vereins in Stuttgart*, vol. 222. Tübingen, 1901.
Calmette, J. "De Bernardo Sancti Guillelmi filio" (c. 844). 117 pp. Toulouse, 1902. Rev. by F. Lot, *Le Moyen Âge*, 2e Ser., VIII, 148–54 (1904). Cf. Calmette, *Annales du Midi*, 1906, pp. 145–65.
Child, F. J. Ballads, 11, 33–44 (1886).
Lot, F. See Calmette.
Lüdtke, G. See Texts.

Paris, S. "Le Roman du Conte de Toulouse." *Annales du Midi*, XII, 1–31 (1900).

Sarrazin, G. See Texts, Lüdtke.

Siefken, O. *Das geduldige Weib*, pp. 66–68.

Thomas, A. "Le Roman de Goufier de Lastours." *Rom.* XXXIV, 55–65 (1905).

KING OF TARS

VERSIONS. The earliest known version of the story embodied in the *King of Tars* is found in the *Reimchronik* (Scriptores Rerum Austriacarum, III, c. 192–93), which was written before 1290 by Ottokar von Horneck (Krause, p. 28). Like the English poem this tells of the love of a heathen king for a Christian princess, of their marriage, of the birth of a strange offspring, of its transformation at baptism, and of the consequent conversion of the father. In this version, however, the princess is given to the Tartar king in the hope that she may convert him; the child which she bears is beautiful on one side, rough and hairy on the other; because of it she is accused of adultery and sentenced to death; she then demands that the child be baptized, and her husband, overcome by its transformation, himself immediately receives baptism together with twelve of his knights.

In contrast to this first version, which is told in 255 lines, the Middle English version in 1228 lines, is greatly amplified. It has some notable changes of detail, and shows a strong tendency to turn the story into a pietistic romance. That the story enjoyed a certain real popularity in English is suggested by the three fourteenth-century manuscripts in which it is found. Of these the oldest is the Auchinleck manuscript (1330–40), which is probably not much later than the original version. The Vernon manuscript (1370–80) was derived from the same source as the Auchinleck (A) and is closely related to Additional manuscript 22283 of the British Museum (Ward, *Catalogue*, 1, 763). All three texts were written in the twelve-line, tail-rime stanza with the rime scheme aabaabccbddb, and with considerable use of alliteration (Krause, p. 10). The diction is full of the conventional formulas of expression: the poem begins and ends with prayers and contains an unusual number of purely religious phrases, such as " For Marie, ðat swete ðing," " Jesus ðat dvȝed on treȝ," " Of Jesu Crist in trinite," " bi Jesu ful of miȝt," etc.

Although its substance is ecclesiastical, a minstrel origin for the poem is suggested by its style, by the appreciative praise of gift-giving to minstrels (l. 556), and by the frequent allusions to the teller of the tale or to those hearing it. The original poem was probably composed in the Midland dialect, perhaps in that North-Eastern district from which came *Amis and Amiloun*. The A and V manuscripts show some mixture of forms, northern ones predominating in A and southern ones in V (Krause, p. 19).

ORIGIN. The immediate source of the King of Tars seems to be a story told under the year 1299 in the *Flores Historiarum*. This chronicle was long wrongly ascribed to Matthew of Westminster, but is in reality the work of Matthew Paris, whose Chronicle from the Creation to 1265 was included in the *Flores* [1] and extended to 1303 by some monk of Westminster Abbey. In this account we are told of Paganus, brother of the king of the Tartars, and his love for a Christian princess of Armenia, of the refusal of Paganus to become Christian at the insistence of the maiden's father, of the threatened war, and of the maiden's sacrifice of herself, " salute gentis suae, velut Hester altera," in order to prevent such woe. With the exception of this last detail the story is identical with that in the *Reimchronik* and undoubtedly represents the same Eastern tale brought home to Germany and to England by returning travelers or Crusaders. It is even possible that the Templar whose stories of the East are recorded, also under the year 1299, in the *Annales Angliæ et Scotiæ*,[2] may have been the means of transmission so far as England was concerned.

The story is briefly alluded to in the *Chronica* (1259–1306) of William Rishanger and is retold in terms practically identical with those in the *Flores* in the *Historia Anglicana* (Rolls Series, pp. 77 and 113) of Thomas of Walsingham who died about 1422. As Krause has pointed out, the priority of the *King of Tars* to this version and the omission of the suggestive passage about the voluntary sacrifice of the princess, preclude consideration of this text as a source of the romance.

---

[1] Cf. Krause, p. 28. For bibliographical discussion of the *Flores* and its true authorship see Gross, *Sources of Eng. Hist.*, § 1774.

[2] Ed. by H. T. Riley, W. Rishanger, *Chronica* (Rolls Ser. 1865, p. 400). Krause did not refer to this possibility nor to the version of the story in Rishanger's chronicle, p. 189.

From the twenty-two lines of the Latin text of the *Flores* the Middle English poet has developed his story in characteristic fashion. The beauty of the heroine is stressed and the heathen Sultan is said to fall in love with her simply from hearsay, a situation which recalls that in Trivet's version of the Constance legend [3] and the still more romantic ardor of the plaintive troubadour, Jaufre Rudel.[4] The Sultan is at once the haughty suitor who offers the choice between himself and death to the heroine and the typical Saracen of mediæval fiction.[5] He flies into ungovernable rages, smashes tables, and, when his prayers remain unanswered, beats the images of his gods " till he gan to swete." Romantic scenes are elaborated with the usual descriptive detail: there is a great tournament and a wedding feast to which the bride comes clad " in riche palle " ; there are two battle scenes, that between the King of Tars and the Sultan before the marriage, and the great conflict which later the converted Sultan wages against his own recalcitrant subjects. Like many another heroine of romance the princess dreams (1. 418 ff.) that hounds attack her, but it is a characteristic touch in this particular story that makes her fancy that one of them turns into a white-clad knight and addresses her in terms of pious consolation. The change is supposed to be prophetic of the moment when her heathen husband, having received baptism, is transformed from black to white.

The naïve piety of the tale is perhaps its most striking feature. Indeed, piety seems to have been the author's chief concern, for he scatters religious allusions broadcast through the poem, emphasizes the heroine's saintly resignation and fortitude, contrasts the saving power of the Christian Triune God with the false helpless gods of the Saracens, and sets forth the articles of Christian faith in what is practically a sermon preached by the princess to her penitent husband. The misconceptions of Mohammedanism, characteristic of the period, and the fanatic zeal of the romance bear witness to its connection with the Crusading era. To its primary religious impulse may be as-

[3] Cf. *Emare.*

[4] Cf. O. H. Moore, " Rudel and the Lady of Dreams," *PMLA.* xxix, 527 ff. (1914).

[5] Cf. the Saracen characters in *Richard Coeur de Lion, Beves of Hampton,* etc.

cribed some of those changes which differentiate the romance from the legend. In all the other versions, for instance, the disfigured child [6] is supposed by the father to be the result of the mother's sin. In the English story, in which the Sultan delays his marriage with the princess until she has at least outwardly accepted his faith, the shapeless and inert offspring which she bears is thought by each parent to be the result of the other's lack of faith.

BIBLIOGRAPHY

TEXTS: (1) Auchinleck MS. f. 7, described by Kölbing, *Eng. Stud.* VII, 178; (2) Vernon MS, Bodleian, 3938, f. 304, ed. Ritson, II, 156-203 (1802). Both MSS. were printed by Krause, *Eng. Stud.* XI, 33, ff. (1887). (3) Additional MS. 22283, f. 126, Brit. Mus. described by Ward, *Catalogue of Romances*, I, 767 ff. Cf. Brown, *Register*, II, No. 745.

STUDIES: Cf. Wells, p. 122; 782.
Krause. See Texts.
Schofield, H. *Eng. Lit. . . . to Chaucer*, p. 312.
Ward. See Texts.

---

[6] The episode of the Misbegotten Child is paralleled in *Theseus of Cologne*, a *chanson de geste* of which the first recension must have been composed early in the fifteenth century (Ward, *Catalogue of Romances*, I, 771). Theseus, the son born to King Floridas of Cologne and his wife, a princess of France, is ugly and deformed. A rejected suitor of the queen convinces Floridas that the child is the son of the queen and the royal dwarf. A miracle ultimately restores the child's beauty and he is recognized as the true royal heir.

GOWTHER (ROBERT THE DEVIL)

VERSIONS. Despite the changes in the hero's name, in his ultimate fate, and in the localization of his story, the Middle English romance of *Sir Gowther* is easily recognized as a version of the famous legend of Robert the Devil, a man so possessed of evil that he commits every crime ere repentance comes to him. His story is known, according to Breul's list (pp. 198–207), in one hundred and six texts, though many of these are but modern reprints of older versions. Of these fifty-three belong to France, eleven of them antedating the sixteenth century, sixteen to Spain, — the earliest a sixteenth-century text, — three eighteenth-century texts to Portugal, eleven to England, none of which are earlier than the fifteenth century, five to the Netherlands, thirteen to Germany, these chiefly in the form of Volksbücher, and five are related French and English legends. The modern popularity of this typically mediæval story is one of its most amazing features, and is best explained by the universal love for melodramatic story that combines excitement with unforgettable " doctrine."

The original version of the long *roman d'aventures, Robert le Diable* (Löseth, Paris, 1902), is ascribed by its editor on linguistic grounds to the late twelfth century. In this text there are references to an earlier written source which, indeed, one would presuppose from the style of the narrative itself. The romance, containing over five thousand lines of verse, is extant in two manuscripts, one of the thirteenth and the other of the fourteenth century. In this version the hero's name is Robert, and his parents are the Duke and Duchess of Normandy. The story is localized in Normandy, and Normandy is the heritage which Robert rejects at the end in order to continue in Italy his pious penances and solitude. After his death he is buried in the cathedral of St. John Lateran at Rome, but his bones are later stolen by a rich man from Puy in Velay and placed in the great abbey of St. Robert founded in his honor. In another version, the brief Latin prose exemplum (pr. Breul, p. 208) which the Dominican monk, Etiénne de Bourbon, recorded was told him " a duobus fratribus, a fratre qui hoc se legisse asserebat," the legend is baldly treated. The whole story of Robert's iniquitous early life, a matter of some five hundred lines in the romance, is given in eighteen; and in general no names of persons or places appear except the name Robert and the mention of his penitent journey to Rome. Etiénne's collection of exempla seems to have been made about 1261 (Löseth, pp. xvii, xlvii).

From the same original as the romance and the exemplum came two prose versions, one in the *Croniques de Normandie,* Rouen, 1487 (Breul, p. 57), which was written late in the thirteenth century and several times reprinted, and the other in a fifteenth-century German prose redaction (Borinski, *Germania,* 1892, xxxvii, 44). As Löseth (p. xviii) pointed out, all these texts are characterized by the pietistic ending which tells of Robert's death as a holy hermit. In the romantic versions the hero regularly marries a princess and dies as the ruler of his own land. The earliest of these romantic texts is the *Dit de Robert le Diable* (Breul, *Tobler-Abhandlungen,* 1895), a fourteenth-century poem of over two hundred four-line stanzas. From this were derived the *Miracle de Robert le Dyable* (Paris, *Miracles de Nostre Dame,* 1881, vi) and an inedited *Vie de Robert* written in French verse by Jacques de la Hague early in the sixteenth century. In France the prose romance printed at Lyons, 1496, and Paris, 1497, became the most famous version of the story. It was also widely known outside of France and served as the basis for the popular Spanish, Portuguese, Dutch, and German versions. In the sixteenth century the story was again versified in French, in the eighteenth it was revived, and in the nineteenth century the legend, in one form or another, served for a French pantomime, a ballet, a *mystère,* a ballad, and a grand opera (Breul, pp. 50–67).

In England the story seems to have made its way slowly. Its influence is apparent in the fourteenth-century poem, *Roberd of Cesile,* and in the fifteenth-century poem, *Sir Gowther,* but not until the sixteenth century did the Robert story itself become well known. It was then translated from the French, and published in two editions by Wynkyn de Worde (Esdaile, *Eng. Tales*, p. 120). This English version was turned into a metrical romance (Hazlitt, *Remains*, 1864, 1, 217) by some anonymous writer, and into a long dull prose romance by Thomas Lodge, 1591 (Breul, p. 98).

The Middle English romance of *Sir Gowther* is found in two manuscripts of the latter half of the fifteenth century, both written in the twelve-line, tail-rime stanza form. To Breul (p. 5) the text of B (Royal 17), which is less alliterative than that of A (Advocates Libr.) and somewhat more learned in the conventions of romance parlance, showed signs of revision for a more cultured audience. Breul did not think that the original poem, probably composed in the North-East Midland district, was written much before the beginning of the fifteenth century. No reference to *Sir Gowther* in contemporary literature has been noted; and since the two extant manuscripts belong to practically the same district, the story itself perhaps enjoyed no widespread popularity. To its connection with the Robert legend, *Sir Gowther* makes no allusion. It purports rather to come from " a lai of Breyten " for which, the poet remarks, he had long to seek. On his own account, apparently, he introduces the information that Gowther, while in fool's guise, was called Hob, a popular name which Breul (note to l. 371) thought might be connected with that in a popular song, " Nou kyng Hobbe in ðe mures ȝongeð." The Middle English poet also states that after Gowther's death and burial at an abbey, where he was " a varre corsent parfytt " and where his shrine became a place of healing miracles, he was called Seynt Gotlake. This shows an evident confusion of the hero's name with that of St. Guthlac, founder of Croyland Abbey.

ORIGIN. Until after the publication of Breul's conclusive study of the märchen elements in the *Robert* legend, the story was supposed to have originated in Normandy, the scene of its action, and the hero was identified with various early dukes. One by one these conjectural identifications have been given up, for, as Breul (pp. 107–17) pointed out, the facts concerning the historical characters do not agree with those set forth in the legend. Since Breul's work on the subject, one further attempt has been made to identify Robert with a historical personage.[1] It is not impossible that the name and Norman origin of Robert Guiscard (1015–1089), the remembrance of his savage raids in Apulia, and of his warfare on the invading Turks, may have influenced the literary forms of the *Robert* legend. But it is difficult to believe that the historical character actually gave rise to the legend; for in Italy, where in that case the legend must have originated, there is no trace of it, and the actual details of Guiscard's life and death cannot be identified with those of Robert.

The legend begins with an account of the marriage of Robert's parents, of their long childlessness, of the mother's appeal for a child whether from God or the Devil, and her promise to give the child to the devil if it should be born through his aid. The child thus born comes into the world already possessed by evil. He has extraordinary strength and precocity, and from the first gives evidence in his violence and wickedness of his diabolic origin. After falling to the utmost depths of human depravity, he is roused to a sense of the horror he inspires, forces his mother to tell the story of his birth, and then begins a long and arduous penance.

The Wish-Child or Wonder-Child folk-tales[2] seem to have influenced the beginning of the legend. They tell of a marvellous child born from the union of a mortal woman with an Otherworld being,[3] — a theme of immemorial fairy lore, frankly

---

[1] Borinski, *Germania*, 1892, XXXVII, 60; *Zts. fur Völkerpsychologie*, 1889, XIX, 77; Löseth, p. xxx.

[2] "Grindkopf," Breul, p. 115; "Teigneux," Löseth, p. xxx; cf. Crane, p. 53, for other names applied to the type.

[3] For Celtic instances of the Semi-Supernatural Son, see T. P. Cross, "The Celtic Origin of Lay of Yonec," Univ. of North Carolina, *Stud. in Phil.*, 1913, pp. 54 ff.; also *Revue Celtique*, XXXI (1910). Ogle, "Some Theories of Irish Influence and the Lay of Yonec," *Rom. Rev.*, X, 123–48 (1919), attacked the theory of Celtic influence and cited a large number of stories from classical mythology, from Oriental and Christian sources in which this theme appears. Of special interest for illustration of the mediæval transformation of a god-like father into a devil are the accounts of the birth of Merlin. In Layamon's *Brut* the supernatural father appears as a knight in golden armour; in the prose *Merlin* as a devil who is sent to ruin an innocent maiden. Cf. Toldo, "Leggenda dell' amore che trasforma," *Zts. f. rom. Phil.*, 1903, pp. 279 ff.; "*Yonec*," *Rom. Forsch.*, XVI, 609–29 (1903–4).

pagan and unmoral, — or of a child born through the instru-
mentality of a supernatural being to whom he is thereby promised. After being delivered into the keeping of this creature,
a demon, wild man, or sorcerer, the child touches some forbidden
object, and his hair turns golden (Panzer, pp. 251–54). The
motif of the " Child Vowed to the Devil " appeared in ecclesiastical guise in the thirteenth century, but in Paul Meyer's [4] opinion
these versions, in which the outwitting of the Devil is accomplished by the innocent youth himself or through the intercession
of the Virgin, have nothing to do with the *Robert* legend. In
the latter it is a question not of physical but of spiritual captivity, and the crux of the tale is the hero's spiritual redemp-
tion. The earliest text showing an adaptation along the line
which the *Robert* legend was to take, of the initial *motif* of the
" Child Vowed to the Devil " is the *Imram Húi Corra* (ed. by
Stokes, *Revue Celt*. xiv, 22 ff.), an Irish tale preserved in the
fifteenth-century Book of Fermoy, but possibly as old as the
eleventh century. In this a couple rashly promise their offspring
to the Devil, and the three sons who are born begin, after the discovery of their demoniac origin, a wild outlaw life. The three
are subsequently converted, endure arduous penances, and
eventually start off on those saintly wanderings, the account of
which is the true purpose of the story (Crane).

The romance of *Sir Gowther* follows closely the *Robert* legend
in the account of the childless parents, the prayer of the
Duchess of Austria, etc. Here only is found the scene in which
the Devil, taking the form of the lady's husband, as did Uther
in winning the mother of Arthur, woos the Duchess in the
orchard. On leaving he reveals himself and prophesies the
demoniac nature of his son. These departures have been traced
by some scholars to the influence on *Sir Gowther* of the Breton
lays, from one of which it claims descent (Ravenel). Similarly
in *Tydorel* (ed. Paris, *Rom*. viii, 66 ff.), the queen is wooed in
her garden by a splendid Otherworld stranger who at parting
foretells the birth of his son. Despite its thirteenth-century

[4] Meyer's list of eight versions superseded that of Breul. The folk-tales
of the Wish-Child, *Robert*, and the legends of the Child Vowed to the Devil,
have the same point of departure in the vow of the mother to give her child
to the Devil. An extraordinary modern instance of this theme is given by
Jane Addams, " The Devil Baby at Hull House," *Atlantic Monthly*, 1916.

polish, *Tydorel* represents the Wonder Child story in its distinctly pagan form. No touch of moral obloquy is laid upon the mother for her liaison with the Otherworld lover; no evil effect is traced in the nature of the child. If, however, this tale came under the grey influence of ecclesiastical thought, the splendid lover might readily be transformed, as he is in *Gowther,* into the Devil of Christian theology, the godlike child into a monster of iniquity, and his joy and pride in his high lineage into loathing.

But this view, that the pagan Celtic story was thus Christianized, has been sharply attacked by Ogle on the ground that the orchard scene in both *Tydorel* and *Gowther* should be derived from the Apocryphal legend of Anna, wife of Joachim and mother of the Virgin Mary. This legend was current in western Europe from the fifth century, and made widely known the type story in which the grief of a childless pair leads the wife to desperate prayers and to the coming to her in an orchard (pomerium) of an Angelic Visitor who promises her a child of grace. Though it is difficult to see how the pious author of *Gowther* could ever have borrowed this story directly, as Ogle (p. 43) was inclined to think he did, since such borrowing would involve equating the Angel with the Devil and the Blessed Virgin with the devil-born boy, it is nevertheless certain that this scene in the two romances is more closely paralleled by that in the *Anna* legend than in any other yet cited. From this point of view *Tydorel* must be regarded simply as a wholly secularized fairy tale [5] and *Gowther* as an off-shoot from the secular type.

The central portion of the *Robert-Gowther* story tells of the hero's adventures after his conversion. In this section Breul recognized as the most fundamental part of the story the folk-tale of the Male Cinderella. Living for penance as the humblest menial or fool at the court of the Emperor (of Rome, *Robert;* of Almayn, *Gowther*), the hero is nevertheless able by his masterful deeds in three great battles to save the realm from invading Saracens or from the angry, disappointed wooer of the Em-

---

[5] For an instance of the complete secularization of early Apocryphal legends concerning the Virgin Mary see C. B. Lewis, *PMLA.* xxxvii, 141–81 (1922). He argued that from these legends came the passionate and wholly secular Old French lyrics known as the Weaving Songs (*Chansons de Toile*) and the Fountain Songs.

peror's daughter. In answer to his prayer for divine assistance
he is provided for each battle with horses and armor of different color. Thus equipped, he rides forth, unrecognized, and
saves the day. The dumb Princess, whose power of speech is
miraculously restored, subsequently proves the identity of the
fool with the hero and, in *Gowther,* his absolution having been
pronounced, marries him. The episode of the Three Days'
Battle indicates the parent group of folk-tales for this part of
the story (Weston, pp. 21 ff.) : a Wish-Child, marked by his
golden hair, or some similar attribute, takes service as a menial
in a king's palace. He is loved by the Princess, who alone sees
his golden hair, and ultimately wins her hand, in a contest of
her suitors, or by such service against foreign enemies that the
Princess is given in reward, or by rescuing her from a fairy
castle or a dragon's den. Magical, strangely colored horses are
found for him or he obtains them from his supernatural parent
or captor, or from Grateful Animals. In the romance versions
of the Three Days' Battle [6] the contest is always a tournament
or battle, and the three disguises are provided by the hero himself, or, as in the *Robert-Gowther* legend, by an Angel. From
fiction this picturesque disguise seems to have passed into real
life, for in 1417–18 Malory's patron, Richard Beauchamp, Earl
of Warwick, during his governorship of Calais, under such names
as the Chevalier Vert, for three days challenged French knights
to a tourney.[7]

To adapt this folk-tale to ecclesiastical purposes, it was only
necessary to identify the menial service of the disguised and
heroic youth with the ardent penance of a contrite sinner. The
special nature of the punishment which forced a man to give up
speech and apparent understanding and to live with animals,[8]
in short, to degrade the human to the animal state, had its in-

---

[6] See *Ipomedon.*

[7] Cf. Maynadier, *Arthur of the English Poets,* 1907, p. 223, for comment
on this episode and its romance parallels.

[8] Eating with dogs is the penance of a faithless wife in the *Forty Viziers,*
Behrnauer, *Die Vierzig Veziere,* p. 325 (tale of the 39th Vizier) ; E. Gibb, *Forty
Vezirs,* p. 331 (tale of 34th Vizier). For other references establishing the
oriental origin of the *motif,* and indicating its wide distribution, see Kittredge, *Arthur and Gorlagon,* pp. 251–53, notes. The penances of St. Alexius
and of Valentine in *Valentine u. Namelos* (W. Seelmann, 1884) were of almost
equal severity.

ception in Oriental ideas. From Buddhistic practices, from the legend of the Prodigal Son and his swine, from the legend of Nebuchadnezzar [9] eating grass, the theme passed from the East to the West. Here one of its earliest appearances in vernacular form must have been the lost Carolingian poem on the proud king, Guisbert, a version of which is preserved in the *Reali de Francia*, v. (*Rom.*, II, 355). Breul (p. 130) noted that the beast penance appeared in *Robert of Sicily*, in the legends of St. Albano and of St. Giovanni Boccardoro (ed. d'Ancona, Bologna, 1865; G. Paris, *Revue Celtique*, III, 54), and in the *Dit des III Chanoines* (ed. Jubinal, *Nouv. Recueil*, I, 266). Appropriately, therefore, it found its way into the legend which was to be the preëminent expression of monkish meditation over the problem of extremest sin and the possibility of atonement.

BIBLIOGRAPHY

TEXTS: Mss. (1) Advocates Library, Edin, 19, 3, 1; (2) Royal, 17, B, III, ed. Utterson, I, 157 ff. (1817). Both MSS. ed. by K. Breul, Oppeln, 1886, 1895. Rev. *Eng. Stud.*, XII, 78–83 (1889); *Rom.* XV, 160.

STUDIES: Cf. Breul, pp. 198–207; Wells, *Manual*, p. 784.
Crane, R. S. "An Irish Analogue of the Legend of Robert the Devil." *Rom. Rev.* V, 55–67 (1914).
Deister, B. *Sprachliche Untersuchung des abenteuerromans Robert le Diable*. Diss. Göttingen, 1918.
Kippenderg, A. "Die Sage von Robert dem Teufel in Deutschland und ihre Stellung gegenüber der Faustsage." *Stud. zur vergl. Lit.* IV, 308–33 (1904).
Löseth, E. *Robert le Diable, Roman d'Aventure. SATF.* Paris, 1902. (Introduction, i-xlviii; Text, 1–198).
Meyer, P. "L'Enfant Voué au Diable." *Romania*, XXXIII, 162–78 (1904).
Ogle, M. "The Orchard Scene in *Tydorel* and *Sir Gowther.*" *Rom. Rev.* XIII, 37–43 (1922).
Panzer, F. *Hilde-Gudrun: eine sagen-und literargeschichtliche Untersuchung*. Halle, 1901. (Variants of the Goldenermärchen, pp. 251 ff.)

---

[9] For fourteenth-century English versions of this story, see Gower, *Confessio Amantis* (ed. G. Macaulay, Lond., 1900), bk. 1; Chaucer, *Monk's Tale*, l. 153; the alliterative poem, *Purity* or *Clannesse* (ed. R. Menner, New Haven, 1917), l. 1676. As early as 1100 the Nebuchadnezzar story was carved in the cloister of the abbey church at Moissac (A. Tilley, *Mediæval France*, 1922, pp. 336, 393).

Ravenel, F. L. " Tydorel and Sir Gowther," *PMLA.* xx, 152–77 (1905).

Tardel, H. (1) *Die Sage von Robert dem Teufel in neueren deutschen Dichtungen u. in Meyerbeers Oper.* Berlin, 1900. Rev. *Stud. z. vergleich. Lit.* ii, 503 (1902). (2) " Neuere Bearbeitungen der Sage," *Stud. zur vergl. Lit.* iv, 334–45 (1904).

Thoms, W. *The Lyfe of Robert the Deuyll, A Romance from the edition by Wynkyn de Worde,* reprinted, Edin., 1904; Lond., 1907.

Weston, J. *The Three Days' Tournament,* Lond., 1902.

ROBERT OF CISYLE

VERSIONS. The Middle English version of *Robert of Cisyle* may be considered either a romance or an ecclesiastical legend. In the many forms [1] of this story current in western Europe the hero had various names and titles but these are negligible for purposes of classification. In one type of story, most notably represented by the tale of the Emperor Jovianus in the *Gesta Romanorum* (c. 1300), the humiliation of the proud man who thinks his power supreme is accomplished by means of a bath. While on a hunting expedition he becomes over-heated and plunges into a stream. Deprived of his clothes and insignia and impersonated in court by the one who has taken them, the ruler is unrecognized and suffers in utter destitution until he has learned humility and wisdom. The story appears in the various texts of the Latin *Gesta* (ed. Oesterley, 1872, p. 360) and in various vernacular translations.[2] Closely related to it, though often with many changes of detail, are two Icelandic versions, one of the fourteenth and one of the seventeenth century, and a number of sixteenth-century variants, among them a French *moralité* printed at Lyons in 1584, a song and comedy by Hans Sachs (1549–56), an anonymous Dutch poem probably of the fourteenth century, a Hungarian poem by Stephen Poli (1583), a German version printed by Valentine Schumann (1559) of Leipzig, and various popular versions in Italian and Bohemian. In a sixteenth-century Spanish play by Rodrigo de Herrera the theme of the Proud King Humiliated is interestingly related to the Emperor Frederick II and the story is localized in Sicily (Varnhagen, 1, p. 38).

[1] Varnhagen's *Stammtafel* of European variants, (2, p. 161) included forty-five texts. This was somewhat amplified by Kümmel. Both discussed composite forms of the two main types of the story but only with reference to late modern forms.

[2] Cf. Dick, *Erlanger Beit. z. engl. Phil.* 1890; Herbert, *Cat. of Romances*, III, 202 ff., 214; Graesse, *Gesta*, 1905, n. 262. In the Anglo-Latin *Gesta* the tale is numbered 29 and is sometimes called *Ponnius in Civitate*.

As the type name " König im Bade " is derived from an early scene in the first version of the story, so is the " Magnificat " title for an older version, though this, in some of its later variants, does not always exclude the bath scene. In this version the king hears at church the solemn verse, " Deposuit potentes de sede et exaltavit humiles " (*Luke*, 1, 52), and proudly denies its application to himself. He falls asleep, his place is taken by an Angel, clad in his garments, and the king, waking, rushes forth to find himself mistaken for a beggar and a madman. As in the first group of tales, after his bitter lesson has been learned, he is restored to his former state. The earliest version in this group is a Middle High German poem[3] ascribed to Der Stricker (1240), which may have been derived in part from that same German prose chronicle, now lost, in which Herrand von Wildonie said he found the source for his story *Der Nackte Kaiser* (Corneus), written in the last half of the thirteenth century. Early in the fourteenth century Jean de Condé composed a poem on a proud king of " Sezile," *Li dis dou Magnificat* (Scheler, Brussels, 1866, II, 355 ff.). Jean's source, it is now supposed, was the same " boke " as that which inspired the Middle English version.[4] In 1335 Don Juan Manuel inserted a Spanish prose version in *El Conde Lucanor* (ed. Knust-Hirschfeld, 1900, Ex. ll.). About 1374 Giovanni Sercambi of Lucca[5]

[3] Ed. by H. von der Hagen, *Gesammtabendteuer*, 1850, Nr. 71. For further bibliographical details about Der Stricker and Herrand, see Edwardes, *Summary of Literatures*, Index. Cf. Varnhagen, I, p. 53. In Herrand's version the king is forced to become a kitchen servant and to receive the abuse of his fellows.

[4] Varnhagen, 2, p. 38, expressed disbelief in his earlier idea that Jean's poem was the source of the ME. version. The basis for this change was a consideration of the fact that two ancient traits appear in the latter that are not found in Jean's poem, namely, that the king has the Deposuit translated to him, and that the king is mistreated by his own palace porter. On the other hand there seem to be even more important points of correspondence. The question needs further investigation, especially in connection with the more exact determination of the relationship between the German and French versions of the late thirteenth or the fourteenth-century and the Middle English romance.

[5] The hero of Sercambi's story is Ambrotto, King of Navarra. Not only the name but also the type of the story, which belongs to the Magnificat group yet introduces the bath episode, makes impossible any relation between it and the ME. poem, interesting as it would be, in view of Young's suggestion, *Kittredge Anniversary Papers*, p. 405, (1914), concerning Chaucer's possible indebtedness to Sercambi, to find other evidence of knowledge of the *novelle* in England.

included the story in his *novelle* and at least twice in the fifteenth century it was again retold by Italian writers, one, an
anonymous dramatist (d'Ancona, *Sacre Rappresentazione*, III,
175) and the other, Antoninus, Archbishop of Florence (d. 1459),
who wrote in Latin prose (Varnhagen, I, pp. 45–59). A German
play on the subject was written by John Römoldt in 1563, and
a Danish play by Rudolph Schmidt, *Den Forvandlede Konge*,
was acted in 1876 in Copenhagen.

In England the legend seems to have had special popularity.
Three of the eight manuscripts which contain the Middle
English poem are of the last half of the fourteenth century, i.e.,
Vernon manuscript, Additional manuscript 22283, and Trinity
College manuscript; the others are all of the fifteenth century.
It is probable that the original poem was not composed much
before 1370, the date of the Vernon manuscript. According to
Horstmann, the Vernon and Trinity College manuscripts most
nearly represent that original; in Nuck's opinion the Vernon
manuscript should be in a class by itself, but he was not aware
of Additional Manuscript 22283, which is closely related to the
Vernon manuscript, though, as Ward (*Catalogue* I, 763) pointed
out, not a copy of it. Nuck believed the original poem was
written by an unknown poet in the southern part of the East
Midland district but beyond noting a few stereotyped expressions, he made no effort to characterize the author's style. Few
Middle English poets, however, tell their stories with more freshness and even poignancy of phrasing. The author was no minstrel with a repertoire of stock phrases and themes, but a poet
in whom the best of monastic influences is discernible. Tender,
devout, wistfully credulous about that blessed time when an
Angel ruled upon earth, he tells the story with moving sweetness
and unusual dramatic power. Though he uses throughout the
short riming couplet, he falls occasionally into the use of refrain
lines, as in the Angel's question, " Where is now ði dignite? ", or
the stricken king's piteous prayer, " Lord, on ði fol ðou have
pite," with almost liturgical dignity and obvious stanzaic effect.
He stresses churchly seasons and Scriptural legends. It is on
St. John's Night, Midsummer Eve, that the Angel comes; on
Holy Thursday the Angel's splendid gifts are given in Rome.
From some version of the *Book of Judith* the poet paraphrases

the story of " Sire Olyferne "; again he tells of that "Nabgodon-osare " on whose shame Roberd meditates, and carefully quotes and translates the Latin text of the Deposuit.

The most distinctive influence on the Middle English poem, however, is that of the famous conversion legend of Robert the Devil. In no other version of the King Deposed story does the hero bear the name of Robert and in no other are the humiliations suffered by the king so reminiscent of the penance of the converted " Devil." In both legends the hero is treated as a fool, in *Roberd* he wears a hateful garment " With foxes tayles wyuen aboute ", he endures buffets and jeers from those who should most do him honor, and he eats, like a beast himself, with hounds. On Holy Thursday he is made to enter Rome where his true spiritual penance is to begin. It is probable that the assimilation of the two legends had taken place in the thirteenth century, but in no version is there a deeper perception of the tragic irony of the situation than in this Middle English *Roberd of Cisyle;* nowhere is the language phrasing it more adequate. One does not lightly forget the brief stern speech of the Angel to the raving king nor the plaintiveness of the poor fool's prayer.

The legend was known in England not only through these various texts of the poetic narrative but also through versions of the *Gesta Romanorum* and through dramatic representations. In 1452–1453 a *Ludus de Robert de Cesill* was acted at Lincoln and in the time of Henry VII another play on the same subject was given at Chester. Since no texts of these plays have been preserved, their existence is known only from contemporary allusions and town records.[6] In the nineteenth century another revival of interest resulted from Leigh Hunt's *A Jar of Honey from Mount Hybla* (1848), and from the *Sicilian's Tale* in Longfellow's *Tales of a Wayside Inn* (1863), a version destined to give new life in America to the old story.

ORIGIN. The ultimate origin of the legend of *Roberd of Sicily* is, according to Varnhagen (1, pp. 1–33), to be found in ancient Hindoo beliefs in metempsychosis. He and Köhler have cited a number of Indian tales which turn on the idea of the trans-

[6] Cf. E. K. Chambers, *The Mediæval Stage*, Oxford, 1903, II, 151, 356, 378.

ference of a man's soul from his own body to that of another man or to that of some bird or beast. In one version the hero is a weary old king longing for the renewal of youth. On a hunting expedition a wily magician persuades him to enter the body of a dead youth and immediately enters, himself, into the body of the king and assumes his royal power. But this tale, despite the royal rank of its hero and the hunting scene, is much less close to the legend of the King Deposed than are the various Jewish accounts of Solomon. The Babylonian Talmud, for instance, relates that Ashmodei, king of demons, gained Solomon's ring [7] and place, and that Solomon, after various sufferings, regained his throne.[8] Levi, in an article on " L'Orgueil de Solomon " (Revue des Études Juives, xvii, 1888, pp. 62–63), quoted an even older story from the Talmud of Jerusalem in which it is set forth that an angel, by God's command, took the form of Solomon, and that the king was then driven forth to wander from place to place, mocked always by those to whom he cried, " I, the Preacher, was king over Jerusalem " (Ecclesiastes 1, 12). The type traits which characterize this story, the divine purpose of humiliating mortal pride, the angelic usurper, the mockery of the king, are those which define the European legend of the King Deposed. Levi's belief that the latter offers a striking example of direct mediæval adaptation through the medium of converted Jews or of clerks interested in Rabbinical lore, seems on the whole more probable than Varnhagen's belief (2, p. 47) that some form of the Solomon story passed by way of Byzantium into South Slavic lands and was transmitted through translations from Bulgarian or Servian texts to Europe.

[7] Cf. Köhler's long note on the story of the lost ring recovered from the stomach of a fish.

[8] For summaries of the Solomon legend see The Jewish Encyclopædia, xi, 443 (1905); R. Farber, König Solomon in der Tradition, Vienna, 1902. Köhler, p. 208 ff. gave a useful résumé of the Solomon story from both the Jewish and the Mohammedan sources. He believed the story of Schehabeddin (Thousand and One Nights, Forty Viziers) was closely related to other Oriental sources. A sultan who is to be punished for his sin of doubt, is told to immerse his head in water and he will see marvels. He does so and immediately passes into a kind of trance in which he thinks himself bereft of his kingdom, and finds himself a stranger in a strange land where he lives many years. On recovering consciousness he finds the entire experience has occupied but a moment. This is a curiously rationalized version.

In their various stages of composition the Talmudic legends of Solomon were probably influenced by the ancient Biblical example of the humiliation of King Nebuchadnezzar. In the European development of the King Deposed legend the essential kinship of the two stories was often recognized. In an obscure Viennese version,[9] an anonymous poem of the thirteenth or fourteenth century derived from the poem ascribed to Der Stricker, the king's name is actually given as Nabochodnoser, although in general the namelessness of the king is, as Varnhagen (2, p. 32) pointed out, a characteristic trait of the western versions. In the Middle English texts the interpolated summary, already noted, of the Nebuchadnezzar story is distinctive. As an English version of that story, it is of special interest for comparison with other almost contemporary versions by such poets as Gower and Chaucer [10] and the author of *Purity*. Earlier than this the Nebuchadnezzar theme had certainly affected such legends as that of King Guisbert [11] of France who, having boasted that he did not fear God, thereupon became a leper and lived like a wild beast in the forest until he repented of his pride. It had also influenced the legend of *Robert the Devil*. From the beast penance in this seems to have come the specific suggestion for the details in the French and English versions of *Roberd of Cisyle*.

BIBLIOGRAPHY

TEXTS: (1) Caius Coll. Cbg. 174, edit. Horstmann, *Archiv* LXII, 421; (2) Univ. Lib. Cbg. Ff. II, 38, pr. Halliwell, *Nugæ Poeticæ*, Lond. 1844; Horstmann, *op. cit.* p. 426; Hazlitt, *Remains of Eng. Pop. Poetry*, I, 264, ff. (1864); (3) Univ. Lib. Cbg. JI, IV, 9, Horstmann, *Archiv*, LXII, 417; (4) Trinity Coll. Oxf. 57, variants given by Horstmann in his edition; for date see *Anglia* I, 287; (5) Vernon MS., Bodl. 3938, Oxf., edited by Horstmann, *Sammlung ae. Legenden*, 1878, p. 209 ff.; selections pr. Cook, *Reader*, pp. 168–73; (6) Harl. 1701, Br. Mus., pr. in part Ellis, *Specimens*, III, 143 ff.; Halliwell-Ellis, p. 474 ff.; variants pr. Horstmann, *Sammlung ae. Leg.* 209–19; (7) Harl. 525, pr. Utterson,

---

[9] Cf. J. M. Schottky, *Jahrbücher der Literatur*, Wien, 1819, v, 31. The poem has 240 verses.

[10] See here, *Gowther*, n. 9. Nuck, note to lines 181–84, suggested that Chaucer knew the ME. *Roberd*.

[11] Cf. Gaston Paris, *Romania*, II, 355, in a review of Rajna's *Reali di Francia*. Varnhagen, 2, p. 57, did not discuss the legend adequately.

1839; Extracts in Warton, *Hist. Eng. Poetry*, I, 183 ff. (1840); described Ward, Catalogue, I, 765; (8) Additional MS. 22283, Br. Mus., desc. Ward, *ibid.* A critical edition of the poem was printed by R. Nuck, Berlin, 1887. Trans. F. J. Darton, *A Wonder Book of Romance*, N. Y. 1907. Cf. Brown, *Register*, II, no. 1711.

STUDIES: Cf. Wells, *Manual*, pp. 162–163.

Herbert, J. *Catalogue of Romances*, III, 202, 214, etc.

Jacob, G. *Xoros Kardash*, pp. 104–08. Berlin, 1906.

Köhler, R. " Der nackte König," *Kleinere Schriften*, II, 207–13 (1900).

Kümmell, K. *Drei italienischen Prosalegenden*. Halle, 1906. See König im Bade.

Nuck, R. See above.

Varnhagen, H. (1). *Ein indisches Märchen auf seiner Wanderung durch die asiatischen u. europäischen Litteraturen.* 123 pp. Berlin, 1882; rev. *Eng. Stud.* VI, 259–60.

(2). *Longfellow's Tales of a Wayside Inn und ihre Quellen,* Berlin, 1884. See *Robert of Sicily*, pp. 16–80. Reviews, *Eng. Stud.* VIII, 324–27; *Anglia* VII, Anz. 143–46.

AMIS AND AMILOUN

VERSIONS. The numerous versions of the famous story of *Amis and Amiloun* fall into two groups so nearly contemporary in their earliest forms that it is difficult to determine their relative priority. The most ancient text of all is the *Epistola* written in 1090–1100 by Raoul le Tourtier (Radulfus Tortarius), a monk of Fleury-sur-loire, who celebrated in Latin distichs various famous friends, among them Ami and Amile (Bédier, p. 175, n. 2). Raoul's account is little more than a learned résumé of a story which he says was even then widely known.

His account belongs to the group of romantic versions [1] represented first by three manuscripts, the earliest about 1200, of an Anglo-Norman version, *Amis e Amilun* (ed. E. Kölbing,[2] *Amis*, pp. lxxiii, 111–87), written in short riming couplets; second by a French *chanson de geste,* extant in a single thirteenth-century Paris manuscript (ed. C. Hofmann, Erlangen, 1882), in which the heroes are attached to the Charlemagne cycle; third by an inedited and much longer fifteenth-century manuscript; fourth by a fourteenth-century drama, *Un Miracle de Nostre Dame d'Amis et Amile,* (ed. G. Paris & U. Robert, 1871, IV); and fifth by the Middle English romance. This last, which is closely related to the Anglo-Norman form, seems to have originated in the latter half of the thirteenth century. It was written down in 209 twelve-line, tail-rime stanzas in the dialect of the Northeast-Midland district. Four manuscripts attest its popularity. Of these the best and earliest is the Auchinleck text

---

[1] The most complete bibliography for the French versions is to be found in L. Gautier, *Les Épopées Françaises,* 1897, vol. v, 52–55. Cf. *Hist. Litt.* XXII, 288; P. Schwieger, *Die Sage von Amis u. Amiles,* Berlin, 1885; C. Hofmann, *Amis et Amiles u. Jourdains de Blaivies,* Erlangen, 1882, pp. iv–vi, listed twenty-three versions.

[2] Besides the 1884 edition of the Middle English, Old French, Norse, and Latin texts, Kölbing's most important publications on the *Amis* story were in Paul u. Braune, *Beitr.* IV, 271–314 (1877); in *Engl. Stud.* II, 295–310 (1878–9). In this he argued against Ten Brink's theory that the English poem was derived from the *chanson de geste.*

(1330–40), which was independently derived from the common source of the other three manuscripts (Kölbing, *Amis,* pp. ix–xiv). Of these Egerton 2862 is ascribed to the fourteenth century, Douce 326 to the fifteenth, and Harley 2386 to the sixteenth.

The distinction of the legendary as opposed to the romantic versions of the story, is that the heroes, under the names Amicus and Amelius, are honored as martyrs. The longer version of this group includes a twelfth-century Latin prose legend, the *Vita Sanctorum Amici et Amelii* (Kölbing, *Amis,* pp. xcvii ff.), and its old French prose translation, *Li Amitiez de Ami et Amile* (ed. L. Moland, C. d' Héricault, *Nouvelles françoises en prose du 13e Siècle,* pp. 35–82, 1856); a mediocre Latin versifying of the prose life (Faral), of which a portion was edited with the *Vita* by Kölbing (p. cxi), and a fourteenth-century version in Welsh (ed. Gaidoz, *Rev. Celt.,* IV, 203–44, 1879). A shortened form of the Latin legend, *De duobus pueris, Amico et Amelio,* used by Vincent of Beauvais in the *Speculum Historiale,* lib. XXIII, 162–66, 169, served as the basis for later versions. Among these may be mentioned the thirteenth-century Dutch version of the *Speculum* by Jacob van Maerlant and the Norse *Amicus Saga* (ed. Kölbing, *Germania,* 1874, XIX, 184 ff.), the material of which was transmitted via England and translated in Iceland in the thirteenth century (Leach, *Angevin Britain,* p. 263). The story appears in the series of religious dialogues known as *Der Seelen Trost* (Wackernagel-Stadler, pp. 181–87), written in German prose at the end of the fourteenth or beginning of the fifteenth century, a book of which there were soon versions in High German, Dutch, Swedish, and Danish; in a German poem of about the same date by Andreas Kurzman, a monk of Neuberg; and in an inedited prose version in the Swabian dialect (Kölbing, *Amis,* p. cxx).

Curious versions of the story of *Amis et Amile,* combined with other material, are found in the short Old French poem, *Le Dit des Trois Pommes* (ed. Ulrich), in which the three apples serve as a test for determining a true friend, and in the *L'Ystoire des Sept Sages* (ed. G. Paris, *SATF.* 1876, XXXIII, 167–92), in the story of Alexander, Prince of Egypt, and his friend, Prince Louis of France. It was somewhat closely imitated by the German poet, Konrad von Würzburg, in the thirteenth century in a long poem, *Englehart und Engletrue* [3] (ed. Haupt and Gereke, Halle, 1912), which makes an unexplained change of names and tales, and refers (v. 211, 6492) to an unidentified Latin source. The thirteenth-century *chanson de geste, Jourdains de Blaivies* (ed. Hofmann, Erlangen, 1882), links itself loosely to the *Amis* story, as Jourdains is said to be the grandchild of Amis. An important free adaptation of the *Amis* story appeared in the French prose romance of *Olivier de Castile et Artus d'Algarbe,* printed at Geneva in 1482 and 1492. In this the Two Friends, Olivier and Arthur, are stepbrothers, and Olivier is forced to flee because of the incestuous love of his stepmother. After various adventures he weds a princess and has by her two children. He is imprisoned, and his stepbrother becomes aware of his danger through the change of color of a magic phial. Arthur goes in quest of his friend, is mistaken for him by Olivier's wife, achieves Olivier's release, and himself falls gravely ill. Through a dream Olivier learns that the blood of his children will restore his friend. He slays them, but they are miraculously restored to life. English translations of this text were printed in 1518 and 1695 (Esdaile, *Eng. Tales,* p. 104), a frequently reprinted Spanish translation in 1499 (repr. A. M. Huntington, N. Y., 1902), a German translation from the French by Ziely [4] in 1521, and a popular Italian version in 1552. Gerould (*The Grateful Dead,* 1908, pp. 92–94) discussed the relation of the Spanish version to Lope de Vega's *Don Juan de Castro,* 1623, and to the play *El Mejor Amego el Muerto, c.* 1627, attributed in part to Calderon and based on *Don Juan.* The Spanish *Romance de la linda Melisenda* (Belissant) in which Amiles bears the name Airuelos, has also been recognized as a version of the *Amis* legend (Hofmann, *Amis,* p. v, n.).

ORIGIN. The earliest extant reference to the legend is contained in the poem by Raoul de Tortaire to which reference has already been made. Raoul not only asserted that the legend was

[3] For studies on the work of Konrad von Würzburg, see G. Janson, *Studien über die legendendichtungen Konrads,* Marburg, 1902; Schroeder, *Studien zu Konrad, Göttingen,* 1906; H. Landan, *Die Chronologie der Werke des Konrads,* Göttingen, 1906.

[4] Ziely's work was translated into English by Leighton and Barrett, *The History of Oliver and Arthur,* 1903.

widely known, but he identified the heroes with local personages
in Auvergne and Gascony. In Bédier's opinion (II, 179) and
that of Huet (p. 163) both Raoul's poem and the Latin *Vita
Sanctorum Amici et Amelii* were derived from a French *chanson
de geste* of a character more archaic than the version now known.
This literary version, the work probably of a French jongleur,
originated, it would seem, in the little Lombard city of Mortara.
Here traditionally was the scene of the great battle between
Charlemagne and the Lombard king Didier, in which Ami and
Amile were killed. Here Charlemagne gave them noble burial
and here the miracle of the tombs took place when the sar-
cophagus of Amile mysteriously rejoined that of Ami from which
it had been separated.[5] This was a marvel of course even to
Raoul. For centuries at Mortara the tombs of the two heroes,
canonized as warrior saints, were shown in the church of St.
Albin's to the pious pilgrims who were travelling the Via
Francesca on their way to Rome. The churchly legend which
developed about the two friends emphasized, according to
Bédier's theory, the pietistic theme, " Omnem filium quem Deus
recepit, corripit, flagellat et castigat," especially in regard to the
humiliation of Amile. But the jongleur who took up this story
and who was evidently familiar not only with places along the
pilgrim route but with France and its epic traditions,[6] secularized it straightway. In his hands in the last years of the
eleventh century the legend became essentially feudal and militant and its fame was spread by jongleurs and pilgrims alike.

But if the mediæval secularization of the legend can thus be
accounted for, there yet remains a nucleus of very different
origin. In the romance the two friends [7] are said to be so

[5] The tombs at Mortara are thus referred to not only in the *Vita* but
also by Godfrey of Viterbo (died 1190). Cf. Bédier, pp. 173–74. The fullest
account is in the *Chevalerie Ogier de Danemarche* (ed. Barrois, 1842, vv.
5847 ff.). In this, Amis and Amile, riding unarmed on their way to join
Charlemagne's army after a pilgrimage to Rome, are brutally killed by Ogier.
Bédier (p. 186 ff.) showed the probable influence of the eleventh century
Vita Hadriani on the authors of the *Vita Amici*, on the original *Ogier*, and on
the Italian chronicles which preserve the Carolingian legends.

[6] Cf. Körner's study of place names in *Amis*. The actual Carolingian
references in the *Vita* are supplemented in the *chanson de geste* by such
indirect allusions as that to the traitor Hardé, who is represented as one of
Ganelon's kin.

[7] R. Mertz, *Die deut. Bruchstücke von Athis u. Prophilias in ihrem*

remarkably alike that the wife of one of them mistakes the other for her husband. They are depicted as men of equally noble rank, named somewhat similarly and perhaps allegorically, and are said to have been born on the same day, to have been brought up in the closest intimacy. All this seems referable to the type of story known as the Two Friends (Bolte and Polívka, *Hausmärchen*, I, 528) in which two brothers who exactly resemble each other experience various vicissitudes. One falls victim to enchantment and the other, going in quest of him, is mistaken by his brother's wife for her husband. His use of the Sword of Chastity is in this instance paralleled by the action of Ami who, likewise acting as the husband of his friend's wife, places at night his unsheathed sword between himself and the lady.[8] The combination of the " Sosie " *motif* with that of the Sword of Chastity in both the folk-tale and the romance, makes

---

Verhältnis zum alftrz. Roman, Leipzig, 1904, p. 1, thus classified the two principal groups of mediæval Friendship Romances: (1) Athis and Prophilias, Titus and Gisippus (Boccaccio, *Decameron*, 10, 8), Alexander (Alcander) and Septimus; (2) Amis and Amile, Engelhart and Dietrich, Alexander and Louis (*Sept Sages*), Olivier and Artus. For *Athis* see A. Hilka's edition, Dresden, 1912–16; L. Staël von Holstein, *Le Roman d'Athis, Étude litt. sur ses deux versions*, Upsala, 1909; Liese, *Vergleich der Erzahlung x, 8. bei Boccaccio mit Athis*, Progr. d. städt. Realschule zu Gorlitz, 1901; *Hist. litt.* xv, 179–93; W. Grimm, *Kleinere Schriften*, III, 212–366 (Berlin, 1883); Ward, *Catalogue of Romances*, I, 173. On p. 929 ff. Ward pointed out, as others had done before him, the source story of *Athis* in the *Disciplina Clericalis* (ed. A. Hilka, 1912; cf. Ward, *Catalogue*, II, 247). From this it was copied into various exempla collections such as the *Gesta Romanorum*, the *Alphabet of Tales*, etc. For a long bibliography for these and other analogues to Boccaccio's story see A. C. Lee, *The Decameron, Its Sources and Analogues*, pp. 330–43 (Lond. 1909); F. L. Jones, *Boccaccio and his Imitators*, p. 39 (Chicago, 1910); G. Groeber, *Ueber die Quellen von Boccaccio's Dekameron*, pp. 85–87 (Strassburg, 1913).

[8] B. Heller, " L'Epée Symbole et Gardienne de Chastete," *Rom.* XXXVI, 36–49 (1908); also K. Campbell, *Seven Sages*, p. cxii, Heller (p. 37) believed that it was by way of the *Vita Amici* as adapted into the *Roman des Sept Sages*, that the sword *motif* passed into the literature and popular traditions of Europe. Cf. the Sigurd-Brynhild story, the *Edda*, the *Volsung Saga, Tristan et Iseult, Bovon de Haumtone, Le Roman de la Poire* (ed. Stehlich, 1881) etc., and the religio-romantic legend, *Le Prevot d'Aquilee* (ed. Köhler, *Kleinere Schriften*, I). For romance references see G. Schoepperle, *Tristan*, Index, Separating Sword. Ogle, *Rom. Rev.* x, 131, n. 6 (1919), noted that the situation in the Mabinogi of *Pwyll* was similar to that in *Amis* and " was no doubt derived from the same source." Pwyll appears in the guise of Arawn but lives in perfect chastity with the wife of his friend. In this version there is no reference to the sword.

certain some relationship between them. Since the resemblance *motif* in the folk-tale is clearly and regularly explained by the fraternal relationship, the folk-tale version is probably the earlier form (Huet, p. 168).

Even more important, since it concerns the major portion of the story, is the evidence of the popular origin of the central theme of the story. It concerns the testing of the loyalty of two men who are called upon to make supreme sacrifices for each other, and corresponds closely with the well-known märchen known as Faithful John or the Faithful Companion (Bolte and Polívka, *Hausmärchen*, 1, 42). In this a servant secures a bride for his royal master, saves him from various dangers though at the sacrifice of being himself turned to stone, and recovers life through being bathed with the blood of his master's child. The folk-tales do not explain the doom visited upon the faithful servant; but Potter (p. 484), on the evidence of a song from southern Siberia, believed it probably due to the folk idea of the danger in breaking a taboo of silence. The servant learns in a vision or through the speech of birds or animals of the perils awaiting his master and suffers petrifaction when he betrays this supernatural knowledge. In the literary versions of *Amis* in which essentially this same situation is reproduced, leprosy [9] takes the place of petrifaction, and the variety, as well as the unsatisfactory nature of the reasons given for this affliction, seem to indicate that it was an old traditional element which was not readily understood by the western romancers and so was interpreted in various ways. In any case, as Huet (p. 180) pointed out, the great antiquity and the consistency of the Eastern versions in regard to the petrifaction *motif*, make it impossible to believe that in this episode the East borrowed from the West. Moreover since the antiquity of the *Amis* story makes evident the circulation in France of the folk-tale at a time long

[9] In Raoul's poem the affliction is accidental; in the *Vita Amici* it is a test of piety; in the *chanson de geste* and the *Miracle* it is because Amis, wedding the king's daughter under a false name, commits the crime of bigamy; in the English version it is because he enters falsely into a judicial combat. Cf. Bédier, p. 180. The leprosy *motif*, as it appears in Hartmann von Aue's *Der arme Heinrich* and analogous tales, is fully studied by Wackernagel and Stadler, pp. 217–23. For Hartmann see F. Piquet, *Étude sur Hartmann von Aue*, Paris, 1898; E. Gierach, *Der arme Heinrich, Überlieferung u. Herstellung*, Heidelberg, 1913.

antedating Hartmann von Aue's *Der arme Heinrich* (*c.* 1200), the earliest known German analogue to the *Amis* story, Voretzsche's idea (p. 246) of the folk-tale as originally German can hardly be accepted.

In the chivalric transformation of the *Amis* legend in France, numerous romantic characters and incidents were woven into the secularized legend. In the romance a Jealous Seneschal betrays the love of Amis and the king's daughter. The lady herself is of the type known as the Wooing Princess or the Forth-Putting Lady. A Judicial Combat takes the place of the dangers which threatened the Faithful Servitor, and the lover of the princess gallantly though falsely undertakes to prove her innocent of a liaison with himself. A prophetic dream, in which Amiloun sees his friend beset by wild beasts, warns him of the latter's trouble. A voice from Heaven tells him of the danger of taking his friend's place in the combat. Golden cups which the two friends exchange at their first parting serve later as Recognition Tokens when Amiloun, hideously disguised by leprosy and poverty, comes to his friend's castle. The characters, such as Libias, the Cruel Wife of Amiloun,[10] are developed with power and almost sinister realism, and mediæval customs and conditions are pictured in colorful ways. The most graciously romantic quality in the story comes from its emphasis on friendship as an ideal human relationship, and it is for this quality that the tale is remembered longest as a " chançoun d'amur, de leauté, et de grant douçur."

BIBLIOGRAPHY

TEXTS: (1) A, Auchinleck MS., Advocates Libr. Edin., ed. Weber, II, 369–473 (1810); E. Kölbing, *Altengl. Bibl.*, Heilbronn, 1884 (a critical edition of this and other MSS.); cf. Eng. Stud. IX, 175, 456, 477; XIII, 134; (2) S, Duke of Sutherland's MS., desc. *Eng. Stud.* VII, 191; now Egerton 2862, desc. *Brit. Mus. Cat. of Add. MSS.*, p. 239 (1905–10); (3) D, Douce 326; (4) H, Harley 2186, desc. Ward, *Catalogue*, I, 677. Trans. E. Rickert, *Romances of Friendship;* F. J. Darton, *A Wonder Book of Old Romance*, N. Y. 1907.

STUDIES AND ANALOGUES: Cf. n. 1; Edwardes, *Summary*, pp. 74, 176, 224; Wells, *Manual*, p. 787. Trans. from the French: *Amis and Amile,*

---

10 Cf. Comfort, " Character Types in the Old French Chansons de Geste," *PMLA.* XXI, p. 380.

adapted from the *chanson de geste* and retold in modern French by
J. G. Frazer, Lond. 1903; in modern English by William Morris,
Portland, Maine, 1909, reprinted from ed. of 1894; in modern German
verse, by H. Grein, Kiel, 1902; W. Pater, *The Renaissance,* Lond. 1898,
1902, gives a partial translation of the thirteenth-century prose version
in the Bibliothèque Elzevirienne; trans. from the text of Moland by
E. Mason, *Aucassin,* Everyman Series, 1910, 1912, pp. 173, ff.

Ayres, H. M. " The *Faerie Queen* and *Amis and Amiloun.*"   *MLN.*
    XXIII, 177–80 (1908).

Bédier, J. *Les Légendes Epiques,* II, 170–86. Paris, 1908.

Brechtefeldt, W. *Der Bau des Nomens, u. Verbums in den Chanson de
    Geste " Amis et Amile " und " Jourdains de Blaivies,"* Ein Beitrag
    zur altfrz. Dialectkunde. Diss. 175 pp. Kiel, 1904.

Faral, E. " Le MS. Latin 3718 de la Bibliothèque Nat. Paris." *Rom.*
    XVLI, 244–46 (1920).

Haupt, M. *Engelhard und Engeltrut.* Leipzig, 1844, 1900; Altdeut. Text
    Bibl. XVII. Halle. 1912.

Huet, G. " *Amis et Amile,* Les Origines de la Légende." *Le Moyen Âge,*
    XXX, 162–84 (1919).

Kölbing, E. See Texts.

Körner, K. " Ueber Die Ortsangaben in *Amis et Amiles.*" *Zts. frz. Spr.
    u. Lit.* XXXIII, 195–205 (1908).

Potter, M. A. "Ami et Amile." *PMLA.* XXIII, 471–85 (1908).

Ulrich, J. " Le Dit des Trois Pommes." *Rom. Forsch.* XIX, 622–32 (1906).

Voretzsch, *Einführung,* p. 244–47, 1913, 2d ed.

Wackernagel, W. u. Stadler. *Der arme Heinrich u. zwei jüngere Prosale-
    genden verwandten Inhaltes, S. Silvester, u. Amicus u. Amelius aus
    Der Seelen Trost (Amicus,* pp. 181–87; 226–32) Basle, 1911.

AMADAS

VERSIONS. There are few Middle English romances for which an immediate French source is neither known nor very positively conjectured, but of these *Amadas* is one. The hero bears the name of the lover in the romance of *Amadas et Idoine*,[1] but his story is of an altogether different type. It is found in a fifteenth-century manuscript in the Advocates Library, Edinburgh, and in the Ireland manuscript (Hale, Lancashire) in which various local records were commenced in 1413 by William Ireland. The two texts are written in the twelve-line, tail-rime stanza in the dialect of the North-Western part of England (Stephens, p. 5), possibly in that of Lancashire (Robinson, pp. x, xlii). They seem to have been independently derived from a common source.

The story of *Amadas* is told briefly and vigorously in less than a thousand lines and concerns chiefly the service which Amadas renders to a dead man and the Grateful Dead's subsequent actions. Didactic as it is in theme, the story is enlivened by touches of blunt and almost humorous realism. The poor wife, who has sat for sixteen weeks beside her husband's corpse, says frankly that he " wroght more lyk a fole " in giving his goods to all who asked. The merchant who will not let the body be buried until his debt is paid, like any canny Scot, wishes a sorry grace to all such " wastars," and grieves for the thirty pounds of which he will not see a penny more. The ruined Sir Amadas, who gives his last cent to secure burial for the dead man, sits at last alone in the forest, lamenting his own old follies with refreshing honesty. Pure romance, however, finds expression in such scenes as that in the woodland chapel with its bier and burning candles where Amadas first finds the dead man and his grieving lady, in the appearance of the ghost as a White Knight

[1] Cf. G. Paris, *Furnivall Miscellany*, Lond. 1901. Though no Middle English version exists, the number of allusions to this romance shows how widely it was known in England. The French text of *Amadas et Idoine* (ed. C. Hippeau. Paris, 1863) is summarized in the *Hist. Litt.* XXII, 758 and is the subject of an unpublished Harvard dissertation by J. Reinhard.

who comes to the rescue of the hero, and in the latter's discovery of a shore where from a great wreck the waves have washed a chest of gold, dead knights in armor, rich robes, and live horses, brown, white, and grey. Amadas, when he comes to a king's castle, is taken by his white hand and given royal welcome. In true romantic fashion he wins in the course of time lands, wealth, and a princess for his wife.

In effect, it must be admitted, the story is less a romance than a moral tale. Its moral purport, that kindness even to the dead does not go unrewarded, is reënforced by a simple piety of spirit, sure that " Goddes help his ay nere." Pious ejaculations and allusions, especially to the Rood, are many. The great scene of the romance, in which the White Knight, the ghost of the buried debtor, comes to demand the promised half of Amadas's new possessions, is strongly suggestive of the Abraham and Isaac story. The White Knight will not take the " londes wyde," the towered castles, the wood and waters, the wild deer, the forests, jewels, silver, or red gold, but only half of that which is dearest, the wife and child of Amadas. The lady's gentle resignation as she lies meekly down, covering her eyes with her handkerchief and taking her babe into her arms, Amadas's grief-stricken obedience as he raises his sword to smite them both, are surely reminiscent of the sacrifice of Isaac in mediæval dramatizations. The test accomplished, the White Knight, after a moral peroration, " glod away as dew in son."

The oldest extant version of the theme of the Grateful Dead is Cicero's tale of Simonides (*De Divinatione,* 1, c. 27), who finds a corpse on the seashore, buries it, and is later saved from drowning by the dead man's ghost. Gerould (p. 26), who has made the most exhaustive study of the theme, suggested that this was an independent anecdote which passed down to the Middle Ages through Valerius Maximus (*Facta et Dicta,* 1, 7), Robert Holkot (*Super Libros Sapientie,* Lect. 103), and Chaucer (*Nun's Priest's Tale*). Another early version appeared in the Apocryphal Book of Tobit, c. 76. In this Tobit buries a dead man at night, is imprisoned, and sends his son Tobias to seek help; in disguise the angel Raphael aids the boy in gaining a bride and delivering her from the demon by which she is possessed; and finally the angel and Tobias return and release

Tobit. The simple treatment of the theme was here greatly complicated by the addition of other *motifs*, but as "perhaps the best loved story of the Apocrypha," it had undoubtedly great influence.

Most nearly related to *Sir Amadas* is the group of six stories represented by the fourteenth-century German poem *Rittertriuwe* (von der Hagen, *Gesammtabenteuer*, 1850, 1, 105 ff.) and by the Old French romances, the thirteenth-century *Richars li Biaus* (W. Foerster, Vienna, 1874) and the curious fourteenth-century *Lion de Bourges*,[2] which was translated into German prose[3] in the fifteenth century and printed in 1514 (Hippe, p. 154). A literary source in French must be postulated for these two romances and presumably also for the story of Duke Pippin of Lorraine, told in the Old Swedish *Legendarium*, 1256–70 (Stephens, p. 73), for the fourteenth-century *Novella di Messer Dianese* (d'Ancona, *Rom.* III, 191), and for the English *Sir Amadas*. In all six stories a knight starts for a tourney; in all but the Old Swedish he is a spendthrift who pays for the burial of a dead man at the cost of practically all he possesses; in *Richars*, *Lion*, and *Amadas*, he is later provided for by the ghost in the form of a White Knight; and in all but *Richars* he promises to share his winnings. In *Richars*, in the Old Swedish *Legendarium*, and in *Amadas*, the ghost demands half the lady, and in *Lion* and in *Dianese* either the lady or the property. As Gerould (p. 33) pointed out, the distinctive trait of this group of versions is the combination of the Grateful Dead theme with that of the Spendthrift Knight.

The Grateful Dead theme was used somewhat incidentally in the long thirteenth-century romance of *Walewein* (Jonckbloet,

[2] See H. Wilhelmi, *Studien über die Chanson de Lion de Bourges*, Marburg, 1894; B. Scholvien, *Weitere Studien z. Chanson de Lion de Bourges Teil 1*, Diss. Greifswald, 1905; R. Krickmeyer, *Weitere Studien z. Chanson de Lion de B.*, Teil 1, Greifswald, 1905; E. Hüdepohl, *Weitere Studien z. Chanson de Lion de B.;* analyse des schlussteiles, text der Joieuse-Tristouce-episode (sage vom Mädchen mit der abgehauenen hand), Diss. Greifswald, 1906; E. Stein, *Sprache u. heimat der jüngeren fassung der Chans. de Lion de B.* (Hs.B), Diss. Greifswald, 1908; H. Zeddies, *Weitere Studien z. Chans. de Lion de B.* Diss. Greifswald, 1907; W. Zorn, *Sprache u. heimat des Lion de B.* Diss. Greifswald, 1907.

[3] Cf. I. Beth, "Federzeichnungen der Herpin-Handschrift in der K. Bibliothek zu Berlin." *Jahrb. d. Kön. preusz. Kunstsamml.* XXIX, 264–75 (Berlin 1908); E. Müller, *Überlieferung des Herpin von Burges*, Halle, 1905.

1846; cf. Ker, *Folk-Lore*, v, 121–27) in which the hero mortally wounds a Red Knight who then asks and receives Christian burial. By the aid of a thankful beast no less than by the help of the Red Knight's ghost, Walewein is enabled to accomplish the various impossible tasks assigned to him. In the fifteenth century the theme was combined with that of the Two Friends, although even in *Sir Amadas* itself the romantic eagerness of Amadas to welcome the White Knight, to share with him his all, and his willingness to give even unto the life of his child, suggest the influence of *Amis and Amiloun*. In this connection Gerould (p. 92 ff.) referred to the fifteenth-century prose romance, *Olivier de Castile et Artus d'Algarbe*, and the derivatives which are here discussed under *Amis and Amiloun*. In sixteenth-century English the Grateful Dead *motif* again appeared in that extraordinary composite of folk-lore, farce, and romance, Peele's *Old Wives' Tale*, pr. 1595 (Gayley's *Representative Eng. Comedies*, 1903). There is also a confused but recognizable use of the theme in Massinger's *Fatal Dowry*, 1632, and in Nicholas Rowe's *The Fair Penitent*, 1720.

The folk-lore versions of the Grateful Dead number more than ninety and are of almost universal distribution. Of special interest to English readers are the numerous versions of Jack the Giant Killer which show absorption of the theme (Gerould, pp. 24, 70 ff.)

ORIGIN. It is probable that the origin of the Grateful Dead story is to be sought in ancient beliefs about the sacred duty of burial, and in those customs, as old as the ancient Egyptian law of which Herodotus tells, which permitted a son to pledge for debt even his father's body, and as modern as that still practised in Scotland in the sixteenth century, by which a corpse might be left unburied until the relatives had paid the dead man's debts and the expenses of burial in the churchyard (Gerould, p. 162 ff.). These widespread practices and beliefs are sufficiently similar to allow the supposition that the basic tale was produced sporadically here and there, but the long integrity of the theme " in lands whose inhabitants are connected by blood or social intercourse," may indeed entitle it to consideration as " an organism with a life history of its own." Against those who believe in a Germanic or at least a European origin Gerould (p. 167) argued, on the evidence of the distinctly Semitic origin and coloring of *Tobit*, and of modern Asiatic folk-tales coming from a district practically unvisited by Europeans, that it was originally an Oriental folk-tale.

In tracing the development of the simple theme of the duty of burial and the gratitude of the ghost, Gerould noted its gradual combination with others. The reward obtained by the hero is a wife; sometimes she is possessed by a demon; sometimes she is herself a Poison Maiden [4] from whose fatal embrace the ghost saves his friend; sometimes she is a Woman Ransomed from slavery by the hero to whom he is united only after the ghost saves him from dire peril of enemies (Gerould, ch. IV, V). In other cases the ghost obtains for the hero the Water of Life or achieves for him some other equally Impossible Task.[5] In these more elaborated forms of the reward-story appears the *motif* of the Bargain Contract which calls for a literal division of all the hero's gains. In the Poison Maiden group of stories the sharing of the bride comes from the desire either to purify her or to save the hero from her embrace. Gerould (p. 75) disagreed with Hippe's belief (p. 181) that this motivation was more primitive than that in which the ghost's demand is a test of the hero's willingness to fulfill an obligation.[6]

The combination of the Grateful Dead theme with that of the Spendthrift Knight [7] must have been effected, according to the literary variants, by the middle of the thirteenth century; that with the much older *motif* of the Woman Ransomed, before the fourteenth century.[8]

[4] The term "Poison-Maiden" comes specifically from the story in the pseudo-Aristotelian *Secretum Secretorum* of the maiden reared on venom and sent as a Greek gift to Alexander, who was saved from her by Aristotle. Cf. W. Hertz, *Die Sage vom Giftmädchen,* 1893.

[5] The Impossible Tasks are achieved not only by the aid of the ghost but often by helpful animals similarly inspired by gratitude. Cf. Gerould, p. 159; A. Wünsch. *Die Sagen vom Lebensbaum u. Lebenswasser,* 1904; E. W. Hopkins, "The Fountain of Youth," *Jour. American Oriental Soc.* XXVI. Gerould (p. 119) noted the need of a new study of the Water-of-Life theme.

[6] Gerould (p. 158) thought that stories of the type, "The Child Vowed to the Devil," may have suggested the idea of including the child in the sacrifice to the ghost. See *Gowther* here and Meyer, *Rom.* XXXIII, 163.

[7] See *Cleges.*

[8] Gerould, p. 82, 171. The combination appears in the *Scala Celi* com-

BIBLIOGRAPHY

TEXTS: (1) Ireland Ms. ed. Robson, *Camden Soc.* 1842; (2) MS. Jac. v, 7, 27, Advocates Library, Edin., ed. Weber, 1810, III, 243–75. The two MSS. were printed together by G. Stephens, *Ghost Thanks, or the Grateful Dead*, Cheapinghaven, 1860. Trans. E. Rickert, *Romances of Friendship*, pp. 40–67; J. Weston, *Chief Middle Eng. Poets*, p. 216 ff.

STUDIES: Cf. Wells, *Manual*, p. 787.

Benary, W. "Hervis von Metz u. die sage von dankbaren Toten." *Zts. f. rom. Phil.* XXXVII, 57–92; XXXVIII, 229 (1914).

Cock, A. *De Sage van den te gast denooden doode.* 46 pp. Ghent, 1909.

Dutz, H. "Der Dank des Todten in der engl. Literatur." *Jahresber. d. Staats-Oberrealschule.* Troppau, 1894.

Gerould, G. H. *The Grateful Dead, The History of a Folk Story.* Folk Lore Soc. Lond. 1907. Bibliography, pp. 7–25.

Hippe, M. "Unterschungen zu d. mittelengl. Romanze von *Sir Amadas*." *Archiv.* LXXXI, 141–183 (1888). Rev. *Rom.* XVIII, 197.

Holthausen, F. "*Sir Amadas* und Peele's *Old Wives Tale*." *Archiv.* CXVII, 177 (1907).

Köhler, R. "Die dankbaren Toten u. der gute Gerhard." *Kleinere Schriften*, I, 5–29. Weimar, 1898, 1900.

Stephens, G. See Texts.

---

posed by Johannes Junior (Gobius). In this Saint Nicholas plays the part of the ghost. To rebuild the church of the saint a merchant impoverishes himself. He wins and loses a wife, the daughter of a sultan. He regains her through the help of the saint.

CLEGES

VERSIONS. Unique in Middle English for its combination of humor, piety, and romance, is the pleasant little poem of *Sir Cleges*, which is preserved in two fifteenth-century manuscripts. Common rimes show the derivation of these texts from an earlier English original, but in detail they differ widely, as if written down from memory or oral recitation (McKnight, p. lxxiv). The familiar verse tag, " so seyeth ðe boke " (l. 248), may or may not refer to this lost version, but it is at least possible from a comparison of the two extant texts to conclude that it was composed in the North Midland district about the beginning of the fifteenth century (Treichel, p. 371). The verse is the twelve-line stanza, riming usually aabccbddbeeb.

ORIGIN. Like so many others, *Cleges* is clearly a minstrel tale. Naïvely it praises gift-giving to minstrels and Christmas feasts; naïvely it enjoys the punishment of the surly porter, the traditional enemy of minstrels; and a minstrel " geste " is made partly responsible for the impoverished hero's restoration to fortune. In verse, as in spirit, one hears the voice of some shrewd, singing wayfarer. With catholic taste, he combines in somewhat motley sort themes proper to entirely different literary types. Influenced probably by *Sir Amadas*, he begins with the motive of the " Spendthrift Knight," [1] and touches it with homely tenderness in the picture of Cleges, grieving over his ruined state, being comforted by his gentle wife and little children. As in a *conte dévot*, he tells of Cleges's prayer for help and the answering miracle of the cherry tree [2] hung with

---

[1] McKnight, pp. lxiii ff., noted as other examples of the Spendthrift Knight *motif* Chestre's *Launfal* (ed. *Eng. Stud.* xviii) and the later *Sir Lambewell* (*Percy Folio MS.* ii), the fifteenth-century *Knyght and his Wyfe* (Hazlitt, *Remains*, ii), and a *True Tale of Robin Hood* (Child, no. 154). See here under *Amadas*.

[2] The miracle of getting fruit out of season appears in saint legends, in stories of Impossible Tasks, and of magical accomplishment. Cf. McKnight, p. lxv; Chambers, *Medieval Stage*, i, 252–53; Tatlock, Chaucer Soc. 2nd Ser. 51, p. 55, note 3.

fruit on Christmas day. This is at once the knight's reward for his previous generosity and the means of his rehabilation. The minstrel draws on romance for the dim Arthurian setting of the court of King Uther, whose famous gallantries to Igerne are faintly suggested in the king's gift of Cleges's cherries to a " bryght lady " of Cornwall. Even the name Cleges, which appears in the stories of Chrétien and Malory, belongs to romantic tradition. But as the poet goes on to tell of the hero's encounter with the greedy porter, the usher, and the steward, who each demand a third of his reward before admitting him to the king's presence, and on whose account he asks for a reward of twelve blows, romance gives way to a widely known folktale. As jest, biographical anecdote, fabliau, or moralized exemplum, the story of the " Blows Shared " or " Greed Requited " appears in the English *Gesta Romanorum* [3] and in popular French, German, Spanish, Latin, Greek, Swedish, Italian, Turkish, and Arabic versions. It is one of those universal tales common to all races and all times to which no date or home can be assigned. So far as is now known, *Sir Cleges* is simply one of many independent versions (McKnight, p. lxxii ff.).

BIBLIOGRAPHY

TEXTS: (1) Jac V, 7, 27, Advocates Library, Edin., ed. Weber, 1, 331 (1810); Ashmole 61, Bodleian, Oxf. (576 lines), ed. G. H. McKnight, *Middle English Humorous Tales in Verse*, pp. 39–59, Boston, 1913; The two MSS. were ed. by A. Treichel, *Eng. Stud.* XXII, 374 ff. Trans. by J. Weston, *Libeaus Desconus and Sir Cleges*, Lond. 1902.

STUDIES: McKnight, Introd. lxi–lxxv, and Bibliography, p. 89 ff.

[3] For the " Blows Shared " story in England see the English *Gesta* (EETSES. XXXIII, 413, *no.* XC); the Latin story of *Invidia* of John Bromyard, *Summa Praedicantium*, f. CXIII, b, and the *Pleasant Conceites of Old Hobson, the Merry Londoner* (Hazlitt, *Shakespeare's Jest Books*, p. 40, no. 24). Cf. McKnight, pp. lxix–lxxi. As the latter points out, the story is akin to the tale of the Three Wishes, (Bédier, *Les Fabliaux*, 1895, p. 220), to the *Dit du Buffet* (Montaiglon et Raynaud, *Fabliaux*, 1872–90, Notes) and to the one called "Lucky they are not peaches" (W. Clouston, *Popular Tales*, II, 467 ff.).

ROMANCES OF LEGENDARY ENGLISH HEROES

KING HORN

VERSIONS. *Horn* is one of the best stories that came out of Anglo-Norman England. The manner of its telling varies in different versions, but its narrative vigor does not greatly change. " Blithely " enough it sets forth the story of the boy Horn and the loss of his kingdom, of his bringing up at the court of a foreign king, of his winning the love of a foreign princess, of a false accusation made against Horn and his second exile, of his adventures at the court of another king, of his two rescues of his sweetheart from unwelcome suitors, and of his final recovery of his heritage. Outworn as most of these situations were destined to become in the development of mediæval fiction, in the *Horn* legend they are freshly told and altogether diverting.

The earliest manuscripts of the story in either French or Middle English belong to the thirteenth century. The Anglo-Norman version [1] consists of 5250 alexandrines rimed in "tirades." Its original has in general been ascribed to the twelfth century, though some scholars, on account of the elaborated picture of court life presented in the poem, have placed it in the first half of the thirteenth century (Hartenstein, pp. 19–20). The increasing realization of the influence upon it of the Anglo-Norman Tristan [2] lends likelihood to this later date. In the

[1] This is extant in three long manuscripts and in the Cambridge fragments printed in 1921 by Braunholtz. The poem was first edited in 1845 by Michel under the title *Horn et Rimenhild (RH)*. It was re-edited in 1883 by Brede and Stengel, *Ausgaben u. Abhandlungen*, VIII, and a new critical edition is under consideration (P. Studer, *Study of Anglo-Norman*, Oxford, 1920, p. 28).

[2] Thomas's *Tristan* was written between 1155 and 1170 (Bédier, *Tristan*, II, p. 55); or possibly as late as 1189 (Loomis, *MLR*. XIV, 39; XVII, 26). It is to be regretted that no complete historical study of the names in *RH* has yet been made, for behind them may lurk a good deal of historical evidence, to say nothing of connections with the *chansons de geste*. For a list of the proper names in *RH*, see Mettlich, *Bemerkungen zu d. agn. Lied vom wachern Ritter Horn*, Munster, 1896; rev. *Eng. Stud.* XVI, 306. Heuser, pp. 112–15, emphasized the vital importance of the name-evidence in the French version for any source study of the legend.

extant version the author alludes several times to a written source, his "escrit" (l. 192), his "parchment" (ll. 2993, 3981), and refers to himself as "Mester Thomas" and to his "fiz Gilimot /Ki la rime apre mei bien controuerat" (l. 5240). Who this Thomas was has not been determined. Hartenstein (pp. 23–25) believed that he was a native of southern England, who had possibly been in Brittany; that his native speech was Anglo-Norman, but that he was not altogether ignorant of English since he introduced such words as *horn* (l. 4206) and *God wite* (l. 4013) into his text; that he was a poet familiar not only with the *Horn* story but with legends about Horn's father; finally, that he was old enough when he finished *Horn* to have a son capable of continuing his work. Hartenstein's idea (p. 34) that this Thomas was a traveling minstrel depended chiefly on the many references to minstrels and their accomplishments which come into the story. But its length and elaboration argue that its author was of more leisurely habit of life than most minstrels. He may well have been a courtly clerk like his countryman and possible contemporary, Hue de Roteland, the author of *Ipomedon*.

The French *Horn*, as Soderhjelm observed (*Rom.* 1886, xv, 579 ff.), has in general the spirit of a *chanson de geste* and the romantic character of a story of the Table Round. Epic tendencies are shown in lusty fights between Christians and pagans, in the glorification of prowess, the enthusiastic descriptions of battle after battle in which Christian heroes are individually portrayed, and in the practical absence of all supernatural element save the prophetic "epic dream." Horn himself is conceived primarily as a fighter, and the romance has as a whole an air more militant than romantic. Yet it was definitely influenced by romances of the "courtois" type; its manners and customs are altogether feudal and chivalric; it lingers over all the scenes of courtly life, over the elaborate feasts, the tournaments, the games and sports of the young nobles, over the description of the rooms of the Irish princess Lemburc, over details of costume and feeling (Stimming, *Eng. Stud.* 1, 357–60). The courtly line, "De la belte de Horn tute la chambre resplent" (l. 1053), which recalls a similar gracious bit of fantasy in *Aucassin,* proved too charming for even the abrupt Middle

English redactor to resist (Hall, p. 117). The influence of *Tristan* seems most palpable in the scenes in which the disguised young Horn sings before Lemburc or Rimenhild (Schofield, p. 60). The women characters of the French *Horn* are wholly without the emotional subtlety of those in *Tristan,* but it is suggestive of the sophisticated character of the romance that Rimel has her confidante Herselot, and is attended by a retinue of lovely maidens.

The Middle English version of *King Horn* (KH), like that in French, has been preserved in three manuscripts. The oldest and probably the nearest to the original text is the Cambridge manuscript (C), written about 1260 by an Anglo-Norman scribe (Hall, p. x). Wissmann (1, p. 15) believed that the three texts were independent variants derived from oral transmission, but Zupitza (*Anz. f. deut. Alt.* IX, 181–92) and Hall (p. xiv) emphasized the textual relationship of Laud and Harleian 2253, that famous anthology of lyrics, satires, fables, and saint legends which may have emanated from the priory of Leominster (Hall, p. viii). McKnight (p. xxviii) thought the original Middle English version of *Horn* must have been composed in the last half of the thirteenth century, probably in the Middle South; in Essex, according to Wissman (*Untersuch.* p. 33); in North-West Surrey, according to Hall (p. xliv). The poem is apparently transitional in form, for it is rimed but is not in the " beat verse " of romance rhythm. Some have seen in it " the coming to light again of the primitive Teutonic measure song verse " of the four-stress " Otfrid " type (Luick, Paul's *Grundriss,* 1893, 11, 994, 1004; 1007; Wissman, *Untersuch,* p. 56); others, like Schipper (*Grund. d. Eng. Metrik,* Bonn, 1885), recognized in it the natural development of the Old English alliterative verse under the influence of French prosody with its insistence on syllabic regularity and rime. McKnight (p. xxiii) felt that in the verse of *Horn* alliteration has become an unessential element, and agreed with Schipper (pp. 71–72) that in about 1300 verses the prevailing form, a variety of Siever's A type in Anglo-Saxon verse, has three accents and feminine rime. Schipper's scansion of the poem was also accepted by Hall. West (ch. IV) argued, however, that *Horn* shows a two-stress movement in free rhythm and that in its internal structure the *Horn* couplet is only a natural Middle English development of the Anglo-Saxon four-stress long line when rimed in equalized short lines (pp. 33, 50, 88).

In comparison with the French version, *King Horn* (*KH*) seems as abrupt as it is virile and primitive. Its poet cares nothing for the knowing courtliness of Thomas. Though he has the same story to tell, he hurries through it as to the swift twanging of his own harp. His Horn is " blithe " to be alive, blunt to the point of rudeness, brutal and gay, impatient of everything save fighting, a wholly unsentimental lover who is more interested in rescuing his sweetheart than in remaining with her. The bareness of scene, the simplicity of motive, and lively vigor of action, give the English *Horn* a popular, ballad-like quality.

Because of such archaic effects as these, many German and English scholars have thought the English poem older than the Anglo-Norman version.[3] Such a conclusion not only contradicts such evidence as the manuscripts give, but ignores the French influence in the metre, vocabulary, and spirit of the poem.[4] As Schofield (p. 3) pointed out, romance scholars are unanimous in declaring that the extant French version is earlier than the English. The essential identity of the two stories has always been recognized, but in all the study lavished on their individual traits, aside from the matter of terminology, not more than eight passages have been noted which are peculiar to the English *Horn* (McKnight, p. x). Of these not one changes the story or is more than a natural enough variation for an author as different in poetic character and purpose as the English minstrel was from Mestre Thomas. In their specialized study of the names in the

[3] Child, *Ballads,* I, 192; Billings, *Guide,* p. 5; McKnight, p. xii; Hall, p. liv; Wissman, *Untersuch.,* p. 113; Stimming, *Eng. Stud.* I, 352. Hartenstein, pp. 19–20, 78, 109, recognized the priority of the French version.

[4] For the romance words in the vocabulary see Hall, pp. xxix–xxxi; for metre West, passim. Hartenstein, p. 116, recorded the ninety-five French rimes of *KH,* but thought the number too small to be significant. McKnight, p. x, who assumed that *RH* borrowed from *KH,* listed a number of close verbal parallels between the two poems. Though the unromantic and uncourtly style of *KH* gives the effect of much greater primitiveness than does the style of the French poem, it must be noted that *KH* depends absolutely for content on romantic themes which were not, as far as we know, familiarized in England until after the Conquest. Cf. Schofield, p. 52; McKnight, *Horn,* p. xx.

English poem, both Morsbach (p. 297) and Schofield (pp. 51–53) became convinced that it had come directly from some earlier French version. Schofield, however, continued to believe that behind this inevitable " lost " French version, there must have been a still earlier one in English.[5] Though Heuser did not credit the name studies of Morsbach and Schofield, he admitted (p. 129) the possibility that an early Bretonized lay existed, and that an English redaction was made in the first half of the eleventh century.

In addition to the French and Middle English versions already noted, the story of *Horn* is also preserved in the poem known as *Horn Child* (HC), in certain Scotch ballads of *Horn,* and in the prose romance, *Ponthus et la belle Sidoyne,* written between 1372 and 1390 in honor of the famous Tour Landri family of Anjou (G. Paris, *Rom.* xxvi, 468–70). The earliest manuscript of *Ponthus* is in the magnificent volume, Royal 15, E, vi, of the British Museum, which was presented to Margaret of Anjou in 1445 (Ward, *Catalogue,* i, 130). Not all the French manuscripts of this romance have been noted, but the favor in which it was held is suggested by the seven manuscripts listed by Hartenstein (p. 144) and by the seven French editions appearing between 1478 and 1548 (Brunet, *Manuel du Libraire,* Paris, 1863). In England the story was translated about the middle of the fifteenth century in a version of which two copies survive in manuscripts. The same version is also found in Wynkyn de Worde's edition of 1511 and in another edition of 1548 (Esdaile, *List of Eng. Tales before 1740,* p. 113). About 1465 *Ponthus* was translated from French into German by Eleanor, daughter of James I of Scotland and wife of Archduke Sigismund of Austria. Eleanor's translation was frequently copied and printed in various revisions, among them the sixteenth-century *Buch der*

---

[5] The basis for this belief is not clear. In passing, Schofield, p. 36, referred to the English names in the story and implied, pp. 29, 51, not only that the recurrent pun on the hero's name in *RH* and *KH* was in an original English version of the story but that this version preceded the Conquest. The evidence for this was an allusion in the French *Waldef* to English versions of *Tristan, Waldef,* and *Aalof,* a hero who is mentioned in *RH* as the father of Horn. The unsatisfactory nature of this reference is discussed below (*Horn Child,* note 6), but at best it offers an argument from analogy only. Even the proved existence of an Old English *Aalof* saga would not establish the existence also of a *Horn* saga.

Liebe. Through the sixteenth and seventeenth centuries the story in romance or chap-book form continued its popularity (Hartenstein, pp. 146–48). From Germany it passed into Iceland, and there in the sixteenth century an Icelandic *Ponthus* was begun (Mather, p. xli, ff.).

The relation of *Ponthus* to the Anglo-Norman *Horn* was first noted by Weber (*Met. Romances,* 1810, III, 361). Mather, (pp. vi–xvii) showed how carefully the French author used every essential element of the earlier plot of *Horn* but how he changed the localization of the story, substituting Spain for Suddene, England for Ireland, and intensified by the introduction of many French scenes and historical characters the interest for a French audience. His special purpose in retelling it, apart from glorifying the Tour Landri family, was to make it a book of introduction in courtesy; and for this purpose he dwelt on the beauty, accomplishments, and virtues of his hero Ponthus, who is representative of the later, more complicated ideal of knighthood. Mather (p. xlvii) noted a certain sweetness and gaiety of spirit which save Ponthus, despite his virtues, from being " a Grandison out of due time." In the French author's style there was no distinction, but in the English version Mather felt some improvement. Though he would not compare it with Malory's subtly beautiful cadences, he found in it the brisk and fluent virtue of unaffected talk.

The latest versions of the *Horn* story are found in nine or ten Scotch ballads of *Hind Horn*,[6] and in one version known as Colhorn (MacSweeney). In these texts the old story is reduced to a matter of seventy lines or less. The lovers exchange gifts; Horn receives a magic ring; when it warns him of his love's danger he returns, hears from a beggar of her imminent marriage, enters the castle, and begs a drink in Horn's name. The bride recognizes the ring he drops in the cup, and joyously offers to go beg with him " frae town to town." Traits such as the discoloration of the ring, the beggar disguise, the ironic final

---

[6] Child, *Ballads,* no. 17; Hartenstein, p. 88. Nelles believed the likeness between *Horn* and the debased ballad of the *Kitchie Boy* (Child, vol. IV, 400) is more a matter of stock stanzas than of actual relationship. MacSweeney, (p. 210) spoke of the influence of *Hind Horn* in *Young Beichan, Lady Diamond, Robin Hood rescuing three Squires.*

couplet (A 24), seem to link the ballads with *Horn Child* rather than with *King Horn*. Hartenstein (p. 124) believed the ballads originated in a North-English folk-saga from which all extant versions were derived, and Nelles, who has made the closest study of the ballads, accepted the theory of a common source for them and *Horn Child*.

ORIGIN. Whether the original *Horn* story came from the Anglo-Saxons, the Danes, the Norse Vikings, or the Anglo-Normans, is still a matter of dispute. Germanic elements in the story were noted as early as 1811 by Grimm (*Mus. f. altd. kunst u. Litt.* Berlin, II, 303). Stimming (*Eng. Stud.* I, 355) likewise thought that the names were Germanic, and McKnight made the same claim for such dominant *motifs* as the exile-and-return of the hero and the separation and reunion of faithful lovers. In 1911 Grass (p. 38) too urged that *Horn* as a bride-winning story was closely related to *Kudrun* and other Germanic tales. But Wissman's observations (*Anglia* IV, 398) that there is nothing in *Horn* which can be called exclusively Germanic appear still to hold good. In general the topography of the poem has come to be the decisive test of critical opinion. Those who identify Suddene, Horn's own home, as Surrey (Michel, *RH*, p. 454) or Sussex (Ward, *Catalogue*, I, 450) or as South Devon (Suðdefne, Heuser, p. 119) or any other part of the southern coast of England, believe in the English origin of the story and relate its events to the Anglo-Danish period. Hartenstein (p. 29) and the latest editors of the Middle English poem, Hall (p. lv) and McKnight (p. xvii), expressed themselves in favor of this English derivation.

The belief in the Danish origin of the legend rests on the identification of Suddene as Suðdene, the land of the South-Danes, who are mentioned in *Beowulf*. Ten Brink (*Hist. Eng. Lit.* I, 150) was convinced that " the North Sea, its neighboring waters, and their shores, were the scene of the action." Horn himself was tentatively identified by Suchier (*Gesch. d. frz. Lit.*, p. 111) with the Danish Horm who went in 851 to Ireland where he was hospitably received and fought victoriously against the Norwegian Vikings. Deutschbein (pp. 15–26) made the same suggestion and went on to trace the gradual Christianization of the narrative and its absorption of the names and characters of later Norse-Irish history. For instance, the " Arald, crown prince of the foreigners of Erinn," who was killed at the great battle of Glenmama in 1000, was equated by Deutschbein with Arild, son of King Thurston of Ireland, in the romance, and in a later article Deutschbein (3, p. 55) discovered Horn's true historic prototype to have been the Viking, Eyvindr Úrarhorn. But the evidence concerning Horm or Eyvindr or the Norse Orns mentioned by Schofield (p. 29) is slight at best, and the assumption that the story of Horn's life at the Irish court is the oldest part of the legend, is seriously open to question. The " duplication of climax," once regarded as evidence that independent traditions about Horn had been linked together, was shown by McKnight (p. 224) to be a familiar enough feature in mediæval fiction. Since in all versions the most vital part of the story is Horn's relation to Rimenhild and his rescues of her, it seems difficult to believe that the whole story of their early love was invented as mere duplication of the Irish episode. Deutschbein's belief (p. 4) in the priority of the Irish adventures was due to what seems a mistaken emphasis on the detail that in Ireland Horn had a chance to kill some of the enemies who had slain his father.[7] But this is only a palpable device for linking unrelated episodes together; the real vengeance of Horn belongs to the later part of the story in which he returns to his kingdom and regains it after a general destruction of his foes. If the secondary character of the Irish adventures be admitted, then

[7] Ward, *Catalogue*, 1, 448, also believed that the Irish episode was the oldest part of the story. But the reason he gave, i.e., that Horn regains his love and his heritage through the help of Irish knights, is as open to question as Deutschbein's. In romance heroes acquire troops with incredible ease; troops are mere accessories. In the traditional situation the lover who returns to rescue his sweetheart from an enemy's power is usually alone, just as in the ballad versions Horn is alone. In any primitive version this was probably the case. To the present writer it seems as futile to argue the priority of the Irish Rimel-Lemburc story to the rest of *RH* as it would be to urge that in the *Tristan* legend the episode of the second Isolt was the earliest. The practical identity in *KH* of the names Rymenhild and Reynild shows that even the English poet was familiar with this device of writers using in whole or in part the theme of the Man with Two Wives. (Cf. Matzke, *Mod. Phil.* 1907–8, v, and here, *Lay le Freine*, note 6.) On different grounds, Grass, p. 50, also expressed disbelief in the " historical " origin of *Horn*, and in the priority of the Reynild story.

the theory that they represent the historic kernel of the romance is hardly tenable.

In 1903 Schofield set forth an ingenious argument to prove that the original *Horn* story was an old Norse tale of the tenth century orally transmitted to some Old English poet, and that his Old English version was translated by an Anglo-Norman into the simple version which was the source of the extant Middle English *Horn*. Schofield identified Suddene as the Isle of Man, from which a strong north-west wind might, as the story tells, drive Horn's boat in twenty-four hours to England, Westir as Ireland, and Westernesse (Western Ness) as the Wirral peninsula. Topographically Schofield's theory is in many ways reasonable, but unfortunately it rests, as did the identification of Suddene as Surrey, on the single recorded instance in the manuscript of Gaimar's *Estorie des Engles* in which the one word is used for the other. Schofield (p. 7, 12) pointed out that in form the old name of Surrey, Sudreie, would be identical with the name given by the Norse Vikings to the Isle of Man, Su rey, as one of the Su reyjar, South Isles, and that it would not be impossible for French writers to turn Suðrey into Sudene even as they turned Orkneye into Orceine. He argued further (p. 39) that the events and places in *KH* were of a sort familiar to the Norsemen of the ninth and tenth centuries, and that the Horn story itself was of the same type as that told of the Viking, Gunnlaug Serpent-Tongue (983–1009), whose actual history received poetic embellishment and was orally transmitted for several generations. The realistic impression given by the English *Horn*, Schofield (pp. 43–45) believed, was due to its reminiscences of actual Norwegian depredations of the tenth century, introduced by the Old English poet to whom the story of a Viking's adventures had come.

The *Namenuntersuchung* set forth by Heuser in 1908 did more to advance the true understanding of the *Horn* legend than earlier studies in so far as he emphasized the importance of the earliest extant text, the French *Horn et Rimenhild*, which other scholars, obsessed by the idea of the primitiveness of *King Horn*, have neglected. Heuser insisted that all the supposed historical elements in the different versions are variable, whereas the love story of Horn and Rimenhild remains constant, recognizable in whatsoever form, and persistently dear to people living in England.[8] The roots of the story, he believed, must have been English and have had their growth in Cornwall, where the romantic adventures of Hereward, which Deutschbein (p. 55), Wissman (*Untersuch.* p. 110), and others, have recognized as a variant of the *Horn* story, are clearly localized. Of all explanations of Horn's name, that of Heuser's, which connected it by way of the Celtic *corn* (Latin *cornu*) with Cornwall, is perhaps, the most convincing. Deutschbein's assertion (2, 18) of the lack of any literary connections between the Anglo-Saxons and the people of Cornwall was disproved by the evidence concerning the early history of Cornwall in J. Loth's, *Contributions a l'Étude des Romans de la Table Ronde* (Paris, 1912, p. 65 ff.). The *Ur-Horn* may indeed have been influenced by tales of Scandinavian-Irish wars, but it seems probable that it was in the form practically of a lay and that its nucleus was romantic rather than historical.

The significant *motifs* and details in *King Horn* are for the most part easily defined. The Exposure of the boy hero in a rudderless boat recalls that of the boy Sceaf, of Arthur's exposure of the children born on May day, and that of many another unfortunate in history and romance (Hall, pp. 102–03). The lad's arrival at the court of the Foreign King may be matched with that of Beves (Boje, *Beves*, p. 79 ff.). The account of the instructions given for his Education, the description of his Dubbing, the gift to him of the wonder-working Ring, are most fully paralleled by Hall (pp. 108–09; 124–26; 129–30) and by Wissman (*Anglia* iv, 352–57). Horn's rescue of Rimenhild from the unwelcome wooing of King Modi and again from his own false friend, Fikenild, are incidents appearing in a great number of romantic tales which have been studied by Child (*Ballads*, 1, 194) and by Splettstösser (*Der heimkehrende Gatte*, Berlin,

---

[8] Nelles, like Heuser, was content to recognize the primarily romantic character of *Horn*. Many other writers, even those most insistent on the ancient historical origin of the poem, have admitted the impress of the age of chivalry on *King Horn*.

Of importance for the further study of names in *Horn, Havelok, Beves,* the so-called "Viking sagas," is E. Björkman's *Nordische Personennamen in England in alt. u. frühmittel. Zeit,* Halle, 1910. Interesting, too, is such a study as H. O. Wyld's, "Old Scandinavian Personal Names in England," *MLR.,* v, 289–96 (1910), though this is limited to Lancashire names.

1899). In these the regularly recurrent elements are the long absence of the lover, his sudden return and appearance under disguise at the feast celebrating the nuptials of his love, and his revelation of himself to the bride by means of a ring dropped into a wine-cup. The Disguise as a minstrel or a beggar is a device which may have borrowed no more from fiction than from life itself.[9] Of special interest is the similarity already noted between the *Horn* story and the *Gesta Herewardi* (ed. T. H. Hardy, Gaimar's *Estoire,* Rolls Ser. 1888, I, 349–53), which tells of the disguised Hereward's rescue of a Cornish princess at her marriage feast. Layamon's *Brut* (ed. Madden, ll. 30,728–828) tells of Brian, disguised as a pilgrim, who sought his sister at the court of Edwine (Hartenstein, pp. 137–38). Episodes of this sort seem to have been especially popular during the Crusades, and in this, as well as in the typical animosity to " heðene houndes," the *Horn* legend seems to show the influence of crusading times. Like other heroes in such " cheerful edifying romances " as *Beves of Hampton* and *Guy of Warwick,* Horn during his long absence remains loyal to Rimenhild, and the second lady, who is cither offered to him (*KH*) or is won by his own charm (*RH*), is not treated as a psychological problem but simply as a test of the hero's faith (Schoepperle, *Tristan,* I, 166–73).

The most notable folk-lore elements in the legend are the riddles or parables which appear in both the French and the Middle English versions. In *King Horn* the disguised hero tells Rimenhild he has come back to see if his net is still as he left it, his net meaning Rimenhild herself. In the French version Horn meets his rival Modin and, riddling so that the latter thinks him a fool, tells of a net for which he has now returned. Later to Rimel he tells the parable of the Hawk which he hopes to find as good as he left it. Child (*Ballads,* I, 191) noted the

---

[9] No one seems to have noted in this connection the story quoted by Dugdale, *Monasticon Anglicanum,* Lond., 1830, VI, 501, from the Register of Lacock Abbey, concerning William Talbot. In 1186 William assumed the guise of a pilgrim and sought for Ela, heiress of the Earl of Salisbury, who had been taken to Normandy and was there strictly guarded. Having found the right castle, William, who was skilled in songs, put on a minstrel's guise and so won his way within. He succeeded in escaping with the lady and in bringing her back to England, where she was given in marriage to William Longespee.

similarity of the French parable of the net to a story told in the *Gesta Romanorum* in which, after exchanging vows of fidelity with an emperor's daughter, a soldier goes to the holy land for seven years, returns, meets a king who is a rival suitor, and tells the same net story. The Hawk parable is found in the romance of *Jehan et Blonde* (ed. Suchier II, l. 2821), written between 1270 and 1280 by Philippe de Remi, Sire de Beaumanoir. In the fifteenth century a revised version was known as *Romant de Jehan de Paris* (Hartenstein, pp. 138 ff.). Except for these tales and for variants of *Apollonius,* riddles are of comparatively rare occurrence in romance.

The century and more of criticism that has been devoted to *King Horn* has established few facts, though it has brought forth stimulating discussion of the verse form and topography of the poem and the relationship of the versions. At present the tendency is to believe that the *Horn* legend was possibly influenced in the course of its development by Anglo-Danish affairs but that its origin was in romantic rather than historical tradition, and that the early-seeming Middle English version is actually later than the elaborated Anglo-Norman romance by Mestre Thomas. Though in this last version lies probably the most fruitful field for future research, in *King Horn* itself lives one of the earliest and most virile of Middle English romances.

BIBLIOGRAPHY

TEXTS: (1) H, Harley 2253 (1546 lines), ed. Ritson, 1802, II, 91–155; (2) O, Laud Misc. 108, Bodleian, desc. *Archiv.* XLIX, 395–414; ed. Horstmann, Herrig's *Archiv.* L, 39–58 (1872); (3) Univ. Libr. Cbg., Gg. IV, 27, 2 (1530 lines), ed. Michel, *Horn et Rimenhild,* Paris, 1845; J. R. Lumby, *EETS.* XIV, 1866; reëd. G. McKnight, 1901; R. Morris, *Specimens,* 1887, I, 237–86; Maetzner, *Alteng. Sprachproben,* 1867, l. 209 ff. A critical edition was published by T. Wissman, *Quellen u. Forsch.* XLV (1881). The three MSS. were printed by McKnight, *op. cit.* and by Jos. Hall, Oxford, 1901. See Hall, p. xv, for reviews of Wissman; Wells, p. 762, for reviews of Hall. An edition by L. Morsbach of Göttingen was announced in 1902. Trans. L. A. Hibbard, *Three Middle Eng. Romances,* 1911; J. Weston, *Chief. Middle Eng. Poets,* p. 93 ff.; H. Lindemann. *King Horn, eine mittelengl. Romane aus dem 13 Jhdt. ins. deutsche übertragen,* Köln. 1904.

STUDIES: Billings, *Guide*. pp. 23–24; Hartenstein (see below), pp. 3–14; Wells, *Manual*, p. 762; West (see below) for verse studies, pp. xi–xiv.

Azzalino, W. *Die Wortstellung im King Horn*. Diss. 194 pp. Halle, 1915.

Braunholtz, E. G. "Cambridge Fragments of the Anglo-Norman Roman de Horn," *MLR.*, XVI, 23–33 (1921).

Breier, W. "Zur Lokalisierung des King Horn," *Eng. Stud.* XLII, 307–09 (1910).

Dahms, O. *Der Formenbau des Nomens u. Verbums in dem anglonormanischen Gedichte "Das Lied von wackern ritter Horn."* Diss. 87 pp. Kiel, 1906.

Deutschbein, M. (1) *Studien zur Sagengeschichte Englands* (Horn, Havelok, Tristan, Boeve, Guy of Warwick). 264 pp. Cöthen, 1906. Rev. *Literar. Zentralblatt*, 1906, sp. 1276; *Deut. Literaturzeit.* 1906, sp. 1578; *Literaturblatt f. ger. u. rom. Phil.* 1907, sp. 280; *MLR.*, 1907, p. 176; *Anglia Bl.* XVIII, 1–13; (2) "Beitrage z. Horn und Havelocsage." *Anglia Bl.* XX, 16–24; (3) "Zur historischen Hornsage (= Horn B)," *ibid.* pp. 55–59 (1910).

Grass, P. *Horn u. Hilde in ihrer Stellung z. germ. Sagengeschichte*. Diss. 51 pp. Münster, Borna-Leipzig, 1911.

Hall, J. See Texts.

Hartenstein, O. *Studien zur Horn Sage, ein Beitrag z. Litteraturgeschichte des Mittelalters*. (*Kieler Stud. z. engl. Phil.* IV.) Heidelberg, 1902.

Heuser, W. "Horn u. Rigmel (Rimenhild); eine Namenuntersuchung," *Anglia* XXXI, 105–31 (1908).

Luick, K. "Berichtigung zu King Horn," *Anglia Beiblatt* XIII, 332–33 (1902).

MacSweeney, J. J. "Hind Horn," *MLR.* XIV, 210–11 (1919).

Mather, F. J. "King Ponthus and the Fair Sidone," *PMLA.* XII, 1–150 (1897). Rev. G. Paris, *Rom.* XXVI, 468–70.

McKnight, G. H. "Germanic Elements in the Story of Horn," *PMLA.* XV, 221–32 (1900). See also Texts.

Morsbach, L. Die angebliche Originalität des frühmitteleng. King Horn," *Beitr. z. rom. u. engl. Phil., Festgabe f. Foerster*, p. 297 ff. Halle, 1902.

Nelles, W. C. "The Ballad of Hind Horn," *Jour. of American Folk-Lore*, XXII, 42–63 (1909).

Northup, C. S. "King Horn, Recent Texts and Studies" (with a comparative table of line numbers for nine editions), *Jour. Ger. Phil.* IV, 529–41 (1902).

Schofield, W. H. "The Story of King Horn and Rimenhild," *PMLA.* XVIII, 1–84 (1903).

Tamson, G. "A Passage in the Middle Eng. King Horn," v. 701–04, *Anglia* XIX, 460 (1896–97).

Vising, J. *Studier i den franska romanen om Horn*. I. Goteborg, 1903; II (1904), Prolegomena zu einer edition des roman von Horn (1905).

West, H. S. *The Versification of King Horn.* Diss. 92 pp. Baltimore, 1907.

Wissman, T. (1) *Untersuchungen zur ME. Sprach- u. Litt. Geschichte*, Strassburg, 1876; *Quellen u. Forsch.* XVI. (Cf. Wells, p. 762, for reviews.) (2) "Studien zu Horn," *Anglia* IV, 342–400 (1881). (3) See also Wissman's editions of *Horn*, Texts.

Wüst, P. *Die deut. Prosaromane von Pontus v. Sidonia.* Diss. Marburg, 1903.

HORN CHILDE

VERSIONS. Chaucer's reference in *Sir Thopas* to *Hornchilde* has given it a bad eminence, justified, so most critics have felt, by the "degenerate minstrelsy" of the poem itself.[1] It consists of 1136 lines in the tail-rime stanza (aab aab ccb ddb), and the single extant text is in the Auchinleck Manuscript (1330–40). The poem therefore must have been composed before 1340, and its borrowings from *Sir Tristrem* (ed. Kölbing, p. lxiv), to which it alludes by name (l. 311), show that it was written after 1290 (Hartenstein, p. 78). The author, who refers to his "boke" (l. 277) and who makes Horn study both "harpe and romance," was familiar with the stock phrasings of Middle English diction. Caro (pp. 347–50) noted a large number of these and indicated also the extensive use in the poem of assonance and alliteration. At times the poet rather helplessly repeats his own expressions, and there is little variety or vigor in his style. In general critics assign his home to the Northern district, but Caro (p. 342), who alone has made any serious study of linguistic evidence, assigned it to the southern part of North England, near the East Midland boundaries (Hartenstein, pp. 78–79).

As early as Bishop Percy's time *Horn Childe* (*HC*) was recognized as "an altered and somewhat modernized version of *King Horn*," or, more accurately, of the *Horn* legend (Hartenstein, p. 77). Its story of Horn's adventures is essentially the same as that in the earlier versions, though it is varied by some individual touches. Like so many of the lesser poets of his time, the author has an unhappy genius for the concrete and trivial at the expense of the imaginative effect. Horn, he tells us, discovers Rimnhild, whom her father has cruelly beaten, "liggeand on hir bede, Mouðe and nose al forbled;" Horn himself on another occasion stays at home for a blood-letting. The Irish king

---

[1] Cf. Hartenstein, p. 85; Schofield, p. 66; Wissman, *Untersuch.* pp. 94–100; Ward, *Catalogue* 1, 458–60.

Finlac, wounded so that the blood " ran ouer his eiȝe " orders
that his daughter " schuld a plaster ta." The poet goes to excess
in localizing the scenes of his story; the Danes invade Northumberland at " Clifland bi Tiseside," fight with Horn's father at
" Alertonmore," and leave their bones where men yet see them
lie " bi Seyn Sibiles kirke." Haðeolf hunts on " Blakeowemore "
heath, holds feasts at Pikering and at York, fights and dies at
" Stainesmore." Horn as a child is carried far south into England, and later as an exile, goes to Snowdon in Wales.[2] The
same excess is shown in the poet's interest in unimportant characters such as Horn's young comrades, whose individual fortunes
are unnecessarily narrated. Yet with all this detail the poem is
not prolix, and makes a real attempt to combine local color and
patriotic feeling with true romantic spirit. One scene at least
is pleasantly told: Rimnild in her bower breaks a pomegran-
ate and offers Horn true knightly gifts, a goshawk, greyhounds,
a black steed, an ivory horn with silk and golden baldric, and
Weland's sword, " Bitterfer." At parting she gives Horn a ring
which will show him by its change of color how she keeps faith.
He in return bids her watch a well, overgrown with ivy, which
will, as long as it is shadowless, be symbolic of his truth.[3] In
the typical vein of popular romance too are the beggar who
brings Horn word of his lady's danger, and the surly porter
whose bones Horn so cheerfully breaks. In somewhat courtly
fashion the poet amplifies the king's speech in regard to the
fealty of Horn's comrades or the account of Horn's joust in the
wood or of the tournament in Wales.

No other version of *Horn Childe* is known, though the Scotch
ballads, already discussed in connection with *King Horn,* were
certainly in some way related to the poem.

ORIGIN. The first two hundred and fifty lines of *Horn Childe,*
according to Schofield (p. 75), embody genuine historical traditions not connected with the *Horn* legend until the composition
of this particular poem. Its remaining portion has a large

---

[2] For proposed identifications of these places see Deutschbein, p. 90;
Hartenstein, pp. 82–3; D. Haigh, *Anglo-Saxon Sagas,* Lond. 1891, pp.
62–70.

[3] For similar tests of faith or of chastity see *Percy Folio MS.* ed. Furnivall, 1868, II, 300–04; Child, *Ballads,* v. Index.

number of important traits which connect it with the Anglo-Norman version of *Horn*. Many names are the same for both; alike too are the scenes in which Rimnild gives her gifts and that in which Horn, disguised as a beggar, meets his rival, King Modiun and " riddles " him the parable of the net. Whatever the minor changes in *Horn Childe,* these parables with *Horn et Rimenhild* make indisputable its author's knowledge of the French text.[4] With *King Horn,* on the other hand, there are few resemblances in diction and none in plot detail not also to be found in the French text. The features listed by McKnight as peculiar to *HC,*[5] may, with two exceptions, be regarded as due to omission. In an abridgment such as this, therefore, they prove nothing in regard to source material.

The two matters in which *Horn Childe* most differs from the French version are its transformation of the scene of the story and its historical introduction. This deals first with a victory of King Haðeolf over Danish raiders, and next with his defeat and death at the hands of King Malkan and Irish foes. The poet was evidently familiar with the territory the traditions of which he wished to use. Schofield (p. 68) noted that most of the places mentioned in *HC* belong to the North Riding of Yorkshire, and identified Horn's father, King Haðeolf, with Earl Eadulf (*c.* 966) of Northumberland; Malkan with King Malcolm I or II of Scotland; Thorbrand, who usurped the land after Haðeolf's death, with the Thorbrand, who, in a pseudo-historical tract ascribed to Simeon of Durham (Ed. T. Arnold, Rolls Ser. 1882, 1, 215), was killed by Aldred, son of Uchtred, the valorous successor of Eadulf. Details from different texts of wholly different date and origin, have to be fitted together to make these identifications possible. Schofield (p. 72) thought that the poet derived his details not entirely from oral traditions but from Anglo-Saxon poems of the same type as the *Battle of Maldon* (991, Anglo-Saxon Chronicle). Just what use a fourteenth-century poet could have made of these songs is not clear. Deutschbein accepted Schofield's placing of the story but pointed

---

[4] Cf. Hartenstein, p. 118; McKnight, p. xv, for variations of critical opinion.

[5] McKnight, *Horn,* p. xiv, mistakenly listed as peculiar to *HC* the scene of Rimmeld's gift-giving which is directly based on that in *RH*.

out that the tract ascribed to Simeon, which tells at length of the
raid of Malcolm II and the siege of Durham, describes an English victory under Uchtred, whereas *Horn Childe* tells of the
English defeat in which Haðeolf was killed. Deutschbein (p. 91)
found in Fordun's late fourteenth-century *Chronica Gentis
Scotorum* (ed. Skene, *Historians of Scotland,* Edin. 1871–72, 1,
182) a more satisfactory reference to a defeat inflicted on the
English by Malcolm II in the neighborhood of Stanmore. As
for the account in *Horn Childe* in which Haðeolf is first represented as conquering the Danish invaders, an episode which
Schofield (p. 68) had somewhat tentatively connected with the
thirteenth-century saga of *Olaf Tryggvason* (trans. Sephton,
Lond. 1895, ch. 64), Deutschbein (p. 93) found its historical
antecedent in the account of a victory achieved by Athelred in
the neighborhood of Alverton (= Allerton) and celebrated by a
feast in York. Although Langtoft, who recorded this episode
(*Chronicle* ed. T. Wright, Rolls Ser. 1866–68, 1, 310), himself
ascribed it to the reign of Athelred I (866–71), Deutschbein
believed that it should be dated in the reign of Athelred II (978–
1016). It is no wonder that by this method " all difficulties
disappear."

The modicum of fact so far established is simply that the
introductory portion of *Horn Childe* does not refer to a special
locality and does contain apparent reminiscences of Danish and
Irish raids. But it seems altogether improbable that the author
drew his material from oral tradition, from Anglo-Saxon songs,
or from any of the texts yet cited. He was, as the rest of the
poem shows, of wholly unoriginal mind and art, and it is safe
to say that this puzzling introduction had some single French
source as easy to abridge as was the French *Horn* itself.[6]

A final word may be said about the evidence that there was

[6] Hartenstein (p. 121) believed that there was a northern Volkssage of
the *Horn* story, that the author of *HC* used it and also, perhaps, the lost
" Chanson Aalof." Schofield, pp. 74–75, noted the lack of any evidence before
HC which would connect the Hafeolf story in *HC* with the Horn legend.
The Aalof story, as Thomas tells it, is as courtly and sophisticated
as *HR* itself. This the *HC* poet might have abridged as he did *HR*,
with change of the original names and places. He might also in a twelfth- or
thirteenth-century French chronicle have found some account of Haðeolf.
But in any case the immediate source used by this poet writing about 1300
cannot have been of very " primitive " character.

once a "saga" of some sort about Horn's father. The oldest extant text of the Horn legend, *Horn et Rimenhild,* refers extensively to Aaluf (Aalof). He was born in a forest, the son of an unknown father and of Goldeburc, daughter of Baderolf, emperor of Germany. He was brought as a foundling to King Silaf (Silaus), happily reared, and became distinguished for his feats of prowess. He was slandered by the traitor Deneray, but nevertheless received for his wife the Princess Samburc, and later became king. During his ten years' rule he became the father of Horn, and the "cumpagnun" and sworn friend of King Gudereche who was later to welcome Horn and tell him something of his father's history. After a heroic fight with invaders Aalof was killed (Hartenstein, p. 60).

It has always been a question whether the story of Aalof was of independent origin and attached to the *Horn* legend by Mestre Thomas, or whether he simply elaborated hints found in his source story. Schofield (p. 56–58) favored the first theory, since the names in the Aalof story are predominantly Germanic and not of Norse origin. He thought them as foreign to the primitive story as would have been the adventures of Hadermod, Horn's son, which Thomas said his own son Gilimot would record. Thomas's reference (l. 192) to his *escrit* would seem to imply an earlier written account of Aalof, for which Schofield found evidence in a passage of the French *Waldef.* The argument seems hardly to take into account the fact that the Aalof story in *Horn Childe,* so far as Hartenstein (p. 60) and others have been able to reconstruct it, is not merely a "suitable" but an almost exact counterpart of the *Horn* story, and that the device of duplication, not merely of climax but of theme, which so often appears in mediæval fiction, could fully account for it. By the time when Mestre Thomas wrote, it was an established custom to write romances dealing with fathers, sons, and even grandsons.[7] Thomas himself intended such a triology in writing

[7] Schofield (p. 58) referred to the stories of Galahad, son of Lancelot, of Lohengrin, son of Parzival. It may be noted that nearly all of the thirteenth-century romances which introduce the *enfance* theme develop the history of the hero's parents almost as fully as that of the hero's son. This is true not only of the prose *Tristan* and of the prose *Lancelot,* but also of the French and Latin romances about the *enfance* of Gawain. Cf. Meyer, "Enfances Gauvain," *Rom.* xxxix, 1–32 (1910); J. D. Bruce, "De Ortu Waluuani," *Hesperia,* 1913.

of Aalof, Horn, and Hadermod. Thomas may have had his earlier written account of Aalof, but the reference in *Waldef*[8] is doubtful confirmation, since its only trustworthy statement is that the current French romances of *Tristan, Waldef,* and *Aalof,* were " molt amées." In the absence of any other known French version of the Aalof story, the *Waldef* passage may as well refer to Thomas's own account as to anything else. So voluminous a romancer was Thomas that mere references to Horn's father in any antecedent text might well have been elaborated by him into the story which he tells. He was amply familiar with contemporary romance;[9] he had in the *Horn* story itself a good model to imitate, and his Aalof story must not, therefore, despite its Germanic names, be taken as serious witness either to antiquity or to reality.

BIBLIOGRAPHY

TEXTS: (1) Auchinleck MS. f. 317–22, ed. Ritson 1810, III, 282–320; Michel, *Horn et Rimenhild,* 1845, pp. 341–89; J. Caro, *Eng. Stud.* XII, 323–66 (1888–89); J. Hall, *King Horn,* Oxford, 1901, pp. 179–92.

STUDIES. Cf. Billings, *Guide,* pp. 11–12; Hartenstein (see below); Wells, *Manual,* p. 763.
For references to Deutschbein, Hartenstein, McKnight, Nelles, Schofield, see *Horn* bibliography.

---

8 Cf. Hartenstein, p. 110; Schofield, p. 50. For the fifteenth-century Latin translation by John Bremis, the monk of Thetford, see *Historia Regis Waldef,* ed. R. Imelmann, *Bonner Stud. z. Eng. Phil.* IV, 1912; "Vom romantischen u. geschichtlichen Waldef," *Eng. Stud.* LIII, 362–39 (1919).

9 Heuser (p. 113, n.) referred to the likeness of two of the women's names to those in the *Havelok* legend. Deutschbein (pp. 254–62) discussed the relations of " Sage u. Lit. Deutschlands u. Englands im 11, 12, u. 13 Jahrhundert." See also Langlois, *Table des Noms Propres dans les chansons de Geste.*

HAVELOK THE DANE

VERSIONS. The legend of *Havelok* tells of a prince become pauper. When his father is killed and his kingdom lost, the boy Havelok is taken to England where he becomes the sturdy scullion of an English lord and is married perforce to an English princess. Her wicked guardian, who is Havelok's lord, hopes thus to fulfill his oath to wed her to the strongest man about and also, by this seeming mésalliance, to degrade the maiden. After many adventures Havelok regains his own heritage and his wife's and dies as king of England and of Denmark.

Of this legend there are four principal versions (Sisam, p. xi–xx). The earliest, an episode introduced in Gaimar's *Estorie des Engles*, ll. 41–818 (ed. Hardy and Martin, Rolls Ser. 1888, Part 1, 1–34), was written between 1145 and 1151 and is preserved in four manuscripts (Heyman, p. 139; Gross, *Gaimar; die komposition seiner Reimchronik*, Erlangen, 1902); the second, a French metrical romance of eleven hundred lines, the *Lai d'Havelok* (ed. Hardy and Martin, op. cit. 1, 290 ff.) was composed late in the last half of the twelfth century (Bell, p. 23); the third is the Middle English romance known as *Havelok the Dane;* and the fourth is a summary of eighty-two lines (pr. Sisam, p. xvii) interpolated before 1400 in the Lambeth copy of the translation of the chronicle of Pierre de Langtoft. This translation was made by Robert Manning of Brunne who himself interpolated a passage which shows that in 1338, when he finished his work, he was familiar with a Middle English version of *Havelok* (Sisam, p. xvi).

Short minor versions of the story are found in some of the later chronicles: in the *Petit Brut d'Angleterre*, written, according to the prologue, in 1310 by Raouf de Boun(e) of Lincolnshire; in the anonymous *Brut* in fourteenth-century prose which was later translated into English and printed in part by Caxton in 1480; in the *Scala Chronica* [1] written in French prose about

[1] Selections from the two *Bruts* are given by Skeat, 1902. For the *Scala Chronica,* see Heyman, p. 116.

1335 by Sir Thomas Grey of Northumberland; in the *Eulogium Historiarum* (Rolls Ser. 1858–63) of the late fourteenth century; and in the *Chronicon* (Rolls Ser. 1889–95) written by Henry Knighton in the same century (Heyman, pp. 109–22). These are unimportant in determining the relationship of the earlier versions but suggest some interesting connections with other legends. Heyman (p. 112) noted that in Raouf's *Brut,* Guy of Warwick is connected with Havelok's son, and that Knighton tells Guy's story immediately after Havelok's. Both Raouf's *Brut* and the anonymous *Brut* in French prose (cf. Brie, p. 362) give Havelok's father the name " Birkebeyn " in agreement with the Middle English romance. The nickname " Birckebeinar " (Birch-legged fellows), which first appeared in England in Roger of Hoveden's *Chronica,* was Norse in origin and was originally given in Norway to a group of outlaws who succeeded in 1184 in making Sverre Sigurdson their king. In Roger's chronicle, which was written after 1192, this king was referred to as Swerus Birkebein.[2]

The relationship of the extant French versions was first seriously studied in 1880 by Kupferschmidt (*Roman. Stud.* IV, 411–30). He believed that a lost French version in verse was the common source of Gaimar and the French *Lai.* Putnam in 1900 accepted these results with one exception. He urged that the Lambeth Interpolation was not derived from Gaimar, as Kupferschmidt thought, but was an independent summary of the lost version. In the main these views prevailed until Dr. Fahnestock's reconsideration of the whole problem in 1915. She derived the *Lai* from Gaimar, and her conclusion was confirmed by Bell's independent studies in 1923. After a comprehensive sketch of the history of the question, Dr. Fahnestock enumerated in parallel columns the lines in Gaimar's account and in the *Lai* that are in close resemblance, and found (p. 105) that one hundred and seventy lines are identical. The fact that in several instances these lines occur in large groups, suggests that passages in the later version were taken bodily from Gaimar's text. To

[2] Heyman, p. 87. Were Raouf de Boun's text of more reliable character (according to Heyman, p. 104, it is found in only one seventeenth-century manuscript, Harley 902), it would establish the fact that the English *Havelok* was in any case composed before 1310, for Raouf took this name Birkenbayne from the English romance.

the romancer's conscious imitation besides of the *Lais* of Marie de France, Dr. Fahnestock (pp. 115–36) traced such evidences of characteristic technique as the prologue and epilogue in the *Lai,* its references to Arthur and to the Bretons, who are said to have made a lay about Havelok, and its introduction of scenes and characters which belong to a courtly environment. Notable among these personages is Grim, Havelok's friend and rescuer, who is represented as a lordly baron. In few instances can the process by which an *estoire* developed into romance be better studied than in these two texts. As far as the *Lai* is concerned, no *Ur-Havelok* earlier than Gaimar's version need be supposed.

The Middle English romance of *Havelok* is preserved in four brief fragments of a late and corrupt text discovered by Skeat in 1911 (*MLR.* vi) and in Laud Misc. 108, the early fourteenth-century manuscript which also contains *King Horn.* In regard to the date of *Havelok,* Hales (*Athenaeum,* Feb. 1889) argued that the reference (l. 139) to " Rokesburw " as the northern frontier proved the poem after 1296, the year in which, as he supposed, Roxburgh first became a border fortress. He believed also that the reference (l. 1178) to a Parliament at Lincoln must be after 1301, the year in which the first Parliament was held there. But it is now known that Roxburgh was in the hands of the English as early as 1174 (Deutschbein, p. 159), and a Parliament was held at Lincoln in 1226 (Van der Gaaf, p. 319). Skeat (1902, notes, ll. 679, 819) thought the poem was written before 1303, asserting that he caught echoes in it from Robert Manning's *Handlyng Synne.* The two parallel passages cited by him seem, however, somewhat meagre evidence. Both Sisam (p. xxiv) and Schmidt (pp. 89–97) quoted with approval Skeat's argument that the extensive use of final *e* in *Havelok,* contrasted with the more limited use in *Handlyng Synne,* proves the earlier date of the romance. But it must be remembered that the earliest manuscript of the *Handlyng Synne* is later than Laud 108, and that, as far as we know, Robert's work may have been only begun, not necessarily finished, in 1303. The dialect of the romance is that of Lincolnshire where the story itself is localized (Schmidt, p. 80 ff.). On the evidence of rime and verb inflection Hupe (*Anglia,* xiii, 193) argued for Norfolk as the home of the poet. The 3001 lines of *Havelok* are for the most part rimed in short couplets in clear imitation of French models, but occasional passages occur, such as ll. 87–105, which have one rime only (Sisam, p. xxvii–xxxix).

Havelok begins with an appeal for a " cuppe of god ale," and the many personal comments of the author, his quaint proverbs, his hearty curses, his homely figures of speech, the easy casual swing of his verse, suggest that he was a minstrel poet of the same sort as the one who probably once packed into his saddle-bags the small compact manuscript which still preserves the poem. *Havelok* was certainly meant for minstrel recitation, not for reading, and for an altogether popular audience. The author knows and likes plain names such as Griffin Galle, William Wendut, and Huwe Rauen, and enjoys scenes in kitchen or cottage or tavern. He describes with gusto the hard ways of a fisherman's life, and of a Lincoln laborer such as Havelok became. In such passages the poet amplified his French source; two detailed descriptions, for instance, one of forty-five lines and one of two hundred, correspond to passages in the French version of thirteen and fifty-six lines (Creek, p. 205). The English Havelok, who is utterly unlike the conventional heroes of romance except in his prowess and the physical marks of his royal origin, is a hard-working, simple-minded person who is frankly horrified at marriage with a wife whom he is too poor to support. Barefoot he goes to Lincoln, clad in the rough coat which Grim the fisherman has fashioned from a sail. Rarely is romance so frankly realistic as is *Havelok,* so familiar in its portrayal of humble life and of actual environment. Because these traits are distinctive and consistent, Creek rightly refused to accept the old belief that they were all due to popular tradition. He insisted that one feels in *Havelok* an author who had a definite attitude toward his story, who deliberately changed what he wanted to change in his French source, and who is recognizable as a " clear-eyed, kindly practical man, interested in common people, thoroughly patriotic, and very religious in character, if not in profession."

The relationship to its source of the English version of the *Havelok* story is still a matter of controversy of which Dr. Fahnestock (pp. 27–32) has given the fullest report. Skeat's elaborate theory (1902, p. xlviii) of the derivation from a lost English original of the English *Havelok* involved four hypothetical stages of development through which the extant text passed. Skeat took heed of the textual influence of Norman scribes but not of any possible contacts between the English and the French versions. Heyman (p. 147) vigorously denied that the English poem, in which none of the names are French and in which passages occur each of which " is found only in one of the three other versions respectively," could be derived from anything save independent English tradition. He neglected the possibility that changes of name may be the result of deliberate intention or even of mere translation, and his argument from parallel passages is unconvincing until the relationship of the versions has been finally established. Because of the known derivation of most Middle English romances from French originals, and of the indisputable existence of the French versions of the *Havelok* story, Creek (p. 196) and others have admitted the probability that the source of *Havelok* was French (Fahnestock, p. 31). Of special interest was Creek's own study (pp. 197–202) showing the remarkable uniformity of geographical references throughout all the versions, and more important still, the evidence that the English version is " honeycombed with inconsistencies and difficulties which point directly to the French version for explanation."

A certain resemblance between *Havelok* and the *Historia Meriadoci*, a Latin romance of the thirteenth century, has given rise to the conjecture that the latter in its original form was a Welsh version of the *Havelok* story (Deutschbein, p. 134; Bruce, *Historia Meriadoci, Hesperia*, 1913, p. xxx). The resemblance is limited to the first episodes of the two stories, in which royal children are deprived of their heritage by a wicked regent, and saved from the death to which he condemns them by compassionate executioners.[3]

ORIGIN. It is evident that by the middle of the twelfth century, when Gaimar wrote his *Estorie*, the *Havelok* story was fully formulated. That it was localized in Lincolnshire may

[3] A. Olrik, *Heroic Legends of Denmark*, tr. L. Hollander, N. Y. 1919, p. 310, noted that the *Hrolfssaga* is connected but slightly with the *Havelok* legend but closely with *Meriadoc*.

have been one reason for Gaimar's telling it, as he was writing under the patronage of Constance FitzGilbert, a Lincolnshire lady (Sisam, p. xxii). Before 1338, according to Robert Manning, himself of Lincolnshire, men indicated in Lincoln as places of interest the stone that Havelok was supposed to have thrown at some enemies, and the chapel where he was married; Grimsby too was held to be the town founded by Grim the fisherman, (*Chronicle*, ed. Hearne, Oxf. 1725, I, 25). The seal of the town, which is at least as old as the time of Edward I, portrays the figures of " Grym," " Habloc," and " Goldeburgh " in commemoration of the English legend. Between the middle of the twelfth and the middle of the fourteenth century, the story was then vitally alive. What was its origin?

The historical conditions suggested by the various versions of the story are not enlightening. The account of Athelwold's reign in the English *Havelok* is simply idealized description but certain other reminiscences in the legend strongly suggest the Anglo-Scandinavian period.[4] Since in all versions the central idea of the story is the elevation of a Danish prince to the kingship of Denmark and of all or part of England, the origin of the legend as a whole must be subsequent to the time when a Danish sovereign actually ruled England. Heyman (p. 88, 91) noted that the first Dane to hold this office was Sven Tveskæg (1013) and that Canute was the first Danish king to be crowned in London as, in the English romance, Havelok is said

---

[4] For brief but interesting comment on *Horn, Beves,* and *Havelok,* as Viking Sagas see H. Leach, *Angevin Britain and Scandinavia,* Index; for *Havelok* in particular see Björkman, Bugge, and Whistler. Miss Ashdown, p. 113 ff., believed that the episode in the *Lai* in which Havelok fights to decide the fate of his kingdom with the usurper Odulf, formed part of the original legend of Anlaf-Havelok, and that the duel of Canute and Edmund Ironside to decide the fate of England, an episode recorded by Henry of Huntingdon and others, was perhaps inspired by the tradition associated with Anlaf. But as Bell, p. 27, pointed out, the one clear thing about the battle recorded by Gaimar and the author of the *Lai* is that it occurred in Denmark, not in England, as it would if it had been part of the local-historical tradition connected with Anlaf. This episode, moreover, is far from being a regular part of the *Havelok* tradition. If it is difficult to accept the legend of the Single Combat even in *Guy of Warwick,* in which it is a very important part of the story, as symbolic of Brunanburh and its subsequent traditions, it is still more difficult to believe in the Havelok-Odulf episode as in any way related to the Anlaf who was defeated at Brunanburh. See *Guy of Warwick,* note 11.

to be. The large number of Norse words in the English *Havelok* " argues that it was composed in some stronghold of Scandinavian influence such as Lincolnshire." But this, as has been said, is rather a suggestion of the distinctive character of the English version, than an argument that this version preserves, more independently than the French versions, the traditions of that place.

The quest for historical " kernels " in a story so apparently realistic has gone on apace with the name of Havelok as the crux of many discussions. In the French versions and the Lambeth Interpolation, Havelok bears the nickname Cuaran (Cuheran, Coraunt), which the *Lai* (ll. 258–60) says was what " li Breton " called a cook. Originally this meant, in Irish, brogue or sandal. Because of the use of this nickname and because the French Avelok is the same as the Anglo-Saxon Anlaf, the Scandinavian Olaf (Irish, Amhlaibh; Welsh, Abloyc), Storm (*Eng. Stud.* iii, 533) identified the Havelok of romance as the Viking, Olaf Sictricson, who was also known as Anlaf Cuaran. Chroniclers and scholars alike have confused this man with his more famous cousin, Anlaf Guthfrithson, who was defeated by the English at the battle of Brunanburh in 937 (Beaven, p. 6). Both Anlafs experienced vicissitudes of fortune, gaining and losing royal power in Northumbria, and their efforts to regain their lands parallel to some extent those of Havelok. But neither man ever had any connection with Denmark and the resemblance between them and the hero of the romance is chiefly a matter of name (Heywood, p. 71, 80 ff.; Beaven, p. 6, n. 22). However tempting it is to find the historic prototype of Havelok in Anlaf Cuaran, it must be remembered that the earlier the texts of the legend, the more romantic they are. It is in the later texts that the tendency grows to emphasize historical aspects and connections. In the chronicles of Rauf de Boun and of Knighton, Havelok's story is told as affording evidence of Canute's claim to the English throne by virtue of Havelok's earlier rule (Ashdown, p. 115, n. 5). The unreliability and confusion worse confounded of these " historical " accounts can be shown even in Gaimar's *Estorie;* for in this, written little more than one hundred years after the close of the Anglo-Danish period in England, the *Havelok* story is placed in what would correspond to the years 495–556 in the Anglo-Saxon Chronicle, and Havelok is endowed with a father Gunter who was conquered by King Arthur. In Gunter still later chroniclers, such as Pierre de Langtoft, recognized the Guthrum who was King Alfred's opponent and the later king of East Anglia (Heyman, p. 82).

Another attempt to find historical antecedents for the *Havelok* legend was made by Deutschbein. He agreed with Heyman that the connection between Anlaf and Havelok was merely nominal, but in the heroine Goldeboru (Argentille in the French versions) he recognized (pp. 103–17) Alfwyn, daughter of Athelflaed, the famous Lady of Mercia. After her mother's death in 918 Alfwyn was dispossessed of her inheritance by her uncle, Edward the Elder. In Caradoc's *History of Wales*, 1697, is recorded the tradition that Edward's wrath had been incurred by Alfwyn's secret marriage to Reynald, king of the Danes. Although it is true that the Anglo-Saxon Chronicle and other authoritative texts refer to the disinheritance of Alfwyn and to certain activities of this Reynald (Reginwald), there is unhappily no other evidence than Caradoc's for the romantic story of Reynald as the husband of Alfwyn and of Edward's anger. Rather are we told in the Chronicle that Reginwald concluded in 924 a firm alliance with Edward whom he chose, according to Florence of Worcester, for his father and lord. Deutschbein (p. 109) admitted that even on Caradoc's evidence Edward was represented as opposing Alfwyn's marriage whereas in *Havelok* the heroine's uncle wickedly forces her into what seems a wretched union. If Edward were historically the friend of Reginwald and the opposer of Alfwyn's marriage, it is difficult to recognize in him the Villain-Uncle of Havelok's wife, the man on whom the hero took such hearty vengeance. In the historical accounts cited by Deutschbein to justify his contention that the legend of Havelok grew out of the history and deeds of Reginwald, the uncle of Anlaf Cuaran, there is little agreement in the names of historical characters [5] with those in the legend, and no agreement, save in

[5] Deutschbein did not discuss the Raegnald Guthfrithson who was received at baptism in 943 by King Edmund and who was for a time the successful rival of Anlaf Cuaran. (Cf. Beaven, pp. 7–9, for an account of this personage who would seem to have almost equal claims with those of the earlier Reginwald for consideration.) In order to strengthen his Reginwald theory Deutschbein noted that various chroniclers report the name of Reginwald's

fragmentary details, in the sequence of events. The fundamental assumption that a legend of the famous Anlaf might usurp the adventures of his uncle, is, of course, entirely possible; but as Reginwald's supposed connection with Alfwyn was Deutschbein's principal reason for asserting that the life of Reginwald more nearly paralleled that of Havelok than did Anlaf's own, this explanation of the "historical" elements in the *Havelok* legend must stand or fall with the Alfwyn story.

In its general outline the exile-and-return type of the *Havelok* tale proves nothing save the popularity of the formula.[6] Havelok, like many another dispossessed young prince, lives humbly in the service of a foreign king. Panzer, in his study of the "Goldener-märchen" listed (*Hilde-Gudrum*, p. 252–54) many bright-haired kitchen boys who, like Havelok, serve their lords. A more literary parallel may be found in the second part of the French epic *Aliscans*, of the kindly giant Rainouart who serves in the royal kitchen, outdoes his fellows in feats of strength and in eating, and finally marries a royal princess (Heyman, p. 97). Bugge (pp. 272–95) set forth the notable likeness between the story of Havelok and the saga of Olaf Tryggvason, who was spirited on board ship by his mother, was captured by pirates, as Havelok was in the French *Lai* and the Interpolation, who served as a slave even as Havelok served as a scullion, and who was distinguished by a strange light which spread over him, even as Havelok was by the light that came from his mouth when he slept. Zenker (p. 97) somewhat elaborately compared

---

father as Guthred or Guthrum, a king of East Anglia. This Guthred Deutschbein identified as the Gunter of the romance and cited in connection with him a story told by Simeon of Durham to the effect that Guthred (son now of Hardacnut) had been sold as a slave to a widow and had been rescued at the instigation of St. Cuthbert. This story Deutschbein thought (p. 118) might have suggested the scullion boy episode in *Havelok*. It would seem then that Havelok owed his name to Anlaf Cuaran, the account of the loss and recovery of his kingdom and his marriage to a disinherited woman to Reginwald, and his youthful experiences as a scullion to Guthred. If Havelok were the result of this strange compilation, then truth is even stranger than the fiction created.

[6] Cf. Nutt, "The Arian Expulsion-and-Return Formula in the Folk-and-Hero Tales of the Celts," *Folk-Lore Record*, Lond. 1881; A. Olrik, *op. cit.* p. 309, for Danish parallels; Deutschbein, pp. 120–31, cited examples from the legends of *Olaf Tyggvason, Tristan,* of *Aurelius Ambrosius,* brother of Uther-Pendragon, of *Waldef,* of *Beves.*

this early portion of Havelok with Livy's similar tale (Lib. I, cap. xxxix) of Servius Tullius (Cf. Heyman, p. 99). Despite his noble birth, Servius, like Havelok, grew up as a servant; was recognized as royal by a flame playing about his head; won fame as a warrior and ultimately married a king's daughter. Deutschbein (p. 168) pointed out the inconsistency between Zenker's acknowledgment that Servius's flame simply corresponds to the gold hair of the boy in the folk-story, and his insistence that Havelok's flame must be a literary borrowing. In the French versions of the story, Havelok is distinguished not only by the flame but by his ability to blow a great horn and thus prove himself the true heir. In the English romance he bears on his shoulder a bright " kingmark " which more than satisfied Grim of his origin. In *Richars li Biaus* (1. 670), as Heyman noted (p. 101), the hero's lineage is recognized from the light in his face and the shining crosses on his shoulder. In the related poem, the *Lion of Bourges*,[7] the heir is known both by a cross and by his power to blow the horn, but it is improbable that this late romance is, even in these details, an offshoot of the *Havelok* story. Fiction has always identified true heirs by these and similar devices. In French and English versions of *Havelok* alike the hero's lineage is revealed to his wife through a dream or vision. In the French versions the dream of animals attacking the hero is a portent of dangers to come familiar enough in romance, but the later account of the homage paid by animals and of the trees that bowed to the hero, is a bit of elaboration not commonly met.[8] In the English romance Havelok's dream of himself, with his arms stretched out to embrace all England, is curiously matched by the dream of William's mother in both the French and the English versions of *William of Palerne* (Heyman, p. 107).

A certain similarity between the legend of *Hamlet* and that of *Havelok* has been used by Zenker to support his theory that the two stories are fundamentally related. They both concern Danish princes who marry in England and return and regain

[7] For *Richars* and *Lion* see *Amadas*, n. 2.

[8] Cf. W. Baake, *Die Verwendung des Traummotivs in der engl. Dichtung bis auf Chaucer*, Diss. Halle, 1906, ch. iii; W. Henzen, *Ueber die Träume in der altnord. Sagalitteratur*. Leipzig, 1890.

their heritage. In particular the legends introduce the same stratagem to deceive an enemy. In both cases dead men are set up on stakes in order to suggest the arrival of new forces. Heyman (p. 96 ff.) noted how the same *motif* appears in *Ogier le Danois,* in which the hero made dummies of wood and horsehair and placed them on the walls of Castlefort (Gautier, *Épopées,* III, 240 ff.), in the Provençal *Philomena,* and in other widely distributed literary and popular tales.

BIBLIOGRAPHY

TEXTS: (1) Laud Misc. 108, ed. Madden, Roxburghe Club, Lond. 1828; Skeat, *EETSES.* IV, 1868, Oxford, 1902 (rev. *Anglia BL.* XIV, 10); Skeat, revised by K. Sisam, Oxford, 1915 (rev. *MLN.* XXXI, 252); Holthausen, Old and Middle Eng. Texts, Lond. 1901 (rev. *JGP.* III, 510); Heidelberg, 2nd ed. 1910; (2) Cbg. Univ. Lib. 4409 (19), three fragments, ed. Skeat, *MLR.* VI, 455-7 (1911), pr. Sisam, p. 103. Trans. E. Hickey, Lond. 1902; F. J. Darton, *Wonder Book of Romance,* N. Y. 1907; L. A. Hibbard, *Three ME. Romances,* Lond. 1911; J. Weston, *Chief ME Poets,* Boston, 1914.

TEXTUAL AND LINGUISTIC STUDIES:

Bradley, E. " On Havelok," l. 2333, *Trans. Phil. Soc.* 1903-04.
Browne, W. H. " Havelok's Lament," v. 570-04, *MLN.* XXI, 23 (1906).
Foerster, W. " Zu Havelok," v. 2461, *Archiv,* 107, 107 (1901).
Grattan, J. " Minor Notes on Havelok," *MLR.* IV, 91 (1908).
Holthausen, F. " Zum Havelok," v. 321, 504, *Eng. Stud.* XXX, 343 (1902);
   Archiv, CI, 100; *Anglia Bl.* XI, 306, 359; XII, 146; " Emendations
   to the text of Havelok," *Furnivall Miscellany,* Oxford, 1901, p. 176.
Horn, W. " On Havelok," v. 247, *Anglia* XXIX, 132.
Koeppel, E. " Havelok-randglossen," *Anglia Bl.* XXIII, 294 (1912).
Littlehale, H. " On Havelok," v. 2495, *Trans. Phil. Soc.* 1902-03, p. 161.
Morsbach, L. " Bemerkungen zum Havelok," *Eng. Stud.* XXIX, 368-74
   (1901).
Napier, A. " Havelok Notes," *MLR.* XI, 74 (1916).
Schmidt, F. *Zur Heimatbestimmung des Havelok.* Diss. 98 pp. Göttingen,
   1900.
Wolff, A. *Zur Syntax des Verbums im alteng. Lay of Havelok.* Diss. 69
   pp. Leipzig, 1909.

STUDIES AND ANALOGUES: Cf. Billings, *Guide,* pp. 23-4; Edwardes, *Summary,* pp. 72-74; Fahnestock (see below), pp. 31-32; Heyman (see below), pp. i-ix; Sisam, (see texts), pp. v-viii; Wells, *Manual,* pp. 763-64.

Ashdown, M. "The Single Combat in Certain Cycles of English and Scandinavian Tradition and Romance," *MLR*. XVII, 113–30 (1922).

Beaven, M. "King Edward I and the Danes of York," *Eng. Hist. Rev.* XXXIII, 1–9 (1918).

Bell, A. "The Single Combat in the Lai d'Havelok," *MLR*. XVIII, 22–29 (1923).

Björkman, E. "Nordiska Vikingasagor i England," *Nordisk Tidskrift*, 1906, pp. 440–50.

Brie, F. "Zum Fortleben der Havelok-sage," *Eng. Stud.* XXXV, 359–71 (1905).

Bugge, A. "Havelok and Olaf Tryggvason," *Saga Book of the Viking Club*, VI, 257–95 (1910).

Creek, H. C. "The Author of Havelok," *Eng. Stud.* XLVIII, 193–212 (1915).

Deutschbein, M. See *Horn* bibliography.

Fahnestock, E. *A Study of the Sources and Composition of the Old French Lai d'Havelok.* Diss. 138 pp. Bryn Mawr, 1915.

Gaaf, W. van der. "Parliaments held at Lincoln," *Eng. Stud.* XXXII, 319–20 (1903).

Heyman, H. *Studies on the Havelok-Tale.* Diss. 153 pp. Upsala, 1903.

Putnam, E. K. (1) "The Lambeth Version of Havelok," *PMLA*. XV, 1–16 (1900). (2) "The Scala Chronica Version," *Trans. Amer. Phil. Assoc.* 1903, p. xci.

Sisam, K. See Texts.

Skeat, W. See Texts.

Whistler, C. "Saga of Havelok the Dane." *Saga Book of the Viking Club*, III, 395–412 (1902).

Zenker, R. *Boeve-Amlethus*, Die Havelok Saga, pp. 91–111.   See *Beves* bibliography.

BEVES OF HAMPTON

VERSIONS. The hero who bears the name of Beves of Hampton (Boeve de Hamptone, Hanstone) might well be described as an international character. The wide wandering of his story was like his own fabled adventuring from Hampton to Damascus. Versions in English, Welsh, Irish, French, Dutch, Scandinavian, Italian, attest the popularity of him who became even in Russia the most acclimated hero of the chivalric epic (Wesselofsky; cf. *Rom.* xviii, 313). The story of the loss and recovery of his inheritance, his fights with Saracens and dragons, his marriage with a converted princess, his gaining of innumerable possessions, is distinctive chiefly for its amazing absorption of familiar *motifs* and for its blending of elements drawn from romance, fairy tale, saint legend, and heroic epic. Few stories better illustrate the catholicity of mediæval taste; and in this, perhaps, lay the secret of an influence which may be traced, not only through the wealth of manuscript material but through many literary allusions to the poem and through the representation of its incidents in different artistic forms.[1]

The length, the number, and the variety of the vernacular versions of *Beves* make the problem of their classification extremely difficult. Since the publication in 1899 of Stimming's edition of the Anglo-Norman version of *Beves*, the story has been the subject of many elaborate investigations, but for the purpose of enumeration it is convenient to disregard the maze of controversy and to note as the three principal versions the Anglo-French (*AF*), the Continental French (*CF*), and the Italian (Matzke, *Mod. Phil.* x, 20).

[1] Scenes from *Beves* appear in the Smithfield Decretals and in the Taymouth Horæ (See here *Guy,* n. 10). *Notes and Queries,* 8th ser. xi (1897) referred to the hangings of Juliana de Leybourne, 1362, which were worked with the legend. W. G. Thompson, *Tapestry Weaving,* p. 26, mentioned two pieces of arras of *Beves* of the time of Henry V. The *Bull. de la Soc. des Antiquaires de France,* 1909, p. 237, shows a small stone mould (*c.* 1359) of the Musée de Cluny on which Beves and two lions appear. An inscription refers to " Bueve."

The first group, as Stimming made clear, has four branches, a thirteenth-century Anglo-Norman poem extant in two long supplementary fragments (ed. Stimming, 1899), a fourteenth-century prose version in Norse (ed. Cederschiöld, 1884), another of the thirteenth-century in Welsh (R. Williams, 1892), and one in Middle English verse (ed. Kölbing). The last, in the Auchinleck manuscript, has the first 474 verses in a six-line stanza and the remaining 4146 lines in short couplets. The popularity of the version, belonging originally, it would seem, to the south of England (Kölbing, xiii ff.), is attested by the six existing texts and by the six which Kölbing assumed as antecedent in order to explain the extant readings. These six manuscripts fall into two classes (A and SN; Mo-ME-C), in which the earliest, the (A)Auchinleck manuscript, is less near to the lost thirteenth-century Middle English original than is the fifteenth-century (M) Manchester manuscript, or even Pynson's old print. This original, from which the later manuscripts take over numerous references to a French original, was, in Stimming's opinion, derived from a lost Anglo-Norman version (x), the source also, through various lost intermediaries, of the extant Anglo-Norman and Welsh texts, and of the Norse account. The Middle English poet seems to have shortened his original at will, to have elaborated certain episodes, and to have made three important additions: (1) the account of Beves's first battle fought on Christmas day for the honor of God; (2) his great fight with the dragon of Cologne, an episode which suggests to the poet comparison of his hero with Lancelot, Wade, and Guy of Warwick; and (3) the heroic defense made by Beves and his sons against the London citizens when they are roused against him by the accusation that Beves has killed the king's son, a scene graphic enough to suggest some contemporary riot. Despite its prolixity and its constant borrowings from the commonplaces of Middle English romantic diction, which Schmirgel pointed out in Kölbing's edition, (pp. xlv–lxvi), the poem has a certain vigor of its own. Its popularity with a mediæval audience is not to be wondered at, nor is it strange that the traditional delight in this hero persisted even in the Elizabethan period.[2] An instance of

---

[2] Beves and Guy had an almost equal popularity, and the heroes were often mentioned together. See Crane, Bibliog. of *Guy*.

the foreign interest in the Middle English *Beves* is a fifteenth-century Irish translation (ed. Robinson).

The Anglo-Norman (AF) text is generally thought to represent an independent version of the same story as that told by the continental French texts. Of these, nine manuscripts in verse and two in prose are now known. They fall apparently into three groups. The first is represented by the thirteenth-century Paris manuscript (P^1) published by Stimming in 1911. This version, Behrens (p. 77) believed, originated between 1230 and 1250, on the southern borders of Picardy. The second version, represented by an inedited and incomplete manuscript in Rome (R), another (W) of the fifteenth century in Vienna, and by another thirteenth-century Paris manuscript (ed. Stimming, 1913), was thought by Oeckel (p. 78) and Meiners (p. 239) to have been by the scribe, Pierot du Ries. The possibility that Pierot might have been the author was dismissed by Stimming (2, p. 4, 200). This version tends constantly to amplify the original by new episodes and so much delights in ecclesiastical detail that its author was presumably of the clergy. " Lokal patriotismus," however, gives now and then a secular touch to his story. The third group comprises the *Beves* texts of the thirteenth and the fourteenth centuries found in manuscripts at Carpentras (C), Turin (T), and Venice (V); and finally a fragment now at Modena (Wolff and Paetz). Of these continental texts Boje (pp. 136–37) believed the oldest and truest form to be represented by the Rome and Paris manuscripts of the second group, and the original text to be the work of one man only. As a whole this continental French version is somewhat longer than *AF*, and, unlike it, places the hero's home on Gallic soil and names his stepfather Doon de Mayence. In the *AF* version Doon is Emperor of Almayn, and Beves's home is at Littlehampton (Hampton-sur-Mer, v. 2811), not more than two and one half miles from Arundel, the city named, according to the English romance, in honor of the race won by Arundel, Beves's famous horse. Finally it may be noted that the two fifteenth-century French prose versions of *Beves* and the five known sixteenth-century editions belong to the same redaction as the manuscripts P, R, W (Boje, p. 13).

The Italian version is preserved in at least six texts, of which the earliest is the fragmentary thirteenth-century Venetian manuscript (ed. Reinhold). The only complete form is the *Buova d'Antona* in the *Reali di Francia,* a late fifteenth-century composite which draws on the French as well as the Italian versions. The Italian version is shorter than the French; it differs in names and in sequence of events; and is, in the opinion of Rajna (*Ricerche intorno ai Reali di Francia,* pp. 135-40, Milan, 1872), of Jordan, and Matzke (3, p. 32), the prior form "independently transmitted from the original version of which the common source of *AF* and *CF* is another offspring."

Of the later popular versions of *Beves,* the first Dutch edition, printed at Antwerp, 1504, was derived from the *CF* version; and the sixteenth-century Russian and Jewish folk-books were from the Italian (Wesselofsky, *Rom.* XVIII, 302-14, 1889). In 1881 the Italian was translated into Roumanian (Groeber, 1901, 11, 3, 386). The fullest account of these and all the other versions is given by Boje (pp. 1-13).

The influence of *Beves* has been traced in the Middle High German poem, *Graf Rudolph* (cf. Bethmann, *Palæstra,* xxx; Deutschbein, p. 191), but the similar scenes are of the fairly conventional type concerning a Christian hero and a heathen princess. The Provençal poem, *Daurel et Beton* (ed. P. Meyer, Paris, 1880), is in part clearly a sequel to *Beves* (Jordan, 1, 102). Brockstedt's account (pp. 96-103) of this relationship is more convincing than his idea that the *Siegfriedlied* and the *Nibelungenlied* are variations of the Anglo-Norman *Beves.* The forest death of Beves's father, Beves's fight with the dragon of Cologne, and the bridal of Josian with Earl Miles, are in truth analogous to scenes in the German poems, but the inference made from the resemblance is over-large. Boje (p. 137) believed that the influence of the French forms of *Beves* was to be clearly traced in certain incidents in five poems; in *Florent et Octavian* (*Hist. Litt.,* xxvi, 316), in *Parise et Vienne* (*Rom. Forsh.,* xv, 1904), in *Ciperis* (*Hist. Litt.,* xxvi, 31), in *Valentin u. Namelos* (ed. Seelmann, 1884, p. 68) and, most interesting of all, in *Aucassin* (ed. Suchier), in the episode in which the heroine, disguised as a maiden minstrel, goes in search of her lost lover. On the whole, however, the influence of *Beves* is best attested by the long line of its own self-perpetuating versions.

ORIGIN. *Beves of Hampton* is a typical *roman d'aventure* which moves within a certain " Ideenkreis " of a well-defined character. In his comparison of it with one hundred and eighty-seven Old French romances Boje distinguished the following characteristic details and incidents: the forest hunt, p. 62; the murder of Beves's father, the marriage of his mother with her husband's murderer, the stepfather's hostility to Beves, pp. 62–64; the disguise of Beves, coloring his face, p. 67, etc., to save his life; the exhibition of his blood-stained clothes as a proof of death, p. 66; the rude porter, p. 71; the feast broken up by a tumult, p. 66; the selling of the boy and his stay at the court of a foreign king, the love for him of the Saracen princess, the defeat through Beves of her cruel suitor, the false accusation brought against the lovers, the letter of death carried by Beves to a heathen king, pp. 74–80; the overthrow of the idols by Beves, p. 82; his imprisonment in Damascus, his escape and the vain pursuit, pp. 91–100; the beating of the idols by the heathen king, p. 100; Josian's forced marriage and the magic protection of her virginity, p. 106; Beves's disguise as a palmer and his horse's recognition of his master, pp. 108–09; the drugging of Josian's guard, p. 112; the elopement of the lovers, pp. 109–12; the grotesque giant Escopart and his comic baptism, pp. 113–14; Josian's second forced marriage, the killing of her husband, and Beves's rescue of Josian from the stake, pp. 115–17; Beves's homecoming, the rage of the usurper who throws a knife at the messenger, p. 90; the overthrow of the usurper by Beves in battle or by a judicial combat, pp. 82–88; the great race won by Beves's horse, p. 118; the horse theft attempted by the king's son, p. 131; the killing of the king's son, pp. 120–23; the second exile of Beves, the forest birth of Josian's twin sons, the separation of the family, pp. 123–24; Beves's nominal marriage with another lady, Josian's disguise as a minstrel, her search for her lost love, the recognition and reunion of husband and wife, pp. 128–31; the old age of Beves, the angelic warning and his death, pp. 132–33.

As no text of *Beves* antedates the thirteenth century, as linguistic studies, no less than a literary study of *motifs* such as Boje's, suggest nothing antecedent to 1200, it is probable that the original poem was not composed before that date. But numerous attempts have been made to find in the extant versions the signs of much more ancient origin. Suchier's belief (1, p. cxcv) based on the evidence of such names as Ivor, Bradmund, Rudefoun, etc., that the poem was basically a Viking saga, may be offset by reference to Langlois's *Tables des noms propres dans les chansons de geste*, Paris, 1904, from which it appears that these names appear in Old French poems for which no Viking origin can possibly be alleged. Deutschbein (p. 198) sought to connect the story with certain historical German antecedents and suggested identification of Doon, represented in *Beves* as the Emperor of Almayne who murders Beves's father in the forest in order to marry his mother, with Otto (Odon) the Great (929–947) who exiled his step-son, Duke Ernst of Swabia, or with the father of Ernst II of Swabia who was killed on a hunt and whose son revolted against his step-father, the Emperor Conrad II. Boje (pp. 62 ff.), however, proved the essentially literary character of this introductory part of the romance.

The question of origin has been constantly associated with the localization of the story. The apparently ample evidence of English place-names,[3] which led Stimming (pp. 183–85) to believe the poem of Anglo-Norman origin, has been brought into dispute by the contention that the Italian version, in which the English are supplanted by Continental names, is representative of the oldest and most authoritative version. Rajna in 1872 was one of the first to point out in his studies on the *Reali di Francia* that Hamtone or Hanstone might better be identified with Hunstein or Hammerstein on the Rhine than with Southampton, and others have stressed the importance of the clearly non-English elements in the romance. Nevertheless, Matzke, who did most to establish the independent value of the Italian version, thought (*Mod. Phil.*, x, 54) the question of insular or continental origin still an open one. Less cautious scholars, by considering limited portions of the story in the *AF* or *CF* group, which they take to represent the original nucleus of the story, have arrived at interestingly varied opinions. Settegast (pp. 282, 383) derived the history of Beves's first exile from an Armenian tale in which a king was killed on a hunting expedi-

[3] Cf. J. Westphal, *Englische Ortsnamen im Altfranzösischen*. Diss. Strassburg, 1891.

tion, the throne was seized by an usurper and a young prince, the true heir, escaped in disguise as a shepherd boy. By the most dubious sort of etymology (p. 354) the names in this tale were made in some instances to coincide with those in *Beves,* and so made to argue an eastern origin for the romance. Deutschbein (p. 182), emphasizing different elements in this same part of *Beves,* the ill treatment of the boy by his relatives, the feast which he breaks up by shaming his enemy, was reminded of Karl Mainet and of an episode in *Jourdain de Blaivies.* The account of Beves's relations with his royal stepfather still further suggested (p. 198) the twelfth-century German poem, *Herzog Ernst,* (ed. Bartsch, 1869), which relates the adventures of Ernst of Swabia, traditionally the rebellious stepson of Otto the Great. In *Graf Rudolph, c.* 1170 (Palæstra xxx) the eastern adventures of the hero, his escape from prison, his rescue of his beloved from a forced marriage, parallel to some degree similar incidents in *Beves.* These stories of Mainet and Ernst and Rudolph, which were known in their earliest versions in the district between Flanders and Picardy, were supposed by Deutschbein (p. 204) to have been carried to England by Flemish colonists who settled in Pembrokeshire in the neighborhood of Haverford (Aberford, in *AN. Beves*). There the stories were localized, and to some extent, perhaps, influenced by tales of the *Horn* type. The commonplace likeness between *Beves* and *Horn* in the hero's expulsion from home, his adventures at the foreign court, his banishment, his rescue of his betrothed, led Hoyt, on wholly insufficient grounds, to conclude that the home of the two stories must have been in England and that *Beves* was " but a romantically developed form of the Horn Saga."

The historical kernel for the story of Beves's second exile is to be found, according to Jordan (*Archiv,* cxiii, 98), in the story recorded under the year 870 by Regino of Prüm (*Mon. Germ.* I) of Carolus, the Frankish prince. In this anecdote a courtier, whose horse has been stolen in jest by the prince, unluckily wounds the royal youth and has to flee for his life. Deutschbein (p. 209) accepted Jordan's view and noted that Prüm was not far from the district from which he fancied some episodes in the first part of *Beves* to have been originally drawn. The theft of a famous horse as an episode in itself was, as Boje (p. 131) indicated, a popular incident.

Legendary sources for *Beves* have been found far and near. Zenker (p. 44) maintained that *Beves* and the Hamlet (Amlethus) legend told by Saxo Grammaticus were versions of the same story (p. 32), and that the common source probably originated in England. In the two stories the hero becomes the stepson of his father's murderer, vows vengeance, has a violent altercation with his mother, is sent (but for different causes) to a foreign court bearing a letter of death (Uriasbrief), escapes, and finally returns to accomplish his revenge on the step-father, the usurper of his heritage. Zenker believed that of these incidents the most distinctive was the use of the Uriasbrief, and paralleled it (p. 45) with numerous oriental tales, with the Greek Bellerophron story (pp. 283, 313), and the French *Dit de l'Empereur Coustant* (*Rom.*, VI, 162 ff.). But later students have shown that in most of these instances, with the exception of the Greek story, the letter, so rewritten as to command great rewards for the bearer, opened to him a new career of successful adventure. Such is the tale twice found in the Amlethus legend, but in *Beves* the original letter was delivered by the hero, and almost caused his death. This simpler use of the *motif* seems to be derived either from the ancient Biblical story (2 *Sam.* XI, 15) of David and Uriah or from " a folk-lore tale current in the East and introduced into *Beves* in the time of the Crusades."

A second important argument of Zenker's that *Amlethus* is the source of *Beves*, rested on the supposedly similar incidents of the double marriage of the two heroes. In *Beves* the hero, separated from his wife and children, comes to a city (*AF*, Aumberforce, *CF*, Civile); its ruler, one of many " Forth-Putting " ladies, offers herself to him, having been attracted by his military prowess; he enters reluctantly into a pretended marriage with her (*AF* version); and his true wife appears in time to prevent its consummation. In *Amlethus* the hero enters willingly into the second marriage, and the interest of the episode lies entirely in the Valkyrie-like character of the lady who, because of her vow of chastity, has long caused the death of all her suitors. The essential unlikeness of the episodes makes it improbable that one was derived from the other. To Jordan

(2) the distinctive element in *Beves* was the hero's separation from his family — the separation and reunion *motif* that dominates such stories as *Guillaume d'Angleterre, Sir Isumbras, Die Gute Frau,* etc., narratives which are always in this episode in some way related to the Eustachius legend.

Although Zenker believed that the larger portion of *Beves* was to be derived from the northern Hamlet legend or its variants in the stories of *Havelok, Hrolf Hraka,* or the Icelandic *Anloði,* which he thought basically related, he accounted for many of its eastern elements by traces which he detected in the Hamlet legend itself of the ancient Persian Chosro story found in the "King's Book" of the poet Firdausi (*cir.* 1011). This Chosro account in turn seems to show a fusion of the Brutus and Bellerophron legends. Beves's childhood resembles that of Chosro; for each has a faithful protector in the person of his father's friend, each acquires a wonderful horse whose recognition of his master is sometimes of vital consequence, each hero marries a king's daughter.

The Eastern names, the localization of so many incidents in eastern places, the perceptible flavor of the Crusading spirit in *Beves,* have led to other attempts to identify special incidents. Beves's imprisonment in Damascus was traced by Settegast (pp. 282, 338) to the similar experience of Bischen as recorded in Firdausi's book, and more significantly by Brockstedt (p. 35) to the French *Floovent.* In the Italian *Bovo* (Jordan, i, p. 17) the princess Malgaria loves and protects the imprisoned Beves; in *Floovent* the princess Maugalie, similarly tender-hearted, aids the hero to escape. The possible influence on the *Ur-Bueve* of *Floovent* or other stories of this exceedingly popular type must be admitted. Warren's study (*PMLA.* xxix, 340–59) of the Enamoured Moslem Princess, showed that the type story greatly antedated the Crusading era, as he traced its earliest western form to the sixth *Controversia* of Seneca, the Rhetorician, and the earliest Crusade version to the account of Bohemond in the *Historia Ecclesiastica, c.* 1135, of Orderic Vitalis. Brockstedt's argument, however, that the Italian version of *Beves,* because it borrowed the episode from *Floovent,* is a late form, was disputed by Matzke (*Mod. Phil.,* x, 25) who urged that the role of Malgaria must have belonged to the French source of the Italian

poem, since she is to be recognized as the necessary second heroine of the story (which he believed the fundamental one in
Beves), the so-called Legend of the Man with Two Wives (" Lay
of Eliduc," *Mod. Phil.*, v, 211–39). In this type a youth exiled
from his own home wins through his valor the love of a princess.
He is slandered and is again forced to go into exile. In another
court he wins the love of another lady but remains loyal to the
first. He returns in time to rescue her from an unwelcome marriage, or she appears in time to prevent his marriage to the
second lady. To Matzke (3, p. 41 ff.) the starting point of the
legend is simply the doubling of the exile-and-return formula,
and the consequent doubling of the love adventure of the hero.
The doubled form appeared in such tales as *Horn, Ille et Galeron,*
and, with certain variations in *Tristan, Eliduc, Lai del Fraisne,*
and its derivative, *Roman de Galeran.* A comparison of the
different versions of *Beves* seems to show that its original form
was structurally of the same type as these.

Some of the earliest processes of accretion in *Beves* are set
forth in Matzke's study of the St. George legend. In its ancient
Eastern forms this legend had known only the monster-killing
and martyrdom episodes, but in the course of its development in
the west it absorbed the *Beves* story and became a typical
roman d'aventure, as it appears, for instance, in Richard
Johnson's *Seven Champions of Christendom,* London, 1592. In
Beves, on the other hand, the influence of the saint legend is
especially obvious in the scene in which Beves overthrows the
heathen idol, in the account of his sufferings in the prison of
Damascus, and his fight with the dragon of Cologne.

In regard to the authorship of *Beves,* the most important suggestion of recent years was that made by Boje. He urged that
the original French version was the work of a single author sufficiently acquainted with contemporary romance to borrow from
it freely. His belief that *Beves* was not a racial saga, that it
was not of German, Anglo-Saxon, Celtic, or Viking origin, nor a
gradual combination of elements drawn from Persian-Armenian,
nor Græco-Roman story, but a literary romance, the work of
one man, is in line with the whole tendency of modern
criticism.[4]

---

[4] Cf. Bédier, *Les Légendes Épiques*, Paris, 1908–13; L. Foulet, *Roman de
Renard*, Paris, 1914; F. Lot, *Étude sur le Lancelot en prose*, Paris, 1918.

BIBLIOGRAPHY

TEXTS, MIDDLE ENGLISH: (1), A, Auchinleck MS., ed. Turnbull, Maitland Club, Edin., 1838, rev. *Eng. Stud.* II, 317; E. Kölbing, *EETSES.* XLVI, XLVIII, LXV, 1885–86, 1894, rev. *Anglia,* XI, 325; *Eng. Stud.* XIX, 261; *Rom.* XXIII, 486; (2) C, Caius Coll. Cbg. 175, desc. *Eng. Stud.* XIV, 321; (3) S, Egerton 2862, desc. Brit. Mus. *Catalogue of Add. MSS,* 1905–10, p. 238, formerly the MS. of the Duke of Sutherland, desc. *Eng. Stud.,* VII, 191 ff.; (4) N, Royal Library, Naples, MS. XIII, B, 29; (5) C, Cbg. Univ. Libr. MS. Ff. II, 38; (6) M, Chetham Library, Manchester, MS. 8009, ed. Kölbing, *op. cit.;* cf. *Eng. Stud.* VII, 198. Early printed editions: L, "Douce fragments," no. 19, Bodleian; O, undated edition by Pynson, Bodleian. Editions from 1689–1711 listed by Esdaile, *English Tales,* pp. 163–64. Trans. L. Hibbard, *Three Middle Eng. Romances.*

FRENCH: Stimming, A. (1) "Der Anglo-Normannische Boeve de Haumton," *Bibliotheca Normannica,* VII, Halle, 1899; (2) "Der festländische Bueve de Hantone," Fassung I, *Gesellschaft f. rom. Lit.* XXV (1911); (3) Fassung II, *ibid.* XXX (1912); XLI (1918); Fassung III, *ibid.* XLII (1920).

IRISH: Robinson, F. N. "The Irish Lives of Guy of Warwick and Bevis of Hampton." *Zts. f. celt. Phil.* VI, 180–320 (1907). Text and trans. See also, *Eng. Stud.* XXIV, 463.

ITALIAN: Reinhold, J. "Die franko-italienische Version des Bovo d'Antone." *Zts. f. rom. Phil.* XXXV, 555–607; 683–714; XXXVI, 1–32 (1912).

STUDIES: Billings, *Guide,* pp. 40–1; Boje (see below) for MSS., pp. 1–13; Studies, pp. 43–49; Wells, *Manual,* pp. 765–66.
Behrens, L. *Ort u. Zeit der Entstehung der Fassung I des festländischen Beuve de Hantone.* Diss. 135 pp. Göttingen, 1913.
Bodtker, A. "Ivens Saga u. Bevis Saga in Cod. Holm. Chart. 46," *PB. Beiträge* XXXI, 261–71 (1906).
Boje, C. "Ueber den altfrz. roman v. Bueve de Hamtone." *Beihefte z. Zts. f. rom. Phil.* XIX, 145 pp. Halle, 1909. Rev. *Rom.* XLII, 314; *Zts. f. frz. Spr. u. Lit.* XXXV, 49.
Brockstedt, 1. *Floovent Studien.* Kiel, 1907. 2. *Von mittelhochdeut. Volksepen französischen Ursprungs.* Kiel, 1912. *Beves,* pp. 60–159. Rev. *Archiv.* CXXI, 170–72.
Deutschbein, M. *Studien z. Sagengeschichte Englands.* Die Wikingersagen: Horn, Havelok, Tristan, Boeve, pp. 181–215, Guy· of Warwick. Cöthen, 1906.
Favaron, G. *L'elemento italiano nel period popolare toscano del epopea romanzesca; Saggio sul Buovo d'Antona.* 61 pp. Bologna (1900).

Gerould, G. See *Isumbras* here.

Groeber, G. *Gründriss,* II, 386 (1901).

Hibbard, L. A. "Beves of Hampton and the Nibelungenlied," *MLN.* XXVI, 159–60 (1911). "Jaques de Vitry and Boeve de Haumtone," *MLN.* XXXIV, 408–11 (1919).

Hoyt, P. C. "The Home of the Beves Saga," *PMLA.* XVII, 237–46 (1902).

Jordan, L. I. "Ueber Boeve de Hanstone," *Beihefte z. Zts. f. rom. Phil.* XIV. 197 pp. Halle, 1908. Rev. *Archiv.* CXXII, 412, *Zts. f. frz. Spr. u. Lit.* XXXIV, 25. 2. "Die Eustachiuslegende, Christians Wilhelmsleben, Boeve de Hanstone u. ihre orientalischen Verwandten," *Archiv.* CXXI, 340–62 (1908).

Kühl, H. *Das gegenseitige Verhältnis der Handschriften der Fassung II des festländischen Bueve de Hantone.* Diss. 63 pp. Göttingen, 1915.

Matzke, J. E. I. "Contributions to the Legend of St. George," *PMLA.* XVII, 464–535 XVIII, 99–171 (1902–03). 2. "The Legend of St. George; Its Development into a Roman d'Aventure," *PMLA.* XIX, 449–78 (1904). 3. "The Oldest Form of the Beves Legend." *Mod. Phil.* X, 19–54 (1912–13).

Meiners, J. E. *Die Handschriften P (RW), Fassung II d. festländischen Bueve de Hantone.* Diss. 268 pp. Göttingen, 1914.

Oeckel, F. *Ort. u. Zeit. d. Entstehung der Fassung II d. festländischen Boeve v. Hantone.* Diss. 88 pp. Göttingen, 1911.

Paetz, H. "Ueber das gegenseitige Verhältnis d. venetianischen, d. frankoitalienischen u. d. französischen gereimten Fassungen d. Bueve de Hantone." *Beihefte z. Zts. f. rom. Phil.* L. 133 pp. Halle, 1913.

Reinhold, See Texts, Italian.

Robinson, See Texts, Irish.

Sander, G. *Die Fassung T des festländischen Fassung d. Bueve de Hantone.* Diss. Göttingen, 1913.

Settegast, F. *Quellenstudien z. gallo-rom. Epik.* Leipzig, 1904. Ch. XVI, 338–69, *Beves, Generides.*

Schültsmeier, F. *Die Sprache d. Handschrift C d. festländ. Bueve de Hantone.* Diss. 200 pp. Göttingen, 1913.

Stimming, See Texts, French.

Wolf, S. *Das gegenzeitige Verhältnis d. gereimten Fassungen d. festländ. Bueve de Hantone.* Diss. Göttingen, 1912.

Zenker, R. "Boeve-Amlethus, Das altfrz. Epos Boeve de Hantone u. der Ursprung der Hamletsage." *Literarhist. Forschungen,* XXXII, 480 pp. Berlin, 1905. Rev. *Archiv.,* CXVIII, 226; *Eng. Stud.,* XXXVI, 284.

GUY OF WARWICK

VERSIONS. Though Chaucer in the fourteenth century was already jesting at *Guy of Warwick* as a " romance of pris," it is ironically true that in sheer popular favor the story for long years outlasted anything of his. Frequently re-issued by the early printers,[1] treated as serious history by the Elizabethan chroniclers known to Skelton, Udall, Puttenham, Drayton, Shakespeare, dramatized by Day and Dekker, 1620, turned into stall ballads (1592) and again into heroic poems such as Samuel Rowlands's *Famous History of Guy Earle of Warwicke,* 1608, revived by eighteenth-century antiquarians, and happily read as pure fairy tale by nineteenth-century children, the romance had a history of which greater works might well be proud. Crane's study of the vogue in England of this " popular classic " gave a valuable picture not only of the extraordinary persistence of a mediæval story in modern times, of a popularity that stretched from the thirteenth to the nineteenth century, but of the successive transformations by which the story kept pace with the changing tastes of different audiences. Though it passed from the hands of one rather dull redactor to another, its diversity of episode continued to attract the adventurous, the romantic, the pious alike. Moreover, until the end of the Renaissance, the story made a strong patriotic appeal to all Englishmen, for Guy, by his fight with Colbrond, was thought to have saved his country from the Danes. By the middle of the thirteenth century he was one of the most accredited heroes of English legend. By 1410, according to Dugdale (*Baronage,* 1,

---

[1] Cf. Crane, p. 128 ff.: Pynson's edition, printed shortly before 1500, was " in all essentials identical with a version in short couplets composed as early as the fourteenth century "; Wynkyn de Worde, *c.* 1500; Copland, 1562–69; Caswood. " After 1575 the metrical versions ceased to be reprinted " (Crane, p. 141). Reeves, *MLN.* XI, col. 405, disposed of Morley's unsupported assertion (*Early Prose Romances,* 1889, p. 27) that the earliest edition of *Guy* in English prose was printed by Copland. Brown (p. 15) showed that the source of Morley's chapbook version was Rowlands's *Famous History.* See also Crane, p. 130, and Esdaile, *Eng. Tales printed 1475–1642.*

243), his fame had spread even to Jerusalem, for there a reported descendant of his was received with great honor.

The mediæval versions of *Guy* begin with those in French verse of which thirteen manuscripts are now known.[2] Winneberger's study of seven of these manuscripts led him to believe that they fall into two groups; and Weyrauch (p. 81), on comparing them with the Middle English manuscripts of *Guy,* found that the latter were in general translated from the second group of French texts.[3] Since of the five Middle English manuscripts, the earliest is the Auchinleck manuscript (1330–40), the first Middle English version was probably composed about 1300. The first English references to *Guy* are to be found in Robert of Brunne's translation of Langtoft's Chronicle, *c.* 1338, and in the *Speculum Vitæ, c.* 1350 (*Percy Folio MS.* 11, 510, 512). Of the English versions of the romance one, in short riming couplets, concluded somewhat abruptly in the Auchinleck manuscript with Guy's killing of the dragon that came " out of Irlond " and his presentation of its head to Athelstan at Warwick. This couplet version (*A*) served as the basis for the fourteenth-century copies made in the Auchinleck manuscript (f. 107–46), in the fragmentary Sloane manuscript, and in the fifteenth-century manuscript of Caius College, Cbg. 107, which included Guy's later history. According to Brandl, *Grundriss,* § 37, it was, perhaps, composed in southern Warwickshire.

Another version (*a*), of a slightly more northern origin,[4] fashioned in twelve-line tail-rime stanzas, is found only in the Auchinleck manuscript (ff. 146–67). Beginning practically at the point where the story in *A* had stopped, except for a brief

[2] Seven OF. MSS. were listed by Tanner, pp. 49–51, of which one (Bibl. Nat. Paris, MS. fr. FR. 1476) was a fifteenth-century prose translation. Twelve OF. MSS. were given by Winneberger, p. 2, and Weyrauch, p. 67. These lists were corrected by Herbert, *Rom.* 35, 68, who added an account of the former Edwardes MS., now additional MS. 38662 of the British Museum, (Acher). Jenkins, *Mod. Phil.* VII, described a fragmentary MS. found in the Library of York Minster. Among the OF. prose versions of *Guy* should be listed Royal MS. 15 E VI of the British Museum.

[3] This includes O (MS. Bennet 50. 6, CCCCbg. late thirteenth century); R (Regent MS. 8 F IX, Br. Mus., early fourteenth century); o and f (Rawlinson D, 913, Bodl. Oxf., early fourteenth century.)

[4] Wilda, *Ueber die oertliche Verbreitung der 12-zeiligen Schweifreimstrophe in Eng.* Breslau, 1888, pp. 46–55, thought this version arose in a region bordering upon Essex.

recapitulation of Guy's early life, this version told of the hero's marriage to his lord's daughter Felice, the proud-spirited lady who had insisted that he win fame enough to compensate for his lower birth, of his pious resolve to abandon his bride for whose sake he had so long forgotten the service of God, and of his subsequent adventures until his death's day as penitent warrior and hermit. After this came the story of Guy's son Reinbrun (ff. 167–75), a short romance in itself of 127 twelve-line tail-rime stanzas. In addition to these two versions Zupitza in 1873 distinguished two others in couplet form, a third represented by the fragmentary fourteenth-century text, now Add. MS. 14408, and a fourth found in the fifteenth-century manuscript, Ff. 2, 38, Cbg. Univ. Library. Weyrauch in his study of the relationship of all the versions, decided that the second or *a* version was the result of an independent translation of the French original. His conjecture that it was composed by the scribe who copied *A*, has been disputed by Möller (p. 5) on the basis of differences in style, phraseology, rime, and dialect. In Möller's opinion (p. 105), *A, a,* and *ao,* as he designated *Reinbrun,* were by different authors. He also pointed out (pp. 47–81) that though the correspondence between *a,* the strophic part of *Guy,* and the Middle English version of *Amis and Amiloun* was much greater than Kölbing had supposed, it pointed not to identity of authorship, but to the conscious use of *Guy* by the author of *Amis.*

The number of extant French and Middle English manuscripts but approximately suggests those once known. *Guy* is frequently listed in such mediæval catalogues [5] as have come down to us, two texts, for instance, *Guy, Earl of Warwick,* and *Guy and Colbronde,* appearing in the little library of English books of John Paston (Crane, p. 126). The popularity of the story was far from insular. In the fifteenth century it was translated into Irish from a Middle English version (Robinson). It strongly influenced the famous Catalonian tale of *Tirant lo Blanch,* [6]

[5] Savage, *Old Eng. Libraries,* pp. 229–31; cf. also *PFMS.* II, 510, for reference to texts at Bruges and Brussels.

[6] Reproduced in facsimile by the Hispanic Soc., N. Y., 1904. See Swan, *Gesta Romanorum,* II. 527, and Spence, *Legends and Romances of Spain,* p. 193 ff.; J. A. Vaeth, *Tirant lo Blanch,* Columbia Univ. Diss. N. Y., 1918, p. 72, 97–111; A. Thomas, *Spanish and Portuguese Romances of Chivalry,* Cambridge. 1920, pp. 32–40.

Valencia, 1490, which in turn was translated into Castilian, Italian, and French. Though the hermit warrior whom the young Tirant of Brittany met near Windsor was called William, Earl of Warwick, his old adventures were those of Guy. Like Guy he had gone to the holy land, had returned to live as a hermit near his own castle, had been forced to fight mightily against an invader of his country, etc. The eastern adventures of the young Tirant suggest those of the youthful Guy.

Not only in romances but in *exempla* and in chronicles are versions of *Guy* to be traced. In the Latin and vernacular texts of the *Gesta Romanorum* appeared a curious synopsis of the romance which abbreviated into a page or so the thousands of lines devoted to Guy's early history. It related in detail, however, the story of his meeting with his dispossessed friend, Tirri, of the latter's dream of treasure, of the soul-animal which ran from Tirri's mouth into a knoll where the friends were to discover weapons for Guy, of the treachery by which Guy was thrown into the sea, and of his victory over Tirri's enemy. As Tanner observed (pp. 41–42), this amazing tale with its absurd moral was certainly not, as Warton (*Hist. Eng. Poetry*, 1, 286) first supposed it to be, an early outline of the champion's history, but a condensation based on the known romance itself. In a number of manuscripts of the *Gesta* the hero's name was lost and he was called Josias or Rosias. This version was popular enough to have a life independent even of the *Gesta Romanorum*. It appears as a separate narrative in the fifteenth-century German prose narrative published by Mau, and served as the basis for the mystère of Jean Louvet which was written in Paris in 1537 (Hibbard, p. 183).

The English chronicles make frequent allusion to Guy and especially to his fight with the Danish giant Colbrond, but since no reference of this sort antedates the fourteenth century, it may be safely inferred that the chronicles borrowed from the romances. The earliest of these pseudo-historical accounts seems to have been that written by Gerard of Cornwall in his *Historia Regum Westsaxonum*. Of this the eleventh chapter, the *Historia Guidonis Warwick*, is still preserved.[7] Nothing is known

---

[7] In a manuscript of Higden's *Polychronicon*, now MS. 147 of Magdalen College, Oxf., and in Cott. Vesp. D IX f. 41 (10) in the British Museum.

of the writer save that he is referred to in the *Liber de Hyda,* a late fourteenth-century compilation, and in Thomas Rudborne's *Historia Wintoniensis, c.* 1454. These references are Kingsford's only reasons for suggesting in the *Dictionary of National Biography* that Gerard lived about 1350. Tanner believed (p. 33) that Gerard should be identified with that shadowy Walter of Exeter of whom Bale, in the *Index Brittannicæ Scriptorum,* recorded that he (Walter) had written in 1301 " apud S. Caradoc in Cornubia " a *Vitam Guidonis Comitis de Warwyck* at the instance of Baldwin, " civis Excestriensis urbis." More acutely Tanner (p. 29) noted that Gerard's text was simply a Latin translation of the French romance. What relation, if any, this Latin prose version had to the " canticum Colbrondi " which the minstrel Herebertus [8] sang in 1338 in the hall of St. Swithin's, is of course impossible to say. After Gerard the story of Guy's fight was told by Knighton (*Chronicon,* before 1366), by Rudborne, 1454, by Hardyng (*Chronicle,* before 1465), and by John Rous.[9] Even in the sixteenth century, as Crane noted (p. 134), it was seriously recorded by such chroniclers as Fabyan, Grafton, Holinshed, and Stow. It is of interest to find that between 1442 and 1468 Gerard's text was translated at the request of Margaret, Countess of Shrewsbury, who claimed descent from the old English hero. The poet in this case was John Lydgate, who, despite a few pseudo-Chaucerian flourishes, managed to retell the story in eight-line stanzas with equal fidelity and dullness. The poem survives in six manuscripts (Robinson). A little *Geste of Guy and Colbrond* is in the Percy Folio MS. (II, 527-49).

Illustrations from the romance of *Guy of Warwick* have not infrequently appeared in mediæval art. A number of scenes were introduced in the Taymouth Horæ, *c.* 1330, and others in the Smithfield Decretals (Br. Mus., MS. 10 E IV).[10] Dugdale

[8] Hazlitt-Warton, *Hist. Eng. Poet.* 1871, II, 97, III, 168; cf. E. K. Chambers, *Medieval Stage,* I, 56. Kölbing (*Germania,* Neue Reihe, XXII, 193) thought the poem *Guy and Colbrande* (*PFMS.* II, 527) was derived from an older version closely related to that used by the poet of the A version.

[9] For Rous see *Dict. Nat. Biog.* Two versions are extant of his Roll of the Earls of Warwick. The Rous Rol, 1477-85, was published privately (Rows Roll) in 1845, and by Wm. Courthope, 1859.

[10] These references are due to the kindness of R. S. Loomis, whose studies, especially in connection with the Tristan legend, are doing much to illumine the relationship of mediæval narrative and art. See below, notes 14 and 17.

(*Antiquities of Warwickshire*, 1, 237) recorded that a suit of arras containing the story of Guy and hanging in Warwick Castle, was given by a special grant to Thomas Holland, Earl of Kent (Pat. 21, Ric. 2). In Rowlands's poem (Ch. IX), reference was made to the arras at Warwick which depicts the fight of Guy with the dragon (Brown, p. 19). Warton (*Hist. Eng. Poetry*, 1824, 1, 93) recorded that within his memory a rude painting of the fight of Guy and Colbrand was to be seen on the walls of the north transept of Winchester Cathedral.

ORIGIN. In the traditionally famous fight of Guy with Colbrond, Tanner (p. 21) and others sought to find the historical nucleus of the romance. Anglo-Saxon chronicle and song record the great victory of Brunanburh, 937, won by Athelstan over the Viking invader, Anlaf, and since the romance uses the names of both Athelstan and Anlaf, the temptation to identify the historic and the fictitious event has been strong. But the romance localizes the scene near Winchester, which was certainly not the site of Brunanburh, and makes the fate of England dependent on the issue of a single combat.[11] Deutschbein (p. 221) furthermore pointed out that the duel in fact and fiction was wholly unfamiliar to the Anglo-Saxons and that its presence in the romance precludes

---

[11] G. Neilson, *Trial by Combat,* Lond. 1890, pp. 23–30, and Deutschbein, p. 223, show the flimsiness of the evidence purporting to prove that the judicial single combat was known in England before the Norman Conquest. If the duel itself, if the names of the adversaries and the place of the Guy-Colbrand fight cannot be associated with Brunanburh, it is impossible to accept the legendary account as even symbolic of the historic battle. For romance texts describing the Island Combat see G. Schoepperle, *Tristan,* II, 339–67; for the Single Combat see O. Leibecke, *Der verabredete Zweikampf in der altfrz. Lit.,* Göttingen, 1905; M. Pfeffer, "Die formalitäten des gottesgerichtlichen Zweikampfs," *Zts. f. rom. Phil.* IX (1885), 1–75; G. Fundenburg, *Feudal France in the French Epic,* Princeton, 1918, pp. 92–99; Ashdown, p. 128. Miss Ashdown, p. 126, n. 2, disputed Deutschbein's contention that *Guy* was after the Conquest; she argued that the Single Combat was widely known in Scandinavia before the Norman Conquest and that the Colbrand episode, in which Colbrand represents the Danish nation, may as well have been inspired by Scandinavian as by Anglo-French tradition. But the fact remains that the Anglo-Normans were the first shapers of the *Guy* legend and that they gave it the form of pure romance. The single combat in Middle English romance appears in *Guy of Warwick,* in *Beves of Hamtoun,* in *Tristrem,* in *Torrent of Portyngale,* in *Partonope of Blois,* in *King Alisaunder,* in *Duke Rowlande and Sir Otuel,* and traces of it are to be found in *King Horn* (Cf. ed. by Hall, p. 143) and in the English *Troy Book* (EETS. cxxi, l. 8477).

the possibility that the episode was drawn from the tenth-century tradition. Conscious archaism and patriotic purpose in *Guy,* as in the romance of *Athelston* itself, sufficiently explain the use of the historic names, and the popularity of the fateful Single Combat in mediæval story accounts for its association with Guy. Ward's attempts (*Cat. of Romances,* I, 475) to identify Rohaud of Warwick, the father of Felice, as that actual Thurkill of Warwick (Domesday Book, ff. 240–41) who had a granddaughter Felice, and Siward of Ardern as that Siward of Wallingford who in the romance was Rohaud's steward, explained nothing in regard to the motivation of the romance but did possibly indicate a certain amount of antiquarian information on the part of the French poet. The romance is evidently intended to exalt the lords of Wallingford and Warwick; and records of the two founders of those families, of Thurkill of Warwick and of Wigod of Wallingford, himself the Cupbearer of Edward the Confessor, and the most probable prototype of Guy in the romance, must have been many in both family and monastery, in the monastery of Abingdon, for instance, to which Thurkill and his son, Robert d'Oily, had been benefactors, and in Oseney Abbey, where the Abbot Wigod (1138–69) was possibly a descendant of the earlier Wigod (Freeman, *Conquest,* IV, App. C; Deutschbein, p. 218). It is precisely in tracing the shrewdness with which such fabricators as the author of *Gui de Warwick* adapted historic names [12] to present purposes, that some of the most interesting problems in connection with mediæval romance have yet to be worked out. In general, however, the author of *Gui* patched together his borrowings from purely romantic and pietistic material.

No source study of this long-winded romance has yet been made, but it is possible to define certain familiar *motifs* and details and to illustrate the author's method of work. The initial description of Felice, taught the Seven Arts by wise men of Toulouse, and of Guy, with whom thirty maidens fell simultaneously in love, is an obvious courtly elaboration. Felice is a typical Proud Princess who rejects a more lowly born suitor, and Guy, swooning with love sickness, an altogether French and

[12] Brown, p. 22, noted a possible Irish original (Collbran) for the name Colbrand and found in it confirmation of the Brunanburh theory.

not a mediæval English lover. After he and his young friends are knighted, in a scene which Hall (*Horn,* note to l. 499) thought was directly imitated from that in *Horn,* Guy in his quest for fame goes to Rouen and wins there in tourney a priceless falcon, a steed, and greyhounds, to say nothing of the Princess Blaunch-flour, whom he rejects. Her name here is used incidentally, as later on is that of Amis, a gallant young lord who aids Guy in rescuing friends from prison, but the use of the names suggests memories of the two famous romances, *Floris* and *Amis.*. Whatever the relationship between the Middle English versions of *Guy* and *Amis,* the fundamental influence of the older legend is evident besides in the way in which the Friendship *motif* is embodied in *Guy.* Though less moving and more militant than *Amis, Guy* is as much a romance of friendship as of love, for it tells at length of the sworn fellowship of Guy and Tirri, a devotion which began with Guy's rescue of Oisel, Tirri's lady, from outlaws, and went on through other rescues of Tirri from prison, and of Oisel from a forced marriage to the treacherous Duke Otun of Pavia. In the *Gesta Romanorum* and versions related to it, the story of Guy and Tirri was of primary importance.

The adventures of Guy on the Continent and in the East belong to a far-ranging, geographical type of story of which *Beves of Hampton* is a notable example. Most realistic, perhaps, are those episodes which tell of Guy's capture of the German Emperor, of the fight with his host, Earl Florentin, and of his meeting with Tirri near the city of Spires.

The first adventure takes place in Argonne. Duke Segwyn is unjustly attacked by the German Emperor, and Guy goes to his assistance. After numerous battles the Duke learns from a spy that the Emperor plans a hunt, and Guy vows to bring him to dine with Segwyn. The next day, at the moment when the Emperor sees himself surrounded with armed men, Guy approaches, olive twig in hand. The Emperor somewhat surprisingly accepts the invitation to enter the city and there he is royally served by his formidable vassal. The next day the Duke, clad only in his shirt, and with a rope around his neck, pleads before the Emperor for peace. He is forgiven and is presently wedded to the Emperor's daughter. Throughout all the narrative of *Guy,* German scenes and characters are stressed, but the penance of the Duke recalls a French incident. His appearance and his plea suggest comparison with the historic story of the burghers of Calais before Edward III in 1347, although earlier instances of similar scenes can be cited.[13]

The second adventure is likewise sufficiently graphic to suggest a definite though not yet identified source. Guy, who has pursued a boar into Brittany, kills the beast and slays at the same time the arrogant son of Earl Florentin who has been sent to bring the hunter to court. Guy thereafter accepts the hospitality of Florentin and is in his hall when the dead youth is brought in.[14] There follows a dramatic scene. Florentin learns the identity of the slayer and hurls an andiron at Guy's head. Guy escapes with difficulty from the castle and in a subsequent fight with his pursuers generously remounts the old earl for the sake of the dinner that has been given him. There are many parallels to the fury of Florentin in his attack on a guest protected by the laws of hospitality or of truce,[15] but no parallel to the episode as a whole has yet been noted. Nearest to it is the episode in *Floovent*, ll. 1046–1194, in which Richier, who has unwittingly slain the son of his host, Emelons, proves his innocence by fighting and receives the pardon of Emelons.

It is futile to attribute anything in *Guy,* save the mere art of compilation, to its author. His method of borrowing may be

[13] G. Neilson, "Submission of the Lord of the Isles to James I: Its Feudal Symbolism," *Scottish Antiquary*, xv, 113, noted the surrender of Milan in 1162 as told by a Flemish chronicler, *Rerum Germ. Belgicum*, vi, 183 (1607): the rabble appeared in their shirts and with ropes around their necks. In romance literature the chivalric penance appears in the *Voeux du Paoun*, 1300–05, in the Scotch translation, the *Buik of Alexander,* in *Richard Coeur de Lion,* etc.

[14] This adventure is one of those illustrated in the Decretals, fol. 16, 17. The OF. text may be found in MS. Regent F ix, fol. 133.

[15] Boje, *Beuve de Hantone,* p. 90, cited thirty-one instances. Especially important are those in *Ogier*, p. 174 (ed. Barrois, 1874) and in *Octavian*. Further correspondences between *Beves* and *Guy* as noted by Boje are as follows: (here § numbers refer to Boje, page references to *Guy*); § 2, Guy's coloring of his face, p. 328; § 3, Herhaud's disguise as a palmer, p. 415; Guy's stay at the court of a foreign king, p. 167 ff., a long story which includes the episode in which Guy is sent on a Message of Death, p. 217 (Boje, *Uriasbrief,* 79); § 7, the carbuncle gleaming on a helmet, p. 590, or on the roof, p. 657; § 12, the knife-throwing; § 13, the dreadful prison, p. 334; § 15, the vain pursuit, p. 313; § 16, the idols beaten, p. 212; § 25, the freeing of the beloved, p. 343; § 27, the killing of the king's son at a game of chess, p. 427; § 31, the old age and death of the hero, p. 612.

illustrated by his account of the meeting of Guy, the penitent, and his unfortunate friend Tirri, the episode which became so well-known through the version already referred to in the *Gesta*. Of the antiquity of this tale there is no question, for it is the story of King Guntram's Dream told in the eighth century by Paul the Deacon in his History of the Langobards. Paul's story remained essentially unchanged in all the mediæval chronicles recording it and slipped from one of them into the French *Gui*.[16] The romance version simply altered the names of the personages and omitted the description of the watching soldier who draws his sword to make a bridge across the stream for the soul of the sleeping Guntram. Likewise the Treasure incident in the romance is an unmitigated bit of borrowing.

The whole paraphernalia of romance appears in *Guy*. For supernatural elements the author uses chiefly dreams, dragons, and giants. In dreams angels give convenient information or wild animals, attacking the hero, give intimation of his danger. Gigantic champions appear, such as the Saracen Amoraunt or the African Colbrond. In the tale of Guy's fight with Amoraunt, a story still popular in the seventeenth century (Percy Folio MS. II, 136–43), the hero's magnanimity is made apparent by the permission he grants Amoraunt to drink, a permission later refused to Guy. A certain almost humorous exaggeration occurs in the account of Colbrond's coming to combat " so michel ðat non hors miʒt him bere," and bringing more than two hundred weapons. Amazing arms are possessed by Guy and his adversaries, Alexander's helmet, King Clarel's hauberk, the swords of Hector and Hercules. The hero fights later with a mighty dragon come " out of Irlonde." Like Ywain, Guy saves a lion from a dragon and henceforth, until it is treacherously slain, it serves him with doglike devotion.[17]

The Eastern elements in the story are commonplace. Guy goes to the relief of Constantinople when it is besieged by a cruel Sultan; inevitably Guy defeats the heathen hordes; the

[16] Hibbard, *Romanic Review*, 1913, IV, 189.

[17] The lion episodes are illustrated in the Taymouth Horæ, fol. 12–14, and in the Smithfield Decretals, fol. 80–85. For studies on Grateful Animals see O. M. Johnston, " Ywain, the Lion and the Serpent," *Zts. f. frz. Spr. u. Lit.* XXXI, 157–66 (1907); A. C. L. Brown, " Knight of the Lion," *PMLA*. XX, 702; G. Baist, " Der dankbare Löwe," *Rom. Forsch* XXIX, 317–19 (1911).

Sultan rails upon his gods and breaks his idols; Guy is sent on a message of death to the Sultan but beheads him as he sits in his splendid pavilion. Guy's last eastern fight is at Alexandria where he serves as champion of King Triamour whose son has killed the son of another Sultan at a game of chess. In all this the setting and the abuse of the Saracens are characteristic of the Crusading spirit in romance, but the episodes have nothing of Eastern character. The offer to Guy of the hand of the Christian Emperor's daughter, the jealousy of the false steward, Morgadour, his accusation to the Emperor that Guy is dishonoring the Princess, make a somewhat absurd combination of contradictory *motifs,* some of which seem borrowed from *Horn* and *Beves.*

The latter part of the story changes wholly from the romantic tone to the pietistic. As one of the most famous knights of the world Guy weds Felice, only to leave her during the wedding festivities from a sudden overwhelming sense of contrition for the worldliness of his life. In this part, as in the account of Guy's return as a poor and unknown pilgrim to beg at his own castle gates, the influence of the St. Alexis legend on the probably monastic author has been recognized.[18] Whatever may have been the relationship of the old French texts of legend and romance, it is possible in the Middle English version to feel some direct connection. For instance, in the Laud MS. of *St. Alexis* (*EETS.* lxix) the departing young husband says:

" And half ðe godenesse ðat I do
 Graunte ðee god almiȝth." (*Alexis*, l. 233)

In *Guy* he uses almost the same words:

" And of all the goodnesse that I doo shall
 I graunte the euere haluendell." (*Guy*, Auch. MS. 7430)

It is, perhaps, merely a humorous chance that brings into the subsequent story of St. Alexis an account of Jonah and into that of *Guy* the meeting with Earl Jonas.

[18] Groeber, *Grundriss*, ii, 776. For the Alexius legend see Wells, *Manual*, p. 809. The Middle Eng. texts were listed by C. Brown, *Register*, vol. ii, Index.

The story of the ultimate return of Guy to England, of the king's entreaty that the poor pilgrim undertake the fight with Colbrand, of the old man's heroic victory and swift withdrawal to a hermitage, was referred by Deutschbein (p. 225) to the epic type preserved in the *Moniage Guillaume*.[19]   In this the old warrior William hears in his hermitage of King Louis's desperate need of a champion against the heathen leader whose army is besieging Paris.   William overthrows the enemy and returns unrecognized to his hermitage, though the king learns subsequently the name of his deliverer.   The same type of story appears in the account of the monk Ogier's last fight against the heathen besieging Meaux.[20]   In actual life many a war-worn old hero must have similarly renounced the world, but it is probable that the tales of such triumphant exploits were chiefly the product of monastic imagination at work on epic legend.   The resulting type of story seems to have been clearly defined by the middle of the twelfth century and to have been amply familiar to the original French author of *Guy of Warwick*.[21]

BIBLIOGRAPHY

TEXTS: (1) A, a, Auchinleck MS. ed. Turnbull, Abbotsford Club, 1840; Zupitza, *EETSES*. 42, 49, 59; (2) C, Caius College, Cbg. 107, ed. Zupitza, *ibid.;* (3) S, Sloane MS. 1044, ed. Zupitza, *Sitz. d. Wiener, Akad. d. Wiss. Ph. Kl.* 74, 624–29 (216 lines); (4) P, Add. MS. 14408, ed. Phillips, Middle Hill, 1838; reprinted by Turnbull, 1840; (5) C, MS. Ff. 2, 38, Cbg. Univ. Libr. ed. Zupitza, *EETSES*. 25, 26 (11, 976 lines).   Early printed editions: W, Douce fragments, no. 20, Bodleian; d, Copland's edition.   Cf. Zupitza, *Sitzungsberichte*, p. 641, 632–39; Schleich, *Palaestra*, 139.

---

[19] For bibliography to 1908 see Bédier, *Les Légendes Épiques*, I, 90.   The whole volume is devoted to an epochal study of *Le Cycle de Guillaume d'Orange*.

[20] See Bédier, "Ogier le Danois et l'Abbaye de St. Faron de Meaux," *Légendes*, II, 305–310.   Of special interest is the evidence of the familiarity of Alexander Neckham, the Englishman who taught in Paris in 1180–86, with this Ogier legend (cf. *De naturis rerum*, ch. CLVII, Rolls Series, 1863).   See T. Walker, *Die altfrz. Dichtungen vom Helden im Kloster*, 1910.

[21] All the Middle Eng. texts of Guy refer to Tirri's coming to England after Guy's death and to his taking Guy's body back to Lorraine where he built a splendid abbey in which monks were forever to sing for Guy's soul.   See Bédier's remarks on the tombs of Amis and Amiloun, *Legendes*, II, 170 ff., and of Ogier and his friend Benoit, II, 294 ff.

STUDIES AND ANALOGUES: Billings, *Guide*, 25–32; Wells, *Manual* 15–19, 764.

Acher, J. "Acquisition des MSS. de Mr. Dunn par le musée Brittanique, Gui de Warwick, Add. MS. 38662," *Revue des langues romanes*, LVI, 513–14 (1913).

Ashdown, M. "Single Combat in English and Scandinavian Romance." *MLR.* XVII, 113–130 (1922).

Brown, A. C. L. "The Source of a Guy of Warwick Chap-Book," *Jour. Ger. Phil.* III, 14–23 (1900).

Chap-Books and Broadsides, *Harvard Univ. Bibliographical Contributions*, No. 56, p. 29, No. 484–89 (1905).

Crane, R. "Vogue of Guy of Warwick from the Close of the Middle Ages to the Romantic Revival," *PMLA.* XXX, 125–94 (1915).

Deutschbein, M. *Sagengeschichte*, pp. 214–34 (1906).

Herbert, J. A. "An Early Manuscript of Guy of Warwick," *Romania*, XXXV, 68–81 (1906).

Hibbard, L. A. "Guy of Warwick and the Second Mystère of Jean Louvet," *Mod. Phil.* XIII, 181–87 (1915).

Kölbing, E. "Amis and Amiloun und Guy of Warwick," *Eng. Stud.* IX, 477–78 (1886).

Jenkins, T. A. "A New Fragment of the Old French Gui de Warwick," *Mod. Phil.* VII, 593–96 (1910).

Liebermann, F. "Guy of Warwicks Einfluss," *Herrigs Archiv.* 107, 107.

Mau, P. *Gydo und Thyrus, ein deut. Ausläufer d. altfr.-mittelengl, Freundschaftsromans Guy v. Warwick.* Diss. (69 pp.) Jena, 1909.

Möller, W. *Untersuchungen über Dialekt u. Stil des mitteleng. Guy of Warwick in der Fassung der Auchinleck-Handschrift u. über das Verhältnis des strophischen Teiles des Guy zu der mitteleng. Romanze Amis und Amiloun.* Diss. Konigsberg, 1917 (107 pp.). For Reinbrun, see pp. 36–47.

Penn, H. C. "On the Dialect of the Auchinleck and the Caius MSS. of Guy of Warwick," *PMLA.* XX, p. xxviii (1905).

Reeves, W. "The So-Called Prose Version of Guy of Warwick," *MLN.* XI, 202–04 (1896).

Robinson, F. N. "On Two Manuscripts of Lydgate's Guy of Warwick," *Harvard Studies*, V, 177–220 (1897). "Irish Lives of Guy of Warwick," *Zeit. f. celt. Phil.* VI. Halle, 1907.

Tanner, A. *Die Sage v. Guy von Warwick.* Diss. 68 pp. Heidelberg, 1877.

Weyrauch, M. *Die mitteleng. Fassungen der Sage v. Guy of Warwick u. ihre altfr. Vorlage.* Diss. Breslau, 1901. Rev. *Eng. Stud.* xxxii, 405 (1903).

Winneberger, O. *Über d. handschriftenverhältnis d. altfr. Guy de Warwick.* Frankf. a.M. 1889.

Zupitza, J. "Zur Literaturgesch. des Guy of Warwick." Wien, 1873 (*Sitzungsber, d. Kais. Akad. d. Wiss. Phil. Hist. Kl.* LXXIV, 623–45).

REINBRUN

Versions. The romance of *Reinbrun, Gij sone of Warwicke,* is found in Middle English only in the Auchinleck manuscript (1330–1340). It contains 1524 lines in twelve-line tail-rime stanzas and was, perhaps, written in South Warwickshire (Brandl, *Grundriss,* § 37). Like *Guy of Warwick* it is a redaction of an older inedited version in Old French. Möller (pp. 36–45) urged that its author should not be identified with the redactor of the *a* version of *Guy.*

After a pious plea for blessing on those who read, and a rapid summary of the events leading to Reinbrun's birth, the story begins with a colorful account of the " richesse " brought to London by the merchants to whom Athelston gives permission to fare through his land. Arrived at Wallingford, they send a Spanish mule to Heraud who was left, after Guy's death, in charge of the town and of Guy's seven year old son. After they have spoken " stille " with the porter, they steal the child and set sail for Russia. But a great storm drives them to Africa where Reinbrun is given to King Argus's daughter, a maid who knows much of " menstralcie " and " of romance reding."

In England, meanwhile, Heraud, grieving desperately for the lost child, goes to the king's parliament and advises Athelston concerning the defence of the realm against a threatened attack of the Danes. Heraud is accused by envious lords of having sold Reinbrun for his weight in gold and of being a traitor to his lord. Edgar, Heraud's steward, challenges for his master's sake the Duke of Cornwall and Heraud himself starts forth to seek Reinbrun. Arrived in Africa, he is so long imprisoned by the Emir Parsan that his hair grows down to his girdle, " Grisliche he was of siȝte." When the Emir at last learns that his prisoner once served Guy of Warwick, he arrays Heraud richly and sends him forth to fight the forces of King Argus. In a great battle he almost kills Argus but the latter is saved by the youth Reinbrun. In the midst of a great fight Heraud learns the name of the boy and recognition follows. They return to the Emir, Argus is slain, and Reinbrun and Heraud start for England.

The next adventure tells of the coming of these two knights to a castle owned, as the porter tells them, by a most sorrowful lady. Her lord, Amis of Mountayne, once Guy's young friend, has disappeared, captured presumably by an old enemy of Guy's. Reinbrun goes to seek Amis, swims a river " sterne and grim," sees a castle with crystal walls, rafters of cypress, jasper posts, a great carbuncle shining from the front, and with a tree full of singing birds standing near the gate. Reinbrun learns from Amis whom he finds alone in the hall that this is the home of a fairy knight, Gayer, and that in this house one may stay without ever growing old. Reinbrun catches up a magic sword and the room shines with light. Pursued by Gayer, Reinbrun fights with him as " fresch ase grehonde to hare," until Gayer begs in Guy's name for mercy. Reinbrun restores Amis to his lady, and again the youth and Heraud start on their way.

In Burgundy the country is devastated and the Earl, shut up in one castle, is aided by a gallant youth of twenty. None may pass him without fighting. In a great combat between Reinbrun and the youth it is discovered that the latter is Heraud's son, Haslak. Taunted with his father's long absence, the boy had dubbed himself knight and gone forth to seek Heraud. After a joyful recognition, the three men return to the Earl, defeat his foes and finally set sail for England.

ORIGIN. The wholly unoriginal quality of *Reinbrun* is evident from this summary. The account of the merchants who steal the child and the tale of Heraud's long search for him, are in palpable imitation of the *Tristan* legend. The selling of the boy to the Saracen king and the princess's care for him recall the story of *Beves*. The fights of Reinbrun first with his foster father and later with Heraud's son, are somewhat unhappily duplicated variants of the Father and Son Combat. Reinbrun's adventure in releasing Amis from the fairy castle is interesting chiefly because of its clear indications of the fairy landscape (the dark river, the impossible richness of the castle, the tree of singing birds) and for the English poet's mild attempts at rationalization. In the Old French text of *Gui* in the College of Arms, Amis tells his friend that without a kiss from Reinbrun, Amis will be turned into a serpent. This suggests, though in oddly inverted form, *Le Bel Inconnu* and the variants summarized by Schofield (*Libeaus Desconus, Harv. Stud.* IV, 1896) which tell of the serpent lady who can only be disenchanted by a kiss. But until the Old French texts have been more extensively printed it is impossible to say how far the process of omission and of rationalization has gone in the Middle English *Reinbrun.*

BIBLIOGRAPHY

For texts and studies see *Guy of Warwick.*

ATHELSTON

VERSIONS. A single manuscript written in the North Midland dialect in the last half of the fourteenth century, contains the only known version of *Athelston* (Zupitza, p. XIV). The initial prayer for grace, the familiar appeal, " lystnes, lordyngs," the rime phrase, " I wol ʒow tel," the use of the popular twelve-line, tail-rime stanza with occasional lapses into stanzas of eight, six or even four lines, and the use likewise of a great number of well-worn alliterative phrases, are signs of professional minstrelsy.[1] The author refers to his source as " in book iwreten " or " in romaunce as we rede," and also as a tale " men me told." This discrepancy may well indicate, despite the conventionality of the phrases, the use of both oral and written sources.

The plot of *Athelston* is strikingly simple and unified. A jealous courtier makes accusation against King Athelston's relatives. The king orders their execution but is forced by Alryke, Archbishop of Canterbury, to allow his sister, his brother-in-law, and their children, the ordeal by fire. This they pass successfully; the traitor's wickedness is revealed and he suffers the doom he had prepared for others. In this direct and graphic story there are no foreign elements. The names are typically old English for Athelston and his sworn brothers, Alryke, Wymound, and Egelan(d), and the poem abounds in local color. No romance refers more familiarly to places of interest in London, to Westminster, to Charing Cross, to Fleet Street. The detailed mention of towns through which royal messengers take their way from London to Canterbury or Dover, shows that the author must have had more than a hearsay knowledge of the famous

---

[1] Zupitza's invaluable list of minstrel commonplaces, in conjunction with those given by Schmirgel, *Beves of Hampton* (*EETS.*), by Kölbing, *Arthour and Merlin, Sir Tristrem*, by Führmann, *Die allit. Sprachformeln in Morris' E. E. Allit. Poems and Sir Gawayne and the Grene Knight*, Kiel, 1896, Hall's *Horn*, Schleich's *Ywain and Gawain*, offer much material for that possible classification through diction of the different schools of romance makers in England which was suggested by Dr. Rickert, *Emare*, note to l. 9.

pilgrim route. In style also, in its omission of all the elements of chivalry and romance, in its rude vigor, its occasional brutality, its liking for scenes of tumult and rapid action, in its simple motives and naïve credulity, the tale has distinctive qualities of English popular fiction which are found in such Middle English romances as *Havelok, Richard Coeur de Lion,* and *Gamelyn.* An occasional line like that which tells how the queen in a moment of danger casts off her " gerlondes of cheryes," has the apt brevity of a ballad phrase. Ballad-like also are the wild horse-killing rides, the hasting messengers, and the effective suspense of the three ordeals by fire.

ORIGIN. In name at least the Athelston of the romance has been identified with the famous Æthelstan, king of England from 925 to 939,[2] conqueror at Brunanburh (937), and the storied king for whom Guy of Warwick fought with the Danish giant Colbrand. He was the hero, according to William of Malmesbury, of many old songs and legends, and among these Zupitza (p. xiv) noted two which were concerned with conspiracies against the king. In these tales, however, there is no single point of agreement with *Athelston* except in the common likeness of all stories of kings, jealous courtiers, and false accusations. As a matter of fact Athelston in the romance, though he bears so famous a name, is not the real hero of the story; that place is taken by Archbishop Alryke, whose fearless defiance of the king was possibly modeled on the great traditional example of Thomas Becket in his quarrel with Henry II. In any case, as Gerould has pointed out, *Athelston* has a strong ecclesiastical bias; it exalts the clergy above royalty itself, and its climactic scene is in the nature of religious, rather than romantic, marvel.

These facts give the clue to the origin of the romance in the famous Winchester legend of Queen Emma and the Ploughshares (Hibbard, p. 227). The tale was first told (*c.* 1200) by Richard of Devizes, a monk of Winchester, and was copied from him by various Benedictine chroniclers such as Ranulf Higden of Chester (1327) and Richard of Cirencester, a monk of Westminster

---

[2] See Beaven, " The Regnal Dates of Alfred, Edward the Elder, and Athelstan," *Eng. Hist. Review,* 1917, xxxii, 517–31.

(1355–1400). In this legend Emma, mother of Edward the Confessor, was accused of various crimes and conspiracies by Robert of Jumièges, Edward's special favorite. She exculpated herself by the ordeal of the fiery ploughshares and together with the good Bishop Alwyn of Winchester, who had been accused with her, received the king's penitent submission.

In structure *Athelston* is practically identical with this story. In details the romance was altered for the deliberate purpose of disguise. The part of the wicked churchman, Robert of Jumièges, was given to the layman, Wymound; the part of the gullible King Edward to Athelston, who was made not only gullible but brutal; Queen Emma's part was divided between Athelston's wife and his sister, and the whole legend was shifted from Winchester to Westminster. In this transformation of the story it is possible to detect certain details which could only have come from Westminster monks and, in all probability, from Richard of Cirencester himself. Of such sort is the unusual name Alryke which, in an obscure Westminster chronicle used by Richard, is the name of the monk, elected in 1050 by his fellows to be ruler over them, who was displaced by Robert of Jumièges. With true ironic fitness it is in the romance Alryke, as Archbishop of Canterbury, who brings to nought the plans of Wymound, the fictitious counterpart of Robert.

This clever manipulation of the original story shows clearly enough that *Athelston* was influenced by the learning and the taste of some Westminster monk, presumably Richard. But the characteristic style of the romance, the introduction of such popular incidents as the swearing of " brotherhood "[3] by the four " messengeres," Athelstan, Wymound, Egelan, and Alryke, and the rude violence of the king to his wife, must be referred to

[3] For general discussions of blood brotherhood and sworn brotherhood see Gerould, p. 194; Peebles, " Blood Brotherhood," pgr. *PMLA*. 1913; J. Flach, *Le Compagnonnage dans les Chansons de Geste, Études Romanes,* Paris, 1891; Stowell, " Personal Relationships in Mediæval France," *PMLA*. xxviii, 388–416 (1913); G. F. Fundenburg, *Feudal France in the French Epic,* Princeton, 1918, p. 67, 79–84. Flach's article, which also appeared in his *Origines de l'ancienne France* (Paris, 1893, II, 427–90), set forth *Le Comitat germain,* then the primitive Scandinavian rite of blood brotherhood, ii, 439, then *Compagnonnage sous les rois francs,* and in the last two chapters, examples of poetic friendships such as those of Roland and Oliver or Amis and Amile.

minstrel authorship. Westminster,[4] like other great monasteries of the day, kept minstrels in pay, and at Westminster, we must believe, lived the unknown minstrel who produced the present version of *Athelston*. At Winchester itself, as late as 1338, the original Emma story, the " gestum Emmae reginae a iudico ignis liberatae," was sung by the minstrel Herbert in the hall of the priory of St. Swithin's.[5]

BIBLIOGRAPHY

TEXTS: MS. 175 Caius College, Cambridge, ed. Hartshorne, *Ancient Metrical Tales*, Lond. 1829; Th. Wright, *Reliquiae Antiquae*, Lond. 1895, 11, 85 ff.; J. Zupitza, *Eng. Stud.* XIII, 331–414 (1889); Lord Francis Harvey, *Corolla S. Eadmundi*, Lond. 1907, p. 525 ff. Trans. Rickert, *Romances of Friendship*, p. 67 ff.

STUDIES: Cf. Billings, *Guide*, pp. 32–36; Wells, *Manual*, pp. 23–25.
Gerould, G. H. " Historical Reminiscences in the ME. Athelston," *Eng. Stud.* XXXVI, 193–208 (1906).
Hibbard, L. A. "Athelston, A Westminster Legend," *PMLA.* XXXVI, 223–244 (1921).
Zupitza, J. "Die Romanze von Athelston," *Eng. Stud.* XIV, 321–344 (1890).

---

[4] Chambers, *Mediæval Stage*, I, 56: L. Pound, " *The Eng. Ballads and the Church*," *PMLA.* XXXV, 182 (1920).

[5] Warton, *Hist. of Engl. Poetry*, 1840, p. 81; see also Chambers, *op. cit.*

RICHARD COEUR DE LION

VERSIONS. Three specific allusions to a French source and at least ten references to an original " geste " or " boke," indicate that the Middle English romance of *Richard* was preceded by an Anglo-Norman version. The allusion to a French source is confirmed by the preservation of a number of phrases, " Seynyours, tuez," and even of whole verses, such as the Angel's cry to the Christians, " Suse, Seynours, has tost armes " (l. 3012), and by the large number of French rimes (Paris, *Rom.* xxvi, 361, n.). That this original poem was written in England is evident from the blatantly partisan nature of *Richard* with its praise of the English and its derision of the French as braggarts and cowards (l. 3849–65). As a date for it, Paris (p. 361) suggested " about 1230 "; Loomis (*JEGP.* xv, 456–8) about 1250. Before the end of the century it was translated into English, and it was known presumably in this form to the author of the chronicle called Robert of Gloucester's (Brunner, p. 73). The evidence of distinctively Kentish forms suggests that the author was a man of Kent (Loomis, *ibid*, p. 463). Kölbing, in his edition of *Arthour and Merlin* (Leipzig, 1890, p. LXXIII ff.), set forth his belief that this Kentish translator was identical with the author of the two Kentish poems, *Arthour and Merlin* and *King Alisaunder,* other biographical romances of strangely-born heroes.[1] In these texts a number of passages are parallel to those in *Richard.* Especially notable is a lyric passage on the " merye-tyme of May," on bird-song and ladies' bowers, strewn with " red roses and lylye floures " (l. 3759–72), which is closely related to similar effusions in the Kentish poems. But it must be noted that the Kentish author was not the only one to use such passages, and that in the muscular and occasionally rather brutalized narrative of *Richard,* the passage stands out with an

---

[1] Kölbing's argument from the similarity of theme, so far as this depended on the supernatural birth of the hero, is discredited if Paris's theory be accepted that the birth story in *Richard* is a late accretion.

effect of startling difference. It was more probably due to a
redactor familiar with the Kentish romances than to the man
who translated the Anglo-Norman original of *Richard*. With
the exception of the first twenty-four lines, this first English
version is represented by the fragments, 696 lines, in the (L)
Auchinleck manuscript (1330–42).[2]

In addition to this manuscript there are six others which preserve the story of *Richard* in Middle English. All these, except
(E) Egerton 2862, a late fourteenth-century manuscript, are of
the fifteenth century. In 1509 and 1528 the poem was printed
by Wynkyn de Worde, and again in 1568–9 by Thomas Purfoote
(Arber, *Stationers' Registers*, Lond. 1875, i, 179). According to
Brunner, the latest editor of the romance, these texts present
two versions, *a* represented by manuscripts CB–W, and *b*, by
L–ED–AH, which differ greatly in content. The nearest ap-
proach to a complete version is Wynkyn de Worde's edition of
1509. After a brief prologue the Auchinleck manuscript passes
directly to a résumé of the events leading up to the Third Crusade. The manuscripts of the *a* type amplify the story by beginning with an account of the fairy lady, Cassodorien, who
reaches England in a marvelous ship with ropes of silk, samite
sails, and ivory mast; she becomes Richard's mother, and stays
until she is forced to behold the Sacrament; she then flies away.
This version tells also of the Salisbury tournament where Richard
receives the stout blows of two Lincolnshire knights, Thomas de
Moulton and Fulke Doilly, and welcomes them as his comrades
in arms, of Richard's pilgrimage to the Holy Land, of his imprisonment by the King of Almayne, and of Richard's revenge.
These accretions amount to 1233 lines. They seem due chiefly
to the redactor's liking for oral and written tradition of a fabulous sort, and to an especial desire to glorify the two South
Lincolnshire knights, whose names appear in records from 1190
to 1240. In what has been accepted as the translation of the

[2] Brunner (p. 17 ff.) did not accept this estimate of the Auchinleck MS.
as indicative of the original character of the romance. Although in general
he agreed with Paris that it was approximately faithful to historical facts,
he accepted the wildly unhistorical account of Richard's birth as part of the
original tale, mainly, it would seem, because MSS. of the *b* version include
lines 35–1268. See *JEGP*. xv, 458–62, for further refutation of this point of
view.

original Anglo-Norman version these names do not occur, nor does history know of them as famous crusaders. Their glory in *Richard* must have been inspired by a minstrel, who was enjoying, as Ward (*Catalogue*, 1, 946) suggested, the patronage of their descendants.[3] Loomis (*JEGP*. xv, p. 465) noted that the two families were actually connected through the marriage of Lambert de Multon (d. 1247) with the widow of Geffrey de Oilli. In addition to these earlier episodes, those enumerated below in the discussion of the fabulous elements of the romance, are likewise to be ascribed to the same poet, who is known as the " interpolator " or the " Lincolnshire minstrel." This seems a somewhat unfortunate nomenclature since, whatever his interests, his dialect was, in Brunner's opinion (p. 48), of the southeast, and not, as Lincolnshire would suggest, of the northeast. The verse form of the two versions, *a* and *b*, is the short riming couplet. At the beginning of the Auchinleck copy there are two twelve-line, tail-rime stanzas.

ORIGIN. Between the death of Richard I in 1199 and the earliest English romance accounts of his life, many chronicles of the Third Crusade were written by men of English, French, and Eastern origin. In these histories, to greater or less degree according to the national bias of the writers, was preserved the record of the wildly reckless deeds, the boisterous courage, the brutality and fantastic chivalry, which made Richard of England one of the most picturesque of royal Crusaders. Fact in his case was often stranger than fiction, as subsequent story-tellers were quick to perceive. In consequence their tales have a certain historical value, sometimes as the record of an attitude of mind and the growth of a personal myth, and again as distorted but recognizable images of actual fact. The shorter, more sober *b* version of the Middle English romance of *Richard*, like its various antecedents, undoubtedly omits much, is inexact in chronological detail, and somewhat subject to patriotic exaggeration concerning its hero, and to depreciation of his rivals and enemies, but on the whole the narrative is fairly authentic. It tells with measurable fidelity of the preparations for the Cru-

---

[3] For the complicated history of the Multone family see N. Neilson, *A Terrier of Fleet*, Lond. 1920, p. lxxxii ff.

sades in Europe, of Richard's stay in Sicily, of the conquests of Cyprus, of the taking of Acre (1191), the massacres of Saracen prisoners, the march to Jaffa, the attempted fortification of Ascalon, the relief of Jaffa, largely through the personal prowess of Richard, and his summons home when news comes of the treacherous activities of his brother John. The question, however, as to how much of this record is due to the extant chronicles of the thirteenth century, such as Ambroise's *L'Estoire de la guerre sainte*, 1190-2, or the *Itinerarium Peregrinorum et Gesta Regis Ricardi*, or Richard of Devize's *De Rebus Ricardi I*, 1189-92, or the *Imagines Historiarum*, 1188-1202, of Ralph of Diceto, how much to lost chronicles, and how much to memory of the actual events, has long been a matter of dispute. Jentsch's attempt to find in the *Itinerarium* the principal source of the romance was disposed of by Gaston Paris (*Rom.* XXVI, 369-85), who showed that the alleged correspondences between the two are necessarily incidental to the treatment of the same historic events and personages, and that the differences in the order of events, the respective omissions and elaborations, are inexplicable if the *Itinerarium* be considered the source of *Richard*. In Paris's opinion the Anglo-Norman poet made up his story from oral tradition and was in general independent of written documents. He may, however, have made use of one text treating of the siege of Acre before the arrival of Richard and the French king. In Brunner's study (pp. 51-70) of the romance a long list was given of the details which in his opinion were to be classified as historic, pseudo-historic, or purely fabulous. Chiefly with regard to the latter, his work on the sources supplemented that of Gaston Paris, who disregarded these fictitious details on the ground that they did not appear in the original Anglo-Norman version with which he was primarily concerned.

It is evident that in the thirteenth century the story of Richard, stimulated by patriotic enthusiasm for the memory of a king whom popular imagination was making into a kind of victorious Roland, was constantly increasing its content and popularity. Though Richard's own mother, to whom reference is made in the *b* version of the romance (l. 2041), was a sufficiently famous subject for song, the legend of his demon birth was in circulation at an early date. Richard's contemporary, Giraldus

Cambrensis (*De principis instructione*, III, cap. 27, ed. Warner, 1891, p. 300), quoted the King's story of the demon lady who was one of his Angevin ancestors (Paris, *Rom.* XXVI, 357). She, like his mother in the *a* version, may be related to all the Fairy Mistresses of romance but is more particularly like the Lamia type of lady best known, perhaps, in the Lusignan legend of Melusine (Edwardes *Summary*, p. 284) as set forth about 1387 by Jean d'Arras. Legends of Richard's prowess rapidly became wide-spread and were represented in art as well as story. Thus his duel with Saladin, which is recounted in early fourteenth-century chronicles such as Peter de Langtoft's (Rolls Ser. II, 102) and Walter de Hemingburgh's (ed. H. Hamilton, Lond. 1848, p. 183), was sufficiently well-known in 1250 for Henry III to order the story painted on the walls of Clarendon palace. It also appeared in the Chertsey Tiles, in the Louterell Psalter (*c.* 1340), and in various other manuscripts (Loomis, pp. 513–19). The famous story of the lion fight from which Richard drew his nickname, was represented in the Chertsey Tiles, in the late thirteenth-century Peterborough Psalter, and on a boss in the cloister of Norwich Cathedral (*ibid.*, pp. 519–22). The date at which this incident became a part of the tale of Richard's captivity is undetermined. Historically the captivity episode belongs to his return from the Crusade in 1192; in the romance it is an incident of his return from a pilgrimage made supposedly before the Crusade. He travels as a palmer, is imprisoned by King Modard of Almayne, and is exposed to the attack of a lion sent into his cell. Richard wraps around his arm the forty silk handkerchiefs brought him by the king's daughter. When the lion attacks him, he tears out its heart, stalks into the king's hall, and salts and eats the heart before the astounded court. The feat suggests comparison with traditional exploits of Samson and David, but in such pictures and carvings as are known, the scene represents " Richard, that robbed the lion of his heart " in fairly recognizable fashion.

The elaborated *a* version shows how strong a magnet the story of Richard was, not only for floating scraps of tradition about the king, but also for anecdotes and *motifs* which had originally no connection with him. The barbaric account of Richard's cannibalism when he dines on Saracen heads " all hot " (l. 3427)

and forces imprisoned foes to eat of Saracen flesh, recalls the
grim account given by Adémar de Chabannes (III, 55, ed. Cha-
vanon, p. 178) of an eleventh-century Norman who in Spain
forced imprisoned Moors to eat the flesh of countrymen (Paris,
Rom. xxvi, 359, n.). In another passage in *Richard* (l. 3089)
the substitution of a " Sarezynʒonge and ffat " for pork, suggests
comparison with the *Chanson d'Antioche* (ed. G. Paris, 1848,
II, 3). Similarly antedating Richard's own time is the old
anecdote of the bee-hives (l. 2906) thrown into a besieged city,
and the account (l. 2150) of the steward whose nose was cut off
by the Emperor of Cyprus. Paris (p. 389) has likened this unfortunate to *Estatin l'esnasé* of the first Crusade. On the other
hand, later than Richard's time was the Castel Pilgrim of the romance, for the Castle was not made or named until 1218; and
later too was the concept of St. George as patron saint of the
English. The saint was not, officially, thus recognized until
after 1222 (Matzke, *Beves, PMLA.* xviii, 155).

The process of accretion is, however, most clearly indicated in
the use of various romance *motifs*. The boat which brings the
fairy lady to England is matched in its strange splendor by
those in *Guigemar* (Warnke, *Lais*, p. lxxix), *Parténopeus*, etc.,
where its purpose is likewise to bring lovers together. In his
Salisbury tournament Richard wears successive disguises of
black, red, and white, as do most of the heroes of the Three
Days' Tournament theme. When he goes on his first journey to
the East, he wears the usual pilgrim disguise. English ballad
stories of Kings Incognito parallel, if they do not anticipate, the
rude speech between Richard and the minstrel who comes begging
to his fire. Betrayed by the minstrel and imprisoned by King
Modard of Almayne, Richard manages in an Exchange of Buffets [4] to kill the King's son, — a deed which commonly introduces in romantic narrative the hero's flight or exile, —
and to engage in a love affair with Modard's daughter,
a typical " wooing princess." [5] In the account of Richard's

---

[4] For the ancient and widespread game of pluck buffet, see G. L. Kittredge, *Sir Gawain and the Green Knight*, Cambridge, 1916, p. 21 ff. 119,
123, 221. See also Child, *Ballads*, III, 55, 77.

[5] McKnight, *Horn*, n. to l. 264, thought that the scene in which the
Princess bids the jailer bring her his captive, disguised as a squire, is possibly
borrowed from *Horn*.

revenge journey into "Almayn," of the edict of Modard who forbids the inhabitants to sell Richard any food, and of Richard's circumvention of the order, the Middle English poet has apparently made a somewhat stupid adaptation of a *motif* used in *Aimeri de Narbonne,* and repeated in chronicles which variously ascribe the adventure to Robert the Magnificent (1034), to the Norwegian kings, Harold (1034) and Sigurd (1111), to the Swabian founder of Donanwerth Abbey (1027), and to the Emperor Frederic II, (Paris, *Rom.* IX, 515). In each case the edict of a rival king or noble is evaded by the unparalleled wealth and recklessness of the newcomers. No price for food is too great for them; if fuel fails, they burn houses, etc. Again the scene in which the infuriated Emperor of Cyprus hurls his knife at Richard's messenger (l. 2120) is paralleled in *Beves of Hampton,* in *Generides,* and many other romances. Richard's overthrow of a marble image (l. 6265) in a Saracenic city recalls Beves's overthrow of the idol in Damascus, a deed which harks back to the legend of St. George. The defeated defenders of Castel Orgylous appear, as do so many other unfortunates enacting in fact or legend the so-called "Chivalric Penance," [6] "barffoot, ungyrt, withouten hood" (l. 4181).

Throughout the romance the supernatural element is but rarely of distinctive sort. When the English hero departs finally from Almayn, he is given two Magic Rings for protection from fire and water, though this bit of popular detail has no further significance in the narrative. Prophetic dreams, angelic warnings or commands, save Richard from danger or send him into battle at the propitious moment. In his direst need St. George comes to his aid. Of more unique character is the description of the Demon Horse presented to Richard. The presentation itself seems a reminiscence of an incident in the *Estoire de la Guerre Sainte* which tells of a chivalrous Moslem who gave a horse to his heroic enemy (Paris, *Jour. des Savants,* p. 489, n. 3). As for the demon colt itself, demon steeds are familiar enough in folklore, and even in Arthurian romance Perceval almost comes to his doom through a demon horse, but in no other case is the creature treated with such graphic and comic detail as in

[6] See here, *Guy of Warwick,* n. 13.

Richard. The colt's ears are stuffed with wax, a forty foot tree is trussed across its head, and it is a sorry demon indeed that Richard rides to a duel with its master (l. 5535 ff.). According to the evidence of the Chertsey Tiles, these fantastic details must have appeared in the duel story about 1275 (Loomis, p. 512).

Richard is one of the most militant of the Middle English romances. Throughout its 7212 lines it is so filled with the pitiless and fanatic spirit of the Crusades that its pages teem with abuse of the Saracen " dogs," caricatures of their leaders, and absurd laudations of the Christians. It is so militant that it seems almost untouched by courtly or chivalric influence. The one passage in praise of May, to which reference has already been made, and a single brief love affair of Richard's, are the only romantic elements in the story. Few heroes, even in Carolingian epic, are represented in more violent mood than the Lion-Heart. He smashes tables in his rage; he cuts through iron chains before the gates of beleaguered cities; he is the very " scourge of God " upon his enemies; he abuses his allies at the first sign of cowardice or indecision. Of all this, and of the business of mediæval siege warfare, of fights on land or sea, of the great catapults with which Richard won his victories, of poisoned wells, and trenches choked with dead, the romance tells with frankest relish. That the author's taste was shared by others, the number of extant manuscripts would seem to show, but there is hardly enough evidence as yet to indicate the existence of a local cult of Richard in the South Lincolnshire district.[7]

BIBLIOGRAPHY

TEXTS: (1) L, Auchinleck, MS. pr. Laing, *Owain Miles and Other Fragments,* Edin. 1837; Kölbing, *Eng. Stud.* VIII, 115–9; (2) E, formerly Duke of Sutherland's, now Egerton 2862, desc. *Brit. Mus. Catalogue of Add. MSS.,* 1906–10, p. 238; (3) C, Caius College 175/96, desc. M. R. James, *Cat. of Library of Gonville and Caius Coll. Cbg.,* 1907; largely printed by Weber, 1803, II, 148–278 (11136 lines), and used as a basis for the critical edition published by Karl Brunner (see below);

---

[7] For further study of Richard's place in fiction, see Needler's dissertation, Brunner, pp. 73–75, and E. A. Baker's *Guide to Historical Fiction,* Lond. 1914, p. 18.

(4) H, Harley 4690, fragment; (5) A, College of Arms, HDN. 58 desc.
W. H. Black, *Cat. of Arundel MSS.*, Lond. 1829, pp. 104–110; (6) B,
Add. MS. 31042, desc. Herrtage, Sege of Melayne, *EETS.* xxxv, p.
viii; (7) D, Douce MS. 228, Bodleian, fragment. The British Museum
MSS. are described by Ward, *Catalogue*, 1, 944–50. Trans. in part,
J. Weston, *Chief ME. Poets.*

STUDIES: Wells, *Manual*, p. 786.

Brunner, Karl. *Der mittelengl. Versroman über Richard Löwenherz*,
    Kritische Ausgabe nach allen Handschriften, mit Einleitung, Anmer-
    kungen u. deutscher Übersetzung. 604 pp. *Wiener Beiträge z. eng.
    Phil.* xli, Wien u. Leipzig, 1913. Rev. *Eng. Stud.* xlix, 126–42;
    N. Y. Nation, July 30, 1914; *JEGP.* xv, 455–66.
Jentzsch, F. "Die me. Romanze Richard Coeur de Lion u. ihre Quellen,"
    Eng. Stud. xv, 161–247 (1891).
Lodeman, F. E. "Le Pas Saladin," *MLN.* xii, 21–34, Introduction: 84–
    96, Text: 209–229; 273–81 (1897).
Loomis, R. S. "*Richard Coeur de Lion* and the *Pas Saladin* in Medieval
    Art," *PMLA.* xxx, 509–28 (1915). Illus.
Needler, G. H. *Richard Coeur de Lion in Literature.* Diss. Leipzig,
    1890.
Paris, G. "Sur un Épisode d' *Aimeri de Narbonne*," *Rom.* ix, 515–46
    (1880). Cf. *Richard*, version *a*, 1475 ff.
    "La Légende de Saladin," *Journal des Savants*, 1893, (mai–août).
    "Le Roman de Richard Coeur de Lion," *Rom.* xxvi, 353–93
    (1897).
Thomas, A. "La Légende de Saladin in Poitou," *Jours. des Savants*, pp.
    467–71 (1908).

GAMELYN

"Gone, the merry morris din;
Gone the song of Gamelyn."
— KEATS.

VERSIONS. The tale of *Gamelyn*, the dispossessed youth who sturdily regains his heritage, is found in sixteen Chaucerian manuscripts. All apparently are derived from the same original and none are of earlier date than the fifteenth century (Hammond, *Chaucer Manual*, p. 425). In the *Canterbury Tales* the story is commonly inserted after the fragmentary Cook's Tale, and critical opinion has varied as to whether it was intended for the Cook, or, as seems more probable, for the Yeoman. But even if Chaucer's interest in the story may be assumed from its presence among the manuscripts of his own works, it is certain that the poem had received no revision at his hands. Since Tyrwhitt's Introductory Discourse to his edition of the *Canterbury Tales* (1775–8), *Gamelyn* has been rejected from the Chaucerian Canon. Skeat (*Chaucer*, III, 400) noted that its dialect was more northern than that used by Chaucer and that words of French origin were in smaller, and those of Scandinavian origin in larger number, than in Chaucer's usage. The name of Gamelyn,[1] apparently derived from the Scandinavian Gammel-ing (son of the old man), is found in records in England as early as the tenth or eleventh century (Björkman, *Nordische*

[1] Prideaux, *Notes and Queries*, Ser. 7, II, 423, suggested that the name comes from that of Candelou, a family related to that of Fulke Fitzwarin, the famous outlaw in whom Prideaux recognized the original of Robin Hood. His reason was that Leland's spelling for Candelou was Gandeline and that this spelling is found also in *Robin and Gandeleyn*, a ballad which Prideaux thought represented figuratively the struggle between Fulke and an early rival. In the ballad the name of the adversary of Robin and Gandelyn was Wrennok and this name apparently was also that of the son of Fulke's temporary successor. But since the ambushed and easily murdered Robin of the ballad was certainly not the Robin Hood of tradition, neither was he representative of Fulke, who had a long and prosperous career after his early troubles, nor was Gandelyn representative of a friendly Candelou.

Personnenamen, p. 45). In temper, no less than in language, *Gamelyn* suggests that its author was of a neighborhood or of a nature in which the old native strain had been little changed by French influence.

The extant texts of *Gamelyn* must have been derived from a fourteenth-century version. The language is certainly not more archaic than that of *Havelok,* the romance with which *Gamelyn* has been most frequently compared. Skeat (*ibid*) argued that the latter should be dated after 1340 because it borrows (lines 277, 764) from a poem on the *Evil Times of Edward II* (Percy Soc. 28, 1) the commonplace line, " By Seint Jame in Galys that many a man hath sought." This poem, found in the Auchinlek manuscript (1330–40), is generally ascribed to the year 1320, but its priority to the lost original version of *Gamelyn* has so far only been asserted, not proved. Such historical filiations as the narrative of *Gamelyn* suggests, point, as will presently be shown, to the early years of the fourteenth century; but realistic as the poem seems, its descriptive details offer no historical data. Lindner (*Eng. Stud.* II, 321) tried to find in the description of the manor house, about the possession of which so much of the story centers, features suited to a thirteenth-century house; but as a matter of fact neither here, nor in the passage describing the moot-hall where Gamelyn's trial was held, is the evidence sufficiently detailed to do more than add to the general vividness of the setting. So local is this in character, with its references to village wrestling green, to the woods and fen beyond the manor, to the villagers " ryding jolily " in " cartes and in waynes," so devoid of the French romantic touch, that it is difficult to believe that it emanates from any French original. Nevertheless Skeat (*ibid.*) on the basis of the French names of Gamelyn's father, Sir Johan of Boundes, and of his brother Ote(s), was inclined to believe in an Anglo-French original.

Gamelyn is roughly divided into six parts by such minstrel admonishments to his hearers as, " litheth and lesteneth," and occasionally, " holdeth your tonge." The story is told in rimed couplets. The single lines have an irregular number of syllables as in the old alliterative verse, but alliteration itself is found chiefly in the numerous stock phrases. In the first half-line there are commonly four stresses, and in the second, three. The couplets, therefore, sometimes approximate the ballad stanza, and touches of ballad style are not infrequent. We find the verve and simplicity of phrasing, the use throughout more than half the poem of the dialogue form, the frequency of minstrel tags, the repetition of easy rimes, as Lindner (*ibid.*, p. 101) has shown in his rime index, and well-worn adages of popular wisdom, such as " after bale cometh bote." In style, spirit, setting, *Gamelyn* is as surely English as the *Geste of Robin Hood.*

Although the early printers were so aware of the popular appeal of the *Geste* that they frequently reprinted it, they seem altogether to have neglected *Gamelyn,* even in the black letter editions of Chaucer, and it must have been from one of the later manuscript forms that Thomas Lodge refashioned it into the first part of his prose romance, *Rosalynde or Euphues Golden Legacie,* 1590. True Elizabethan that he was, Lodge, under the influence of Euphuistic style and of Italian pastoral convention, refurbished and refined the old story out of its un- couth roughness. Stout Gamelyn became the graceful Rosader ; his brothers John and Ote, the fanciful Saladyne and Fernan- dyne ; their English manor a house in Bordeaux. Fighting gave way to a romance which was altogether lacking in the blunt old story, and Rosalynde, beloved of Rosader, and her friend Alinda began those dainty wanderings in the forest of Arden which drew at last Shakespeare himself to sing of them. In *As You Like It* (1599–1600) the pretty idealized love story introduced by Lodge reached its ultimate fulfillment in the beauty and mirth of Rosalind and Orlando.

ORIGIN. Though traditional character types and incidents play so large a part in *Gamelyn,* there are many elements in it which savor chiefly of fact. The tale begins, to be sure, with a true folk-tale situation, for Gamelyn is that youngest son who is perennially subjected to the malice of his older brothers. But Gamelyn's story is developed with the literalness of life. His oldest brother sordidly cheats him out of a comfortable country property, and the youth's complaints about his unsown lands, his oaks cut down, his broken parks, his decayed houses, and his slain deer, remind one of the accounts in the Patent Rolls of

Edward I, II, and III, which record similar abuses wrought against property in private feud or by careless keepers. There is nothing in the poem, as there is in *Havelok* about kingdoms or dispossessed royal heirs, nothing of battles and knights. The parallels between the two stories, the facts that the two heroes are wrestlers, that both use clubs instead of weapons in their rough and tumble fights, that the two poems share certain colloquial expressions, such as the quaint " so brouke I myn ye " (l. 334), rise from a common source in popular taste and not from literary influence. *Havelok* draws clearly on romance tradition, *Gamelyn* on everyday realities. Gamelyn broods over his wrongs, pulls his young beard, flies into an ungovernable rage, chases his brother round his own manor yard, and up the stairs into a loft where hastily " he schette the dore fast." The scene is differentiated by its homely realism, as is the whole disinheritance story in *Gamelyn*, from the conventional use of the same situations in romance and folk-tale. In the records of the thirteenth and fourteenth centuries the cheating of minors is a constantly recurrent offense; and though no exact historic parallel to *Gamelyn* has been found, there is absolutely nothing in this part of the story for which contemporary circumstance could not have furnished ample suggestion.

Gamelyn's exploit in overcoming a famous wrestler is a popular detail which may very possibly go back to some local, well-known tale. The *Geste of Robin Hood* (Fit II, st. 135–42) tells of a wrestling match between all the best yeomen of the West Countree (West Riding of Yorkshire), of a stranger who wins the match, of his danger from angry competitors, and of his rescue by a noble knight for love of Robin Hood. Within twenty-eight lines in the *Geste* there is an amount of detail concerning the prizes and the wrestling much greater than in the hundred lines devoted to the incident in *Gamelyn*. The lines in the *Geste* sound like the summary of an older, longer ballad on the same subject.[2] Though the *Geste* is too different from *Gamelyn* to be identified with it, the resemblance in this incident points to the common use of an older traditional tale.

Other traditional elements may be easily recognized. On Gamelyn's return from the match he is refused, by his brother's

[2] W. H. Clawson, *The Geste of Robin Hood,* Toronto, 1909, pp. 47–8.

orders, admittance to his home. Like Beves and many another hero, he pitches the Surly Porter into a well.[3] Sir John pretends that he has sworn to have Gamelyn bound hand and foot, and in the moment of their apparent reconciliation asks Gamelyn to permit the act so that he (John) may not be foresworn. Thus bound, Gamelyn, like a humble Samson, endures the insults of his brother's friends as they feast about him. Later, when, though released by the faithful old servant, Adam (the) Spenser, he still stands, feigning captivity, the irony of the situation suggests the many popular tales in which a man, supposedly poor and friendless, is taunted by those from whom presently, to their dire discomfiture, he is to regain his inheritance. The incident has always had the same appeal of grim humor whether in the tale of royal Odysseus, unrecognized among the evil suitors in his own Ithacan hall, or in the legend of the Heir of Linne (Fit ii, 84–129), who recovers his lands from the greedy Abbot of St. Mary's.[4] The sarcastic mirth with which the author describes Gamelyn sprinkling holy water " with an oaken spire " on the unlucky heads of his foes, Leach (p. 657) noted as one of the qualities suggestive of the kinship in temper of *Gamelyn* and Scandinavian story.

Gamelyn's fight with the Sheriff, his flight to the wild wood, his fellowship there with amiable and sportive outlaws whose master he presently becomes, his hostility to the rapacious clergy, his feud with the unjust Sheriff, his loyalty to the king, illustrate incidents and feelings which seem closely akin to those in the *Geste of Robin Hood* or to the earlier ballads which were its source. The well-known allusion in *Piers Plowman* (B, v, 401) proves that these were current before 1377, the date of the B text, but the question of their relationship to the lost fourteenth century original of *Gamelyn* has so far remained an open one. In his edition of the tale Skeat (p. xi) suggested that the namelessness of the outlaw chieftain, whose place Gamelyn took, implied that the romance represented an earlier stage than the ballads with their hero of familiar name. This was to argue that every outlaw figure, however shadowy, must be identified with Robin Hood alone and to ignore the many

---

[3] Child, *Ballads,* III, 95, n.
[4] Cf. Clawson, p. 45.

sources in contemporary fact and fiction for such a figure.[5]
Furthermore the outlaw incident in *Gamelyn* is frankly incidental to the disinheritance theme; it is a distinct popular embellishment which in style, incident, and theme reflects the type
of narrative established in the Robin Hood ballads. Since it is
impossible to believe that *Gamelyn* ever gave rise to the ballads,
it only remains possible to find in *Gamelyn* the definite influence
of the ballads, and to recognize their priority. Later on, when
the Robin Hood ballads were yet more widely known, popular
fancy seems to have striven to glorify the outlaw character of
Gamelyn, and to have associated his name with that of Robin
Hood somewhat to the disparagement of the latter. In the
ballad of *Robin and Gandelyn* (Child, No. 115) the outlaw
leader who is murdered by Wrennok and avenged by Gandelyn,
is certainly not the traditional Robin Hood, although the borrowing of the name is a significantly popular touch. In the much
later ballad, *Robin Hood Newly Revived* (Child, No. 128), the
ballad itself is built, as Child remarked, " on the ruins of the
fine old tale of *Gamelyn*." In this Gandelyn outdoes Robin
Hood, is recognized by him as " his sister's son " and is adopted
into the outlaw troup under the name of Will Scadlock or
Scarlet.[6]

The concluding scenes in *Gamelyn* have a distinctive realism
which merits attention. When Gamelyn has fled to the green-

[5] A parallel, for instance, to the fact that Gamelyn after living as an
outlaw leader, made his peace with the king, and was later appointed by
him Chief Justice of the Forest, lies in the well-known history of Adam
Gurdon (d. 1306) who was " disinherited " by Henry III and became a
famous outlaw, but who, on being reconciled to Edward I, was appointed
by him for many years Justice of the Forest on circuits in Berkshire and
Wiltshire. (Cf. E. Foss, *The Judges of England*, 1870; *Dict. Nat. Biog.*)
The episode of Adam's famous single-handed fight with Prince Edward
(1266), which was known to nearly all the chroniclers of the reign of
Edward I, is of special interest for comparison with the story of Robin
Hood's buffeting with " our comely king Edward."

[6] The name of a light-fingered Walter Scarlet, committed for burglary
in the house of a chaplain, is found in a commission for clearing the jail
at Norwich, Nov. 8, 1286, and in one for Estedam, Jan. 28, 1287, Patent
Rolls, Edward I, Vol. II. A Will Skarlet de Shategrave appeared as the
accuser in a trial of 1289 in Norfolk. See T. F. Tout and H. Johnstone,
State Trials of the Reign of Edward I, 1288–1293, Camden Soc., 1906, p.
120. This adds two more to the rather profitless endeavors to equate historical names with those found in the Robin Hood ballads.

wood, his brother John proclaims him " wolf's head." At the next
" schire " Gamelyn goes boldly to the moot-hall, is arrested and
delivered over to the keeping of his good brother, Sir Ote. From
him he returns to the greenwood, and at the time set for his
trial Ote is bound in his place. For this trial Sir John packs
the jury: " He was faste aboute — For to hyre the quest to
hangen his brother " (l. 785). At the trial itself there is a
wild scene. Gamelyn fiercely rebukes the Justice, saying, " Thou
hast yeven domes that ben yvel dight," and thereupon throws
him over the bar and breaks his arm. Then seating himself in
the Justice's place, he makes of his own men a jury and dooms
the false Justice to be hanged, together with his brother, the
sheriff, and the twelve false " sisours." Allowing for popular
extravagance and for the irresistible temptation from the story-
teller's point of view to make the accused become the accuser,
and the victim the judge, we may recognize in all this something
which again seems reminiscent of fact rather than fancy. The
account of the false sheriff, the bribed jury, the trial and punishment which judge and jury are made to suffer, recalls the no-
torious scandals of 1289 when the charges of bribery and cor-
ruption brought against certain chief justices and sheriffs led to
a series of trials lasting over three years and to the infliction
on the guilty of heavy fines and penalties.[7] Many of the contemporary chronicles refer to the affair, and in Norfolk, especially, whence so many complaints came, the memory of the
whole sorry business must have been long lived. Legal injus-
tice, of course, was a sufficiently familiar commonplace of
mediæval life, but the rarity with which popular writers treated
it, gives the more importance to its bold presentment in *Gamelyn,*
and the more reason to find for this episode some possible substratum of fact. So far as story goes, as Leach (p. 354) suggested, the relish for court proceedings in *Gamelyn* is best
paralleled by the interest in the doings of the Thing shown by
the authors of *Njals Saga* and *Grettis Saga.*

[7] Cf. Tout and Johnstone, passim. Various cases are given, indicating
unfair trials, removal and substitution of jurors, intimidation, cheating of
minors, etc.

BIBLIOGRAPHY

TEXTS: (1) Br. Mus. Harley 7334, pr. Wright, *Canterbury Tales,*
1847; by Bell from Wright, 1854; Chaucer Society, 1885. For description, see Hammond, *Chaucer Manual,* pp. 177–8. Skeat, *Oxford
Chaucer,* III, 403, considered this much the best copy of *Gamelyn* and
made it the basis of his editions, Oxford, 1884, 1893; *Oxford Chaucer*
(Text) IV, 645 ff., 1894; (notes) V, 497. (2) Harley, 1758; (3) Royal
18 C ii; (4) Sloane, 1685; (5) Sloane, 1686; (6) Lansdowne 851; (7)
Corpus Christi, Oxford, 196; (8) Petworth, owned by Lord Leconfield.
2–7 are pr. by the Chaucer Society, Appendix to Fragment A of the
Six Text Edition; Appendices to separate issues of these six manuscripts.
(9) Royal 17, D xv; (10) Egerton 2726 contains "a Jacobean copy
of Gamelyn"; (11) Barlow 20, Bodleran; (12) Rawlinson 149; (13)
Laud 600; (14) Christ Church 152, Oxf.; (15) Trinity 49, Oxf.; (16)
Ashmole 45, Oxf. For details concerning these manuscripts, see Hammond, *Chaucer Manual,* p. 425 and pp. 173–192. The first printed edition of *Gamelyn* was that by Urry, *Chaucer,* 1721. Trans. Rickert,
Romances of Friendship, pp. 85 ff.

STUDIES: For bibliography see Hammond, *Manual,* pp. 425–26; Wells,
Manual, p. 766; 25–7.
Leach, H. S. *Angevin Britain and Scandinavia,* Cambridge, 1920, pp.
351–355.
Lindner, F. "The Tale of Gamelyn," *Eng. Stud.* II, 94–114, 321–343
(1878–79).

ROMANCES OF LOVE AND ADVENTURE

APOLLONIUS

VERSIONS. The *Apollonius* story is a famous instance of a tale that for more than a thousand years has kept an almost undiminished integrity and vigor. A Florentine manuscript of the tenth century (Laurentius LXVI) represents a stage undoubtedly late in the development of the story itself, but it is with this, the oldest extant text, that the history of the European versions begins. Over one hundred manuscripts of this Latin prose version, the *Historia Apollonii regis Tyri* (ed. A. Riese, Leipzig, 1893), are known, but many are yet inedited and their classification is still a matter of some dispute. They appear to fall into three groups: the redaction RA, which includes the Laurentian manuscript and a fourteenth-century one in Paris; the redaction RB, represented by manuscripts of the tenth, eleventh, and fourteenth centuries in Leyden, Oxford, and Paris; and a redaction made of mixed texts from which the mediaeval versions are chiefly derived.[1]

Of mediaeval Latin versions in addition to the *Historia* the principal ones are: (1) the *Gesta Apollonii* (ed. E. Dümmler, *Mon. Germ. Hist.* 1888, II, 483–506), a fragmentary poem of 792 verses in leonine hexameter, contained in an eleventh-century manuscript; (2) the abbreviated version in tercets introduced about 1186 by Godfrey of Viterbo into his chronicle history of the world, the *Pantheon* (Singer, 2, pp. 150–177); and (3) the prose narrative in that famous collection of stories, the *Gesta Romanorum*, compiled early in the fourteenth century (Klebs, p. 334 ff.). Although the *Apollonius* (ed. Singer, 2, pp. 68–105; Smyth, pp. 93–112) is found in only one of the late fourteenth-century manuscripts (Colmar 10) of the *Gesta*, its appearance there and in the widely distributed Latin editions of

[1] Cf. Klebs, pp. 18–47. Schreiber noted Klebs' disproof of Riese's assertion of the superiority of the RA redaction. It is in fact no more "original" than is the second group of versions of the *Historia*. Both RA and RB appear to be independent versions of a lost original. The Viennese manuscript edited by Schreiber belongs to the "mixed" texts.

the next century, shows that it must have been known better and at an earlier date than would appear from the extant manuscript evidence (Klebs, p. 353). It was according to Singer (2, pp. 68–149), the *Gesta* version of *Apollonius* that served as the basis for the Dutch translation of the *Gesta* that was printed in 1481, 1483, and 1484, for the oldest French version of the *Gesta*, the free fifteenth-century French translation of the *Gesta*, *Le Violier des Histoires Romaines Moraliséez*, and for the English version by Lawrence Twine, *The Patterne of Painefull Adventures*, London, 1576, 1595, 1607. Free treatments of the *Gesta* version of *Apollonius* appear also in the Danish Volksbuch, Copenhagen, 1627, in a similar Swedish version in 1747, in an Hungarian version of 1591, and in Polish and Russian texts of the seventeenth and eighteenth centuries (Murko, *Archiv f. slavische Phil.* 1892, xiv, 405 ff.; Klebs, pp. 362–83).

No less than the numerous Latin texts of the *Historia* do the vernacular versions of *Apollonius* attest its popularity through the Middle Ages. In England its history began at an exceptionally early date. From some Latin manuscript of Group iii, in either the tenth or the eleventh century, was made an Old English prose translation, now extant in two long fragments.[2] In the Middle English period a version was fashioned from the RB redaction (Klebs, p. 460). Of this only a fragment (ed. Smyth, pp. 49–55) of some two hundred and fifty lines in iambic tetrameter verse is left. It is written on two vellum leaves once used as the cover of a book. The language of this text seems to antedate that of Gower and to be of the Southwest Midland district (Smyth, p. 49). The concluding lines state that the poem was " translatyd Almost at Engelondes ende," by one who was vicar at "Wymborne mynstre " (Dorsetshire). In style the poem resembles the usual rimed chronicle. Gower produced in 1390–1393 a long and fairly well told version of *Apollonius* in his *Confessio Amantis*, Bk. viii, 271 ff. (ed. Macaulay, Oxford,

---

[2] Corpus Christi College, Cambridge, MS. 201, ed. J. Zupitza, *Archiv*, xcvii, 17–35 (1896); cf. *Anglia* i, 463; also " Welcher Text liegt d. altengl. Bearbeitung der Erzählung v. *Apollonius* zu Grunde," *Rom. Forsch.* iii, 269–79; R. Märkisch, "Die ae. Bearbeitung der Erzählung v. *Apollonius*," *Palaestra*, vi (Berlin, 1899). The Old English version of *Apollonius* has special interest as presaging, before the Norman Conquest, the introduction into England of the spirit of romance. See Peters, p. 51, for monastic catalogues of the eighth or ninth century referring to copies of *Apollonius*.

1901). This was professedly based an Godfrey's *Pantheon,* but it is evident from the number of details omitted in the *Pantheon* but found in the *Historia,* that Gower was drawing on the earlier Latin narrative (Macaulay, p. 537). It was Gower's version, presumably, which brought forth Chaucer's much debated fling at " swich cursed stories." [3] A fifteenth-century English verse translation of *Apollonius,* surviving in MS. Douce 216 in a fragment of one hundred and forty lines, was noted by Warton-Hazlitt (*Hist. Eng. Poetry,* 1871, II, 303) and by Klebs (p. 472). A prose romance, *Kynge Appolyn of Thyre,* translated from the French by Robert Copland and printed by Wynkyn de Worde in 1510, Twine's prose novel, already mentioned, the partly Shakespearean play, *Pericles, Prince of Tyre,* 1609, in which the change of the hero's name from Apollonius to Pericles was a reminiscence of the great Athenian statesman and of Pyrocles, one of the heroes in Sidney's *Arcadia* (Lee, p. 10,), the novel, *Pericles,* by George Wilkins, 1608, which was based in part, according to Baker (*PMLA.* 1908, XXIII, 103), on Wilkins's own dramatic version of Twine's book, and finally George Lillo's play, *Marina,* 1738, make up the list of the eight or nine versions of the story in England (Smyth, p. 48). The most important single influence on these sixteenth century versions was Gower's poem which, having been printed by Caxton in 1483 and again reprinted in 1532 and 1554, was the most readily accessible version.

The extant Continental texts of *Apollonius* represent probably but a small part of those once in existence. Numerous allusions in Old French and Provençal poetry of the late twelfth and the early thirteenth centuries show knowledge of the story.[4] An

---

[3] Cf. E. P. Hammond, *Chaucer Manual,* pp. 278–79; Wells, *Manual,* p. 699.

[4] Cf. Marden, p. xxv–vi; Lewis, pp. 147–50; Singer, 2, passim. One of the earliest Old French references to *Apollonius* is in *Philomena* which refers to the delights of *Apoloines* and of *Tristanz.* Cf. Faral, *Rom.* XLIII, 443–45. The former romance may actually have influenced the *Tristan.* Like Apollonius, Tristan after a great storm and a shipwreck comes to land, is received by a kindly king, plays before the court, and later in the Irish court is admired by a princess and becomes her instructor. In the *Apollonius* the wicked Dionysias, jealous of the loveliness of the young Tarsia, who had been left by her father, Apollonius, in the care of Dionysias, orders her slave, Theopilus, to kill Tarsia, but the maiden is carried off by pirates and the slave reports her death. In *Tristan* Iseult orders two serfs

allusion in the *Poème Moral* (ed. W. Cloetta, 1887), *cir.* 1200, to " les vers d'Apoloine u d'Aien d'Avinion," has been happily confirmed by the discovery of a fragment telling of the riddle-solving of Apollonius in an Old French metrical version of the tale (Schulze, p. 226). A French prose translation (ed. Lewis, *Rom. Forsch.* xxxiv) of the Latin romance exists in four manuscripts of the fourteenth and fifteenth centuries and in three free versions, of which one, in a Brussels manuscript, is unconvincingly ascribed by Lewis (p. 222) to Adam de la Hale (*Rom.* xliii, 444). Neither the versions, however, nor the references, fully indicate the influence of the romance in French literature. In the early thirteenth-century *chanson de geste, Jourdains de Blaivies,* many adventures of the hero, his shipwreck, his arrival in a foreign land, his test of skill with the king, his marriage with the princess, their separation and reunion, and the rescue of their daughter from a fate similar to Tarsia's, appear to be borrowed from Apollonius (Smyth, p. 80 ff.). A belated French version purporting to come from " une histoire tirée du Grec," was inserted by Belleforest in his *Histoires Tragiques,* 1582 (Klebs, p. 421).

In Germany the story was known as early as the twelfth century, for the poet Lamprecht alluded to it in his *Alexanderlied,* v. 1009 (ed. Kinzel, 1884), and the author of the Middle High German poem, *Orendel* (cf. Edwardes, *Summary,* p. 321), combined episodes drawn from our story with those of a fictitious Crusading king, Orendel of Treves. The earliest complete and independent version (ed. Singer, 1906) was that of a Viennese physician, Heinrich von Neustadt (1300), who stated at the end of some twenty thousand lines of verse that he was the first to translate the story from Latin into German. The value of this poem has been variously estimated; Klebs preferred the older Latin version, but Bockhoff (pp. 1–25) found Heinrich's an important mediaeval embellishment of the ancient story. The adventures of Apollonius with the gigantic peoples, Gog and Magog, with centaurs and sirens, with which Heinrich

---

(in Eilhart's version, two poor knights) to take Brangwein into the forest and bring back evidence of her death. Cf. *Emare* here, note 14. Teubert, *Crescentia Studien* (see *Florence of Rome* bibliography), p. 7, asserted that the *Crescentia* legend showed the influence of *Apollonius* in the account of the shipwreck of the heroine and of her meeting with a fisherman.

filled in the fourteen years of Apollonius's wanderings after he had left his infant daughter, Singer (3, pp. 29–70) believed were drawn from a lost Byzantine romance. As there is no external evidence, however, to support this conjecture, Pettingill's citation (3) of at least one instance in which the poet proved himself possessed of a measure of originality has special interest. In the episode of the combat between a man and a woman which takes place before the hero and his knights, Heinrich evidently drew for the rules of the whole strange procedure on contemporary law and the possible reminiscence of an incident recorded in the *Chronik de Berne* (1288). But despite the elaboration of Heinrich's story, it was not until the fifteenth century that *Apollonius* was really popularized in Germany. This happened through the increasing number of texts of the *Gesta,* through the very popular version (Augsburg, 1471) by Heinrich Steinhöwel, who asserted that he followed " Doctor Gotfrids von Vitterben " but more probably used both the *Gesta* and the *Historia,* and through two fifteenth-century German prose translations of the *Historia* (Smyth, pp. 25–30).

Among other early vernacular versions of *Apollonius* the following are the most important: an old Danish ballad (Grundtvig, *Danmarksgamle Folkeviser,* II, 466; Klebs, p. 379) which concerns itself with the shipwreck of the hero and has certain affiliations with the Old French poem, *Jourdain de Blaivies,* and the German *Orendel* (cf. Meyer, *Zts. f. deut. Altertum,* XXXVII, 325–56); a Spanish poem of the early thirteenth century, the *Libro de Apolonio* (ed. Marden, 1917), based on Latin prose versions and significant chiefly for its peculiar metrical form, " de nueva maestria," and for its moralizing tendencies; references in Alfonso the Wise's *Grande e General Estoria,* showing that it was intended to introduce the story there (Marden, p. xxxiii); a Portuguese version made in the fourteenth century by Roberto Paym of Gower's *Confessio Amantis* and later turned into Spanish prose (ed. Birch-Hirschfeld, Leipzig, 1909); a Spanish prose version in the *Patrañuela,* 1576, of Juan de Timoneda (Klebs, pp. 384–411); three fourteenth-century Italian prose translations based on the *Historia* (Cf. L. del Prete, *Apollonio in volgare italiano,* Lucca, 1861; Salvioni, *Versione Tosco-Veneziana,* Turin, 1889), one of which served as the source of a

Greek metrical version of the fifteenth century; and a fourteenth century Italian poem attributed to Antonio Pucci (Klebs, pp. 422–450). This poem was often reprinted down to the eighteenth century. In modern Greek there are two sixteenth-century versions of the *Apollonius* story (W. Wagner, *Mediaeval Greek Texts*, Lond. 1871, 1) and a modern folk-tale (Klebs, pp. 451–58).

ORIGIN. The earliest reference to the story of *Apollonius* is found in sacred lyrics of Venantius, Bishop of Poitiers, 566–568, who sadly compared his wanderings in Gaul to those of Apollonius. A grammatical index, *Tractat de dubiis Nominibus*, of somewhat later date, makes passing mention of the " balneum in *Apollonio* " (Smyth, pp. 21–23). It would seem then that a Latin version of the story must have been known in western Europe as early as the end of the fifth or the beginning of the sixth century. This was slightly Christianized, though Klebs (p. 189 ff.), in his very comprehensive study of the romance, showed that some features, such as the episode of the fisherman's sharing his garment with Apollonius, supposedly inspired by the legend of St. Martin (Riese, p. xviii), or of Apollonius's vow not to cut his beard or hair, a vow considered by some to hint of Judaic custom, do not prove any pietistic influence.[5] Klebs (p. 189 ff.) found the only evidence of Christian influence in the oldest texts in the recurrent use of " Deus," and in the description of " quendam angelico habitu," who warns Apollonius to return to Ephesus. The many allusions to pagan gods, to Neptune, Lucina, Apollo, Diana, in whose temple the wife of Apollonius is supposed to serve as a priestess, the descriptions

---

[5] Rohde, p. 447, conjectured that the whole of the Antiochus episode was introduced by a Christian scribe who thus motived Apollonius's long absence from home through the hero's fear of the incestuous king whose criminal secret he had discovered. In the Greek romance of *Antheia and Habrocomes*, which closely parallels a large part of *Apollonius*, the hero's absence from home is due to the command of an oracle. But when so many pagan features were left unchanged in *Apollonius* it would seem incredible that this long episode should have been introduced simply to do away with the pagan oracle. Bürger, p. 17, n. 22, suggested that the wicked Antiochus and his daughter from the first belonged to the romance as figures of dramatic contrast to the virtuous Apollonius and Tarsia. On the Incest theme itself see Baum, " The Legend of Judas Iscariot," *PMLA*. XXXI, 593 ff. (1916); O. Rank, *Das Inzest-Motif in Dichtung u. Sage*, Leipzig, 1912; See *Emare* here, note 6.

of pagan feasts and rites of burial, the atmosphere and localization of the story in Antioch, Tyre, Tarsus, Cyrene, Ephesus, Mitylene, unquestionably point to pagan antiquity for the origin of the story. To Rohde (p. 441), as to the majority of scholars, the civilization suggested by the romance, the love of arts and letters, the actual resemblance of the tale to Greek sophist romances, indicate a pagan Greek original of the second or third century. Greek tales of that period [6] drew upon much the same "universal apparatus of romance, pirates, sea storms, apparent death, the separation and reunion of lovers" (Smyth, p. 11). Klebs (p. 191), however, attacked this theory of Greek origin on the ground that the references to Roman coins, the nature of the inscriptions which in the story were put upon monuments raised to Apollonius and his daughter, Tarsia, the incidental allusions to specifically Roman customs, the literary style of the narrative, with its rhetorical plays on words, its Virgilian descriptions of the storm, of the awakening love of the Princess for the storm-tossed hero, like Dido's for Æneas, were possible only for a pagan Latin author of the first part of the third century. This author, in the opinion of Klebs (p. 299), was aware of the literary effectiveness of the Incest theme used by Seneca and by Ovid, and of the farcical relief afforded by the character of the bawd in Plautine comedy. From such sources then he drew ideas for the episode of the Incestuous Father which begins the story, and for the scene, thrice occurring in the plays of Plautus, in which an innocent maiden preserves her purity in a brothel. From this original Klebs (pp. 215 ff.) believed there were made various intermediate versions in which the story gradually acquired that popular tone of a Volksbuch evident in the earliest extant text.

The conclusion that there was a Latin version of *Apollonius* in the third century is now generally accepted. But the discovery in 1890–1900 [7] of new fragments of the Greek romance

---

[6] Cf. the Babylonian Histories of the Syrian, Iamlichus, 166–180 A.D.; the Ethiopian tales of Heliodorus, 250–300; the *Leucippe and Clitophon* of Achilles Tatius (after the fourth century). Convenient references are in S. Wolff's *Greek Romances in Elizabethan Fiction*, N. Y. 1912. Cf. Rohde, p. 441; Smyth, p. 12.

[7] Cf. Williamowitz's review of *Fayum Towns and Their Papyri* by Grenfell, Hunt, and Hogarth, London, 1912, in *Göttinger Gelehrte Anzeigen,* 1, 30 (1901); also Bürger. For the text of *Chaereas* see *Fayum Towns,* pp. 76–80.

of *Chaereas and Callirrhoe* which seem to prove that its composition must have been before 150 A.D., has again raised the question of an even earlier text for *Apollonius*. Since these fragments antedate any known to Rohde, there is a heightened possibility of a Greek original for *Apollonius*. In this, in Bürger's opinion (p. 26), the familiar märchen *motifs* and the literary style were sufficiently similar to the Greek tale which was the source of Apuleius's version of the Amor and Psyche[8] story in the *Golden Ass,* to justify considering them as a special, and probably contemporary, group of the second century. From this Greek *Apollonius* Bürger thought Zenophon of Ephesus in the third century drew the episodes in his romance, *Antheia and Habrocomes,* which have, on any other supposition, a wholly unexplained resemblance to those in *Apollonius*.[9]

Whatever the " original " *Apollonius* may have been, it is generally conceded that the riddles which appear in the mediaeval versions did not belong to it. In the RA redaction there are ten of these riddles, in the RB group seven, in the mixed texts a number which varies upwards from three (Klebs, p. 178). The riddles were derived from the one hundred *Enigmata* of Symposius and were probably composed in the fourth or fifth century. In the story the riddles are proposed to her father by the unrecognized Tarsia who thus endeavors to drive away his melancholy.[10]

Strange, shapeless, improbable, as in its entirety is " the mouldy tale," as Jonson called it, of *Apollonius,* there is need in any final estimate to pay tribute to the venerableness of its history and to the enduring appeal made by what might well be called the first of our western *romans d'aventure.* The words

[8] For the folk-tale elements in Amor and Psyche see *Partonope* here, note 12. Bürger noted that in *Apollonius* the Wicked Father, the Dangerous Riddle, the Fate of the Suitors, the Jealous Guardians of the heroine, the plan for her murder, all occur in well-known märchen. See also Rohde, pp. 448 ff.

[9] Cf. Rohde, pp. 409, ff. 440; Smyth, p. 11, for analysis of the story. The likenesses of the two romances forced even Klebs, pp. 298, 306, to admit the possibility of a Greek source. Singer's attempt (3, 1911) to prove the existence of a Byzantine original from supposed traces in the *Apollonius* of Heinrich von Neustadt was not convincing.

[10] See Smyth, *Pericles,* p. 88 ff. on the relation of this peculiar style of dialogue to that employed in the Solomon-Markolf type of story.

that Shakespeare or another put on the lips of " ancient Gower " still apply to it:

> " It hath been sung at festivals,
> On ember-eves, and holy-ales;
> And lords and ladies in their lives
> Have read it for restoratives.
> The purchase is to make men glorious;
> Et bonum quo antiquius, eo melius."
>
> — *Pericles.*

BIBLIOGRAPHY

TEXTS: (1) Fragments of two leaves printed by J. O. Halliwell-Philipps, *A New Boke about Shakespeare and Stratford-upon-Avon,* 1850; printed also by A. H. Smyth (see below). For the Old English version see note 2. (2) Gower's *Apollonius,* see Macaulay below.

STUDIES AND ANALOGUES: Cf. Betz, *La Litt. Comparée,* Index; Edwardes, *Summary,* Index; Wells, *Manual,* p. 784.

Beck, J. W. *Quaeritur an recensio christiana Historiae Apollonii Regis Tyri in Gallia orta esse possit.* Album — in honorem H. von Herwerden. Rheims, 1902.

Bockhoff, A. und S. Singer (see below). "Heinrichs v. Neustadt Apollonius u. seine Quellen, Ein Beitrag z. mittelhochdeut. u. byzantinischen Literaturgesch." *Sprache u. Dichtung,* VI, 1911. Rev. *Zts. f. rom. Phil.* XXXVIII, 381 ff.; *Literaturbl.* XXXIV, 363.

Bürger, K. *Studien zur Geschichte des griechischen Romans,* Teil II, *Die litteraturgeschichtliche Stellung . . . d. historia Apollonii.* Blankenburg, 1903.

Herbert, J. *Catalogue of Romances (The Gesta Romanorum),* vol. III, pp. 183–282. Lond., 1910.

Klebs, E. *Die Erzählung v. Apollonius, Eine geschichtliche Untersuchung über ihre lateinische Urform u. ihre späteren Bearbeitungen.* Berlin, 1899. Rev. *Anglia Bbl.* X, 233.

Lee, Sidney. *Shakespeare's Pericles.* (Facsimile, Introd., Notes) Oxford, 1905.

Lewis, C. B. "Die altfrz. Prosaversionen des Appollonius — Romans nach allen bekannten Handschriften." *Rom. Forsch.* XXXIV, 1–277 (1913). Rev. *Rom.* XLIII, 443.

Macaulay, G. *Works of John Gower (Confessio Amantis)* II, 393 ff. Oxford, 1901.

Marden, C. *Libro de Apolonio, An Old Spanish Poem.* Baltimore, Paris, 1917–1922.

Patterne of Paineful Adventures by Lawrence Twine, 1576, repr. J. Collier, 1843, repr. New Rochelle, N. Y., 1903.

Peters, R. *Die Geschichte des Königs Apollonius, Der Lieblingsroman des Mittelalters.* (Introduction and German translation.) Leipzig, 1904.

Pettengill, R. W. (1) *The Apollonius von Tyrland of Heinrich v. Neustadt, A Study of Its Sources.* Unpublished Harvard diss. 1910.
(2) "Zu den Rätseln im Apollonius des Heinrich v. Neustadt," *JEGP.* XII, 248–51 (1913).
(3) "The Source of an Episode in Heinrich's v. Neustadt's Apollonius," *JEGP.* XIII, 45–50 (1914).

Rohde, E. *Der griechische Roman u. seine Vorläufer.* 3rd ed. Leipzig, 1914.

Ropohl, F. *Das Verhältnis d. Assonanzteiles z. Reimteile im altfrz. Apolloniusroman (Jourdains de Blaivies).* Diss. 95 pp. Kiel, 1909.

Schreiber, E. W. *Zum Texte d. Historia Apollonii* (Summary and extracts from a twelfth century Viennese MS.) Korneuburg, 1909.

Schulze, A. "Ein Bruchstück des altfrz. Apolloniusromanes." *Zts. f. rom. Phil.* XXXIII, 226–29 (1909).

Singer, S. (1) *Heinrichs von Neustadt Apollonius von Tyrland. Deutsche Texte des Mittelalters,* VII. Berlin, 1906.
(2) *Apollonius, Untersuchungen über das Fortleben des antiken Romans in spätern Zeiten.* Halle, 1895.
(3) See Bockhoff above.

Smyth, A. H. *Shakespeare's Pericles and Apollonius of Tyre, A Study in Comparative Literature.* Philadelphia, 1898.

THE SEVEN SAGES OF ROME

VERSIONS. The great mediaeval vogue of the various versions of the *Seven Sages,* which in actuality is a collection of tales rather than a romance, once rivalled that of *Apollonius.* Literally hundreds of texts are known, representing in fact or theory almost every age and race. Bewildering as even Gaston Paris admitted this chaos of versions to be, it is nevertheless possible to note certain clear lines of demarcation. The primary division is between the versions of the East and the West. In the Eastern group eight versions are found of the *Book of Sindibād.* In general they tell of the philosopher, Sindibad, to whom the education of a young prince is entrusted. Death nearly befalls this young man when his royal stepmother falsely accuses him of attempting to seduce her, but his life is saved by seven sages who for seven days rival with tales of false women those concerning false counsellors which the Queen tells her husband. On the eighth day the Prince speaks in his own defense and the Queen is exiled or killed. The eight versions are as follows:[1] *Sindban* (English translation, *Folk-Lore,* VIII, 99 ff.), a tenth-century Syriac text; the Greek *Syntipas* (ed. Eberhard, *Fabulae,* 1872), possibly of the last half of the eleventh century; a Spanish text, *Libro de los Engannos* (ed. A. Bonilla y San Martin, Barcelona, 1914), written in 1253 and seemingly derived from the same lost Arabic text which was the source of *Sindban;* a Hebrew version, *Mischle Sindbad;*[2] a Persian prose

[1] Cf. Chauvin, VIII, 1–21; Campbell, pp. XII–XIV, for full bibliographical details; also the standard study of Comparetti, *Ricerche intorno al libro di Sindibad,* Milan, 1870; Eng. trans. *Folk-Lore Soc.* IX, Lond. 1882; Ward, *Catalogue of Romances,* II, 192 ff.; Hilka, I, pp. VIII, XXI.

[2] Ed. with German translation by P. Cassel, Berlin, 1888. Questions of date and origin are much disputed in regard to this version. Hilka (I, p. X) agreed with those who believed it to be of Arabian origin, and put its composition in the first half of the thirteenth century. Faral, *Rom.* XLII, 147, asked whether Hilka's 15th century Latin version was not a late translation from the Hebrew by an author familiar with and influenced by a western form of the story. Campbell, p. XVI, noted as characteristic

text of As-Samarquandī of the late twelfth century; another in the *Touti-Nameh* (Eighth Night) of Nachsebī (d. 1329), and, most important of the Persian texts, the poem, *Sindibād-nāmeh*, 1375 (Campbell, pp. xii–xiv). A late Arabic version known as the *Seven Vezirs* is extant in three versions of the *Arabian Nights Tales*. Of the eight texts the first four are the oldest and most authentic, and of these the *Mischle Sindbad,* from the point of view of European story, is the most interesting, for it has been held to be the most probable intermediary between the Eastern and the Western versions. In Hilka's opinion (1, p. x) the early fifteenth-century Latin manuscript, discovered by him in 1911, was derived from the Hebrew text and most truly represents the intermediate stage.

In the Western versions of the *Seven Sages* there is no mention of Sindibad, and the Sages have individual names, a trait which in the East appears only in the Hebrew version. The Sages tell only one story each instead of two or more, as in the Eastern texts; the instruction of the Prince is entrusted to them, not to the one philosopher, Sindibad; and only four of the original tales (*Canis, Aper, Senescalus, Avis*) reappear in the fifteen tales that are normally told in the Western redactions.[3] In Europe there are at least forty different versions, preserved in upwards of two hundred manuscripts and nearly two hundred editions (Campbell, p. xvii). In 1866 began the first serious attempts at the classification of this material, a task more nearly achieved in regard to certain versions by Gaston Paris in his edition of *Deux Rédactions du Roman des Sept Sages, SATF.,* 1876, than by any one else. The most complete summaries of the literature relating to the subject were given by Chauvin in 1904 and by Campbell in his 1907 edition of the Middle English versions.

---

features of the Hebrew version: the individual names of the sages; the rivalry of the sages in attempting to procure the task of instructing the prince; the defense of the prince by the sages, not by the king's counsellors; peculiarities in the stories of *Aper* and *Avis.*

[3] The traits differentiating the versions may be roughly summarized as follows: number and order of stories; the subject-matter of the stories; the localization of the framework tale; the names of the personages, of the king, queen, prince, sages. These details differ widely. For comparative tables of the tales in the Eastern versions see Bedier, *Les Fabliaux,* p. 136; for those in the Western versions, Campbell, p. xxxv; Smith, p. 5.

The first European version of the *Seven Sages* is found in the *Dolopathos,* a Latin prose work now extant in six manuscripts. It was written about 1190 by Joannes de Alta Silva and translated not long afterwards by the French poet, Herbert.[4] In the *Dolopathos,* as in the Eastern versions, the prince has only one instructor, here the poet, Virgil, but of the nine tales told only one, *Canis,* is found also in the *Book of Sindibād.* Four of the stories (*Canis, Gaza, Puteus, Inclusa*) in the *Dolopathos* agree with those in the later western redactions of the *Seven Sages,* and it seems probable that the Latin text was simply an independent derivative of a version which must have been current before John wrote (Campbell, p. xx). The second group of versions is represented by an Old French poem (K), *Les Sept Sages de Rome* (ed. Keller, Tübingen, 1836), which Paris[5] believed was composed about 1155, though the one extant manuscript is of the thirteenth century. From the same source as K came a third version in a single French prose text, the " version dérimée " (ed. G. Paris, *Deux Redactions,* pp. 1–55), and also possibly the large fourth group (A*) of versions of the type represented by the fifteenth century Italian prose texts of the *Libro dei Sette Savj de Roma* (ed. d'Ancona, Pisa, 1864). To this fourth group also belong two other early Italian versions, an Old French prose version still preserved in a large number of manuscripts (cf. Plomp, p. 18 ff.), two early Swedish versions (ed. Klemming, Stockholm, 1887), a Welsh version,[6] and one in Dutch verse (Campbell, pp. xxxii–iv). The earliest manuscripts of the Swedish, Welsh, and Dutch versions do not antedate the fourteenth century, nor is the Auchinleck manuscript, the earliest of the nine texts containing the story in Middle English, of earlier date.

From his work on these texts, Campbell, however, concluded

---

[4] The *Dolopathos* was edited by H. Oesterley, Strassburg, 1873 (rev. Gaston Paris, *Rom.* II, 481–503) and by Hilka, 1913. For Herbert's version see *Li Romans de Dolopathos,* ed. Montaiglon, Paris, 1856. For bibliography see Chauvin, VIII, pp. 30–31; Campbell, pp. XVIII–XXI.

[5] *Litt. frç. au Moyen Age,* 2e. ed. p. 247.

[6] This was a prose redaction written by the Welsh priest, Llewelyn. He borrowed almost verbatim the scene in which the young Queen visits an old witch to ask about the King's son, from a passage in *Kulhwch and Olwen* in the *Mabinogion.* The Welsh version appears in five manuscripts, the earliest dating from the fourteenth century. Cf. Campbell, p. XXXIII; Loth, p. 351.

that there was originally a thirteenth-century English manuscript (V) from which eight of the extant texts (C, R, A, E, B, F, D, Ar), were derived, though of these only two, C and R, were copies of the same manuscript (*Ibid.*, p. xl). The Aslone manuscript (As), was, he thought (p. xli), derived from an Old French manuscript of the A* group. All the Middle English versions are in the octosyllabic couplet, and it seems probable that their parent version was written in Kent; the three manuscripts, A, Ar, E, are most clearly Kentish in dialect; B, F, are southern, perhaps Kentish; D, is of the Southeast Midland; CR is northern, and As, Scottish (Campbell, pp. xxxvi–xl). Nothing is known of the authors of these versions, and there seems little to support Kölbing's conjecture (*Arthour and Merlin*, 1890, p. civ) that A was written by the author of the Kentish versions of *Arthour and Merlin, Alisaunder,* and *Richard Coeur de Lion* (Campbell, p. lviii). A chronological classification of the manuscripts shows that A, R, D, were of the fourteenth century, C, Ar, F, E, of the fifteenth, and R and As of the sixteenth.

In addition to the four versions already noted, Gaston Paris classified the remaining Latin, French, and Italian versions of the story in five groups.[7] Of these the large group represented by the *Historia Septem Sapientum* (H) is of most interest in its relations to English literature. The oldest of the twenty-eight Latin manuscripts of the *Historia* dates from 1342 [8] and the Latin text, printed first at Cologne in 1475, was frequently reprinted and almost endlessly translated (Buchner, p. 301).

[7] The five groups are: (1) the fourteenth-century abridgment of a lost Latin text made by the Dominican, Joannes Junior, in the *Scala Celi;* (2) a Latin redaction known as the *Historia Septem Sapientum,* the largest of all the groups; (3) the *Versio Italica;* (4) the French redactions of the type of the first Leroux de Lincy text, *Roman des Sept Sages,* Paris, 1838; (5) the *Male Marrastre* (Paris, *Deux Redactions,* p. xxv). Paris considered the *Dolopathos* apart from the eight types represented by the other European versions discussed by him.

[8] In Oesterley's edition of the *Gesta Romanorum* at least thirty-five manuscripts of the *Gesta* are described in which all or a part of the *Seven Sages* appears in its Latin form (Campbell, p. xxiv). It should be noted that the earliest known text of the two famous collections of stories is the Innsbruck codex of 1342. Cf. G. Buchner, *Die Historia septem sapientum nach der Innsbrucker Handschrift,* Erlangen, 1889; Herbert, *Catalogue of Romances,* 1910, III, 184 ff. The literary history of the two collections is remarkably parallel. In the Middle English versions of each collection appear two of the same stories, *Virgilius* and *Canis.*

Schmitz enumerated twelve manuscripts, Fischer seventy-two editions of the German prose translation, and Campbell (p. xxv) noted the metrical German version of Hans von Bühel (1412), a tragedy by Sebastian Wildt (1560) and others. The *Historia* was translated into French prose and at least eight French editions dating from 1492 (ed. Paris, *Deux Redactions*, pp. 55–205) survive. A Spanish version (Burgos, 1530) ran through six editions, and a Dutch translation through fifteen or more editions after 1479. Two Swedish versions were made in the fifteenth century, a Danish version in the seventeenth century, an Icelandic version (Campbell, p. xxvi), and numerous translations into Slavic languages. Of these last the oldest extant text is a Bohemian manuscript of the fourteenth century. From a Polish translation, which itself passed through eight editions, came a Russian version now represented by some forty manuscripts of the seventeenth and eighteenth centuries (Murko, *Sitz. Ph.-hist. KL. Abhandl.* x, Vienna, 1890, pp. 12–92). An Armenian version translated from one of the printed texts of the *Historia* was made in 1614 (Macler-Chauvin, pp. xiv–xx). The Continental popularity of the *Historia* in the fifteenth and sixteenth centuries especially is reflected by numerous contemporary editions in England. From the Latin *Historia* was made the translation printed by Wynkyn de Worde, an edition which served as the source for many of the later English versions in verse and prose.

ORIGIN. Whatever the sources of the widely varied single tales in the different versions of the *Seven Sages*, the framework [9] itself is Eastern in origin. Not only is the oldest Oriental text, the Syriac *Sindban*, two centuries older than the earliest European version, but even in the western versions of the story, the motivating impulses remain inherently Eastern. These balanced tales of designing women and evil counsellors are typical of Oriental cynicism, and typical, too, of the East are the Brah-

---

[9] For other European instances of stories in a frame-work see Hammond, *Chaucer Manual*, 1908, p. 150; Wells, *Manual*, p. 185; Schofield, *Eng. Lit.— to Chaucer*, p. 337; Voretzsch, *Einführung*, p. 416. The frame-work device is found in the *Marques de Rome* (ed. J. Alton, Tübingen, 1889), one of the five continuations of the *Roman des Sept Sages* (Paris, *La Litt. frç.*, 1882, p. 109; Tatlock, *MLN.* xxxvi, 96. n. 5).

minical glorification of wise teaching, and the despotism which
makes the issue of life or death dependent on mere story-telling.
But where or when the original Eastern version was composed
we can only conjecture. Some scholars have found an ultimate
basis for it in the Indian story of Kunāla and Acoka, and conjectured that in India a parent text was fashioned as early as
the fifth century B.C. (Campbell. p. xi). But the available evidence shows us no more than that the extant texts of the *Sages*
were descendants in some sort from a lost Arabic version written
by one Musa (Moses) in the eighth century.

There are various theories concerning the transmission of the
story to Europe. Paris [10] thought that after it had passed
through various forms, Persian, Syriac, Arabic, Greek, it finally
received in the Byzantine kingdom a new form, and that this
Greek version, after it had passed from the Eastern Empire into
Italy, became the source of the Western versions. In the opinion of other scholars, it was not the Greek but the Hebrew version, or, as stated above, a Latin translation of this text, which
formed the bridge between the Eastern and the Western versions. In Campbell's opinion (p. xvi) the changes in the latter
were too great to be accounted for if the author of the original
Western text had been working from any actual text. Rather,
he thought some returning Crusader heard the story in the East
and told of it on his return. Campbell granted (p. xvii) the
" slight probability " that it was some form of the Hebrew version which was thus transmitted. However that may be, it is
probable that the legend had reached western Europe by the
middle of the twelfth century, and possibly somewhat earlier if
Paris's date for the original version of the Old French metrical
romance be accepted. In this, as also in the majority of the
derivative versions, the setting of the tale is laid in Rome, and
names for the principal characters are, like that of Diocletian
the Emperor, drawn from Roman history and legend (Campbell,
p. xxii). In the later texts names from Romance literature begin to intrude themselves. In the Middle English versions, for
instance, the name Florentine for the Prince is probably derived
from the romance of *Octavian* (Campbell, p. 150). Of far
greater importance, of course, is the substitution, in all but four

10 *La Litt. frç. au Moyen Age,* p. 82.

instances, of new tales for the fifteen Oriental stories in the *Book of Sindibād*.

The sources and analogues of these popular tales show upon investigation little connection with mediaeval romance. They belong primarily to the *fabliau* or *exemplum* type and are often anecdotal and bourgeois in character. Only in three or four instances in any of the versions have romance analogues been pointed out, and these in general show the retroactive influence of romance on the tales. The story (*Canis*) of the faithful dog which saves his master's child somewhat remotely parallels an episode in the Latin romance of *Arthur and Gorlagon*.[11] The story of *Virgilius* in the Middle English versions describes brazen men, one with a bow and arrow, one with a magic mirror, which are said to have been set up by Virgil for the protection of Rome. Human automata, as Hertel and Bruce [12] have shown, are familiar features in mediaeval romance, but it is probable, as Bruce (p. 521) observed, that the conception of automata had become a commonplace in the romances before it influenced the Virgil legend. In the story of the *Children turned into Swans* (*Cygni*), which first appeared in the *Dolopathos*,[13] we have the earliest version of what became the introduction to the famous *Knight of the Swan* legend. In the story of Alexander and his friend, Prince Louis of France (Paris, *Deux Redactions*, pp. 167–92), there is direct borrowing from the equally well-known legend of *Amis et Amile*.[14]

A final word may be said concerning *Vidua*, the twelfth story in the *Seven Sages*. Despite its gruesome horror *Vidua* has been

---

[11] Campbell, p. lxxix. In the Latin romance a tame werwolf attacks the king's steward, who is the lover of the Queen. The beast's attack is motived by loyalty to his master just as in the more simple tale the Faithful Animal rescues his master's child. Cf. Kittredge, "Arthur and Gorlagon," *Harvard Studies*, VIII, ch. VIII, "Defense of the Child"; Chauvin, VIII, no. 31.

[12] Cf. A. Hertel, *Verzauberte Örtlichkeiten u. Gegenstände in d. altfrz, erzählenden Dichtung*, Diss. Göttingen, 1908; Bruce, *Mod. Phil.* X, 511 ff.; Comparetti, *Virgilio nel medio evo*, 1896; G. Leland, *Unpublished Legends of Virgil*, N. Y., 1900; Campbell, p. xcv; and for further notes on the general subject of automata see *Floris* here, note 20. Bruce (p. 521) found the earliest instance in which the invention of automata is ascribed to Virgil in the *Image du Monde*, which was not composed until 1245. Comparetti thought the composition of the Virgilian automata was Oriental in origin.

[13] See *Knight of the Swan* here, note 3.

[14] See *Amis and Amiloun* here. Cf. Chauvin, VIII, no. 235.

called "perhaps the most popular of all stories." [15] It tells of
a woman whose grief for her husband is so assuaged at his very
grave that she will presently allow his body to be subjected to
indignity for the sake of a new lover. The tale goes by the
type name of the *Widow* or *Matron of Ephesus*, the heroine
of the classical versions. Since 1879, much controversial argument has been expended to prove some connection between this
brief, cynical tale and the long, highly romantic and chivalric
romance, *Iwain*, of Chrétien de Troyes. Without necessarily
accepting all of Brown's contention [16] that the latter is a Celtic
Fairy Mistress tale, one may recognize from his discussion of
the essential incongruity between *Vidua* and *Iwain* that the two
stories are of altogether different provenance.

BIBLIOGRAPHY

TEXTS: (1) A, Auchinleck MS. (2646 lines), ed. Weber, III, 1–153;
cf. Kölbing, *Eng. Stud.* VI, 443 ff.; extracts, Ellis, *Specimens*, III, 1 ff.;
(2) R, Rawlinson Poet. 175 (new number 14667), Bodleian; cf. *PMLA.*
XIV, 459; (3) D, Camb. Univ. Libr. Dd. I, 17, ed. Wright, *Percy Soc.*
XVI (1845); cf. *Eng. Stud.* VI, 448; (4) C. Cotton Galba E. IX (4328
lines), ed. Weber, 1810, III, 1 ff.; K. Campbell, *Seven Sages of Rome,*
pp. 1–145, Boston, 1907; rev. *MLN* XXIV, 153; (5) F, Camb. Univ. Libr.
MS. Ff. II, 38 (2555 lines), extracts pr. Halliwell, *Camden Soc.* XXX,
p. XLIII; Wright, *Percy Soc.* 1845, XVI, p. LXX ff.; Petras, *Über die
mittelengl. Fassungen d. Sage von den Sieben Weisen Meistern,* p. 60
ff. Breslau, 1885; (6) Ar, Arundel 140, Brit. Mus.; E, Egerton 1995,
Brit. Mus. (complete, 3588 lines); (8) B, Balliol Coll. Oxf. 354,
(complete, 3708 lines); (9) As, Asloan, Malahide Castle, Ireland,
desc. Varnhagen, *Eng. Stud.* XXV, 321 ff. The later English versions
include: (1) a prose translation printed by Wynkyn de Worde, 1505–
1515, repr. Villon Soc., Lond., 1885; (2) a lost edition by Wm.
Copland, 1548–61; (3) a metrical version by John Rolland of Dalkeith,
composed about 1560, reprinted seven times before 1631; (4) a lost
dramatic version (cf. Henslowe's *Diary*, March, 1599–1600); and
twenty-six prose editions from 1653 to the early part of the nineteenth century (Campbell, pp. LX–LXV).

[15] Cf. Joseph Jacobs, *Caxton's Æsop,* I, 13; Campbell, p. CI; E. Grisebach,
Die Wanderung der Novelle von der treulosen Wittwe durch die Weltlitteratur,
2 ed. Berlin, 1889; Chauvin, VIII, No. 254.

[16] "Iwain, A Study in the Origins of Arthurian Romance," *Harvard
Studies,* VIII, Boston, 1903, ch. 1.

STUDIES AND ANALOGUES: Cf. Chauvin (below); Edwardes, *Summary*, pp. 110, 191, 427; Wells, *Manual*, p. 792.

Bertoni, G. "Un Manuscrit du *Roman des Sept Sages* en prose." *Zts. f. rom. Phil.* XXXI, 713–15 (1907).

(2) "Sulla lingua del *Roman des Sept Sages* in versi (ediz. Keller, 1836)." *Studj Romanzi* VI (1910).

Bonilla y San Martin, A. *Libro le los engaños & los asayamientos de las mugeres.* Barcelona, 1904.

Botermans, A. J. *Die Hystorie van die seven wijse mannen van Romen,* (ed. 1479). Haarlem, 1898. Rev. *Rom.* XXVIII, 448.

Buchner, G. "Beiträge z. Geschichte der *Sieben Weisen Meister.*" *Archiv,* CXIII, 297–301 (1904).

Campbell, K. (1) See above, Texts (4). Unless it is otherwise stated, references are to the Introduction in this edition.

(2) "A Study of the *Seven Sages* with Special Reference to the Middle English Versions." *PMLA.* XIV, 1–107 (1899); *Rom.* XXVIII, 166; *Anglia Bbl.* X. 38.

(3) "The Source of the Story of *Sapientes.*" *MLN.* XXIII, 202.

Chauvin, V. *Bibliographie des Ouvrages Arabes,* vol. VIII, 1–213. Leipzig, Liège, 1904.

Evans, J. G. "Report on Manuscripts in the Welsh Language." *Historical MSS. Commission,* pp. 3–4, 33–34, 101 (1902).

Fischer, H. *Beiträge z. Litteratur der Sieben Weisen Meister. Die handschriftliche überlieferung der Historia septem sapientum.* Diss. Greifswald, 1902. Rev. *Archiv* CXIII, 29.

Hilka, A. H. (1) "Historia septem sapientum. 1, Eine bisher unbekannte lateinische Übersetzung einer orientalischen Fassung der *Sieben weisen Meister* (Mischle Sendabar)." *Sammlung Mittellateinischer Texte,* IV. Heidelberg, 1912. Rev. *Rom.* XLII, 147.

(2) II. Johannis de Alta Silva, *Dolopathos,* nach den festländ. Handschriften. *Sammlung,* V (1913).

(3) *Die Wanderung der Erzählung von der Inclusa aus dem Volksbuch der Sieben Weisen Meister. Breslau,* 1917.

Loth, J. "La Version galloise des *Sept Sages de Rome* et le Mabinogi de Kulhwch et Olwen." *Revue Celt.* XXIII, 349–52 (1902).

Mackinnon, D. *Catalogue of Gaelic Manuscripts in Scotland,* p. 152. Edin., 1912.

Macler, F. (1) *Contes Syriaques: Histoire de Sindban.* Paris, 1903. (2) *La Version Arménienne de l'Histoire des Sept Sages de Rome.* Mise en française. Introduction par V. Chauvin. Paris, 1919.

Massey, Isabella. *Text-u. Quellenstudien zu dem anonymen mitteldeut. Gedicht von den Sieben Weisen Meistern.* Diss. Marburg, 1913.

Mikolajczak. *De Septem Sapientum fabulis quaestiones selectae.* Diss. Breslau, 1902.

Napier, A. S. "A Hitherto Unnoticed Middle Eng. Manuscript of the *Seven Sages* (Rawl. Poet. 175)." *PMLA.* XIV, 459–64 (1899).

Paris, Gaston. *Deux Rédactions des Sept Sages de Rome.* SATF. Paris, 1876.

Plomp. H. P. *De middelnederlandsche Bewerking van het gedicht van den* VII *Vroeden van binnen Rome.* Utrecht, 1899. Rev. *Rom.* XXVIII, 449.

Schmitz, J. *Die ältesten Fassungen des deut. Romans von den Sieben Weisen Meistern.* Diss. Greifswald, 1904.

Smith, H. A. "A Verse Version of the *Sept Sages de Rome.*" *Rom. Rev.* III, 1–67 (1912).

Turkish version, English translation. *The History of the Seven Wise Masters of Rome.* Kasan, 1900.

Ulrich, J. *Proben der lateinischen novellistik des Mittelalters ausgewählt u. mit anmerkungen versehen.* Leipzig, 1906.

Voretzsch, C. *Einführung in das Studium d. altfrz. Lit.* (1913), pp. 414–17; p. 457.

FLORIS AND BLAUNCHEFLUR

VERSIONS. The gracious tale of *Floris and Blauncheflur* was once widely known and loved in mediaeval Europe.[1] The oldest version is a French poem composed between 1160–70, now found in three Paris manuscripts (A, B, C). Of these the oldest (A, Bibl. Nat. 375), containing 3342 verses, was written at the end of the thirteenth century. Du Méril (*Floire et Blancheflor*, Paris, 1856) called this the " version aristocratique " (A), and a second version (B), also composed in the late twelfth century, but now found only in one manuscript of the first half of the fourteenth, the " version populaire " (ed. Du Méril, p. 125 ff.). Fundamentally the story of the two versions is the same, a tale of two children who become passionately attached to each other, of their separation lest the royal lad wed the girl of inferior station, of his search for her and their ultimate reunion in a far-off land. But the two versions differ in style and individual incidents.[2] The first is an idyllic romance with the emphasis on sentiment and aesthetic detail; the second, full of action and stirring incident, is somewhat obviously modelled on the contemporary *chansons de geste*.[3]

The nature of the origin of these versions and of their rela-

[1] Reinhold, p. 9, listed sixteen allusions to the story by Provençal poets but there is no proof that there was ever a Provençal version of the story. The best comparative studies of the various versions of *Floris* are: H. Herzog, *Die beiden Sagenkreise von Flore u. Blanscheflur, Germania*, 1884; H. Sundmacher, *Die altfrz. u. mhd. Bearbeitung der Sage, Göttingen*, 1872; and those by Reinhold and Ernst.

[2] The episode of Floire's attempted suicide in the lion pit is usually cited as the distinctive episode of the extant first version. Distinctive in the second are the false accusation brought against Blanchefleur that she had attempted to poison the king; the judicial combat which Floire fought for her as her champion, an incident due perhaps to the influence of stories of the type of the *Erle of Tolous;* and the warfare in which Floire becomes involved in the East. Cf. Reinhold, ch. III.

[3] Cf. Gaston Paris, *Rom.* XXVIII, 443. It is of interest, in connection with the Carolingian cycle, to note that Floire and his love are said to be the parents of Berte, the mother of Charlemagne.

tion to each other, has long been a matter of heated controversy.[4] Were they independent derivatives of a common source? Was the second version derived from some more primitive version of the first or from the extant version in combination with another group? Was the second version, as Du Méril thought, a reworking and transformation of the first in order to adapt it to an audience of less cultivated and courtly taste? In 1906 Reinhold sharply attacked this traditional classification of the French versions and maintained (p. 82, ff.) that the popular version was not less chivalric than the first, and that variations in it were simply because of a redactor's imperfect memory of the first version.[5] From a prayer for " bons ostax " in the B version, he thought (p. 115) that this one may have been especially destined for the entertainment of pilgrims to Compostella. In both versions Blancheflor's mother is captured by Saracens from pilgrims similarly bound, and it may have been the potential interest of this episode which inspired some enterprising jongleur to recount the story. Interesting as is this hypothesis in connection with Bédier's theory for the development of the *chansons de geste,* the second French version is in itself generally felt to be of inferior literary quality.

The antiquity of the French versions is indicated not only by internal evidence but by the fact that the story had passed before the end of the twelfth century from France into Germany. About 1170 was composed a Low Rhenish poem (ed. Steinmeyer, *Zts. f. deut. Altertum,* 1877, xxi, 307 ff.), of which only 368 verses remain. It was based undoubtedly on French sources. Early in the thirteenth century the German poet, Konrad Fleck, freely paraphrased the tale in 8006 lines of Middle High German verse (ed. W. Golther, Kürschners *Deut. National-Lit.* iv, Abt. 3, Berlin, 1889) in a version known through two fifteenth-century manuscripts, through a fifteenth-century prose version (ed. Herzog, *Germania,* xxix, 218–26), and through two thirteenth-century fragments discovered, one in 1898 (Lambel, *Festschrift z.* viii *allg. Neuphil.-tage in Wien,* pp. 37–58) and another by Zwierzina in 1904 (cf. Rischen, 1913). From the

---

[4] Cf. Reinhold, p. 82 ff., for a history of the question.

[5] In the opinion of Gaston Paris, *op. cit.* p. 444, Version ii was a hybrid made from memory by a poet familiar with Version i and with the source of the Spanish-Italian group. Cf. Herzog, *op. cit.* pp. 4–11.

same source that Fleck used, another poet, Diederic von
Assenede, about 1250 composed a simpler version of 3983 verses
in Middle Low German (ed. Moltzer, Groningen, 1879; Leendertz, 1912). A Low German poem, *Flos unde Blankeflos* extant
in five manuscripts of the fourteenth and sixteenth centuries, was
thought by its most recent editor, Decker (1913), to represent a
unique and primitive form of the *Ur-floire*. It refers explicitly
to a " fransoische bokelin " as its source. On linguistic grounds
Decker (p. 131) dated the poem in the last decade of the thirteenth century. Ernst (pp. 50–53) contended that a portion
of this version was translated from a Ripuarian poem, a fragment of 184 lines (ed. Schafstädt, 1906), with which it has some
verbal similarities. Finally, among the German versions may
be noted two groups of Volksbücher, one an adaptation of
Fleck's poem, and one from Boccaccio's Italian rendering of
the story of *Floris*. With the exception of this last group, all
these German texts presuppose a French source antedating the
extant A version. But it is evident from the problems brought
up by new texts and new studies that the last word has not
been said on their history or on their special relationships with
the French and English versions.

The story of *Floris and Blauncheflur* appeared in England
about the middle of the thirteenth century, in the last half of
which were written the oldest extant manuscripts, Cott. Vitell.
and C (McKnight, p. xli). These texts are unfortunately very
fragmentary, but their gaps may be supplemented by two other
manuscripts (A and T), which are respectively of the fourteenth
and the fifteenth century. After collating these texts for his
edition of the poem (1885) Hausknecht concluded that C represents one group, and the other three manuscripts a group X
in which A and Cott. Vitell. form a sub-group. The manuscript
C agrees more frequently with the French source than do the
others. In Hausknecht's text the poem contains 1296 verses
written in short couplets and in the dialect of the East Midland
district (McKnight, p. xli).

The omission in the English romance of any of the traits
peculiar to the second French version indicates that its source
is to be sought in the oldest French form. Of the three texts
(A, B, C) belonging to that version, the English poem shows

the closest agreement with B. But as Hausknecht (pp. 137–140 ff.) pointed out, its agreement in three passages not contained in either manuscript A or B, but found in the German texts of Fleck and Diederic, suggests that it was derived from their common French source.[6]

Whatever text was its direct antecedent, the English version, which closely follows the order of events and in some places the very phraseology of the extant French texts, is nevertheless a free and characteristic rendering. McKnight (p. xxxix)[7] gave an interesting list of the passages omitted, modified, or condensed by a poet who had in view a practical-minded audience and who evidently felt that for Englishmen the tender sentimentality of the French text, its ornate descriptions of gems and precious stuffs, of the wonderful cup, to which the French poet devoted sixty-seven lines and the Englishman but seventeen, or of the marvellously lovely garden of the Emir, would be somewhat over elaborate. But even so he keeps much of the charming idyllic quality of the original. The atmosphere of love and youth and innocence is, if anything, enhanced by the English poet's simplicity of style. His Floris is as boyishly inexpressive in his grief at the (false) news of Blauncheflur's death as is Chaucer's young Dreamer;[8] his little Blauncheflur sums up all her resolution not to wed the Emir by vowing, in familiar English phrase, not " to change old love for new." Throughout the poem, in fact, the speech of the characters is singularly fresh and natural, and the descriptive passages, though so much condensed, keep enough gaily colored detail to make them vivid. One of the earliest of the extant Middle English romances, *Floris and Blauncheflur,* is also one of the best. The continued popularity of the legend in England is suggested by the allusion to it in the fourteenth-century romance, *Emare.* In this a beautiful robe is described which has been embroidered with the stories of famous lovers, Amadas and Idoine, Tristan

---

[6] Cf. Hausknecht, p. 134 ff.; Reinhold, p. 32; Ernst, p. 62 ff., for varying views concerning the source of the English poem.

[7] McKnight followed Hausknecht's list, p. 143 ff.; Reinhold, p. 33, criticized severely the lack (to him) of imaginative and poetic feeling in the English version.

[8] Cf. v. 239 (Trentham MS.) with the *Book of the Duchesse,* v. 1309. In Floris himself no one can suspect that " artless artfulness " which Kittredge (*Chaucer's Poetry,* 1915, p. 53–54), attributed to Chaucer's Dreamer.

and Isolt, and, as no less famous, with that of Floris and Blauncheflur.

The remaining groups of Continental versions of the story belong to Italy, to the Scandinavian countries, and to Spain. In Italy it developed in one version known as the *Cantare di Fiorio e Biancifiore* (Crescini, Bologna, 1899; Crocioni, 1903) written in *ottava rima* by a popular poet, probably early in the fourteenth century. (Crescini, II, 25–6.) From a version derived from the same source as the *Cantare* Boccaccio fashioned between 1338–41 the *Filocolo*,[9] his first prose romance. It is generally supposed that the lost common source was a Franco-Italian poem (Crescini, I, 163; II, 10, 239), probably nearer in some instances to the original French version, and certainly more complete than the abridged *Cantare* version.[10]

With the Italian versions belongs the Spanish prose romance, *Flores y Blancaflor*, printed at Alcalá in 1512, and translated into French in 1554 (Ernst, p. 4). The Spanish text was originally of much greater antiquity, though the name Flores, preserving the *s* of the French nominative, indicates, as Gaston Paris pointed out (*Rom.* XXVIII, 446), a date subsequent to that of the French versions. Paris's summary [11] of the traits which distinguish the Spanish romance, the *Cantare*, and the *Filocolo*, from either of the two French versions, argued that a lost French text, as distinctive in character as the two that are extant, was

[9] Ed. by E. De Ferri, Turin, 1921–22. Cf. Hausknecht, p. 37; H. Cummings, *Indebtedness of Chaucer's Works to the Italian Works of Boccaccio*, Univ. of Cincinnati Studies, x, 1916, ch. 1.

[10] Cf. Paris, *Rom.* XXVIII, 439. A fuller but slightly different version found in the fourteenth-century Greek romance, *Flores and Platziaflore* (ed. W. Wagner, *Mediaeval Greek Texts*, Lond. 1870). Herzog believed the first French version and the Italian-Spanish groups to be variants of a more ancient Greek romance which had, before the fourteenth century, experienced two redactions. Crescini, II, 4, noted that the name Blancheflour, common to the two twelfth-century French versions, practically makes this hypothesis impossible.

[11] *Rom.* XXVIII, 441. In the Spanish-Italian group Blancheflur's parents are of Roman nationality; her mother (in the French versions an unnamed French lady) is called Topazia; widowed and captured at the same time, she later dies in giving birth to Blancheflur; the maiden gives Floire a ring which will indicate to him when she is in danger; the master, not the father, of Floire discovers the boy's love for the maiden; she is held captive in Babylon in Egypt (Cf. p. 444, n. 1); she has for servant a girl named Gloris (in the French versions her friend and equal is called Claris); she and Floire at the end of the story receive the imperial power of Rome.

once known; but again the complex question of their inter-relation is open to doubt.

From Scandinavian countries come the following versions: two Norse sagas, one written before 1319 and still preserved in complete form (ed. Köbling, Halle, 1896), and another of which only a fragment remains (ed. G. Storm, Copenhagen, 1874); a Swedish poem (ed. E. Olson, Lund, 1921) which was translated about 1311 from a lost Icelandic original and later translated into Danish (ed. C. Brandt, *Romantisk Digtning*, Copenhagen, 1869–77). All of these versions were derived from a French source, but their variety and distribution indicate the popularity of the story in the North.

ORIGIN. Before 1897 the story of *Floire et Blancheflor* was variously supposed to have come from Provençe, from Germanic myth, from Spain, from a lost romance of Byzantine origin, and from Persia.[12] In 1897–99 Ten Brink and Huet [13] independently advanced the belief that it was originally an Arabic tale. They derived the Tower of Maidens, in which Floire discovered his lost sweetheart, from an eastern harem, and found a striking parallel in at least four Arabic tales for the episode in which Floire, getting himself concealed in a basket of flowers, gains admittance to the Tower. The incident is practically the same in the Arabic tales, though certain details vary widely. The girl is a harem slave, the youth a merchant or money changer; in all the stories but one he enters the harem disguised as a woman or as the Khalif himself. There are besides such correspondences as these: in one story the ruse episode is preceded by an account of the lovers' childhood and of their youthful passion for each other; and in two stories, as also in *Floire*, the hero, when he arrives within the harem, goes or is taken to the wrong door. In the oldest French version of *Floire* and in the derivative versions, the tower with its many rooms, its armed guardians, its lovely inmates, their services to the Emir, their equality with each other, and the geographical allusions (in the French versions to Babylon of Asia), seem to point

[12] The most recent summary of these opinions is given by Johnston, 2, pp. 126–29.

[13] See respectively, *Geschiedenes der Nederlandsche letter kunde*, p. 115 ff., Amsterdam, 1897, and Huet, *Rom.* xxviii, 349–59 (1899).

to the customs, the locality, and the story *motifs* of the Arabic East. Especially notable from this point of view is the fact that Floire, in starting on his long quest to regain Blancheflor, assumes a merchant disguise, a kind rare indeed in the chivalric romances of the west, but used innumerable times in eastern story (Huet, *Rom.* XXVIII, 355; XXXVI, 95).

The Arabic hypothesis for the origin of *Floire* is engaging but not wholly satisfactory. In 1906 Reinhold pointed out that no single Arabic tale is of the same structural type as *Floire*, although single incidents may be paralleled here and there; he urged strongly the improbability that the tales, especially those of the Arabian Nights collection, were known in twelfth-century France; [14] and finally he asserted that the idea of the Tower of Maidens as a supposedly Eastern harem is as anomalous as that of the monagamous but murderous Emir who in the romance is said to kill his wife each year before taking a new bride. Though the modification of a harem into a Maidens' Tower would not seem a very startling modification for a western poet to make, Reinhold preferred to think the idea came from the *Book of Esther* in which the House of Maidens is clearly distinguished from that of the king's concubines. He found still other parallels between the *Book of Esther* and the romance in the accounts of the feasts of Ahasuerus and the Emir, which were broken up, in one case by Vashti's disobedience, in the other by the discovery of Blancheflor's lover in the Tower, and in the description of the assembling of a court of judges. Though Reinhold's destructive criticism has much to commend it, there is nothing in this suggested derivation of *Floire* from *Esther* that brings conviction. Neither the characters nor the incidents of the two stories are in any genuine sense alike.

To explain the actual story of the lovers, Reinhold turned to that of Cupid and Psyche as told by Apuleius in the *Golden Ass*.[15] In this as in *Floire* the love story includes the mésalliance *motif*, the separation of the lovers through parental influence, the quest of one lover for the other, the entrance of the

[14] Huet, *Rom.* XXXV, 97, assembled the evidence showing that the collection of the Thousand and One Nights was certainly anterior to the fifteenth century. The composition of the oldest portion has been assigned to the tenth century.

[15] See *Partonope of Blois*, note 13.

seeker into a dangerous place (Psyche into the house of the irate goddess Venus, her greatest foe, Floris into the Emir's Tower), and the winning of that foe's forgiveness through the lover's great devotion. But the comparison offers at best a far-fetched likeness which ignores the fundamental märchen elements in Psyche's story. Her marriage with the god, her breaking of the prohibition which he laid upon her, her painful quest and achievement of impossible tasks, have no parallel in the romantic and thoroughly mediaeval adventures of the opulent young Floris.

Far nearer to *Floris* in chivalric and aesthetic interest and in actual detail is *Aucassin and Nicolette*,[16] the unique and lovely *chantefable* of thirteenth-century France. Each romance tells of the passionate devotion to each other of a high-born lad and a girl in lowly case, of the cruel lordly father who separates them, and of the youthful lover's romantic quest. These correspondences convinced Brunner (*Ueber Aucassin and Nicolette,* Halle, 1880) that *Floire* was the source of *Aucassin,* and made Johnston (1911, 2, p. 129) suspect the opposite. He noted that in several instances in the initial pilgrimage scene, in the attack of the Saracens, the account of the birth of the two children and the linking of their destinies, like those of Amis and Amile, by their simultaneous birth and by their similar names,[17] the author seems to have elaborated mere suggestions for these things in *Aucassin.* In the main, however, scholars believe in a common source for the two poems.[18] It seems probable that this source was influenced by some twelfth century version of Ovid's tale of Pyramus and Thisbe. In one extant text [19] the

[16] Cf. the seventh edition by H. Suchier, Paderborn, 1909, p. vii, for bibliography to 1909; also ninth edition, 1921. In regard to the date of *Aucassin* Madame Lot-Borodine pointed out (p. 86) that as Nicolette's disguise as a jongleur is borrowed from that of Josian in *Beuve de Hanstone, Aucassin* must be of later date than *Beuve.* As regards its source, Bullock, in an able review (*MLN.* xxxvi, 497) of the 1921 edition of *Aucassin,* showed that "the whole question of Arabic influence on the story is still open."

[17] Cf. A. Krappe, "The Legend of Amicus and Amelius," *MLR.* xviii, 152 (1923); J. Harris, *Cult of the Heavenly Twins,* Cambridge, 1906, p. 58, on the use of similar names, especially for twin children.

[18] Cf. Lot-Borodine, p. 79; Johnston (2), p. 129.

[19] *Pyrame et Thisbé, poème du XIIe siècle,* ed. C. de Boer, Paris, 1921. Cf. E. Faral, *Rom.* xli, 32–57 (1912), and *Sources Latines des Contes et Romans Courtois du Moyen Age,* Paris, 1913, pp. 5–63. Faral (*Sources,* p.

author clearly develops the idyllic note, making much of the childhood devotion of the pair, and so turns the classic tale into a little tragic idyll, the prototype of the happy idylls in *Floire* and in *Aucassin* (Lot-Borodine, pp. 93–98).

Notable in the *Floire* legend are three descriptive passages. One concerns the beautiful tomb shown to the hero as the grave of his sweetheart. In the French A text (Du Méril, p. 24) this is described as shining like the sun, so rich is it in precious stones. On it are carved the figures of two beautiful children holding flowers in their hands and moving when the wind blows so that they embrace each other and speak " par nigremance." [20] This passage Reinhold derived from the account in the ancient romance of *Apollonius* of the pretended tomb of Tarsia which was shown to her grieving father. It has also been compared with the tomb of Didon and Camille in the *Eneas*.[21] Another

---

32) thought that *Floire* was influenced by *Pyramus* in the episode of the hero's attempted suicide and in his apostrophe to his " grafe " (v. 785–98). For later vernacular texts of *Pyramus*, see Faral, pp. 35–36.

It is perhaps of some interest to note that the *Pyramus* story was retold in English not only by Chaucer and Gower but also by John Metham, a self-styled scholar of Cambridge. He was writing about 1448–49 under the patronage of Sir Miles and Lady Stapleton. His romance, *Amoryus and Cleopes*, in seven-line stanzas, is recognizable as a version of the *Pyramus* story, though in it the tragic is changed to a happy ending, for a hermit miraculously restores the two dead lovers. The tale is absurdly amplified by the introduction of much pseudo-learning. The author was interested in "palmestrye," physiognomy, fortunate days, astrology, etc. Only one manuscript of this romance is known. It is summarized by Furnivall, *Political, Religious, and Love Poems, EETS.* xv, 301–08 (1866). For other versions see Flügel, " Pyramys and Tysbé," *Anglia* xII, 13–20, 631 (1889).

20 Cf. J. D. Bruce, " Human Automata in Classical Tradition and Mediaeval Romance," *Mod. Phil.* x, 511–26 (1913). Bruce did not discuss these figures on the tomb but referred (p. 518) to a golden image of a harper which appears to Floire through the entertaining magic of an enchanter, " Et harpe le lai d'Orphéy." Other automata noted by Bruce are in the *Pèlerinage de Charlemagne*, the *Eneas* (an archer on the tomb of Camilla, v. 7691), *Tristan. Alexandre, Huon de Bordeaux, Diu Crône, Cleomades,* and various versions of the Grail romances. Many of these automata resemble those ascribed to the magic art of Virgil. Cf. Comparetti, *Vergilio nel medio evo*, 2nd ed. Florence, 1896; Faral, *Sources latines*, pp. 328–35, *les automates; arbres; oiseaux; personnages humains*. This section of Faral's book is part of an interesting study on " Le Merveilleux et ses Sources dans les Descriptions Romans Frç. du XIIe Siècle," pp. 307–78. On this general subject see also Easter, *A Study of the Magic Elements in the Romans d'Aventure*, Diss., Baltimore, 1906. Cf. *Seven Sages*, note 12.

21 Cf. A. Dressler, *Der Einfluss des altfrz. Eneas-romanes auf die altfrz.*

passage (Du Méril, p. 19), describing a cup on which was wrought the judgment of Paris and the beauty of Helen of Troy, shows that interest in classical story characteristic of the oldest French version but almost lost, unfortunately, from the English texts. The third passage describes the garden about the Tower of Maidens (Du Méril, p. 65 ff.). The garden has streams of water from Paradise, gravel formed of jewels, a Tree of Love, a Well of Chastity. Spring there is eternal. Johnston suggested the possible influence on this, as on other descriptions of twelfth century French romance, of conventionalized descriptions of the Celtic Otherworld. But again such indications as we have point to the East (Patch, *PMLA.* 1918, XXXIII, 623–4). The marvels of the East were becoming known through the Alexander romances and through Crusaders' and travelers' tales of the sort that ultimately gave rise to such accounts as those of Friar Oderic or Mandeville concerning the unearthly magnificence of Prester John, of the Great Khan, and the Old Man of the Mountain (Rickert, p. XLII). Like the Emir, they have marvellous palaces and gardens, light-giving jewels, a Well of Youth, and companies of young maidens for their service. Readily indeed would such picturesque details blend with a story to which the earliest European redactors obviously wished to give the charm and mystery of the far-off East, however much they imbued it with the sentimentality and chivalry of the West.

BIBLIOGRAPHY

TEXTS: (1) Cott., Cotton Vitellius D III, ed. J. R. Lumby, *EETS.* XIV, 1866; reëd. and all texts printed, G. McKnight, *EETS.* 1901; (2) A, Auchinleck MS., ed. C. H. Hartshorne, *Ancient Metrical Tales,* Lond., 1829; D. Laing, *A Penni Worth of Witte,* Abbotsford Club, Edin., 1857; (3) C, Cambridge Univ. MS. Gg. 4, 27, 2; (4) T, Trentham MS. belonging to the Duke of Sutherland, Trentham Hall, Staffordshire, now MS. Egerton 2862, desc. *Brit. Mus. Cat. of Add. MSS.* 1905–10, pp. 238–89. A critical edition of the MSS. was made by Hausknecht, *Sammlung engl. Denkmäler,* Berlin, 1885. Rev. *Eng. Stud.* IX, 92. Trans. E. Rickert, *Romances of Love;* F. G. Darton, *A Wonder Book of Romance.*

Lit., Leipzig, 1907, pp. 135–39. The Middle English texts preserve but a mere mention of the tomb.

STUDIES AND ANALOGUES: Cf. Edwardes, *Summary*, Index; Wells, *Manual*, p. 785.

Basset, R. "Les Sources Arabes de *Floire et Blancheflor*," *Revue des Traditions Populaires*, XXII, 24 ff. (1907).

Boekenoogen, G. J. *De Historie van Floris ende Blancefluer* (naar den Amsterdamschen druk van Ot Barentsz. Smient uit het 1642 uitgegeven). Leiden, 1903.

Bongini, D. *Noterelle critiche sul Filocolo di Boccaccio, precedute da una introduzione storico-bibliografica sulla leggenda di "Florio e Biancofiore."* Aosta, 1907.

Bonilla y San Martín, A. *La Historia de los dos enamorados Flores y Blancaflor*. Madrid, 1916.

Crescini, V. *La redazione velletrana del cantare de "Fiorio e Bianci-fiore,"* II. Rome, 1905. See also *Il cantare di "Fiorio e Bianci-fiore,"* Bologna, 1889–99. Rev. *Rom.* XXVIII, 1899, pp. 439–47.

Crocioni, G. "Il Cantare di *'Fiorio e Biancofiore'* secondo un MS. velletrano." *Soc. filol. romana*. Rome, 1903.

Decker, O. *Flos unde Blankeflos. Krit. Ausg.d. mittelniederdeut. Gedichtes.* 166 pp. Diss. Rostock, 1913.

Ernst, L. "*Floire u. Blantscheflur:* Studie zur vergleichenden Litera-turwissenschaft." *Quellen u. Forschungen*, CXVIII. Strassburg, 1912.

Huet, G. "Encore *Floire et Blanchefleur*," *Rom.* XXXV, 95–100 (1906). See also *Rom.* XXVIII, 349–59 (1899).

Johnston, O. M. (1). "The Description of the Emir's Orchard in *Floire et Blancheflor*," *Zts. f. rom. Phil.* XXXII, 705–10 (1908).
(2). "The Origin of the Legend of Floire and Blanchefleur," *Matzke Memorial Vol.*, pp. 125–38, Leland Stanford Univ., California, 1911.
(3). "Notes on *Floire et Blancheflor*," *Flügel Memorial Vol.*, pp. 193–99, Leland Stanford Univ., California, 1916.

Leendertz, P. "*Floris ende Blancefloer* van Diederic van Assenede." *Bibl. van middelnederlansche Letterkunde*, Leiden, 1912. Rev. *Rom.* XLII, 155.

Lot-Borodine, M. *Le Roman Idyllique au Moyen-Age, Floire*, pp. 9–74. Paris, 1913.

McKnight, G. H. See Texts. Introd. pp. xxx–xliv.

Reinhold, J. *Floire et Blancheflor, Étude de Littérature Comparée.* Diss. 178 pp. Paris, 1906. Rev. *Rom.* XXXVII, 310–12; *Litteraturbl. f. germ. u. rom. Phil.* XXIX, 156–57; *Zts. f. Rom. Phil.* XXX, 153. Cf. Ernst (above), p. 9, n. 3.

Rischen, C. H. *Bruchstücke von Konrad Flecks "Floire u. Blansche-flur."* Germanische Bibliothek, III, 4. Heidelberg, 1913.

Schafstädt, H. *Die Mülheimer Bruchstücke von Flors u. Blanzeflors.* Progr. des Mülheimer Gym., 1906.

Zwierzina, K. "Frauenfelder Bruchstücke von Flecks *Floire*," *Zts. f. deut. Alter.* XLVII, 161–82 (1904).

SIR ORFEO

VERSIONS. The earliest extant version in Middle English of the *Lay of Sir Orfeo* is found in the early fourteenth-century Auchinleck manuscript. The poem contains 602 lines in short riming couplets and is to be ascribed to the South-Midland district (Zielke, p. 55). The two fifteenth-century manuscripts, Harleian 3810 and Ashmole 61, seem to be minstrel variants of a second version (y) derived from the same source as the Auchinleck text (Zielke, p. 25). The original poem was probably composed about the end of the thirteenth century.

Coming at a time when " imitation and not originality was the rule in English writing," the grace and beauty of *Orfeo* are the more exceptional. Brief yet vivid, the little tale is inimitably fresh in style and content. So artless it seems, that a ballad-like quality has been claimed for it (*Cambridge Hist.*, 1, 328). Ballad-like it is in the simplicity of its theme, — a king's rescue of his queen out of fairy land, in the bright distinctness of its few characters, Orfeo himself, his queen, Heurodis, a fairy king, a porter and a faithful steward, and in an occasional humorously laconic phrase. But the poem is not without indications of conscious artistry. Such descriptions as that of the hundred-towered, crystal-shining castle of the fairy king (v. 387 ff.), or of the fairy company riding on snow-white steeds (v. 109 ff.), show deliberate pictorial sense, and in the passage (v. 245) which contrasts Orfeo's life in his royal hall with his misery on the desolate, freezing moor, there is conscious pathos. If *Orfeo* is minstrel verse,[1] it is of very high order and far removed from such a true offspring of popular verse as the ballad into which it was ultimately fashioned.

---

[1] Ker's illustrative reference (*Eng. Lit. Mediaeval,* p. 127) to the lines in *Orfeo* on the wandering minstrels who must proffer their glee, however inhospitable their reception, is far from proving that the author of *Orfeo* was a minstrel. Necessarily the poem says much of minstrelsy, but so, also, and in a very different tone, does *Sir Cleges*, a typical minstrel tale. The quality and effect of *Orfeo* is far less popular than *Cleges*.

The ballad of *King Orfeo* (Child, *Ballads,* No. 19) was not written down until late in the nineteenth century, in Unst, Shetland; but in its choral and dramatic form it is, as Gummere (p. 224) pointed out, of ancient structural type, its story evidently an oral, traditional version of the lay. The ballad contains seventeen two-line stanzas with an unintelligible refrain that may originally have been composed of Danish words. Of these stanzas two, twice repeated, tell of Orfeo's playing:

> " And first he played da notes o noy,
> An dan he played da notes o joy.

> An dan he played da göd gabber reel,
> Dat meicht ha made a sick hert hale."

In other words the ballad is almost exclusively interested in Orfeo, the music-maker, and presents the episode in which his skill recovers for him Lady Isabel, in the most abbreviated narrative form.

ORIGIN. A few specifically English touches such as that which turns Thrace into Winchester, " a cite of noble defens," or that which makes Orfeo summon his people to a " parlement " to appoint a new king when he shall be dead, are but slight modifications of a story recognizably classical in origin. Through Ovid (*Metamorphoses,* x), Virgil (*Georgics,* IV, 454 ff.), and Boethius (*Philosophiae Consolationis,* III, metre XII), the favorite classic authors of the Middle Ages, the tragic Greek legend of Orpheus and Eurydice was widely known. In England [2] as early as the ninth century King Alfred had translated it from Boethius, and in France we have it alluded to in the tenth century by the monk, Froudmont of Tegernsee (Zielke, p. 130). By the twelfth century it had been turned from Latin into French verse and there are extant two Old French fragments of the classical story (Kittredge, p. 182, p. 1). But obviously no version that kept to the classical form could adequately

[2] For the history of the *Orpheus* legend in English literature see Wirl's dissertation. He discussed the Alfredian and Chaucerian versions of Boethius, the *Lay of Sir Orfeo,* the *Orpheus* fable of Robert Henryson (Scottish Text Soc., vol. LVIII, 1908), which was entirely uninfluenced by the *Lay,* and various allusions to the legend by writers of the fifteenth, sixteenth, and seventeenth centuries.

account for the Middle English version nor for the Breton lay from which it claims descent.[3]

The English poem shows that the Greek legend has been transformed under the influence of a different racial culture and belief. The dim Hades of Greek myth has become a glowing enchanting Otherworld; [4] the sad Greek gods of the dead have turned to beautiful, passionate, and mysterious fairy beings. Folk superstition has intruded itself in the scene in which the Otherworld king gains power over Heurodis, the mediaeval Eurydice, not because she dies, but because she falls asleep under a " fairy tree." [5] In his study of *Orfeo* Kittredge indicated not only the general influence of what seems to be primarily Celtic folk-lore, but the specific modification besides of the classic legend under the probable influence of one of the most famous tales known to Irish minstrels, the *Wooing of Etain* (*Tochmarc Etain*),[6] written down in at least one extant manuscript before

[3] Cf. v. 1–24 and v. 595. The opening lines, which generalize on the usual contents of Breton lays, are practically identical with those which make up the Prologue of the *Lay le Fresne*. Foulet, p. 46 ff., believed they belonged to the French original of *Sir Orfeo* and were borrowed from *Fresne*. Miss Guillaume, p. 463, noted that as the Prologue occurs only in the two fifteenth-century texts of *Orfeo*, as it is inferior to the text given in *Fresne*, and as the text of *Orfeo* shows direct borrowing from *Fresne*, it is more reasonable to suppose that the Prologue itself in *Orfeo* was borrowed from the other poem.

[4] The pagan Irish Otherworld was a fairy realm which lay beneath or beyond the sea, or was hidden in a mound. For details concerning its pleasant landscape and the Perilous Passage which commonly led to it, see A. C. L. Brown, " Iwain," *Harvard Studies in Phil. and Lit.* VIII (1903); L. Paton, *Studies in the Fairy Mythology of Arthurian Romance*, p. 83 ff., Boston, 1903; T. B. Cross, " The Celtic Origin of the Lay of Yonec," *Revue Celt.* XXXI, 461, n. 3; Hibbard, " The Sword Bridge of Chrétien de Troyes and Its Celtic Original," *Rom. Rev.* IV, 178 ff. (1913). Even H. R. Patch, who discredited in his study of " Mediaeval Descriptions of the Otherworld," *PMLA.* XXXIII (1918) the idea of Celtic influence on these descriptions, admitted (p. 612) that the idea of a fairy hill was peculiarly Celtic, and noted that in the *Lay*, Orfeo followed the fairy throng " in at the roche " as the only means of penetrating the fairy hill. There is, however, a genuine reminiscence of the classic legend in *Orfeo* in the description of the fairyland as a place of the dead and of the court held by the fairy king.

[5] Kittredge, p. 189, thought this " a Celtic survival," although he admitted that the idea of danger of sleeping under special trees, because it exposed one to the power of the fairies, was not an exclusively Celtic idea. For arguments against considering this "orchard scene " in any way Celtic see Ogle's arguments (*Sir Gowther* bibliography).

[6] See *Bibliography of Irish Philology and Printed Literature*, ed. R. I. Best, Dublin, 1913; Schoepperle, *Tristan*, II, 422, n. 3.

1106. In this, as in *Orfeo,* Etain, the happy wife of Eochaid, high king of Ireland, is stolen away by Midir, a fairy king, to whom in a former life she has been wedded.[7] Like the fairy king in *Orfeo,* Midir sings to her of his marvellous Otherworld realm; like Heurodis, Etain, though guarded by her mortal husband's warriors, is spirited away through the air, and is recovered at last from a fairy hill. The recovery itself, accomplished in the *Etain* story by a siege of the fairy hill, is not paralleled in the later romance. *Orfeo* draws for this part of the story, it would seem, on an earlier episode in the Irish legend. At his first coming to Eochaid's court, Midir, disguised, lures the king into the rash promise to give Midir whatsoever he should desire if Midir wins a game of chess. Eochaid admits the sanctity of the promise even when Midir asks for Etain. So also in the *Lay,* Orfeo, disguised as a minstrel, wins the rash promise of high reward from the fairy king. Like the mortal Eochaid, the fairy king keeps his promise even though Orfeo promptly demands the stolen lady. " Stories of a woman thus won and lost by a ruse between mortals and immortals seem to have been a favorite type among the Celts " (Schoepperle, *Tristan,* II, 428). The same theme is found in numerous Celtic tales of which the most famous, perhaps, are the Irish Diarmid and Grainne story, the Welsh tale of the wedding of Pwyll in the *Mabinogion,* and the French and Norse versions of *Tristan.* In *Orfeo* the abduction episode and its happy sequel, for which there is no parallel in the classic legend, seem to represent characteristic Celtic adaptations.[8]

The evidence of Celtic influence makes more credible the reference in *Orfeo* to an original " Breton " lay as its source, especially as this is supported by a reference in the *Lai de l'Espine* (ed. R. Zenker, *Zts. f. rom Phil.* XVII, 233) to a musical *Lai*

----

[7] There is no suggestion in *Orfeo* of any former relationship between Heurodis and the fairy king. But this detail from the Old Irish stories survives in some versions of the Rape of Guinevere in connection with the lover who appears as Meliagrance in Malory, *Morte Darthur,* XIX, ch. 2. In the older versions of this episode she is stolen by a supernaturally splendid person who as lover or husband has a claim to her prior to Arthur's. (Webster, " Arthur and Charlemagne," *Eng. Stud.* 1906, XXXVI, 348 ff.; Schoepperle, II, 528–31).

[8] Cf. Schoepperle *Tristan,* II, 541–4; for a detailed comparison of the abduction episode in *Orfeo* with that in the stories of Tristan and Guinevere.

d'Orphey sung by an Irish harper (Kittredge, p. 201). It is conceivable that the bilingual Breton minstrels may have turned the Orpheus story into the form of a lay which the Irish minstrel learned and sang, or that the latter himself, knowing the form and assured popularity of the " Breton lays," may have worked the transformation of the original story. In Bretonizing the original legend it was infused with Celtic " magic " and turned, as were all the extant lays, into swift-flowing French couplets. From this form the story then passed into Middle English. It is probable that the English version owes to its French original those special qualities which make it " nearly perfect as an English representative of a Breton lay — its brevity and romantic charm " (Ker, *English Literature, Mediaeval,* p. 127).

BIBLIOGRAPHY

TEXTS: (1) Auchinleck MS. ed. Laing, *Select Remains of Ancient Popular Poetry of Scotland,* Edin. 1822, 1884; O. Zielke, Breslau, 1880 (a critical edition); M. Shackford, *Legends and Satires,* p. 141 ff., Boston, 1913; A. Cook, *A Literary Middle English Reader,* Boston, 1915; (2) Ashmole 61, Bodleian, ed. Halliwell, *Illustrations of the Fairy Mythology of A Midsummer Night's Dream,* Lond., 1895; (3) Harleian 3910, Brit. Mus., Ritson, II, 248 ff., 1884. Trans. E. E. Hunt, Cambridge, Mass., 1909; E. Rickert, *Romances of Love,* p. 32 ff.; Weston, *Chief ME. Poets,* p. 133.

STUDIES AND ANALOGUES: Körting, *Grundriss,* p. 160; Wells, *Manual,* p. 783.
Foulet, L. "The Prologue of *Sir Orfeo,*" *MLN.* XXI, 46–50 (1906).
Guillaume, G. "The Prologues of the *Lay le Freine* and *Sir Orfeo,*" *MLN.* XXXVI, 458–64 (1921).
Gummere, F. B. *The Popular Ballad,* Boston, 1908.
Ker, W. *English Literature, Mediaeval,* p. 127–29, N. Y., 1912.
Kittredge, G. L. "Sir Orfeo," *Amer. Jour. Phil.* VII, 176–202 (1886).
Marshall, L. E. "Greek Myths in Modern English Poetry," *Studi di filologia moderne,* V, 203–32 (1912).
Schofield, W. *English Literature — to Chaucer,* pp. 184–86. N. Y., 1906.
Wirl, J. "Orpheus in der engl. Literatur," *Wiener Beiträge,* XL (1913); rev. *Archiv,* CXXXII, 239.

PARTONOPE DE BLOIS

VERSIONS. The story of Parténopeus de Blois and his fairy love, Melior, has been called one of the most beautiful romances of the Middle Ages. The Paris Arsenal manuscript (A, ed. Crapelet, Paris, 1834), containing 9744 verses, is the oldest extant text. It begins with an account of Parténopeus, the young nephew of King Clovis of France, and ends, after a great combat between the hero and the Sultan of Persia, with the celebration of a triple marriage, of Parténopeus to Melior, of the young king of France to her sister, the wise Urake, and of the hero's faithful friend, Gaudin, to Persevis, Urake's maid of honor. Bödtker (1, p. vi) thought that the vivid style and picturesque descriptions of this ending make it one of the most striking passages in Old French literature, but he held that it was added by a Picard poet to the original version of the poem.

The author of this original version was formerly supposed to be Denis Piramus, the undoubted author of *La Vie Seint Edmunt*. As Ward (*Catalogue*, 1, 700) pointed out, a misinterpreted reference in the *Vie* to the popularity of *Parténopeus* was the principal basis for this ascription, and Haxo (p. 350 ff.) noted that a comparison of the language of the two poems alone would serve to show that they could not have been written by the same author. Haxo was inclined to identify Denis with Magister Dionisius, a monk of St. Edmund's Bury from 1173 to 1200, and to date the *Vie Seint Edmunt* after 1175, or, if Marie's *Lais*, to which it also refers, were not written until as late as 1180, after 1190. Denis's allusion to *Parténopeus* is the earliest known and indicates that the poem must be dated at some time before his own work.[1] Kawczynski (1) believed the romance

---

[1] Groeber, *Grundriss*, 1902, p. 589, thought that *Florimont*, a romance written about 1188 by Aimon de Varennes, shows in part the influence in style and structure of *Parténopeus*. *Florimont*, similarly written in praise of a lady, brings in classical names and allusions, and involves the hero in a love affair with a *fée* who gives him magic gifts.

was composed in 1153 by an author attached to the Count of Blois (Rom. XXXI, 475–6).

Parténopeus is also contained in six other French manuscripts, the relationships of which have been studied by Pfeiffer.[2] They constitute the B redaction which does not diverge notably from that of the A text until v. 9163 of the latter. This divergent part is known as the Continuation. In B there is no single combat and the Sultan departs meditating vengeance. Parténopeus is wedded to Melior and much of the remaining part of the story is devoted to telling of the return of the Sultan, and to recounting the adventures of Anselet,[3] the heathen lad whom Parténopeus tricked into receiving baptism, and then, himself bent on suicide, abandoned. Of the six manuscripts, the longest, G, contains 11,848 lines in octosyllabic couplets and 768 lines in Alexandrine verse. It is closely related to P, a manuscript also in the Bibliothèque Nationale, Paris, but the two texts are independent derivatives of a common source (Pfeiffer, p. 37). From his study of a Tours manuscript in which the story is carried further than in any other French text, Sneyders de Vogel (p. 17 ff.) attempted to prove that the B Continuation, although preserved only in manuscripts later than A, was nevertheless the work of the original poet. His argument rested chiefly on analogies in style and in point of view between the first part,

[2] *Ueber die handschriften des altfrz. romans Parténopeus.* Diss. Marburg, 1884; *Ausgaben u. Abhandlungen aus d. Gebiete der rom. Phil.* XXV (1885). Seven MSS. were cited by Pfeiffer and by Bödtker, 2, p. 1. In connection with Nr. 7516, Nouv. acq., Bibl. Nat., Paris, see *Rom.* IX, 509 and XXXI, 473 (1902). This MS. was listed in 1407 among the books of Francesco Gonzaga I of Mantua. In Pfeiffer's opinion the oldest redaction of *Parténopeus* is represented by A (the Arsenal MS.), the younger B by MSS. BPG.

[3] Anselet is an important character for the classification of the different versions. In the A text the poet promises to tell more of Anselet's adventures but does not do so (English version, Bödtker, v. 7069). The fact that more is told about him in the B Continuation was one of Sneyder de Vogel's reasons for believing in its authenticity. He suggested that the episode in B in which Anselet kills his faithful greyhound, Noon, may have been interpolated by some one familiar with the *Canis* story in *Les Sept Sages.* In the Norse saga, towards the end of the story, Anselet is identified with Gaudin who in the other versions is represented as another faithful friend of Parténopeus (Eng. version, v. 9396 ff.). Bödtker, 2, p. 34, expressed the opinion that in the original version of *Parténopeus* Anselet and Gaudin were two distinct personalities. Their early history and relation to Parténopeus seem, however, amazingly alike.

practically identical in A and B, and the Continuation as set forth in the Tours manuscript and the still longer text now preserved only in a Dutch version.[4]

The first effective classification of the Continental versions of *Parténopeus* was made by Kölbing (" Uber die verschiedenen Gestaltungen d. Partonopeus-sage," Bartschs *Germanist. Studien,* Suppl. *Germania,* II, 55 ff.). There seem to have been two versions of the story; to the first of these (Y) belong all the French manuscripts of the A and B group, a mid-thirteenth century German version,[5] the Dutch version, a free Italian adaptation[6] of the late fourteenth century, and the longer English version.[7]

This English version (ed. Bödtker) is contained in five fifteenth-century texts, of which the oldest one, now in University College, Oxford, was written about the middle of that century. Wülker's suggestion (*Anglia* XII, 607 ff.) that Gower knew the English version of *Partonope,* was disputed on chronological grounds by Kölbing (*Eng. Stud.* XIV, 435 ff.). In the absence of any other evidence than that of the manuscripts, there seems no reason to suppose the English version antedated the fifteenth century. From his study of the manuscripts of *Parténopeus* printed before 1888, Weingärtner concluded that no extant Old French manuscript is the source of this Middle English version. He showed by detailed comparison with Crapelet's edition many instances of practically verbal translation from the French, but noted too that the English poet, though faithful to the order and content of the French story, was not merely a translator. Weingärtner (p. 13) and Schofield (p. 308) both comment on

---

[4] The extant Dutch fragments (ed. Bormans, Brussels, 1871) contain about 9000 lines. *Cf.* A. van Berkum, *De middelnederlandsche Bewerking van den Parthonopeus Roman en hare verhouding tot het oudfransche origineel.* Diss. Leyden, 1897.

[5] Written by Konrad von Würzburg from a German version made for him by Heinrich Marschant. Kölbing (*Germ. Stud.* II, 96) thought it probable that this written version was closely related to the extant Dutch version. He did not agree with Bartsch's assertion, in the latter's edition of Konrad's poem, concerning the superiority of Konrad's poem to its French original. *Cf.* H. van Look, *Der Partonopiar Konrads von Würzburg u. der Partonopeus de Blois.* Diss. Strassburg, 1881.

[6] *Cantare de lo Bel Gherardino,* ed. F. Zambrini, Bologne, 1867. The poem has been attributed to Antonio Pucci. *Cf.* Bödtker, 2, pp. 2–4.

[7] *Cf.* Kölbing, " Ueber die engl. Versionen der Partonopeussage," pp. 80–92, *Beiträge z. vergleich. Geschichte der rom. Poesie u. Prosa des Mittelalters,* Breslau, 1876.

the poet's occasional willingness to omit ornamental descriptive detail, and they signalize the passage (v. 6168 ff.) in which those who care for hearing about the minute details of a lady's dress are referred to the French original. Such adaptations and abbreviations in the English version were made, according to Schofield, to meet the taste of one who was "neither very refined himself, nor wrote, it would seem, for gentlefolk." But the very length and nature of this Middle English poem in which, as Weingärtner (p. 45) himself observed, the author shows a special predilection for reflective and allegorical passages, more or less invalidate such criticisms. Like Chaucer, the poet regards his "olde bokes" with serious deference; in them "ys goode doctrine" (v. 34). He does not in reality condense that "olde booke," "In ffrenshe also, and fayre endyted" (v. 501), which was his source, for he followed it in such leisurely, Lydgatian fashion that his own text runs to 12,192 lines. A careful study of *Partonope* would show, it seems to the writer, not only Chaucerian influence in the phraseology, but also a real appreciation of the artistic effectiveness of the French poem. The poet pauses for such rhetorical passages as the anaphoric lines in which Melior laments (v. 6046), "My joye, my boldenes, and all my game"; he lingers over the description (v. 689 ff.) of a moonlit forest night, of the meadow where the grass grew stirrup-high, and later of that "delectabell contre" ruled by Melior. Though the excess of detail grows tedious, though there is little vivacity in the long-winded conversations, and the adventures are, like those in the French original, too interminably drawn out, this Middle English version must be considered an important and far from unworthy rendering of this particular story. It was undertaken, so the poet tells us (v. 2335 ff.), because his "sovereyne" thought the story too little known and commanded him to draw it from French into English.

The second and shorter version of *Partonope* was also, in its Middle English form, derived from a French source from which Kölbing (*Beiträge*, p. 90) thought it preserved the word "enchauntement," v. 95. This lost French version was not less widely dispersed, according to the same scholar, than was the longer one, as is shown by the number of independent derivative versions to which it gave rise. These are alike in

that the opening part of the story tells of the father of Melior
and of her accession to the throne. The scene of the story is
Greece, and the events which follow Melior's decision to take
a husband, are about the same as those which in the longer version are related to Parténopeus by Melior after her magic arts
have brought him to her side. In Middle English this version
is preserved in a fragment of 308 lines in a manuscript (c. 1450)
now at Vale Royal (Bödtker, 1, p. viii). The same version (Z)
is found in a Danish poem (ed. C. Brandt, *Romantisk Digtning*,
Copenhagen, 1870, II, 33 ff.), written in 1484 and twice printed in
the sixteenth century, and in the two redactions of an Icelandic
version now extant in two fifteenth-century manuscripts and in
several others of later date.[8]   Bödtker (2, pp. 45-47) believed
the Danish and the Icelandic forms were derived from a lost
Norwegian version of the thirteenth century. Like the short
English version, this Norwegian Saga was in all probability
derived from a lost Anglo-Norman version. In general these
Scandinavian texts treat the brilliant social aspects of the French
romance with something of the austerity of the North. They
omit the love complaints and the more elaborate descriptive
passages; they change innumerable small details, — for instance,
it is by means of a magic, light-giving jewel, instead of by a
lantern, that the hero first sees his love (Bödtker, 2, p. 26);
they diverge more widely than do the texts of the Y version
from the original tale. In Spain, where the Z version became
widely known, the Spanish redactor introduced into his story
" many traits that did honor to his patriotism and Catholicism "
but at the expense of fidelity to the original story.   Buchanan's
list of eight Spanish editions dating from 1514 to 1844 illustrates the popularity of the romance. It is probable that the
original Castilian text differed very little from the extant edition printed at Toledo in 1526 (Bödtker, 3, p. 235).

ORIGIN. The romance deals chiefly with the love of Parténopeus, the young nephew of King Clovis of France, for Melior,
a queen whose fairy nature is indicated by the unparalleled
richness of her abode and by certain magic arts through which

---

[8] Cf. Kölbing, *Ueber die nordischen Gestaltungen de Partonopeussage*,
Strassburg, 1873.

she can make herself, her servants, and even Parténopeus, invisible.[9] As concerns the ultimate origin of the story, the most significant episodes are the following: Parténopeus is brought to a mysterious and magnificent abode by supernatural means; is served by invisible but assiduous hands; becomes the lover of Melior on condition that he will not for a given period attempt to see her; breaks this prohibition at the instigation of his mother; beholds Melior's beauty in the momentary light of the lantern given him by his mother; is cast forth the next day in shame and despair from Melior's palace; endures great hardships; and ultimately regains his lady's favor. All this has been given a Christian [10] and typically mediaeval character, even to the introduction of a gorgeous tournament as the final test of Parténopeus for Melior's hand. It has, nevertheless, generally been recognized as a mediaeval transformation of the beautiful legend of Cupid and Psyche, first found in Apuleius's *Metamorphoses* (ed. S. Gaseler, *Loeb Classical Libr.*, Lond.,

[9] The rest of the lady's powers are merely necromantic. She can cause illusions of various sorts, make a room seem of gigantic size or the sun seem to shine at midnight, cause the apparition of great tourneys, of wild beasts, etc. (cf. Eng. version, v. 5946 ff.). The same art of illusion is practised by the fairy lady in *Le Bel Inconnu* (BI) for the purpose of playing tricks on her lover, but neither in her case nor in that of Melior, does the power seem to be regarded as more than a special accomplishment. For such arts alone Melior could no more be considered a *fée* than could the Orleans clerk in Chaucer's *Franklin's Tale* or Colle Tregetour in the *Hous of Fame*, who are said similarly to practice the art of illusion. For other instances of its use, see Schofield, *PMLA*. xvi, 419 (1901); Tatlock, "Astrology and Magic in Chaucer's *Franklin's Tale*," *Kittredge Anniv. Papers*, 1913, pp. 341, 349. Faral, *Sources Latines*, p. 318, pointed out that Melior's knowledge of necromancy might be compared with that of Medea in the *Roman de Troie* (v. 1216), and the belief that it was based on her mastery of the Seven Arts with similar ideas expressed in *Eneas* (v. 2199), and in *Troie* (v. 1219).

[10] Melior, like Yonec (Cross, *Revue Celt.* xxxi, p. 414), is at great pains on the occasion of her first meeting with her lover to explain her own complete orthodoxy. But the mother of Parténopeus is certain that Melior is a devil practising enchantments on her son. She explains her fears to the Bishop of Paris who thereupon so works on the religious fears of Parténopeus that he is at last persuaded to take his mother's magic lantern and try to behold his love (Eng. version, 5650–5865). In *Peter von Staufenberg* (ed. Schroeder, Berlin, 1894), a Middle High German romance of the fourteenth century, the same pietistic treatment of a similar story is observable. On the advice of a priest Peter comes to believe that the fairy wife who has so richly endowed him is a devil of hell. (Cf. Cross, *Mod. Phil.* xii, 592, n. 2)

1915, p. 185 ff.).[11] Divested of the moral and allegorical elements added by the African Apuleius or by his unknown Greek
predecessors, the legend itself is reducible to well-known folk-
tale types [12] which are combined in a distinctive fashion. Parténopeus, as is shown below, might be explained piecemeal by
reference to mediaeval lays and romances, but in the Psyche
legend alone is there an indisputable parallel for the mysterious
marriage, for the nature of the marriage taboo, for the night
scene in which it is broken, and the anguished separation of the
lovers.   It may well be questioned how and when Apuleius's
story came to France,[13] but it seems impossible to doubt that

[11] The assertions by Groeber, Voretzsch, p. 384, and Schofield, p. 307,
that this is not the case, are unconvincing. The differences between the
classical and mediaeval versions of the story may be fully recognized without invalidating the claim that the episodes of *Parténopeus*, as listed above,
are structurally related to those of the Psyche legend or to the folk-tale
from which it came. Pschmadt in his study, *Die Sage von der verfolgten
Hind*, 1911, p. 97, called attention to the unmistakable similarity between
the fairy palace as described in the Psyche legend and in *Parténopeus*. B.
Stumfall, " Das Märchen von Amor u. Psyche in seinem Fortleben,"
Münchener Beiträge, XXXIX, pp. 8-13, Leipzig, 1907, asserted that the author
of *Parténopeus* drew on a folk-tale of the Psyche type but not on the story
of Apuleius.

[12] One of the fullest discussions of these folk-tale types is to be found
in the notes by A. Gough to L. Friedländer's *Roman Life and Manners*,
Lond., 1913, vol. IV, 99-123. Roughly speaking these tales may be grouped
under such captions as the following: The Lady and the Monster; The
Magic House and the Invisible Servants; the False Sisters; The Jealous
Mother-in-law; The Broken Prohibition; Impossible Tasks. Gough believed
that a genuine folk-tale formed the basis of the Apuleian narrative and noted
(p. 115) that the group of Danish, Norwegian, and Swedish folk-tales analyzed by him, are most closely akin to the story of Apuleius. They all
contain the important feature that the young heroine is advised to look at
her lover by a light at night. Cf. Andrew Lang's introduction to the reprint of William Aldington's translation of *Cupid and Psyche*, Lond., 1897.
The theme of the Secret Lover appears in the folk-tales discussed by Köhler,
Lais-Marie, pp. cvi-cxviii; Schoepperle, *Tristan*, I, 150-51; Cosquin, *Rom.*
X, 117-31 (1881).

[13] Kawczynski, 2, p. 193 ff., urged that the work of Apuleius was known
to the author of *Parténopeus*. He also believed that it exerted some influence on *Aucassin, Floire et Blancheflor, Le Chevalier au Cygne, Berte aus
grans piés*, and on *Huon de Bordeaux*. Huet in 1909 strongly questioned
the extent and even the fact of this influence. He pointed out that only
two MSS. of the *Metamorphoses* antedate the thirteenth century, and that
the first known mention of it is that by Vincent of Beauvais. He believed
that the *Metamorphoses* was practically unknown in Europe before this
period. In 1917 he admitted the possibility that the legend might have been
known through other sources than the Apuleian narrative, for instance,

it was known in some form to the author of *Parténopeus*. His introductory summary of the Trojan story and the name which he gives to his hero, taken from that of one of the Seven Champions against Thebes,[14] indicate an interest in classical legend that must be related to the contemporary popularity of romantic redactions of the Matter of Antiquity.[15] The *Roman de Troie*, the *Roman de Thèbes*, the *Roman d'Énéas*, written in the sixth or seventh decade of the twelfth century, had successfully combined classic legends with purely romantic, mediaevalized stories of love and courtship, and offered not only the incentive, but the model, for similar attempts.

The striking reversal in *Parténopeus* of the specific rôles of Psyche and the God of Love is possibly to be accounted for by reference to the supposedly Celtic stories which exercised so potent an influence on the romance. It is to be regretted that no detailed study of *Parténopeus* from this point of view has yet appeared, though the essential fact has been recognized. Schofield (p. 307) remarked: " In induction and other features it resembles the Breton lays of *Guingamor, Guigemar,* and *Lanval;* in development, the romances of *Ivain* and *The Fair Unknown*." The resemblance between *Parténopeus* and the lays is especially close in the earlier part of the story. Parténopeus, in pursuit of a fairy boar sent by Melior, loses himself in the forest of Ardennes, until at last he finds on the shore a mysterious ship which carries him to Melior's magnificent city. The

---

through the *Mythologiarum* of the African compiler, Fulgentius, who drew his abbreviated story, the *Fabula deae Psicae et Cupidnis,* from Apuleius. Though thus admitting the possibility of Apuleian influence, Huet still inclined to the belief that *Parténopeus* represents the combination of a Psyche folk-tale with the history of a *fée.*

[14] Kölbing (*Germ. Stud.* II, 57) suggested that the hero's name comes from the city of Partenay, the lords of which at various times had some connection with those of Lusignan to whom was attached the famous legend of their fairy progenitor, Melusine, the serpent woman. But the Melusine legend is too late, it would seem, to have influenced *Parténopeus.* Whatever was the origin of the local myth, the earliest known literary treatment of the story is the prose romance of *Melusine* by Jean d'Arras. It was compiled about 1387, printed at Geneva, 1478, " englisht " about 1500 (*EETSES.* LXVIII). Cf. J. Kohler, *Der Ursprung der Melusinensgage; Eine ethnologische Untersuchung,* Leipzig, 1895; Baudot, *Les Princesses Yolande et Les Ducs de Bar de la famille des Valois, I, Melusine,* Paris, 1900.

[15] Cf. Dressler, pp. 130–35; Otto (*op. cit. Ipomedon* Bibliog.), p. 59, for the special influence of the romances of *Énéas* and of *Thèbes* on *Parténopeus.*

hero's hunt for a fairy animal as the preface to his meeting with the *fée* herself is found in *Guigemar,* in *Guingamour,* in *Graelent,* and in the later romance, *Generides.* The incident is combined with that of the fairy boat in *Guigemar.*[16] In *Graelent,* as in *Parténopeus,* the *fée* makes a curious pretense of anger and of helplessness before the young hero, but, having at last surrendered herself, she confesses that it was by her wish and means that he has been brought to her.[17]. She admits that she had long since heard of his prowess and loved him even when unseen,[18] a confession which closely parallels that of the *fée* in Marie's Lay of *Lanval,* of the fairy *dame d'amour* in *Le Bel Inconnu,* and *Libeaus Desconus,* of the fairy lover in Marie's Lay of *Yonec,* and of the *fée* again in the old French lay of *Melion,* poems for which a Celtic ancestry has been claimed. In all these instances the supernatural lover has the peculiar magnificence, the power, the lordly generosity,[19] which are characteristic attributes of Celtic fairy folk.

[16] Bödtker, 2, pp. 7, 19, noted that in an Icelandic MS. of the seventeenth century the boar which appears in the French, English, and Danish versions, is replaced by a deer, the usual Fairy Messenger of *fées* in Old French romances. See Pschmadt, note 11, above; *Isumbras,* note 1; Warnke-Köhler, *Lais-Marie,* p. lxxix. Magic Boats are familiar properties of romance. Cf. Brown, *Mod. Phil.* xiv, 392, n. 4 (1906).

[17] Schofield, " The Lays of *Graelent* and *Lanval,*" *PMLA.* xv, 129 ff. and Cross, " The Celtic Fée in *Launfal,*" *Kittredge Anniv. Papers,* 1913, p. 385, argued that the powerful Celtic *fée* who wills and achieves what she desires, is, in *Graelent* especially, confused with the swan-maiden type of fairy who is helpless without her feather garment. In *Graelent,* the hero finds the *fée* bathing, is bitterly reproached when he takes her garments and wins her only by force, although she later tells him she had foreordained their meeting. Cross, " Celtic Elements in *Lanval and Graelent,*" *Mod. Phil.* xii, 617 (1914–15), noted that the swan-maiden type, " generally regarded as distinctively of Germanic tradition, figured in Celtic literature before the twelfth century." He was, therefore, inclined to discredit Schofield's belief that *Graelent* had been influenced by some form of the Wayland Smith story (Cross. p. 621).

[18] For the common folk-lore *motif* of Love in Absence see *Ipomedon,* n. 1; Cross, *Mod. Phil.* xii, 612, n. 3. He compared the *fées* in Marie's lays who so frankly woo their mortal lovers with the Forth-Putting Women of Old Irish story.

[19] In *Parténopeus* the hero, during his stay with Melior, is provided with all possible accessories for his daily hunt. On his return to Blois he is met by twelve sumpter horses laden with gold sent by Melior. With this great wealth he is able to recruit a host of followers and to become the foremost soldier of France (Eng. version 2508–3066). In the Lays, Launfal, after his meeting with the *fée,* is provided with magnificent clothes and returns to find

Even more important in this connection is the command which Melior laid upon her lover not to attempt to see her for a given time. On the one hand this seems merely a modification of Cupid's command to Psyche and may hark back to immemorial folk superstitions and marriage taboos. The idea reappears in one form or another in numerous European folk-tales and in such famous legends as those of *Lohengrin* and *Melusine,* but for *Parténopeus* the closest parallel is to be found in just the lays which we have been considering, now accepted, at least by the Celticists, as French adaptations of a Celtic folk-tale of the Offended Fée. Regularly in this tale the prohibition is laid upon a mortal lover by a regal Fairy Mistress and loss of her follows when he breaks her command.[20] Comparison of the *fées* in *Lanval, Desire, Graelent,* and *Guingamor,* with Melior shows that she is essentially of their sisterhood. She endows her lover bounteously; she imposes the strange command; she is relentless when it is broken. That Melior is so rationalized as to seem only an independent young queen, that her command is no more than her own whim, and not a law of her being; that she herself suffers anguish for her self-willed separation from her lover, are inconsistencies, to be sure, but they may be due to the very element which made the old French poets so quick to seize on this particular type of Fairy Mistress story. To minds filled with the precepts of courtly love, the *fée's* command was completely in accord with the insistence of courtly love doctrines on the necessity for secrecy in love. It became a test of love, its breaking by the hero a failure in love for which the direst hardships, love-sickness running even into madness, were but rightful expiation (Cf. Cross. *Mod. Phil.* xii, 641, 1). For the poet of *Parténopeus,* himself a lover who paused, like Renaud in *Le Bel Inconnu,* for numerous long digressions concerning his own sorrowful state and the hauteur of his lady,[21]

---

his men have been finely arrayed. Graelent's Fairy Mistress sends him the best horse in the world, a servant who provides for his every need. Cf. Cross, *Mod. Phil.* xii, 628 ff., The Fairy Gifts.

[20] On the *geis* or special prohibition laid on Old Irish heroes see Schoepperle, *Tristan,* Index. The heroes of *Lanval* and *Graelent* are forbidden to name their fairy loves. Some form of taboo is almost universally characteristic of stories in which supernatural beings enter into relations with mortals.

[21] Cf. G. Paris, *Rom.* xv, 10; Schofield, *Libeaus Desconus,* p. 108. It is of interest to note that the English poet emphasizes (v. 6759 ff.) the passage

this courtly phase of his story was of special interest. He developed it in accordance with the typical ideas and stylistic devices known to him. Thus the lovers in exchanging their first vows so expatiate on the duties and obligations of lovers that they succeed in defining the code of love itself. Thus Melior exhorts her lover to achieve great deeds for love's sake and thousands of lines are subsequently devoted to the description of the wars of Parténopeus against the enemies of France; [22] thus, as a true lover, the hero implores Melior's mercy because on his return to France, he had under the influence of a drug even for a moment " falsely forgot " her; thus Melior laments the loss of all her good when Parténopeus breaks her command, and he himself in wild grief over his exile from her, starves himself until he is unrecognizable and goes off into the forest to die. Equally typical are the long discussions between Melior and her sister Urake concerning the sin and suffering and even the death of Parténopeus, which Urake reports, passages obviously designed for their emotional effectiveness, for the laying of love in the balance against pride or grief or anything else that was conceived as an enemy to love. In *Parténopeus,* as in the Lays, the tragic type of story in which the Offended Fée is irreparably lost, is so far departed from that, after adequate suffering, the true lover regains his fairy love (cf. Cross, *Mod Phil.* xii, 641). This, of course, was in accord with the current understanding of folk-lore and romance that no true lover should go forever unrewarded. It was also in harmony with the Cupid and Psyche story.

In certain structural features *Parténopeus* seems then to combine a traditional classical legend involving a marriage taboo with Celtic narratives of similar theme as they had been modified and developed in the so-called Breton lays. But in style and in much of its content, *Parténopeus* is to be explained by reference to the longer contemporary romances. It is a matter for regret that the relationship between this romance and Chretien's

---

in his original lamenting the folly of these " olde clerkes " who satirize women and their love.

[22] Cf. Brown, "Iwain," *Harvard Studies* viii, p. 129. One of Iwain's greatest exploits is his Single Combat with Gawain. Parténopeus has a tremendous conflict with the noble heathen king, Sornegour, a fight on which the fate of France depends (Eng. version, 3225 ff.)

Iwain or Renaud's *Le Bel Inconnu* or Hue de Rotelande's *Ipomedon* has not been more exactly indicated. Between *Iwain* and our romance some general analogies were pointed out by Voretzsch (pp. 384–86). Laudine, like Melior a rationalized *fée*, similarly recognizes the claim of chivalric honor and accedes to her lover's wish to leave her and return to court; she is unforgiving when he breaks her command to return within a year, as Melior is when Parténopeus breaks her command to refrain from looking upon her for a given time. Laudine is brought to reconciliation, after Iwain has run mad in the woods,[23] only through the long efforts of her friend Lunet, who, like Urake, teaches the hero how to regain his lady's favor. In *Le Bel Inconnu*, besides the personal digressions already noted as common to Renaud's poem and to *Parténopeus,* the two romances have in part the same fairy-like setting, the *Ile d'Or* in the first, and the *Chief d'Oire* in the second. The fairy ladies make similar confessions of love to the hero and pay him a seductive nocturnal visit. Each lady is said to have learned in youth her magic powers and to be possessed of an abode of extraordinary richness. In each romance a Faithful Squire figures largely.[24] In *Ipomedon* the heroine is a capricious young duchess whose pride makes her as difficult to win as the Offended Fée of Celtic or other lineage. Like Melior, however, she too falters and fails in trying to pronounce the lover's name. The scene is too much alike in the two romances not to suggest specific borrowing.[25] Very similar also in the account of the tournament [26] is the episode in which the hero overthrows his greatest opponent and is

---

[23] The madness of the hero was a *motif* which, once used in *Iwain,* had before it "une brillante fortune" (G. Paris, *Furnivall Misc.* 1902, p. 393). Cross, *Mod. Phil.* XII, p. 641, n. 1.

[24] Cf. Schofield, *Libeaus Desconus,* p. 110, on the Squire Robert in *Le Bel Inconnu.* In *Parténopeus* there are two figures of this sort. The heathen boy Fursin, also called Gileamour, allows himself to be christened Anselet (see above, note 3) out of his devotion to Parténopeus (Eng. version, v. 6877 ff.). Toward the end of the story the elderly knight, Gaudin, insists on taking service with Parténopeus and renders him great service (v. 9396).

[25] Cf. Eng. version, v. 8817 ff., 9063–65. Köhler, *Kleinere Schriften,* III, 1 ff., "Das vom Sterbenden nicht vollendete Wort," discussed the episode in *Orlando Furioso.* Cf. *Ipomedon* here, note 6; Carter, p. 254, was inclined to believe that the author of *Parténopeus* borrowed from *Ipomedon.*

[26] Cf. K. G. Webster, "The Twelfth Century Tourney," *Kittredge Anniversary Papers,* pp. 227–342, for a discussion of the tourney in *Parténopeus* and other romantic and historical sources.

ably helped by a friend. In style, in the leisurely elaboration with which the picturesque background of chivalric life is described, in spirit and tone and length, these last two romances especially belong to the same sophisticated and delightful genre.

BIBLIOGRAPHY

TEXTS: (1) Univ. College, Oxford, C, 188 (7096 lines), pr. W. E. Buckley, Roxburghe Club, Lond., 1862; (2) Rawlinson Poet. 14, Bodleian, partly printed by Buckley; (3) Eng. Poet. C, 3 (158 lines), Bodleian, pr. by Buckley; (4) Lord Robartes' MS. now belonging to Viscount Clifden, pr. Wülker, *Anglia* XII, 607–20 (*cf.* Kölbing, *Eng. Stud.* XIV, 435–37 (1890)); (5) Addit. MS. 35,288, Brit. Mus. (12,192 lines); (6) Vale Royal MS., pr. R. C. Nichols, Roxburghe Club, 1873. All the MSS. are printed in full by A. T. Bödtker, *Partonope of Blois, The Middle English Versions, EETSES.* CIX. 1912; (7) Addit. MS. 4860 (18th cent.), *cf.* Ward, *Catalogue,* I, 707.

STUDIES: Wells, *Manual,* p. 785.
Bödtker, A. T. (1) See Texts.
    (2) "Parténopeus de Blois, Étude Comparative des versions islan-
    daise et danoise," *Videnskabs–Selskabets Skrifter,* II, Hist.-Filos.
    Kl. No. 3. Christiania, 1904. Rev. *Rom.* XXXIV, 167; *Deut. Lit.
    Zeitung,* 1905, col. 34–35.
    (3) "Parténopeus in Catalonia and Spain," *MLN.* XXI, 234–45
    (1906).
Buchanan, M. A. "Partinuplés de Bles (A Bibliography of the Spanish
    Chapbook)" *MLN.* XXI, 3–8 (1906).
Catalan version, 1588, reprinted. *Historia de l'esforçat cavaller Parti-
    nobles.* Barcelona, 1912.
Dressler, A. *Der Einfluss des altfrz. Eneas-Romanes auf die altfrz.
    Literatur.* Diss. Borna-Leipzig, 1907.
Haxo, H. "Denis Piramus," *Mod. Phil.* XII, 345–66; 559–83 (1914–15).
Huet, G.   "Le Roman d'Apulée: Etait-il connu au Moyen Age? " *Le
    Moyen Age,* XXII, 22–28 (1909); XXIX, 44–52 (1917).
Kawczynski, M. (1) *Parténopeus de Blois.* 162 pp. Cracow, 1902.
    Cf. *Bull. de l'Académie des Sciences de Cracow,* 1901. A German
    résumé of the Polish scholar's work is given at the end of his
    book. *Literaturbl.* XXIII, 28–33; *Rom.* XXXI, 475–76.
    (2) "Ist Apuleius im Mittelalter bekannt gewesen? " *Bausteine
    zur rom. Phil., Festgabe f. Mussafia,* pp. 193–210. Halle, 1905.
Müller, L. *Sprachliche u. text-kritische Untersuchungen über den
    altfrz. Parténopeus de Blois.* Diss. Göttingen, 1920.
Schofield, W. *English Literature to Chaucer,* p. 307.
Sneyders de Vogel, K. "La Suite du *Parthenopeu de Blois* et la ver-

sion hollandaise," *Revue des langues romanes,* XLVIII (5e Ser. VIII), 5–29 (1905). Rev. *Rom.* XXXV, 617; *Zts. f. rom. Phil.* XXX, 510 (1906).

Weingärtner, F. *Die mittelengl. Fassungen der Partonopeussage u. ihr Verhältnis zum altfrz. Originale.* Diss. Breslau, 1888.

WILLIAM OF PALERNE

VERSIONS. It is not surprising that a romance of the type of *William of Palerne,* charming as it is in places, should have achieved, so far as records show, but moderate recognition.[1] It tells too strange a tale, mingles elements too diverse, perhaps, even for mediaeval taste. A prince turned into a werwolf, a Roman princess in love with an unknown foundling, lovers living in the skins of white bears and picnicing on provisions brought by the kindly werwolf, battles, enchantments, extravagant emotions, — out of such extraordinary things as these is the story wrought.

The original version, *Guillaume de Palerne* (ed. H. Michelant, *SATF.*, Paris, 1876), is a French romance of 9663 lines written about the end of the twelfth century [2] " after the manner of the older romantic school of 1150 to 1180." Impregnated with the doctrines of *l'amour courtois,* it constantly analyzes the emotions and emphasizes the agonies of love-sickness and the joys of lovers in one another's company. In style it is somewhat " precieuse," verbally prolix, full of formal speeches, of interminable digressions, and marked by occasional allegorical tendencies, especially in the consideration of love (Lot-Borodine, p. 264). Though all this is incongruous when combined with the rapid action and fabulous incidents of a typical *roman d'aventure,* the style, no less than the content, was probably

[1] Three copies of the French version were listed in the inventories of 1467 and 1487 of the libraries of the Dukes of Burgundy (Skeat, p. xiv). See below, note 4.

[2] Suggested dates for the poem are as follows: 1178–1200, Skeat, p. xvi; about 1205, Paris, *La Litt. frç. au Moyen Age,* 3e. ed. p. 276; 1212–25, Zingarelli. The only copy of the poem is found in the same thirteenth century manuscript which contains *L'Escoufle.* Warren, p. 97, pointed out that Jean Renart, the author of *L'Escoufle, Lai de l'Ombre,* and *Guillaume de Dôle,* should not be considered the author of *Guillaume de Palerne,* which is different in style and versification from the others. On Jean Renart, see also Bédier, *Lai de l'Ombre, SATF.* 1913, p. x ff. For the influence on *Guillaume* of *Cligés* see Lot-Borodine, p. 247.

designed with special reference to the taste of that "boine dame," the Countess Yolande, for whom, at the end of his tale, the author says he translated it "de latin en roumans." The idea of a Latin source may be discounted for the romance as a whole, but the deliberate suggestion of a classical origin, like the allusions to the power and wealth of the Greek empire, came from the poet's wish to please this special patron. She was the aunt by marriage of that Baldwin VI, count of Flanders and Hainault, who was elected in 1204 Emperor of Constantinople. From her brother, Baldwin V, Count of Hainault, she once received, we are told, the Latin manuscript of a life of Charlemagne which she had translated (Michelant, p. x–xi). These facts go far to explain the courtly elegance and the liking for literary sophistication which are palpably reflected in *Guillaume de Palerne*.

In contrast with the French romance, the English version has in style at least a fresh and almost homely air, though likewise it was the result of noble patronage. It was translated from the French by one William (v. 5521) at the order of Sir Humphrey de Bohun, the nephew of Edward II, for "ese of Englysch men." (v. 165). Humphrey, who succeeded to the earldom in 1335 and died in 1361, was in France in 1349 and in 1359, and might on either occasion have brought the French romance home with him (Skeat, p. ix–xii). The translation of this into the English long-line, alliterative verse synchronized with the revival of English alliterative poetry about the middle of the century in the West Midland district. Despite the confusion of dialect forms in *William*, this region is generally accepted as the original home of the poem.[3]

The Middle English version is now extant in only one midfourteenth-century manuscript, fragmentary at the beginning and in one or two other places but, even so, containing 5540 lines. The lines 5047–5317, in this text, correspond with those in the prose fragment printed presumably about 1520–35 by Wynkyn de Worde. This fragment constitutes the second known English version of *William*. In Brie's opinion a prose version in English intervened between the two texts; this lost version

[3] In "The 'West Midland' of the Romances," *Mod. Phil.* XIX, 1–16 (1921), J. R. Hulbert disputed the traditional assignment of the alliterative romances to the West Midland district. Cf. Menner, *PMLA.* XXXVII (1922).

was simply a prose redaction of the Middle English poem, and not a translation of the French prose version.[4]

Impossible as it is not to recognize the essential incongruity in a story which attempts to combine a courtly love intrigue with a typical *roman d'aventure*, there is much in *William* of peculiarly mediaeval charm and picturesqueness. Dainty pictures linger in one's mind of young William hiding in the wide-branched apple tree to see his love; of Melior laughing out of her white bear-skin disguise, "Am I nouȝt a bold best?"; or of the two lovers, now disguised as a hart and hind, slipping through the moonlight, to hide themselves on a ship sailing from Reggio, or of their joy together " under a louely lorel tre " when they are safe in the Queen's garden at Palermo. It is a matter of course that in such a tale there should be much of chivalry, of wars and heroic combats, of magnificent feasts, of gift-giving to minstrels, etc., but the familiar setting serves only to enhance the unusual elements in the story itself, and, in the Middle English version especially, its actual charm. Of its kind nothing is better in Middle English romance than that scene (vv. 16–70) in which the baby William, stolen by the watchful werwolf and hidden in its den, is tempted into the open by the grasses and flowers blowing in the sunlight. The cowherd and his wife, even the dog which discovers the boy, and, later in the story (v. 2520), the colliers who talk together outside the quarry where the lovers lie hidden, have a humorous realism rare in chivalric story, — perhaps only to be matched in the incomparable *Aucassin*. In other ways, too, in the feeling for nature,[5] in the constant dwelling on the youthful beauty, of the young hero no less than of the heroine, in the gay romantic adventurousness of spirit, there is much that may be compared in the two stories. In these respects the simpler naturalism of the Eng-

---

[4] Brie (p. 322) remarked that thirty-five English prose romances in addition to *William* were composed between the years 1350–1550. The French prose version of *Guillaume* was apparently composed in the fifteenth century and was printed at Paris by Bonfons (no date), at Lyons, 1552, at Rouen, 1620, and again about 1634. Skeat, p. xvii, on the basis of an acrostic signature, ascribed the authorship of this French prose version to Pierre Durand.

[5] For studies on Nature in Middle English see Weichardt, *Die Entwicklung des Naturgefühls in der me. Dichtung vor Chaucer* (einschliesslich des Gawain-Dichters), Kiel, 1900.

lish version of *William* makes it gain rather than lose by comparison with the French *Guillaume*.

ORIGIN. The fact that the Middle English text is simply a more or less direct translation of an extant French original makes the latter serve as a point of departure for any investigation of the origin of the werwolf legend. However much disguised by the accretions of mediaeval romantic narrative, by elaborate setting, by combination with a disproportionate love story with which it can originally have had nothing to do, the nucleus of *Guillaume* is that story which centers round its true hero, Alphonse, the prince of Spain, who was changed in his childhood, through the magical arts of a witch-like stepmother, into a werwolf. His adventures, his revenge, his ultimate recovery of his human form, constitute the material for an independent story of a type paralleled in several other Old French narratives. Without the werwolf, the adventures of Guillaume and the Princess Melior would fall into nothingness. It is the werwolf who saves the baby William from the conspirators who would poison him; it is the werwolf who guides and protects the escaping lovers; it is he who brings about Guillaume's restoration to his heritage. He is, in short, as Michelant remarked, the *deus ex machina* of the love story.

The belief in werwolves [6] is of too great antiquity, and of too universal distribution, to give any indication of its origin. But in general in werwolf stories certain more or less primitive features may be discerned (Tibbals, p. 361). The most primitive type is that in which the man is a true *loup-garou,* and it is a necessity of his nature to become, at recurrent intervals, a wolf among wolves, a " constitutional werwolf." In this type, best represented by the *Lai de Bisclavret* (ed. Warnke, 1900, p. 75 ff.), of Marie de France, the transformation is effected simply by the removal of the man's clothes, the sign of his civilized nature. A second type is represented by those stories in which the transformation is effected by the putting on of a wolf skin, as in the story of Sigmund and Sinfiotli in the *Volsunga Saga;*

---

[6] On werwolves in general see the many references given by Kittredge, p. 169, n. 1, also p. 173, n. 3, pp. 257 ff.; Warnke-Köhler, *Lais der Marie,* p. xcix (1900); Smith, p. 1 ff.; E. O'Donnell, *Werwolves,* Boston, 1912; C. T. Stewart, *The Origin of the Werwolf Superstition,* Univ. of Missouri, Social Science Series II, 1909.

and a third, the least primitive, in which it is caused by external magic, and is entirely involuntary. To this type the story of Alphonse belongs.

The group of werwolf stories discussed by Kittredge, the *Lai de Bisclavret,* the anonymous *Lai de Melion,* preserved in a thirteenth-century manuscript, the Latin romance of *Arthur and Gorlagon,* preserved in a fourteenth-century manuscript, and apparently derived through some lost Welsh intermediary from some old Irish tale of the type represented by the still current Irish tale of *Morraha* or the *Quest for the Sword of Light* (Larminie, *West Irish Folk Tales,* 1893, p. 10 ff.), embodies a form of the werwolf's tale undoubtedly older than that contained in *Guillaume de Palerne.*[7] In these stories the enchantress is a faithless wife who wishes to dispose of her husband. She wheedles from him the secret of that which will transform him, his clothes in *Bisclavret,* a rod made from his life-tree in *Gorlagon,* in *Melion,* a magical ring, " a congenital talisman like the necklaces in the Knight of the Swan " (Kittredge, p. 171). After the husband has been transformed, he takes refuge with a king whom he serves with the intelligence of a man and the fidelity of a beast. In the Irish tale he is made the special guardian of the King's child, and preserves it from harm. After some years of tame domesticity he is roused to wolf-like fury by the appearance of his wife and her lover and violently attacks them. The king protects him from those who would kill him as a wild beast, and forces the lady and her paramour to confess. Through his royal friend or through his wife, the werwolf is then disenchanted. In *Bisclavret* and *Melion* he is taken into a private room and the actual transformation takes place. Instead of being condemned to death, the wife is forgiven on condition that she keep silence (Irish

---

[7] The story of the knight Biclarel, found in the early fourteenth-century *Roman du Renard Contrefait,* practically duplicates that of Bisclavret (Warnke-Köhler, *Lais der Marie,* pp. xcix–ciii). Malory, *Morte Darthur,* bk. XIX, ch. 11, referred to " Sir Marrok the good knyghte that was betrayed with his wyf, for she made hym seuen yere a werwolf." Among other parallels Kittredge, p. 254 ff., noted the Middle Dutch *Walewein* in which a king's son after a scene resembling the " Potiphar's wife incident " in the *Seven Sages* is changed into a fox by his stepmother; also the Icelandic *Álaflekkssaga* in which Áli on his wedding night is transformed by a wizard into a wolf doomed to ravage the lands of his own father and not to escape death unless some one asks pardon for him when he is taken.

tale), or she is divorced and made to suffer various humiliating penances.

The False Wife story in all these versions is certainly prior to that of the Cruel Stepmother variant in *Guillaume de Palerne*, though in other details this romance is closely akin to the original werwolf story.[8] The likeness becomes clearly recognizable after v. 7205 in *Guillaume* (v. 4012 in the English version). The werwolf's obeisance to the King of Spain, whom William has captured and who is in reality the father of Alphonse, corresponds to a similar act in the other stories.[9] The order of events in the romance has been shifted but it is probable that the werwolf's' initial protection of the baby William (vv. 1–120) rose from some confused reminiscence of the independent anecdote known as *The Defence of the Child* which appears in the various versions of the *Seven Sages* and the *Gesta Romanorum* and in a number of Oriental forms. In the Irish tale of *Morraha* the werwolf saves a child from a monster; in *Gorlagon* he discovers the child after the doubly false wife and mother has reported its death (Kittredge, p. 234 ff.). In *Guillaume* no explanation is given of how the werwolf knew conspirators were plotting against the royal boy, yet obviously such knowledge could have come only if the werwolf had been domesticated, as in the werwolf story proper, at the King's court. The episode has been changed from the middle to the beginning of the romance in order to provide for the introduction of the long account of the lovers' adventures, in all of which the werwolf plays the part of a Helpful Animal.[10]

[8] This conclusion rests on Kittredge's study, though he himself barely mentioned (p. 184, n. 2) *Guillaume de Palerne*. G. Paris, *Littérature frç.* § 67, thought the werwolf part of the romance was directly derived from the *Lais* of *Bisclavret* and *Melion*. Ahlström's refutation of this point (*Studier*, p. 81) was quoted with approval by Köhler, p. xiv. The literary derivation may be questioned without destroying the probability of a common source.

[9] The werwolf is hunted by a king who is his father-in-law (*Melion*, Irish tale), his brother (*Gorlagon*). Being hard pressed the wolf seizes the king's stirrup and licks his foot (*Gorlagon*). In *Melion* the werwolf escapes from the hunt led by his father-in-law, but later, when Arthur comes to visit this Irish king, the werwolf falls at Arthur's feet. In this indoors submission *Melion* is nearer to *Guillaume*.

[10] It is probable that the swimming feats of the werwolf in *Guillaume*, swimming across the straits of Messina with the child William in his mouth,

In *Guillaume de Palerne* the Enchantress Stepmother is summoned to Palermo by her captive husband; she is violently attacked by the wolf, and finally made to confess. Guillaume acts as the werwolf's protector when those about would kill him; in fact Guillaume's rôle corresponds exactly with that of the king in the werwolf tale. The scenes of the werwolf's attack upon the woman who has injured him, of his protection, of his recovery of his human form,[11] are practically the same as those of the Old French stories. Finally it may be noted that in this romance, as in the Irish tale, the enchantress is forgiven and escapes, as indeed she does in all the tales, the death penalty for her crimes. In *Melion* and to some extent in the Irish tale Kittredge (p. 176) thought she preserved the character of a Celtic *fée*. In *Guillaume* this Queen Brande, who lives in a rich city by the sea, who is " sage a merveille et bien letree " and skilled in sorceries (v. 287), has herself such dignity and sweetness of address (v. 7469), that one wonders if the concept has not been touched by some faint memory of the Circe myth.

Although only the more obvious parallels of incident and character have been touched on here, it seems sufficiently clear that the author of *Guillaume de Palerne* was familiar with the particular story of which *Bisclavret* and *Melion* were independent derivatives. If, as Kittredge conjectured (p. 262), a Norman text of *Melion* preceded the extant Picard text, we can the more readily account for the means of its transmission to the Normans of Sicily. Casual as are many of the geographical references in *Guillaume,* the author must have had a certain knowledge of the southern land in which he localized his story, — or how explain his references to Reggio, to Cefalu, to Santa Maria della Scala (v. 4636), near Palermo, to Palermo itself? (Zingarelli, p. 257 ff.). Whether Yolande's poet at sometime lived in Sicily

---

v. 115, or leaping from the ship on which he had embarked with the lovers as stowaways, to swim to land (French, 4604 ff.; English, vv. 2728 ff.) are derived from those in other werwolf stories. So in *Melion* the wolf gets passage as a stowaway to Ireland; in the Irish tale the wolf swims back to his own country.

[11] In *Guillaume* the wolf is disenchanted by means of a ring, itself proof against all magic, which his stepmother ties about his neck. So also in *Melion* the ring is the instrument of disenchantment. In all these stories the werwolf resumes his human shape in closest privacy.

and found there his story, or heard or read it in some brief form that was carried north, we cannot say with any certainty.[12]

In combination with this fundamental werwolf story that of the lovers, Melior and Guillaume, is, as has been said, both disproportionate and incongruous. On analysis it reduces to little more than a patchwork of familiar *motifs*, an account of a supposed mésalliance between a princess and her page, of their flight, their disguises, and their final restoration to their families and rightful dignities. The allusions to Guillaume's mother as a princess of Greece and to one of Melior's suitors as a prince of that land, are the result of contemporary interests on the part of the author and do not imply connections with Greek romance. The mésalliance theme, familiar in Greek story, was well-known in western story by the end of the twelfth century. Many western lovers, especially among the Celts, had learned in story at least the joys of a Forest Life,[13] though none it would seem, save Guillaume and Melior, went so far in their return to Nature, as to don the actual skins of animals. Many a lady had had a *confidante* though few with the wit and tact of Alexandrine, Melior's' lively friend. The rescuing of such beleagured ladies as Guillaume's mother and sister, who were besieged in Palermo by the latter's too ardent suitor, was a well-established chivalric incident. The reunion and recognition of long-separated families, in this instance of Guillaume with his mother, from whom he had been stolen in infancy, and of Alphonse, who had by his transformation into a werwolf been thus separated from his father, is used in a way that illustrates not only the mediaeval fondness for this simple theme but the author's special liking for doubling what he conceives to be effective material. To this liking may be ascribed his doubling of the *motif* of animal disguise, for the lovers, having eloped in the guise of white bears, are represented as presently changing to that of a hart and hind. A quaint but singularly inept touch is added when the poet, still too much in love with this device

[12] In his short essay, "La Sicile dans la littérature française," *Rom.* v. 108–13 (1876), Gaston Paris barely mentioned *Guillaume de Palerne*. He considered it a Celtic tale localized in Sicily.

[13] Cf. the adventures of Aucassin and Nicolette, of Beves of Hampton and Josian, and chiefly, of course, those of Tristan and Isolt. On this romance and the many Celtic parallels see Schoepperle, *Tristan*, II, 391–400.

to abandon it, makes the Queen of Palermo, Guillaume's unrecognized mother, don a hind's skin before she attempts to
communicate with her son. Awkward too is the poet's borrowing of the incident of the Faithful Horse,[14] for in *Guillaume*,
though the hero is stolen when a baby, he is nevertheless recognized by his father's horse, Brunsaudebruel, when years later
he returned to Palermo (v. 5405). In his use of Marvellous
Dreams the poet likewise follows patterns long current in saint
legends and romance.[15] The dream of William's mother that
her right arm stretches over Rome and her left over Spain, a
prophecy fulfilled when her son becomes Emperor of Rome and
her daughter Queen of Spain, is particularly close to that of
the hero in the English version of *Havelok* who dreams of one
arm reaching over Denmark and the other over England. Incidentally it may be suggested that the author, in his account
of Guillaume's devotion to the werwolf, and of the exquisite
politeness of the latter at the court of Palermo, may have been
influenced to some extent by Chrétien's *Iwain*, the story of the
famous Chevalier au Lyon.

This enumeration of literary influences on the love affair in
Guillaume and the remarking of various flaws in the story as
a whole should not, however, destroy a final sense that the romance originated in a spirit pleasantly touched by the gracious
charm of unreality. The pure idyllic mood is expressed in the
happy certainty of Guillaume, vowing, as he and his love betake
themselves to the forest:

> " Bien viverons de nos amors,
>   D'erbes, de fuelles et de flors." (v. 3033–34)

[14] French version, v. 5405; English, v. 3225 ff. More aptly in the various
versions of *Beves of Hampton*, the horse Arundel recognizes his master after
seven years' absence. For other instances see F. Settegast, *Quellenstudien z.
gallo-rom. Epik*. Leip. 1904, p. 343; Böje (see *Beves bibliog*. here) p. 108–9;
Deutschbein, *Sagengeschichte*, p. 196; L. Jordan, *Die Sage von den vier
Haimonskindern*, pp. 93, 140, Anm. 2.

[15] Cf. Gerould *Saints Legends*, 1916, p. 37; Heyman, *Studies in the
Havelok Legend*, p. 107.

BIBLIOGRAPHY

TEXTS: (1) King's College, 13, Cambridge, ed. F. Madden, Roxburghe Club, 1832; ed. Skeat, *EETSES.* 1, Lond. 1867; cf. Kaluza, *Eng. Stud.* IV, 280–7. (2) Prose fragment probably printed by Wynkyn de Worde, pr. F. Brie, *Archiv*, CXVII, 318–25 (1907). Trans. by F. G. Darton, *A Wonder Book of Old Romance*, N. Y., 1907.

STUDIES: Billings, *Guide*, pp. 45–46; Edwardes, *Summary*, p. 109 for English version, p. 192 for French; Wells, *Manual*, p. 765.

Brie, F. See Texts.

Buxton, E. M. *Stories from Old French Romance* (Trans. of *Guillaume*), N. Y., 1910.

Delp, W. E. *Étude sur la langue de "Guillaume de Palerne."* Suivie d'un glossaire. 103 pp. Paris, 1907; rev. *Rom.* XXXVI, 448–50.

Kaluza, M. "Das mittelengl. Gedicht *William of Palerne* u. seine frz. Quelle," *Eng. Stud.* IV, 199–287 (1881).

Kittredge, G. L. "Arthur and Gorlagon," *Harvard Studies in Philology and Literature*, VIII, 149–273 (1903). Cf. *Revue Crit.* 1905, LIX, 5–6; *Moyen Age*, 1904, XVII, 66.

Lot-Borodine, M. *Le Roman Idyllique au Moyen Age (Guillaume de Palerne*, pp. 237–65). Paris. 1913.

Skeat, W. See Texts.

Smith, K. "Historical Study of the Werwolf in Literature," *PMLA.* IX, 1–41 (1894).

Tibbals, K. "Elements of Magic in the Romance of 'William of Palerne,'" *Mod. Phil.* I, 355–71 (1903).

Warren, F. "The Works of Jean Renart and their Relation to *Galeran de Bretagne*," Parts I and II, *MLN.* XXIII, 69–73; 97–100 (1908).

Zingarelli, N. "Il 'Guillaume de Palerne' e i suoi dati di luogo e di tempo," *Miscellanea di Archeologia dedicata al Prof. A. Salinas*, pp. 256–72. Palermo, 1906. Rev. *Rom.* XXXVI, 151 (1907).

IPOMÉDON

Versions. The Anglo-French romance of *Ipomédon* (ed. Kölbing und Koschwitz, Breslau, 1889) is one of the comparatively few of which the author is known. Hue de Rotelande (Flintshire) alludes to himself in several passages of the poem, — in one confessing genially:

> " Hue dit ke il ni ment de ren
> Fors aukune feiz neent mut."

He states that his home was at Credehulle (Credenhill), about four miles from Hereford, and refers not only to bits of local history, but to celebrities of that district, to Huge de Hungrie, probably a canon of Hereford, and to that famous worthy, Walter Map, Archdeacon of Oxford in 1197, to whom Hue gives the palm in the " art de mentir" (Ward, *Catalogue*, 1, 734). At the end of the *Prothesilaus*, a metrical sequel to *Ipomédon*, Hue refers to his patron, Gilbert Fitz-Baderon, fourth Lord of Monmouth, " dount sis chastels est mult manauntz e de latyn e de romaunz," from whose library Hue asserts that he received the Latin source of *Prothesilaus*. Gilbert's death in 1190–91 gives, therefore, a *terminus ad quem* for the composition of these romances, and if Hue's reference in *Ipomédon* to the raid of the Welsh king, Rhees ap Gryffth, into the English counties, be that of 1186, as Carter (p. 237) thought, the poem is probably to be dated shortly after that year. The text of Hue's poem, now extant in three manuscripts, contains over ten thousand lines and shows that the author was a graceful writer, well-learned in the taste of a chivalric audience, and skilful in adapting material of proved popularity. A certain gaiety of tone, as in his amused reference to Map, is, perhaps, his special distinction.

The three Middle English versions of Ipomédon's story (ed. Kölbing, 1889) are based on Hue's romance. The longest and most important text is in the fifteenth-century Chetham manuscript (A). The author of this version must have had before him one of the French manuscripts, so exactly does he at times translate and even borrow the very words of his original. Yet his *Ipomadon,* written in 751 twelve-line tail-rime stanzas, is not a slavish but a fairly independent piece of work. It gives good illustration, as Kölbing (pp. lxv–clvii) pointed out, of the English redactor's methods of work, of his free transposition of phrases and details, though he adhered so closely to the narrative content of his original (Kölbing, p. xxxvi ff.) This first version Kölbing (p. clxxiii) thought originated in north Lancashire about the middle of the fourteenth century. The second version (B), *The Lyfe of Ipomydon,* is a poem of 2346 verses in short riming couplets. It is written in the fifteenth-century Harleian manuscript by the same scribe who wrote the first part of the stanzaic *Morte Arthur.* On linguistic grounds it seems improbable that the two poems could have been by the same author (Seyferth, p. 76). This rather pithily condensed version of *Ipomédon* was perhaps made from memory of Hue's long and complicated romance (Kölbing, p. lxv). The third version (C) of *Ipomédon* is in prose. Although the manuscript in which it is contained seems to be older than that of A, the text itself is too brief to be the source of that version. On the other hand it cannot be simply a prose rendering of A, for it has numerous parallels, not included in A, with the French version (Kölbing, p. xlvi).

The three Middle English versions do not, it must be admitted, preserve very much of the special excellencies of Hue's humorous and leisurely romance. They do, however, testify to the long continued liking for the story in which he had woven together with satisfying effectiveness two well-established themes, that of the Three Days' Tournament and the Rescue of a Beleaguered Lady.

ORIGIN. Hue's introductory assertion that he translated *Ipomédon* out of Latin into " romaunz " is generally regarded as a hoax; so also is his statement at the end of the romance that his hero's further adventures may be found in the story of Thèbes. Though Warren's arguments " On the Latin Sources of *Thèbes* and *Énéas* " (*PMLA.* xvi, 375–87) have increased the belief in possible mediaeval Latin versions of these Romances of Antiquity, Hue's own borrowings from the twelfth-century

versions in French make the supposition of a Latin *Ipomédon*
wholly unnecessary. Ward (*Catalogue* 1, 732) thought it improbable that he knew anything of Statius's *Thebaid*. As a
matter of fact a comparison of Hue's Prologue with those of
the *Roman de Thèbes* and the *Roman de Troie* more than explains the source of his inspiration about " Latin " sources.

The first part of *Ipomédon* tells of the love which overcomes
the hero when, like a second Rudel,[1] he hears of the beauty of
La Fière, the young duchess of Calabria, of his service as her
squire until he is driven away by her capricious scorn, and of
his return when a tournament is proclaimed for the winning of
her hand. In this Three Days' Tournament Ipomédon appears
disguised in white, red, and black armor and has horses to match.
At each day's end he disappears from the field and returns to
her uncle's court. Here he pretends that he has spent the day
in hunting and the court ladies laugh him to scorn for his un-
chivalric tastes. In far more primitive form this episode is
found in numerous folk tales.[2] From them it passed into such
romances as Chrétien's *Cligès* (1160), into *Robert le Diable* and
its English version, *Sir Gowther,* into the *Lanzelet* of the poet,
Ulrich von Zatzikhoven, into the French prose *Lancelot, Parténopeus, Richard Coeur de Lion,* and *Roswall and Lillian.* The
special similarity between this episode in *Ipomédon* and one in
Lanzelet suggests that Hue knew the original of *Lanzelet* which
its author states was a French romance taken from England
in 1194 by Hugh de Morville, one of the hostages for Richard
I. But it is also clear that Hue must have known some form
of the folk-tale version in which the episode is regularly connected, as it is in *Ipomédon* but not in *Lanzelet,* with the winning of a princess.[3] In this respect, likewise, *Ipomédon* is

[1] O. H. Moore, " Jaufre Rudel and the Lady of Dreams." *PMLA.* xxix,
527–8 (1914), gave a number of interesting references to literary examples
of the use of the idea of falling in love from hearsay or from a dream.
See *Partonope,* n. 18.

[2] Cf. *Gowther,* note 2. Carter, p. 239, cited a number of collections
in which these tales are found. See also for the popular and the literary
versions, Weston, *Three Days' Tournament,* pp. 34–43; Ward, *Catalogue,* 1,
734.

[3] Carter, p. 248. See F. Lot, *Étude sur le Lancelot en prose,* Paris, 1918,
p. 166, p. 128, for brief discussions of *Lanzelet,* and of the improbability that
Map was the author of its source.

nearer the original form of the story than is *Cligès*. Though the latter is the earliest extant romance to make use of the theme, it seems improbable that it was the source of this incident in *Ipomédon*. *Cligès* tells of a Four Days' Tournament; the episode is an incidental chivalric adventure on the part of the hero and has no romantic significance.

The second part of *Ipomédon* turns on *motifs* well known in Arthurian romance. On hearing that La Fière is wooed by a barbarous suitor, Ipomédon returns to her uncle's court. Here dressed and shorn like a fool, he extorts from King Meleager the promise of the first feat of arms that shall offer. He is assigned, accordingly, to the service of the Maiden Messenger who comes with her dwarf to ask Meleager's aid for his niece. Despite her scorn and bitter tongue, the hero follows her and performs prodigies of valor. With varying details the essential elements of this episode are also found in the Old French poem of Renaud de Beaujeu, *Le Bel Inconnu* or *Guinglain,* written about 1190 or a little earlier, and in the later versions of the same story, the Middle High German *Wigalois* by Wirnt von Gravenberg, *c.* 1210, the Middle English *Libeaus Desconus, c.* 1350, and in *Carduino,* the Italian poem ascribed to Antonio Pucci, *c.* 1375.[4] It is also in Malory's tale of Sir Gareth (Beaumains), the seventh book of the *Morte Arthur*. *Ipomédon* and *Le Bel Inconnu* are approximately of the same date and are, in action and even occasionally in phraseology, closely related. For these reasons Carter (pp. 255–61) believed that for this incident Hue had before him either Renaud's own poem or its French source.

Other episodes in *Ipomédon* are similarly suggestive of other romances. The Combat between Relatives, here between the hero and his half-brother, Campaneus, a climax skilfully prepared for throughout the story, is simply a variant of the familiar Father and Son Combat of epic and romantic literature.[5] Suggestive of the hero of *Tristan* is Ipomédon's skill at skinning

---

[4] For these versions see W. Schofield's "Studies in Libeaus Desconus," *Studies and Notes in Philology and Literature,* IV, Boston, 1895.

[5] M. A. Potter, *Sohrab and Rustum* (The Epic Theme of a Combat between Father and Son. A Study of its Genesis and Use). London, 1902. Potter, p. 207, enumerated twenty-seven instances from folklore and romance of combats between brothers.

game, his disguise as a fool, and the manner of his jesting. The courtly ideals, the emphasis on the courtesy, generosity, beauty, and courage of the hero, the splendor of the court of Meleager, the scenes of hunting and tourney, the maiden-dwarf episode, the analyses of love-sickness, in many ways seem reminiscent of Arthurian romance as developed in the hands of Chrétien and his contemporaries. But the absolute lack of reference to any Arthurian personage and the lack too of that "paraphernalia of wonder," of which romances like the *Charette* or *Iwain* are full, make it doubtful whether Hue had any knowledge at all of these romances. Kölbing (*Ipomadon*, 1889, p. xxviii ff.) thought the author did know them but later studies on the connection of *Ipomédon* with the Romances of Antiquity have called this view into question. It has been pointed out that at least twenty names in *Ipomédon* are drawn from the *Roman de Thèbes*, that every important character in *Ipomédon*, the active king Meleager, who is very unlike the passive Arthur of Chrétien's stories, the great hero, Campaneus, supposedly modelled on Gawain, but unlike Gawain, defeated by the hero of the story, the seneschal Caeminius with his Kay-like "custumers de mesdire," can be paralleled in *Thèbes* or *Énéas*. Moreover the virtues of character and the nature of the love-code in *Ipomédon* are of distinctly less chivalric cast than in the Arthurian tales (Gay, p. 469 ff.). So far, indeed, is Ipomédon from being a conventional lover that he can remark, even when the lady is more than ready to be his, "De femme aveir ne dei haster" (v. 6644), and leave her pining for yet another year. In all this he is much more like an Anglo-Norman Havelok than he is like one of Chrétien's superfine heroes. Ipomédon's zest for adventure, which at the end induces him to appear in the guise of his lady's foe and fight almost to the death with her champion, is far more convincing than is his zeal as a lover.

With *Parténopeus of Blois, Ipomédon* has some likenesses which prove that the author of one romance must have borrowed from the other, though the order of the two poems has not yet been established. In each story there is a proud heroine who by her own capricious pride drives away her lover. She ultimately confesses her love to a confidante but in trying to

say her lover's name breaks down in the middle of it.[6] Kölbing
(p. xxxi) likewise called attention to the further parallel between the two stories in the account of the Three Days' Tournament. La Fière, like Melior in *Parténopeus*, is urged by her
lords to marry and the tournament is called for the purpose of
deciding on a suitable husband. In tone, length, and elaboration, the two romances have much in common.

Like *Parténopeus, Guillaume de Palerne, Floire et Blancheflor, Ipomédon* was formerly placed among the mediaeval French
romances inspired by Byzantine sources (Paris, *La Litt. frç. au
Moyen Age*, ch. iii). The story is now recognized as a clever
" manufactured " romance which admirably illustrates the sophistication of literary art in England at the end of the twelfth
century.

BIBLIOGRAPHY

TEXTS: (1) A, Chetham Library, 8009, Manchester, desc. *Eng. Stud.*
VII, 195; (2) B, Harleian, 2252, desc. Ward, *Catalogue*, I, 755 ff.; pr.
Wynkyn de Worde, 1500; ed. Weber, 1810, II, 281 ff.; (3) C, MS. 25
of Marquis of Bath, desc. Kölbing, *Eng. Stud.* x, 203. The MSS. ABC
were edited by Kölbing, Breslau, 1889. Rev. *Eng. Stud.* XIII, 482–93.

STUDIES: *Cf.* Wells, *Manual*, p. 785–86.
Carter, C. H. "*Ipomedon*, An Illustration of Romance Origins," *Haver-
        ford Essays*, pp. 239–70, Haverford, 1909. This was part of an
        unpublished dissertation, *Ipomedon: A Study of the Poem*, Harvard,
        1904.
Gay, L. M. "Hue de Roteland's *Ipomedon* and Chrétien de Troyes,"
        PMLA. XXXII, 468–92 (1917).
Hahn, W. *Der Wortschatz des Dichters Hue de Rotelande.* Diss. Berlin,
        1910.
Holthausen, F. "Zu mittelengl. Romanzen, *Ipomadon*," *Anglia* XLI,
        463–97 (1917).
Kittredge, G. L. "Anmerkungen zum mittelengl. *Ipomadon*," *Eng.
        Stud.* XIV, 386–92 (1890).
Kölbing, E. See Texts.
Köppel, E. "Zur Textkritik des *Ipomadon*," *Eng. Stud.* XIV, 371–86.
Otto, S. *Der Einfluss des "Roman de Thèbes" auf die altfrz. Litera-*

---

[6] *Ipomadon*, v. 1440; Eng. version, *Partonope*, v. 5782. Miss Gay, p.
486, n. 91, noted that Hue more probably borrowed this episode (v. 1497)
from the account of Lavinia in *Enéas* (v. 8554) than from *Parténopeus* (v.
7247). Cf. *Partonope* here, n. 25.

ture. Diss. Göttingen, 1909. For the influence on *Ipomédon,* see p. 62 ff.

Seyferth, P. *Sprache u. Metrik des mittelengl. strophischen Gedichtes "Le Morte Arthur" u. sein Verhältnis zu " The Lyfe of Ipomydon."* Diss. Berlin, 1895. *Berlinger Beiträge,* VIII.

Ward, H. L.   *Catalogue of Romances,* I, 728–750 (1883).

Weston, J.   *The Three Days' Tournament,* Lond., 1902.

Willert, H.   *"Ipomadon,* Strophe 37," *Eng. Stud.* XXXVIII, 131–32 (1907).

GENERIDES

VERSIONS. In the *Parlement of Thre Ages*[1] and in Gower's forty-third *Balade* (*Works,* ed. Macaulay, Oxford, 1899, 1, 372) the authors list with other great lovers, " Genarid and Clarionas." Though to the taste of a later time the two wear but borrowed robes, the shreds and patches of more authentic personalities, the literary references to them and the two extant fifteenth-century texts of *Generides* imply a fair degree of popularity. That this lasted into the next century is shown by the fact that the book was licensed to Thomas Purfoote in 1568–69, and printed in an edition of which a few fragments are still extant (Wright, p. vii).

The original version of *Generides,* whether in French or Middle English, was probably a fourteenth-century compilation for which the author used chiefly the French texts of current romances. In the A version of *Generides,* represented by the Helmingham manuscript, the rimes, the vocabulary, the whole style and spirit of the piece, show this specifically French influence. The reference in the Prologue to a Latin version of *Generides* made by a monk at Hertford, may best be taken as an imitation of a similar assertion in the French *Ipomédon,* a romance with which *Generides* has several connections. The A version in rimed couplets is over three thousand lines longer than the B version (Trinity College MS. Camb.) in rime royal. Howe's study (pp. 46–97) of their relationship showed a number of small points peculiar to each version, a good deal of variation in the spelling of names, and the absence of much correspondence in rime. He concluded that the two texts repre-

[1] Gollancz in his edition of the poem (Lond., 1915) dated the *Parlement* about 1350. As the Middle English texts of *Generides* bear every sign of late fourteenth or early fifteenth century work, so that Kölbing even suspected in them signs of Chaucerian influence, it must be supposed that the allusion in the *Parlement* was to the lost French version of *Generides.* Among other lovers cited in the *Parlement* list are Amadase and Idoyne, Ipomadoun, Eglamour, Tristram, and Dame Gaynore.

sented entirely independent versions of the original story. In general he thought that the A version kept closer to its sources and had an ampler, less flattened style than the B text, though in this last he found signs of some effort towards unity and proportion, and a sincere if uninspired effort to follow the " boke." Neither version really escapes mediocrity and it is clear that the original author was more than willing to evade any responsibility for either novelty or invention.

ORIGIN. The romance is full of Eastern names and locations, but it is difficult to believe that these have any more significance than the names drawn from Biblical [2] and classical sources. The author had a passion for both personal and geographical names but it does not appear that there was much lore behind his usage. As Zirwer (p. 18) pointed out, the poet tells of an army's sailing from Damascus to India. The confusion and unreality of the Indian and Persian names in *Generides* seem almost enough to discredit at the start Settegast's attempts to find the origin of the story in ancient Eastern legends.

In his *Quellenstudien* (pp. 245–47), Settegast argued that the initial story concerning the birth of Generides should be derived through various unstated intermediaries from the sixth (?) century drama, *Sakuntalā,* which the poet Kālidāsa based on an opening episode of the *Mahabharata,* the national epic of India. In this it is told how the king, Dushyanta, when hunting through the forest, comes upon a place of great loveliness where he finds and wins a beautiful maiden who was living under the care of her holy hermit father. By her Dushyanta becomes the father of the child of prophecy, the wondrous Bharata. The meeting and separation of the lovers, the king's forgetfulness, the woman's quest, the token which recalls her to him, are to some extent parallel incidents in the two stories, though there is nothing in *Generides* to suggest either the many specifically Indian features of its supposed original or its characteristic motivation. Settegast's attempt (pp. 258–66) to derive such names as Sereyne from Selene, or Auferius from that of Avelius, or to equate the

[2] Among the Biblical names given for various warring kings in *Generides* may be noted Abell, Balam, David, Galad (Cf. Bruce, *MLN.,* 1918; Pauphilet, *Queste del Saint Gral,* Paris, 1921, p. 136), Jonathas, Ishmaell, Reuben, Samson, etc.

name of Nathanel with that of Matali, the charioteer of the god
Indra, weakens rather than supports a parallel that is interesting
even if unconvincing. In his opinion the further stages of the
story were as follows.

The Indian story concerning the birth of a marvellous hero
was fused in Persia with the stories of the Persian heroes
Sijawusch and Bischen, whose fame was recorded about 1011 by
the poet Firdausi in the Persian Book of Kings, the *Shāhnāma*
(Eng. trans. by A. G. and F. Warner, Lond. 1906, vol. II, 200).
Like Generides Sijawusch had an unfortunate encounter with a
stepmother who first proffered him her love and then accused
him of evil intentions against her.[3] He went to the court of a
foreign king, fell in love with the king's daughter, and there incurred the hostility of the king (Warner, II, 200–32). The tragical outcome of this last adventure, in which Sijawusch lost his
life (Warner, II, 296–323), was changed to a happy ending in the
case of Bischen who, having become the lover of a princess and
having been betrayed to her father, was rescued from his prison
pit and lived to marry his princess. The story in which these
episodes and characters had merged drifted then, according to
Settegast (pp. 236–41), to Syria, where it absorbed some geographical names, and thence to Constantinople, where it took
over certain elements from the legendary history of the Emperor
Zeno. Between 475–77 the Emperor had been driven from his
throne by a conspiracy of his wicked stepmother and her lover;
he fled and in company with his faithful wife, waited until he
could gather an army for the conquest of his land. Settegast
(p. 238) identified Aufreus, the father of Generides, with Zeno;
Sereyne, the mother of the hero, with Zeno's true wife, Ariadne;
and Aufreus's false wife with Zeno's wicked stepmother. In
what fashion this strange composite of stories thus drawn from
Indian, Persian, and Byzantine tradition came to western Europe,
Settegast did not say, but in accord with other critics he agreed
that the extant English versions must have been derived from
a lost French original.

As a matter of fact it needs no such far-reaching efforts to

---

[3] Cf. Warner, *op cit.*, II, 212, and the *Seven Sages* here. The *motif* is
commonly known as that of Potiphar's' Wife, and appears in such mediaeval romances as *Graelent* and *Launfal*.

account for most of the characters and episodes in *Generides*. They may be tracked, as Howe has shown, in familiar paths of mediaeval romance.

The opening episode of the story tells of the magic hart which leads King Aufreus apart from his fellows and brings him to his predestined mistress. There is much here to suggest direct borrowing from the lay of *Guigemar*, though Pschmadt's study (*Die Sage von der verfolgten Hind*, 1911) and Howe's on The Magic Hunt prove how commonly this *motif* was used as an introductory episode in romance. In *Generides* the lady's companion is one of the Seven Sages, and it is he who prophesies concerning the child she will bear. In *Guigemar* the lady is married to a cruel old Jaloux; in *Generides* it is Auferius who is already married to a wife both false and cruel. In order to explain his liaison with Sereyne, it is not necessary to turn with Settegast to the multiple marriages of the East, nor, with the mediaeval doctrines of courtly love in mind, to explain the lady's claim as due originally to the peculiar marriage celebrated between Sakuntala and Dushyanta. The cheerfully unmoral little episode, as in *Guigemar*, is " moralized," if at all, by the character of the lovers. The decorated room and bed, the magic pillow, the ivory gates of the beautiful house, in the A version of *Generides*, suggest deliberate imitation on the author's part of the lay (Howe, pp. 310–55). That the original author of *Generides* was at this point also influenced by the *Erec* of Chrétien de Troyes (ed. Foerster, 1890, v. 2490), is suggested by the early morning scene between the lovers. Like Erec, Auferius is awakened by his lady's tears.

In the matter of a Recognition Token between the lovers there is in *Generides* a curious variation from *Guigemar*. In the latter the lady plaited a fold in her lover's tunic in such fashion that only she could undo it. In *Generides* the Sage explains (B, v. 194) that the lady's tears can only be washed out by the lady herself. The variation is sufficient to suggest that at this point the poet departed from the lay in order to follow some folk-tale of the type now represented by the *Black Bull of Norroway*.[4]

---

[4] The Scotch version was first printed by Robert Chambers in 1826 in *The Popular Rhymes of Scotland* and has attained a new vogue in Andrew Lang's *Blue Fairy Book*, Lond. 1901. Chambers gave a Scotch and an English version called respectively *The Black* and the *Red Bull of Norroway*, the

Magic shirts are common enough in folk-lore,[5] but in these two stories alone, it would seem, does the same detail occur in the same situation. In both folk-tale and romance the heroine, who has been long separated from her lover, comes at last to the place where he rules; she alone can wash the magic shirt free from its stain of blood or tears, and by this means is recognized by him. In any case the peculiar liking which the author of *Generides* had for the laundress [6] rôle is worth noting. Howe (p. 354) observed that the poet makes a " lavendere " serve in three important incidents, for it was a lavendere who received the new-born Generides from his mother's confidante; it was as a lavendere that his mother regained her lord; and it was another lavendere who helped Generides' own lady to escape from a threatening suitor. It may be added that almost the only touch of realistic humor in the romance comes in this last scene, for the honest woman who is trying to disguise Clarionas as a true lavendere complains outspokenly of the unseemly whiteness of the princess's legs (B, v. 4403).

It is characteristic of the discursive manner of the *Generides* poet that so large a portion of his story is devoted not to the hero but to his father. There are in fact three love stories in the romance, that of Auferius and Sereyne, of Generides and

---

latter an abbreviated and somewhat rationalized version of the former. The Scotch version tells of a maid carried off by the Black Bull, an enchanted Prince of Norroway, of their separation because she breaks his command, of her seven years of service for a smith from whom she finally obtains the iron shoes which enable her to climb the glass mountain on the top of which is the Prince's kingdom. There she finds a witch woman and her daughter who vainly try to wash the Prince's blood-stained shirt, since he has said he will marry the one who can cleanse it. The maiden does it herself and is at last restored to her lover.

A Gaelic version of this story, found in Campbell's' *Popular Tales of the West-Highlands*, IV, 267 ff., was told about 1812 by a serving maid. In this version the hero is transformed into a great grey dog. The dog-hero of this version confirms the evidence of the name Norroway in the Scotch version which led Leyden, in his edition of *The Complaint of Scotland* (*EETSES.* 1872, XVII, 63), to believe that *The Taill of the Thre Futted Dog of Norroway*, to which the *Complaint* refers, was this story. As the " ballads " listed in the *Complaint* were still current in 1548, the folk-tale can be traced back to within a century of the earliest text of *Generides*.

[5] Cf. L. A. Hibbard, " Chaucer's ' Shapen was my Sherte,' " *Philological Quarterly*, 1922, I, 222–25.

[6] Cf. G. Krapp, " Chaucer's Lavendere," *MLN.* 1902, XVII, 102–03, for other uses of the word.

Clarionas, and of Generides' young friend, Darell, and Lycidas, the daughter of the hero's cruel stepmother. In the love story of the hero, one recognizes the predominant influence of the *Tristan* legend. When Clarionas, the young daughter of the Sultan to whose court Generides comes, falls in love with him, " of hir cupp she offeryd him to drynk " (B. v. 693). Whether this be a faint reminiscence of the immortal potion or not, it is clear that the jealous steward who hides in a tree (B, v. 1360), and who persuades the king to spy upon the lovers from a window, is a stupid descendant of Tristan's foe. Later on in the romance, the poet reverts to the same legend in telling how Generides rescued his love from an abductor and made for her a lodge in the wood. In the B version he builds one for himself also and sleeps in it with his drawn sword by his side (Howe, p. 153). Inept as the imitation is, it is evidently the grotto scene of the *Tristan* that the poet has in mind. Like Mark, the angry Sultan comes upon his daughter, and then, moved by pity, exchanges swords with Generides instead of killing him. Howe (p. 153) noted that the inconsistency with which the incident is treated in B, is proof of a different authorship from that of A, in which the author followed his original with at least a fair amount of understanding. But it is to be noted that the B version makes four different references (B, v. 4736, etc.) to the dog which Generides, like Tristan, gave to his lady. Thus in this respect the B version is closer to the old legend than the A text which makes no allusion at all to such a gift. A final, almost ludicrous bit of similarity between the romances comes in the scene in which Clarionas, like a second Isolt, hastens to her lover, who has fallen desperately ill upon hearing of the death of his parents.

Aside from the *Tristan, Generides* follows many other familiar patterns of romance. The lovers are warned in dreams of coming trouble; Generides is imprisoned and kills the False Steward who had accused him of dishonoring the princess; he is released in order to fight against Belen, the Haughty Suitor who demanded the homage of the Sultan and the hand of his daughter; he kills this King of Kings in single combat; he rescues Clarionas from the emissary sent by Belen's son, who assumed his father's throne and also his claim to the lady; Generides follows when again she is carried off; he crosses the sea, and in the disguise of a leprous beggar, wins access to her. In this episode there is some likeness to the *Horn* story where similarly at her wedding feast a bride recognizes her true lover by his ring. The disguise *motif* is used three times in *Generides*, and in each instance seems only a variant of this original (Howe, p. 445). The elopement of the lovers, who find their horses at a garden gate, is slightly suggestive of *Eliduc*. The pursuit by Sir Yuell, the king's emissary, and his treacherous attempt to kill Generides with a secret knife in his hand, is a feeble variant of the familiar Vain Pursuit of which Boje (*Beuve de Hamtone*, p. 96) gave so many examples. The lovers separate in order to permit Generides to go to his father's aid, and their reunion is rendered difficult by the machinations of the Wicked Stepmother. She sends word to each of them that the other is faithless, and it calls for much travelling back and forth on the part of their faithful friends to bring them together again.

Both hero and heroine in *Generides* are provided with efficient friends. Mirabell, as a confidante, serves her lady much more arduously than Alisandrine does Melior in *William of Palerne*, though she has little of the gaiety or pertness that often characterizes such a character in Old French romance. Like the hero in *Ipomédon*, Generides is given into the hands of a governor who accompanies him upon his travels. It is Nathanell who listens to the love-sick hero, who arranges with Mirabell to have him meet Clarionas in the garden, who takes to her the steeds won by the hero in battle, who waits with horses for the eloping lovers, and is ultimately rewarded with the hand of Mirabell.[7] In the course of the story other friends are provided for Generides; they divide the functions properly belonging to Nathanell. Darell, for instance, rushes from India to Persia to find out the true state of his lord's lady, and takes the place of Generides when the hero himself feels impelled to go to Persia. This easy-going doubling of rôles and the absence of any real attempt at characterization leave the personages of the romance simply type figures moving in a puppet show.

[7] Cf. K. Young, *Origin and Development of Troilus*, 1908, pp. 46–47, on the Faithful Squire or Friend in *Eglamour, Ipomedon, Libeaus Desconus, Amadas et Idoine, Cleomades*, etc.

BIBLIOGRAPHY

Texts: (1) Helmingham MS., ed. Furnivall, Roxburghe Club, 1866; (2) Cambridge, Trinity College o, 5, 2, ed. Wright, *EETS*. 55, 70 (1873–78).

Studies: Cf. Körting, *Grundriss*, § 116; Wells, *Manual*, p. 785.

Holthausen, F. *Beiträge zur Textkritik der ME. Generydes-romanze* (ed. Wright). Göteborg, 1898.

Howe, W. D. *Sir Generides; its Origin, History, and Literary Relations.* Diss. Unpublished. Harvard University, 1899.

Kölbing, E. "Zur Textkritik der strophischen dichtung *Generydes*," *Eng. Stud.* xvii, 49–73 (1892).

Settegast, F. *Quellenstudien zur galloromanischen Epik.* Leipzig, 1904.

Zirwer, O. (1) "Zur Textkritik der ME. *Generides-Romanzen*," *Eng. Stud.* xvii, 23–49 (1892).

(2) *Untersuchungen zu den beiden ME. Generides-Romanzen.* Diss. Breslau, 1889.

CHEVALERE ASSIGNE

(Knight of the Swan)

Versions. (I, The Swan-Children.) It is one of the unfortunate chances of mediaeval English literature that of the many accounts of the legend of the *Knight of the Swan* once current in England, only two English versions are now known to exist, one, the short poem of three hundred and seventy lines called the *Chevelere Assigne,* and the other the prose version printed in 1570 by Wynkyn de Worde and called by him *The History of the noble Helyas, Knight of the Swanne.* The text was a free translation made by Robert Copland from the compilation known as *La généalogie avecques les gestes . . . du très preux . . . prince Godeffroy de Boulin: et des ses frères . . . Baudouin et Eustace: yssus et descendus de la très noble . . . lignée du . . . vertueux Chevalier au Cygne.* This book was prepared by Pierre d'Esrey or Desrey of Troyes, and the earliest extant edition was printed at Paris in 1504. From the date 1499 in the preface it is probable there was an earlier edition and there were certainly many subsequent ones (Jaffray, p. 68). Of de Worde's edition and of the reprint by William Copland, son of the translator, Robert, only single copies are now known.[1] Similarly a single fifteenth-century manuscript contains the English poetic version. This was composed in the last half of the fourteenth century and, as its alliterative verse would suggest, was perhaps written in the north-west. The brief extant text, however, is not of the north, but was written by an East-Midland scribe

[1] Gibbs, p. x, wrongly thought that there was no extant copy of the edition by Wynkyn de Worde. The copy belonging to Robert Hoe was reprinted in a beautiful facsimile edition by the Grolier Club in 1901.

The propriety of including this romance among the non-cyclic legends is open to question. It has been included, however, because the original story of the Swan-Children had an origin and early history independent of the Swan-Knight legend, and because the English poetic version preserves this non-cyclic character.

(Krüger, 1, p. 180). Gibbs (p. i), who edited the poem, and Jaffray (p. 53) thought it merely an epitome of the first 1083 lines of the French poem in that wonderfully illuminated manuscript of the British Museum, Royal 15 E VI, which is itself a whole collection of romances. Krüger (1, p. 175) somewhat more carefully derived it from the same source as a Latin version now in the Bodleian, Rawlinson Misc. 358, in which, as in the English poem, the hero's name appears, not as Helyas, but as Enyas (v. 270).

The Middle English poem gives a fairly complete and not unspirited account of the events that had come to be the introductory portion of the *Knight of the Swan* story. It is the legend of the children turned into swans and of the return of all but one of them to human form. The oldest literary version of the story is found in the *Dolopathos* (ed. Hilka, 1913, p. 80 ff.), which was written about 1190 by Johannes de Alta Silva and translated into French verse not long after by the poet Herbert.[2] John's statements that his tales were " adhuc scriptoribus intacta vel forsitan incognita," that they were " non ut visa sed ut audita " (Hilka, p. 107), and the unquestionably primitive, not to say barbaric, character of this particular story, the seventh in the collection, do not preclude the probability that it came to him, not as a folk, but as a jongleur's tale of which there must have been more than one version in order to explain the differences between the later vernacular versions (Huet, p. 208). These were classified in a memorable article by Gaston Paris (1, p. 315) in four groups, each determined by the name of the mother of the swan-children. In the first group, represented by the *Dolopathos* story, all the characters are unnamed; the mother is a *nympha* whom a young lord finds bathing in a fountain, takes home, and marries. She is clearly a swan-maiden, but her way of reading the stars, and the astrological prophecy which she makes concerning her future offspring, as Huet (p. 207) pointed out, indicate a semi-learned adaptation of some early but literary version. When her seven children are born, the wicked mother-in-law substitutes dogs for them and gives the children to a serf to kill. Believing his

---

[2] See the *Seven Sages* here. For bibliography of the versions of the Swan-Children story see Chauvin, *Bibliographie*, VIII, 206–08; Bolte-Polivka, *Anmerkungen-Hausmärchen*, 1913, 1, 427–34.

wife to be an abhorrent creature, the husband has her half-buried in the court-yard and left for seven years to endure the chance mercies of passers-by. The children, who were spared by the serf and later rescued by an old man, are discovered by a servant of the mother-in-law. When the servant takes the golden chains, which had been about their necks from the time they were born, the six boys turn into swans. Their sister leads them to their father's house where, as a little beggar herself, she provides for them and for their tortured mother. Their father's pity is aroused, the true story is revealed, and the magic chains are restored, with the exception of one that had been partly used in the making of a beautiful cup. In consequence one child was left in his swan form. The author's concluding comment, " hic est cignus de quo fama in eternum perseverat, quod catena aurea militem in navicula trahat armatum" (*Rom.* xix, 317), shows that in his time the tale of the Swan-Children was already linked with that of the Swan-Knight. Even clearer indication of this fact is given in the poet Herbert's translation of the *Dolopathos* (Blondeaux, xxxviii, 169).

The second group in Paris's classification receives its name from Eloixe, the heroine of a long French poem, *La Naissance du Chevalier au Cygne* (ed. H. A. Todd, *PMLA.* iv, 1889), extant in two thirteenth-century manuscripts. In this, 3500 lines are devoted to a version of the Swan-Children story which Paris (1, p. 319) thought was probably derived from the same source as the short *Dolopathos* tale. But much that was primitive in the earlier version is softened in this: the mother's character as a *fée* is less clearly recognizable, and her barbarous torture is omitted, as she dies in giving birth to the children. The author of this version was familiar with the romances of chivalry; he tells of jongleurs singing of Oliver and Ogier (v. 3226–8), and contrasts the " fable d'Artu . . . co fu faerie " (v. 3296) with his own veracious tale, an " estoire " which was found at a church founded in honor of " Sainte Marie " at Nimèque (v. 3301). These references indicate that the poem was not written before the end of the twelfth century (Paris, 1, p. 320).

The two remaining forms of the Swan-Children story were independently derived from the source of the *Dolopathos* ver-

sion. The third version, *Isomberte,* though it undoubtedly existed at one time in the form of a French *chanson de geste,* is
now known only in a Spanish prose chronicle, *La Gran Con-
quista de Ultramer,* ch. XLVII–LXVIII (cf. *Rom.* XIX, 320; XVII,
522). It opens with a situation suggestive of the initial *motif*
of the *Mannekin* group of stories in which a royal princess flees
from home to escape a hated marriage.[3] Isomberte, rescued by
Count Eustache from a wood to which she had fled, marries
him and in his absence bears him seven children at once. By
forged letters, again a device that belongs to the *Mannekin*
group of stories, the wicked mother-in-law contrives to order
Isomberte and her children put to death. The children's life
with the hermit, their metamorphosis into swans, is much the
same as in the earlier versions, but it is one of the most distinctive changes in this and the following version, that the child
who escapes transformation is not the girl, but a boy who can
later serve as his mother's champion.

The fourth version, *Beatrix,*[4] is found in several manuscripts
of the *Chevalier au Cygne* (ed. Hippeau, Paris, 1874–77), to
which story it has been completely joined. *Beatrix* opens with
a scene based upon an idea suggested in *Isomberte.* After the
heroine of that version had borne several children at one birth,
she was in consequence accused of adultery[5] and condemned
to death unless she could find a champion to prove her innocence. In *Beatrix* this idea appears at the beginning of the
story in the conversation between Beatrix and her husband,
King Oriant. A beggar woman, the mother of twins, is taunted
by Beatrix with being an unfaithful wife. The taunt is repeated by her own jealous mother-in-law, Matabrune, when in
time Beatrix herself gives birth to six sons and one daughter.
The story then follows the same course as *Isomberte* but with

---

[3] Paris, *Rom.* XIX, 323, n. 4, thought that in the type story the heroine
escapes from the wooing of her own father. See *Emare* here, notes 6, 16.

[4] It was this version chiefly which found representation in art. Cf. the
account of the fourteenth-century ivory casket showing thirty-six scenes
from the romance which is given by Gibbs, *Chevelere Assigne,* p. vii ff.
Cf. *Jahrbuch d. Kunsthistorischen Sammlungen des allerhöchsten Kaiser-
hauses,* XX, 265; XXXIV, 68–69; *Jahrbuch der K. K. Centralcommission f.
Denkmalpflege,* 1912, Beilage, p. 118; F. Bond, *Misericords,* for other references.

[5] See *Lay le Freine* here.

many additional details. Important among these are the name
Hélias, given to the boy, who is represented as a typical forest-
reared youth, of the " Great Fool " type, amazed at horses, armor,
etc.,[6] the long account of the flight and ultimate punishment of
Matabrune, and the angel's command which starts Hélias in a
boat drawn by his untransformed brother-swan off on new adventures. The author of this version claims at least to be the
first to tell this story as the true account of the origin of the
Chevalier au Cygne (v. 28–31). He gives an elaborate account
of the judicial combat in which Hélias in his mother's defense
overcomes Mauquarre, and of his subsequent fight with Mauquarre's brother. In all this the original fairy tale element gives
place to heroic and epic elements.

From the names Oryens, Bewtrys, Matabryne, as well as from
the context of the story, it is evident that the Middle English
poem belongs to this fourth version. Especially to the taste of
the English poet were the scenes of violence and brutality.
With gusto the old Queen accuses Bewtrys and with zeal the
servants " slongen here deepe — in a dymme prysoun " (v. 86).
Young Enyas, coming to act as his mother's champion, when
after many years she is at last brought to the stake, has his
hair torn out by the furious Matabryne ere he can assure her:
" Thy hedde shalle lye on thy lappe for thy false turnes."
To the young hero, Malkedras vows that he cares not the value
of a cherry for the sign of the cross. The poem is wholly without courtliness or chivalry and so popular in manner that a
ballad-like phrase such as, " she nykked him with nay," comes
casily into the text. The incident itself of the small " chyle "
fighting with the burly Malkedras is of the sort that made popular the various versions of the ballad of *Sir Aldingar*. The
pietistic element is strongly marked: God, who saved Susannah
" fro sorwefulle domus," saves also Queen Bewtrys from death;
a hermit and a hind, " whylle our lorde wolde," care together
for the infants exposed in the forest; an angel follows the boy
hero; bells ring without hands (v. 272) during his fight for his
mother, and an adder springs from the cross that Malkedras

[6] See Paris, *Rom.* XIX, 322, n. 2, on the imitation of the beginning of the
Perceval story. For a detailed treatment of the different versions see R.
Griffith, *Sir Perceval of Galles* (Ch. I, The Hero's Forest Rearing), Chicago,
1912. Cf. Bruce, *Evolution Arthur. Romance*, pp. 306, 310, 339.

derides. Roughly but effectively, too, the English poet introduces the note of humor, especially in the comments of the
forest-reared boy who asks about his horse that " etethe on yren "
and of the shield that bears heavily down on his own young
neck. At the end the poet gives a genuine touch of pathos to
the account of the five swans that again become boys when
their chains are restored to them, and of the sorrow of the
sixth whose chain had been partly destroyed. " He bote hym
self with his bylle," we are told, " his feyre federes fomede upon
blode," because " for losse of his cheyne " he must always remain a swan. Nothing in this version anticipates the service he
later renders the brother who is, however, even here, christened
" Chevelere assygne."

VERSIONS. (II, THE KNIGHT OF THE SWAN.) The story of
the knight who came, conducted by a swan, to the assistance
of a lady whom he freed from persecution by killing her enemy
in a judicial combat, of his marriage with her or her daughter,
of his departure when asked a tabooed question concerning his
origin, and of the descendants of this marriage, was known in
two forms in early French and German literature. In the
French versions the originally unrelated tale of the Swan-Children was added to that of the Swan-Guided Knight. The Swan-
Guide was identified with the youth in the fairy tale who did
not regain his human form. The brother whom he served was
called Helias, and it was Helias who rescued the widowed
Duchess of Bouillon, married her daughter, Ida, and through her
became the ancestor of the famous Crusader, Godfrey of Bouillon.
The story, which thus accounted for the origin of Godfrey, became the introductory portion, in the order of events, of the
group of stories about the Crusades of which Godfrey was pre-
eminently the hero. This group or cycle, as it ultimately became,
had five branches represented by (1) *La Naissance du Chevalier
au Cygne*, (2) *Le Chevalier au Cygne et les Enfances Godefroi*,
(3) the *Chanson d'Antioche* (Ed. P. Paris, 1848), in part probably the oldest portion of the whole cycle as it seems originally
to have been composed by Richard le Pélerin between 1125–
1138, (4) *Les Chetifs*, a story of five knights of the first Crusade, of their capture by the pagan king, Corbaran d'Oliferne,
and of their escape, and (5) the *Chanson de Jérusalem* (ed.

Hippeau, 1868), the story of the capture of the city by the Crusaders in 1099.[7]

There are extant nine manuscripts[8] of the metrical version of the *Chevalier au Cygne,* of which none are earlier than the thirteenth century. From the Paris Arsenal manuscript, which bears the date 1268 and includes all the five branches, it is evident that by that time all these divisions of the work were complete. The oldest French version of the Swan-Knight story itself was contained, according to Gaston Paris (2, pp. 407–08), in the *Chanson d'Antioche* (cf. Blondeaux, xxxviii, 165; Jaffray, p. 6). This amounts to not much more than a mere account of the mysterious coming and departure of the Swan-Knight and resembles a similarly brief version introduced into the *Karlamagnus Saga* concerning a knight there known as Gérard Cygne. The legendary hero is claimed in the *Chanson d'Antioche* as an ancestor of Godfrey's in order to match the claim put forth by his military rival, the Duke of Normandy, that as the latter is a descendant of Doon de Mayence his lineage is superior to Godfrey's, and his right to be the champion of the Crusaders is therefore greater. Neither in this nor in two earlier allusions to the story that are known, is there any specific mention of the name taboo or of the famous traditional combat of the Swan-Knight. But the allusions, brief as they are, and the number of extant manuscripts, indicate that by the end of the twelfth century his story was popular and well-known in Lorraine, though it is difficult to say which text is nearest to the original version. The fact that the Berne manuscript, which was considered the oldest text until Smith and Miss Einstein brought the matter into question, refers to an earlier "estoire" preserved at Mayence, has raised the difficult problem concerning the localization of the story in that supposed original. The Berne Manuscript itself, the German poem of *Lohengrin,* and the Chronicle of the Abbey of Brogne (*cir.* 1210) agree with these Paris

[7] Cf. Blondeaux, *Revue de Belg.* xxxviii, 160; Gautier, *Bibliog. des Chansons de Geste,* 1897, pp. 77–81.

[8] Miss Einstein, pp. 725–27, gave the most complete list but she omitted Add. MS. 36615. Cf. *Brit. Mus. Cat. of Add. MSS.,* 1905–10, p. 157. In her opinion the *Enfances Godefroi* was written by a layman between 1161 and 1187. The author of the *Chevalier au Cygne,* either a monk or a clerk, she thought must have written between 1170 and 1182.

manuscripts in localizing the arrival and combat of the Swan-Knight in Mayence; other manuscripts put these scenes at Nimèque (Krüger, Rom. xxiii, 449). Blöte (2, p. 414) believed that the use of the name Mayence was occasional and due to the exigencies of rime, but Paris (2, p. 405) argued strongly that Mayence was in the original French version and that Nimèque was a variation carelessly introduced into a manuscript which gave rise to the use of the name in later texts. In his opinion the Brogne chronicle followed a lost French manuscript of more ancient date than any that is now extant.

Leaving the French versions for the moment, we may note that in the German versions the oldest is the Lohengrin story, written about 1205, in Wolfram von Eschenbach's *Parzival* (ed. E. Martin, Halle, 1900–03). The name of the Swan-Knight, Loherangrin, *i.e.*, Loheraingarin, Garin le Loherin, Garin of Lorraine, is suggestive of the locality from which came the French tale that was presumably Wolfram's source. By making Loherangrin the son of Parzival, the king of the Grail Castle at Monsalvaesch from which the young hero himself departs, Wolfram loosely linked the legend of the Swan-Knight with that of the Grail. The poet tells of the writings on the Grail that bid Loherangrin go forth to champion the young Duchess of Brabant, of the coming of the Swan-boat for him, of his arrival at Antwerp, of his great combat with the lady's foe, of Loherangrin's marriage to the lady, and of his departure when she asks him the tabooed question concerning his name and origin. At a later date in the same century were written *Der Schwanritter* (ed. F. Roth, 1861) by Konrad von Würzburg, and the anonymous poem, *Lohengrin* (ed. H. Rückert, 1858), which follows closely, though with a good deal of incidental elaboration, the version by Wolfram. In these poems the incidents of the story take place at Antwerp, Nimèque, Cologne and Mainz, the persecuted lady is the Duchess of Brabant or her daughter, and by wedding the young woman the hero becomes duke. In Konrad's poem the two sons of this marriage are said to have been the founders of the houses of Cleves and Gueldres. This is the earliest reference to a tradition which grew steadily in political importance (Blöte, 1; Jaffray, ch. viii). In Brabant itself, from the fourteenth century, an independent version of the legend was current in which the Swan-Knight was identified with Brabon Silvius, the first legendary duke of Brabant. In this version the hero is made the contemporary of Julius Caesar and Octavian, is represented as delivering Antwerp from the power of a giant who took the tribute of a cut hand from travellers, and as following a swan which led him to Valenciennes ("dats Swanendale in dietsche"), where he received the hospitality of the two Swanes, mother and daughter, and returned bringing the mother's gift to Octavian and receiving from him the right to marry the maiden (*Cornicke van Brabant*, summarized by Blöte, 7, pp. 24–28). In general this story shows the influence of rationalization and a very incomplete mastery of traditional material. Its fifteenth-century author, Hennen von Merchtenen, refers to the "Clarasien van Jacop van Merlant" as his source for the account of Brabon (Breboen) from which Brabant received its name. Blöte (7, p. 30 ff.), thought this source was actually written between 1320 and 1330 by some unknown author. Many subsequent versions of the Brabon legend are known.

The popularity of the *Chevalier au Cygne* in its non-political forms continued all through the thirteenth and fourteenth centuries. In the thirteenth-century *Karlamagnus Saga*, to which reference has already been made, the legend is connected with the Emperor, and its hero, Gérard Swan, is represented as the friend of Roland and the husband of Charles's sister. In this version nothing is said of the tabooed question and the knight is hailed as coming from God (Blondeaux, XXXVIII, 231). In an Icelandic saga of later date the hero is called Hélis and is said to be the son of Julius Caesar (Jaffray, p. 104). In his *Speculum Naturale* Vincent of Beauvais briefly summarized the Swan-Knight story, localizing it at Cologne and telling simply of the coming and departure of the knight. In neither of these texts is any reference made to the Swan-Children nor is any explanation offered for the swan and the knight he brings (Blondeaux, *ibid.*, p. 164). In the fifteenth century, according to Krüger (2, p. 424), was compiled the huge enlargement of the story found in the Brussels manuscript published by Baron de Reiffenberg (*Monuments pour servir à l'Histoire des Provinces de Namur, de Hainaut, et de Luxembourg*, 1846–50, vols. IV, V, VI), and known also in a manuscript of 1469 now at Lyons.

This version was later refashioned as a prose romance. Among the best known of these prose redactions was that of Pierre Desrey of Troyes.

ORIGIN. The fairy-tale theme of the Swan-Children seems to be of very ancient date and of unlimited extent. The ancient Celtic tale of the Children of Lir, now known only in eighteenth-century texts, attributes the transformation of the children to the hostile magic of a stepmother who is jealous of their father's love for them. The subsequent account of the sufferings of the swans and the religious elements that are introduced into the story, differentiate it entirely from that form in which the theme appears in the *Dolopathos* account. Lot (p. 63), however, pointed out that the divine origin of the Children of Lir explains in a sense the semi-supernatural nature of the mother in the *Dolopathos* version, and that the gold or silver chain by which the transformation of each swan is accomplished, far from having been suggested by the episode in the Swan-Knight legend in which the swan draws the swan-boat by means of a precious chain, was an ancient and original element in the story of the Swan-Children. He paralleled it by the *Serglige Conculaind* in which two goddesses appear to the hero under the guise of swans linked by a chain of gold. To this might be added the account in the *Tochmarc Etain* in which a god-like pair take flight as swans similarly linked together. Other instances have been cited by Blöte (*Zts. für. deut. Altertum*, XXXVIII, 272) and by Poisson (p. 186) who believed the Old Irish legend of divine beings transformed into swans was introduced during the Carolingian period into the Rhine monasteries by Irish monks. To one of these monks, among whom the knowledge of Greek was preserved even through the Dark Ages, Poisson (p. 195) also attributed the naming of the Swan-Knight. The name Hélias, he thought, came from that of the prophet Elias whose name and story had absorbed some suggestions from the myth of the Sun God Helios. Dechelette's evidence (*Revue Archéologique*, Paris, 1909, 1, 305) that in certain primitive representations the solar disc was associated with a boat, supposedly that which conveyed the Sun across the ocean paths from night to day, convinced Poisson (p. 193) that the Swan-Knight legend itself came from a dim surviving memory of the old pagan myth, and that it was, like the story of the Swan-Children, Celtic in origin.[9]

Another explanation for the origin of the Swan-Knight story is that offered by Blöte (*Zts. f. rom. Phil.* xxi, 179). He found it in the history of Roger of Toeni, also called Roger the Spaniard, whose legendary emblem was a swan, who rescued the Countess of Barcelona from a Moorish assault (*cir.* 1018) and who married her daughter. Roger's granddaughter, Godehild of Toeni, married Baldwin, the brother of Godfrey of Bouillon, and Roger's story and emblem thus became associated with the famous Crusader. To Gaston Paris, on the other hand, who was impressed by the gaps and assumptions in Blöte's argument and the lateness of the evidence for it, the Swan-Knight story was an ancient totemic legend of Lorraine, arbitrarily attached in the twelfth century to the house of Bouillon and only later connected with the Toeni family (*Rom.* xxvi, 581). The local legend would naturally be drawn into the cycle of stories growing up about one who was not only Duke of Lower Lorraine but also one of the most famous men of his time. A possible confusion of the word Signe (Crusader's cross) with Cygne, has also been suggested in explanation of the association of the legend with Godfrey (Edwardes, *Summary*, p. 179).

The early history and associations of the Swan-Knight legend, quite aside from the extant literary versions, are full of interest. The first allusion to the story is in a Latin letter written about 1170 by Gui de Bazoches in which Baldwin, Godfrey's brother, is spoken of as " nepos militis ejus, Per vada cui Rheni dux fuit albus olor." [10] About twenty years later William, Archbishop of Tyre, in his history of the first Crusade, referred sceptically to the legend which made the Swan-Knight an ancestor of Godfrey of Bouillon as a well-known fable. The

[9] A different and even less credible folkloristic theory was given by Pestalozzi, p. 150, who believed in the Germanic origin of the tale. To him the Swan-knight was originally a demon or elf who must disappear upon being asked his name; he was also originally identical with the swan, since this was the form he assumed in attempting to enter the world of men. For the later development of this rationalized fairy tale Pestalozzi accepted Blöte's theory of its association with Roger of Toeni.

[10] Cf. Paris, *Rom.* xxx, 406; Blondeaux, *Revue de Belg.* xxxviii, 163; Blöte 5, pp. 185–91; Jaffray, p. 4.

brevity of the allusion to the story in the *Dolopathos* has been interpreted as showing that the learned author had a similar awareness of this fact and so wished to avoid the tale (Huet, p. 309). The popularity of the legend increased with its association with the house of Bouillon and ultimately resulted, it would seem, in the attachment of the story to still other families. In England the legend appeared in connection with the Norman Radulf of Toeni, son of Roger the Spaniard, and founder of the house of Stafford, to whose descent from the Swan-Knight, in a passage in his *Lives of the Abbots*, Matthew Paris (1250) made somewhat belated allusion (Blöte, 4, p. 342). The marriage before 1125 of Matilde, niece of Godfrey of Bouillon, to Stephen of Blois, may well have stimulated English interest in the traditional legends of her family. Extracts copied in the thirteenth century in the *Red Book of the Exchequer* from a monastic register of Feversham Abbey, founded by Matilda and Stephen in 1148, show that the monastery possessed a *Liber de Cigno* which was possibly a royal gift (Liebermann, p. 106). In the fourteenth and fifteenth centuries the Tony family, the Beauchamps, the Bohuns, and the Staffords, used a swan as a heraldic device, and in some instances claimed descent from the Swan-Knight. This was notably true of that Edward, Duke of Buckingham and Earl of Stafford, " linially dyscended of — Helyas, the Knight of the Swanne," at whose instigation Copland made his version of the story of Helyas (Blöte, 4, p. 349).

On the continent similar claims were made from time to time. These have been investigated with interesting results by Blöte (3). Through the marriage in 1179 of Matilde of Boulogne to Heinrich IV of Brabant, the legend came to be associated with the rulers of Brabant. In the twelfth century the old title of Duke of Lower Lorraine was discarded for that of Duke of Brabant, and this, it will be remembered, was the title given to the Swan-Knight after his marriage with the Duchess of Brabant in Wolfram's story. Blöte has distinguished three periods in the development of the story in Brabant, and to the second of these belongs the period of its rationalization. The earliest specific reference to the Swan-Knight as the ancestor of the Duke of Brabant seems to be that of the Flemish poet, Jacob van Maerlent, in the *Spiegel Historial* 1286–90 (Blöte, 7, p. 3).

A similar claim made by the house of Cleves,[11] which has been held to antedate even that of the house of Brabant, has been shown by Blöte (1) to be equally void of mythological significance or of real antiquity.

BIBLIOGRAPHY

TEXTS: (1) Cotton Caligula A II, ed. Utterson, Roxburghe Club, Lond., 1820; ed. H. H. Gibbs, *EETSES.* VI, 1868. (2) *Helias, Knyght of the Swanne,* pr. Wynkyn de Worde, 1512; repr. from copy in the library of Robert Hoe, Grolier Club, N. Y., 1901.

STUDIES: Cf. Billings, *Guide,* pp. 228–29; Edwardes, *Summary,* Index; Wells, *Manual,* p. 777.

Blondeux, F. "La Légende du Chevalier au Cygne," *Revue de Belgique, Brussels,* 1903: (1) "Les Débuts de la Légende," XXXVIII, 158–76; (II) "Les Versions de la Légende," pp. 231–42; (III) "Les Destinées de la Légende," XXXIX, 40–49, 371–80.

Blöte, J. (1) "Das Aufkommen des clevischen Schwanritters," *Zts. f. deut. Alter.* XLII, 1–53 (1898). Rev. G. Paris, Rom. XXVII, 334–5. (2) "Die Sage vom Schwanritter in der Brogner Chronik von c. 1211," *Zts. f. deut. Alter.* XLIV, 407–20 (1900). (3) "Der historische Schwanritter," *Zts. f. rom. Phil.* XXI, 176–91; XXV, 1–44 (1897–1901). (4) "Der Ursprung der Schwanrittertradition in englischen Adelsfamilien," *Eng. Stud.* XXIX, 337–68 (1901). (5) "Der Schwanritterpassus in einem Brief des Guido von Bazoches," *Zts. f. deut. Alter.* XLVII, 185–91 (1903). (6) "Mainz in der Sage vom Schwanritter," *Zts. f. rom. Phil.* XXVII, 1–24 (1903). (7) *Das Aufkommen der Sage von Brabon Silvius, dem brabantischen Schwanritter.* 127 pp. Amsterdam, 1904. Rev. *Litteraturbl.* XXVII, col. 1–3 (1906).

Chauvin, V. *Bibliographie des Ouvrages Arabes.* Liège, Leipzig, 1904. (Bibliography, pp. 206–208).

Einstein, M. *Beiträge z. überlieferung des Chevalier au Cygne u. der Enfances Godefroi.* Diss Berne, 1910. *Rom. Forsch.* XXIX, 721–63 (1911).

Hilka, A. *Historia septem Sapientem,* II, Johannis de Alta Silva, *Dolopathos sive de Rege et septem sapientibus.* 112 pp. Heidelberg, 1913.

---

[11] Cf. Jaffray, Ch. VIII, The Cleves Legend, especially pp. 88–89, for an account of the famous Fête du Faisan, 1454, of the entry of Adolph of Clève as Le Chevalier au Cygne, and of Adolph's own banquet at which there was a representation of the Swan-Knight, his boat, and swan.

Huet, G. " Sur quelques formes de la légende du *Chevalier au Cygne*," *Rom.* XXXIV, 206–14 (1905).

Jaffray, R. *The Two Knights of the Swan, Lohengrin and Helyas. A Study of the Legend of the Swan Knight.* 121 pp. N. Y., Lond., 1910.

Kawczynski, M. " Le Chevalier au Cygne; Huon de Bordeaux." *Bull. de l'Acad. de Cracovie*, 1902.

Kleinschmidt, W. *Das Verhältnis der Baudoin de Sebourc zu den Chevalier au Cygne.* Göttingen, 1908.

Krüger, A. (1) " Zur mittelengl. Romanze, *Cheulere Assigne*," *Archiv.* LXXVII, 168–80 (1887). (2) " Les Manuscripts de la Chanson du *Chevalier au Cygne* et de *Godefroi de Bouillon*," *Rom.* XXVIII, 421–26 (1899).

Liebermann, F. " *Chevalier au Cygne* in England," *Archiv.* CVII, 106–07 (1901).

Lot, F. " Le Mythe des Enfants-Cygnes," *Rom.* XXI, 62–67 (1892).

Mazorriaga, E. *La Leyenda del Cavallero del Çisne.* Transcripción anotada del códice de la Biblioteca Nacional. Madrid, 1914. I, Texte.

Paris, Gaston. (1) *La Naissance du Chevalier au Cygne* (ed. Todd), *Rom.* XIX, 314–40 (1890).
(2) " Mayence et Nimèque dans le *Chevalier au Cygne*," *Rom.* XXX, 404–09 (1901).

Pestalozzi, R. " Geschichte d. deut. Lohengrinsage." *Neue Jahrbücher f. das klass. Alterthum*, Leipzig, XXIII (1909), 147–58.

Poisson, G. " L'Origine celtique de la légende de Lohengrin," *Revue Celt.* XXXIV, 182–202 (1913).

Rank, O. " Die Lohengrinsage, Ein Beitrag zu ihrer Motivgestaltung u. Deutung." *Schriften z. angewandten Seelenkunde*, XIII. Vienna, 1912.

Smith, H. " Some Remarks on a Berne MS. of the Chanson du *Chevalier au Cygne* et *Godefroi de Bouillon*," *Rom.* XXXVIII, 120–28 (1909).

KNIGHT OF COURTESY, or THE CHÂTELAIN DE COUCI

VERSIONS. The gruesome final incident in the *Knight of Courtesy* and stories analogous to it, gives them the name of the Legend of the Eaten Heart.[1] There are at least fourteen literary versions which Matzke (1, p. 1) divided into two groups. In the first the husband kills his wife's lover and gives her his daintily cooked heart to eat. She thereupon kills herself either by falling from a high place or by self-imposed starvation. The most important versions in this group are: (1) the two Provençal biographies, one much longer than the other, of the Provençal troubadour, Guillem de Cabestaing,[2] accounts that are found in documents of the thirteenth and fourteenth centuries; (2) Boccaccio's story in the *Decamerone*, Day IV, Tale 9, of Messer Guiglielmo Rossiglione e Messer Guiglielmo Guardastagno, which the author asserts he took from a Prov-

[1] See G. Cecioni, " Il Cuore mangiato," *Rivista Contemp.*, 1, Sept. 1888; H. Patzig, *Zur Geschichte der Herzmäre* (progr.) Berlin, 1891; Ahlström, *Studier i den Fornfranska Lais-Litteraturen*, pp. 127–29, Upsala, 1892. Matzke (1) reduced Patzig's twenty-three versions to fourteen. Cf. Gaston Paris, *Rom.* VIII, 343–73 (1879); *Histoire Litt. de la France*, XXVIII, 352–90 (1881); Child, *Ballads*, V, 33–35 (1894).

[2] Ed. by C. Chabaneau, *Les Biographies des Troubadours en langue Provençale*, p. 99 ff., Toulouse, 1885. Cf. E. Beschnidt, *Die Biographie des Trobadors Guillem de Capestaing*, Diss., Marburg, 1879. Matzke, 1, p. 4, strongly questioned Beschnidt's conclusion that the shorter biography was the earlier; to Matzke it seemed simply an abridgment of the longer text. Hauvette, *Rom.* XLI, 187, noted another derivative of the Provençal biography in the *Comptes Amoureux de Madame Jeanne Flore*, Lyons, c. 1540. Another variant is to be found in the story told of the Spanish Marquise of Astorga and the Countess d'Aulnoys (*Memoires de la Cour d'Espagne*, I, 203). In this it is the Marquise who in a jealous rage kills her husband's mistress, serves him with the dead woman's heart, and shows him later her severed head. Cf. *Rom.* VIII, 362, n. 4.

ençal source;[3] (3) Sercambi's ninety-sixth story,[4] *De prava amicitia vel societate* (R. Renier, *Novelle inedite,* Turin, 1889, p. 338) which is closely related to Boccaccio's tale but is not identical with it; and (4) an Indian folk-tale concerning the Punjab hero, the Rajah Rasàlu (Swynnerton).[5] In these stories the husband kills the lover, cuts out his heart, and in two versions, the longer biography of Guillem and the Indian tale, shows to the lady the lover's severed head or his mutilated corpse as proof of his death. Matzke (1, p. 8) believed all these versions had a common source but that the western forms were derived from the same lost Provençal intermediary.

Two of the remaining versions in this group are the oldest texts of the story. One is the eight-line Lay of *Guirun* which Isolt sings in the *Tristan*[6] (ed. Bédier, 1, 295) of Thomas. In another late twelfth-century version, the lay of *Ignaure* (Monmerqué et Michel, *Théâtre frc. au moyen âge,* 1842) the theme is grotesquely treated. The lay tells of a knight, the lover of twelve ladies, who is killed by their enraged husbands and his heart given them to eat. After this they refuse all other food. Coarse derivatives of this tale are the story of Linaure, a Provençal troubabour (c. 1190) whose history is mentioned by Arnaud de Mersan (Raynouard, *Choix de Poésies,* Paris, 1816–21, II, 308), and the sixty-second tale in the *Cento Novelle*

---

[3] Gaston Paris, *Hist. Litt.* xxviii, 378, did not believe that Boccaccio followed the extant Provençal story of Guillem, since in the Italian version the hero is not described as a poet. In Hauvette's opinion the differences in name and detail between the Italian and the Provençal text were best accounted for by the probability that Boccaccio worked from his memory of an abbreviated version of Guillem's life. Cf. Patzig, p. 21. For a compact interesting list of versions including many modern analogues see A. C. Lee, *The Decameron,* Lond., 1909, pp. 143–52.

[4] This did not appear in Matzke's list nor in any of the usual studies of the legend. It was briefly cited by Miss E. N. Jones, *Boccaccio and His Imitators,* p. 23, Chicago, 1910; also by A. C. Lee, *op. cit.,* p. 148. In this version by Sercambi the names are unlike those given in the biographies or by Boccaccio. The cruel husband is called Marsilio of Sivereto; the lady, Caterina de' Salimbeni da Siena; the lover, Count Guarnieri di Monte Scudaio. In this the unfaithful wife is given the face of the lover, not his heart, and stabs herself to death.

[5] See also C. Swynnerton, *Folk-Lore Journal,* 1, Lond. 1883; Clouston, *Popular Tales,* Eden, 1887, II, 187. Cf. Hauvette, p. 200, for other variants.

[6] Cf. Schofield, *PMLA.* xv, 122–25. In some instances the severed heart episode was associated with the hero Graelent.

Antiche.[7] In this the hero is a mere rustic, and the amorous ladies instead of dying found a " convent " where the most excessive hospitality is practised.

In the second group of stories the hero, dying at some distance from the lady, commands a servant to take her his dead heart. But the husband intercepts the servant, takes the heart, and has it served to his wife in the same fashion as in Version I. The earliest extant version in this group is the short metrical tale, *Die Herzmähre* (F. Roth, Frankfurt a. M. 1846) by Konrad von Würzburg (d. 1287). This was later turned into an exemplum in the sermon-book, *Sermones Parati de tempore et de sanctis* (No. 124 reprinted by Matzke, 2, p. 18). Konrad's source according to Gaston Paris (*Rom.* VIII, 366) was also the source of the long romance of the late thirteenth or early fourteenth century by Jakemon Maket. This romance, the well-known *Châtelain de Couci,*[8] was the most elaborate of all the literary versions of the story, and was frequently referred to by such writers as Froissart, the Knight of La Tour Landri, and Christine de Pisan.[9] Its influence may be traced in the Dutch adaptation, *Van den Borchgrave van Couchi* (De Vries, Leiden, 1887), a poem of which two long fragments in a fourteenth-century manuscript are known.

From Maket's romance seems to have been derived also the short Middle English version which contains five hundred lines written in four-line stanzas riming abab. Brandl (Paul's *Grundriss* II, 697) thought its dialect that of the South Midland. It was composed in the fifteenth century but the only extant text is that of Copland's edition. Deferring for the moment the comparison of the English with the French romance, we may note the further appearance of versions related

[7] Ed. J. H. Heitz, Strassburg, 1908; German trans. by J. Ulrich, Leipzig, 1905. Cf. *Rom.* VIII, 368; XLI, 193.

[8] Ed. Crapelet, 1829; summarized by Langlois, pp. 186–221. The author's name is known only from an acrostic signature. Early readings gave the name Sakesep. For that of Maket, see Matzke, 2, p. 12, n. 28; Langlois, p. 187.

[9] Cf. Michel, *Les Chansons du Châtelain de Couci,* Paris, 1830, p. xxxiii; cf. Smythe, p. 169. The continued popularity of the romance is shown by the manuscripts listed in such inventories as those of the library of Charles V, 1373, of Marguerite de Male, 1405, or the libraries of Brussels, 1487, and of Bruges, 1567. Michel, p. xxvi.

to Maket's in the *Chronique de France*[10] (to 1380), printed by Claude Fauchet in 1581, and again in the *Anecdotes de la Cour de Philippe-Auguste* (III, 262–320) published by Mlle. de Lussan in 1793. This typical eighteenth-century version started the story upon a new era of popularity.[11] In it the heroine was given the name of Gabrielle de Vergi, and thus was completed the confusion which had already existed between the anonymous Lady of Faïel who was beloved by the Châtelain de Couci, and Gabrielle, the heroine of the delightful and pathetic thirteenth-century romance, *La Chatelaine de Vergi*.[12]

Of the remaining versions of the story, the most important is Boccaccio's famous story in the *Decamerone*, Day IV, Tale 1, of *Guiscardo e Ghismonda*, in which Tancred, the father of Ghismonda, takes the place of the cruel husband. Through the translation of this story in Painter's *Palace of Pleasure*, 1566 (ed. Jacobs, Lond., 1890, I, 180), or Tuberville's *Tragical Tales*, 1576, or a chap-book version, it became the foundation of many English plays[13] and poems. Among these was the little ballad of *Lady Diamond* (Child, No. 269, vol. v, 29) in which, as in the majority of the ballad versions in Italian, Scandinavian, or

[10] Reprinted by Matzke, 2, pp. 6–8, from Fauchet's *Recueil de l'Origine de la Langue et de la Poësie françoise*. Matzke thought this text represented a version older than the romance, and closely related to the Provençal biography. In the *Chronique* the hero, Regnault de Coucy, is not a trouvère, but a warrior who willingly joins in the Crusade of Richard the Lion-Heart; he receives from his lady "ung las de soye," instead of the braid of hair which in the *Châtelain*, the Lady of Faïel gave to her lover; he dies on land, not as did the Châtelain from a poisoned arrow, and on his homeward journey. These and other details make it hard to believe that the *Châtelain* could have been the source of the *Chronique*.

[11] Cf. Michel, p. xxi; Paris, *Rom.* VIII, 371; Lorenz, pp. 119–38. See also Lorenz, *Die altfrz. Versnovelle von der Kastellanin von Vergi in spätern Bearbeitungen*, Diss. 138 pp. Halle, 1909.

[12] Ed. Raynaud, Paris, 1910; 1912 (rev. *Rom. Rev.* VI, 112); trans. by Alice Kemp-Welch, Lond. 1903. On the story in Art, see W. Bombe, La Châtelaine de Vergy en Italie, *Revue des Langues Romans*, LVII, 262–91 (1914); *Gazette des Beaux-Arts*, Sept. 1911, p. 231 ff; see also E. Bertaux, La Femme et l'Art du Môyen-Age français, *Revue de Paris*, Nov. 15, 1909, pp. 367–90. In this romance the exquisitely sensitive heroine dies when she thinks that her lover has revealed, despite her prohibition, the secret of her love. The hero commits suicide when he finds her dead body. The perfect constancy of the two pairs of lovers in the *Châtelain de Couci* and in the *Châtelaine de Vergi* associated them together and probably facilitated a certain confusion about them.

[13] Cf. F. Schelling, *Elizabethan Drama*, N. Y., 1908, Index.

German, the lover's heart is sent in a cup of gold to the lady by her angry father. In the Swedish song, *Hertig Fröjdenborg och Fröken Adelin,* an eighteenth-century broadside, the original trait is preserved, and the lady eats the heart of her lover. The popular versions seem to mingle traits that belong to Boccaccio's two stories or their sources, but in a German meisterlied, *Vom dem Bremberger's end und Tod* (von der Hagen, *Minnesinger,* 1838, IV, 281), of the sixteenth century, there is a curious reversion to the most primitive type of the story. The husband kills the lover, cuts off his head, and gives his heart to the lady to eat (Child, p. 32). The lover in this version is said to be the minnesinger, Reinmann von Brennenberg, who lived in the middle of the thirteenth century and who loved a duchess of Austria. The fact that the hero here is a poet is paralleled in *Guirun,* in the *Châtelain de Couci,* in *Linaure* and *Guillem de Cabestaing,* and seems to represent a distinct line of tradition. In Matzke's opinion (1, p. 8) it was due to an innovation made by the author of the longer biography of Guillem, and probably did not appear in the original version.

The *Knight of Courtesy* is an abbreviated, indeed, an expurgated, version of the *Châtelain.* It is so utterly vague as to names and places of the French story, that it seems probable the English author was simply writing from memory. The worth of his story has been variously estimated. Gaston Paris (*Rom.* VIII, 369) called it "charmant"; Dr. Rickert (p. LI) considered it "poor in everything but sentimentality"; interesting only as "representing an aspect of mediaeval psychology, being a singular combination of morbid hyper-analysis with sheer brutality." It may be granted that the English poet is poor in invention; he intrudes, for instance, the hackneyed account of a dragon fight among the adventures befalling the hero after his separation from his lady-love. But it is also true that he avoids the prolixity of the French poet without losing the essential pathos of the story. The eight thousand lines of the French romance present a brilliant picture of the pageantry of life in the late thirteenth century. It abounds in descriptions of beautiful caroles, of fêtes and tourneys and heraldic devices;[14] it is a characteristic product of *l'amour courtois* with

[14] Among the heroes present are Simon de Montfort and the Sire de Joinville and Jehans de Niyelle (Nesles). Was this the Jean de Nesles for whom

the usual courtly exaltation of lover over husband. Much in the romance is made of the way in which the Châtelain blithely woos the wife of his friend and neighbor, of the rebuffs and disappointments he must endure before the capricious lady grants him her favor, of the songs he makes for her,[15] of the stratagems and disguises which are necessary for the lovers' meeting, and of the friends to whom they frequently confide their emotions.[16]

All the picturesque detail and all the elaborate love-making are omitted by the English poet. His lovers love, but in purity. After their one mutual confession, they meet but once again when, as in the French tale, she gives him locks of her yellow hair to wear henceforth on his helmet. In the French version the hero comes to his death in Palestine as a Crusader of Richard the First of England; in the English story he dies at a siege of Rhodes, presumably that of 1443 (Rickert, p. L).

ORIGIN. The ultimate origin of the Legend of the Eaten Heart is still a matter of debate. Remotely its horror may be paralleled in the story of Tantalus serving his own son Pelops to the gods, or in the vengeance of Atreus when he gave his brother Thyestes the flesh of the latter's sons, or in the tale of Procne who gave her faithless husband the body of their child Itys. Likewise in Norse legend there is a story of Gudrun, who, in vengeance for the death of her brothers, gave to her lord Atli the roasted hearts of their two children (Vigfusson and Powell, *Corpus Poet. Boreale*, 1883, 1, 51). The legend in any of these forms is as ancient as it is terrible, but it is inherently improbable that the pre-Christian tradition had any

---

the *Perlesvaus* was written? The last historical reference to Jean among those cited by Evans (*High History of the Holy Grail*, Everyman ed., p. xii) is for 1225. Cf. Nitze, *MLN.*, XIV, 498 (1899). Prinet, p. 170, pointed out that the description of the arms of Jean is technically at fault.

15 In this the romance follows the fashion first set in the romance of *Guillaume de Dôle* (*Le Roman de la Rose*), *SATF.*, 1893, l. 8–15, — at least according to its author's own assertion.

16 Matzke, I, p. 15, noted the interweaving of characters and themes of typical romances; from the *Tristan* legend, the husband who spies on the interviews of the lovers; the wife's devoted friend and confidante; the ruses for the deceit of the husband, etc. Gobert, the Châtelain's faithful squire, serves the lovers by pretending to be the husband's spy.

direct connection with the mediaeval versions.[17] In them it was drawn into the usual triangle story of husband, lover, and wife, and found credence in a society only too familiar with outbursts of barbarous passion. But the question remains. Did the mediaeval story have its origin in fact or fiction, and if the last, did it come from the East or the West? Ahlström (*op. cit.*) believed that the tradition showed Germanic elements but thought its literary form derived from *Guirun*. Gaston Paris, chiefly because of the supposedly "Breton" lay of *Guirun*, believed in a Celtic origin. This theory he abandoned when the Indian tale of Rasálu came to light, and he voiced his agreement (*Rom.* xxi, 140) with Patzig that the story was originally an Eastern tale which had in some way come to be localized in Provence. The name Rasálu may have caused the story to be localized at Castel-Rossello in the duchy of Roussilon in Provence. Since the home of the troubadour, Guillem de Cabestaing, was not far from that of Raimon de Castel-Rossello, to whom he is known to have addressed some poems, the legendary association of the two was not unnatural. If the part of Rasálu were ascribed to Raimon, the identification of the poet with the lover of Rasálu's wife would follow. But all this is conjecture which is reducible simply to the fact that some form of the name Rossilon must have stood in the source of the Provençal biographies and of the Indian tale (Matzke, 2, p. 8).

The most serious argument against the belief that this source was Oriental was advanced by Hauvette (pp. 199–205). The Indian tale is admittedly dateless. There is in it nothing that is specifically Indian; indeed it belongs to that northern Punjab country which is, on account of its Mohammedan population, the least Indian part of all India. In the extant versions the story of Rasálu gives but comparatively minor place to the central episode of the Eaten Heart; its originators were more interested in the speaking parrot which betrays the wife's infidelity and in Rasálu's long preparations for revenge.[18] It is

---

[17] Hauvette, p. 195, discussed the allegorical idea of the Eaten Heart in connection with its use by such poets as Sordello or Dante (*Vita Nuova*, iii). In these and other references, the essential thought is that the heart will convey to another its own passionate virtue.

[18] In an Eastern tale of the type known as the Dog and the Lady

characteristic, Hauvette thought, that in this single version, the wife's suicide is prompted by her despairing anticipation of her husband's cruelty; in the western versions she dies so that she may never again touch food after tasting that which was noblest on earth. In other words, the Eaten Heart episode is not vitally emphasized in the Indian tale and we may infer that it was not an original, but a borrowed, element in the story.

This borrowed element, in Hauvette's opinion, was a version of Boccaccio's tale brought into India by some of those far-travelling Italians of the fourteenth and fifteenth centuries whose prolonged residence in India is a known fact. Matzke (1, p. 6) had previously dismissed this possibility of derivation on the ground that in Boccaccio's story nothing is said of the lover's severed head, and yet this trait appears in the story of Rasálu. But Matzke himself had proved that the detail belonged to Boccaccio's source story, and this might have been transferred to the East as easily as the Boccaccian tale itself.

There is no known reason, according to Langfors (p. 353), for the original association of the legend of the Eaten Heart with Guillem de Cabestaing, a man of whom history records not much more than the fact that in 1212 he fought at the battle of Las Nevas. If he were the same man as the troubadour, Guillem, to whom some nine love lyrics are attributed, he was at one time the friend of Raimon de Roussilon to whom two of the songs are dedicated (Langfors, p. 8). But no text before the end of the thirteenth century makes allusion to any tragic event happening to Guillem or to the wife of Raimon, a lady who was a widow when she married Raimon and who lived, apparently, to take still a third husband. The transference of the legend to the crusading poet known as the Châtelain de Couci was probably due to the invention of Jakemon Maket. By choosing the Châtelain as a type of amorous chevalier, the author was enabled to introduce into his story the actual songs of the

---

(Kittredge, " Gorlagon," *Harvard Studies*, VIII, 247, 252, n. 1), the faithless wife is betrayed by a faithful dog and is made to suffer a variety of horrible punishments. Only in a western version, the Latin text of the *Gesta Romanorum* (Oesterley, p. 355-6) does the punishment in the least resemble that of the Eaten Heart legend. In the *Gesta* the lady has to eat from her lover's skull. In the Latin romance of *Gorlagon* (Kittredge, p. 245), the lady had constantly to hold before her at table the bloody head of her lover.

Chevalier.[19] He localized the romance in Vermandois, a district of which he himself, to judge from his rimes, his knowledge of the country, etc., was a native (Langlois, p. 187). His choice for heroine of a lady of Faïel (Fayet), a place near St. Quentin, may have been due to the same interest in locality. In Maket's day Faïel had a château and was not without some importance (*Rom.* VIII, 361). But whatever the realism of place or the accuracy of observation of thirteenth-century manners and customs or the sophistication of sentiment in the *Châtelain de Couci*, its author did not succeed by virtue of these things in impressing his story on the imagination of men. That long-lasting impression came from the terrible and tragic theme he had borrowed and from its sad celebration of the loyalty in love " de quoi on doie faire conte."

BIBLIOGRAPHY

TEXTS: (1) Bodleian, edition printed in 1568 by William Copland; ed. Ritson, 1802, III, 193–218; Hazlitt, *Remains*, 1866, II, 64–87; trans. Rickert, *Romances of Love*, 1908, p. 141 ff.

STUDIES: Cf. Wells, *Manual*, p. 787.

Hauvette, H. "La 39e Nouvelle du Décaméron et la légende du Coeur Mangé," *Rom.* XLI, 184–205 (1912).

Langfors, A. "Le Troubadour Guilhem de Cabestanh," *Annales du Midi*, XXVI (1914): I, Les Chansons attribuées à Guilhem de Cabestanh, pp. 1–51; 189–99; II, Les Quatre Rédactions de la Biographie, pp. 199–225; III, Guilhem de Cabestanh Personnage Historique, pp. 349–356. Rev. *Neuphil. Mitteil.*, Helsingfors, 1915, p. 38.

Langlois, C. V. *La Société Française au XIIIe Siècle d'après dix romans d'aventure*, 2e ed. Paris, 1904; *La Châtelain de Coucy*, pp. 186–221; 3e ed. 1911.

---

[19] The romance refers to the Châtelain's name as Renault. Gaston Paris (*Rom.* VIII, 353) accepted this as the name of the Crusading poet. Fath, *Die Lieder des Castellans von Coucy*, Heidelberg, 1883, showed that the name of the historic trouvère was Gui de Couci who died and was buried at sea during the Fourth Crusade. Matzke, 2, p. 14, found no better explanation for the use of the name Renault than that it was " probably frequent in the well-known Coucy family." Since the same name appeared in Fauchet's *Chronique*, Matzke pointed out that Maket could not have been the first to associate a Renault de Coucy with the Eaten Heart tradition, though he was probably the first to identify Renault with the poetic Châtelain de Coucy. It may be said that few romances are more in need of historical and critical study than the *Châtelain*. It has not been edited since 1829.

Lorenz, E. *Die Kastellanin von Vergi in der Literatur Frankreichs, Italiens, der Niederlande, Englands u. Deutschlands; mit einem Anhange, Die "Kastellan von Couci" sage als "Gabrielle de Vergi" Legende,* pp. 117–38. Halle, 1909.

Matzke, J. (1) " The Legend of the Eaten Heart," *MLN.* XXVI, 1–8 (1911).
(2) " The Roman du Châtelain de Couci and Fauchet's Chronique," *Studies in honor of A. Marshall Elliot,* I, 1–18. Baltimore, 1913.

Prinèt, M. "Les Armoires dans le doman du *Châtelain de Coucy,*" *Rom.* XLVI, 161–79 (1920).

Siefken, O. *Das geduldige Weib,* pp. 69–71.

Smythe, Barbara. *Trobador Poets* (Guilhem de Cabestanh, pp. 169–181). N. Y., Lond., 1911.

Swynnerton, C. *Romantic Tales from the Panjab.* Westminster, 1903.

Zanders, J. *Die altprovenzalische Prosanovelle; eine literarhistorische Kritik der Trobador-Biographien,* pp. 113–27. Halle, 1913.

THE SQUYR OF LOWE DEGRE

VERSIONS. Late but not least in fame or significance among the English metrical romances is the *Squyr of Lowe Degre*. It was printed by Wynkyn de Worde about 1520, by William Copland between 1555 and 1560, was licensed for printing to John Kynge in 1560, and listed in 1575 by Robert Laneham with other still popular romances.[1] The greater Elizabethan poets not infrequently referred to it, though often in somewhat jocose vein (Mead, p. xiii). The only extant texts, however, are the short fragments of de Worde's edition (W), the Copland edition (C), 1132 lines in short riming couplets, a poem which closely follows the older text, and a short version presumably derived from oral tradition, in Bishop Percy's Folio Manuscript (P). The two versions (CP) seem to be independent derivatives of an early tale (x) which had probably the same general outlines as the version P. The original version was presumably in the form of a short tale told in verse which gradually developed through romantic accretions into the form of C. The composition of this original poem Mead (pp. lii–lxxvii) ascribed to the fifteenth century. The old theory, held by Tunk even as late as 1900, that the poem belonged to the fourteenth century, rested on no better ground than the supposition that Chaucer's amusing list of garden herbs and of songless birds in that " fair forest " through which Sir Thopas rode, was a parody on the descriptive catalogue lists of trees and birds in the *Squyr of Lowe Degre*. Though this East-Midland romance is, as Mead's notes show, a perfect mosaic of the romantic conventions which Chaucer burlesqued so gaily in *Sir Thopas*, there is nothing which proves that the *Squyr* was antecedent to Chaucer's poem. In fact the linguistic evidence of the *Squyr*, as well as its gen-

---

[1] Cf. H. S. Murch, *Knight of the Burning Pestle*, Yale Studies, New York, 1908, pp. lxx ff. Laneham's letter contains a list of the ballads and story-books owned by the Coventry mason, Captain Cox. Among his romances were also *Bevis of Hampton, Knight of Courtesy, Eglamour, Triamour, Isumbras*, the *Seven Wise Masters*.

eral imitative quality in style, point to a fifteenth-century date. There are at least twenty-six words which, with two or three exceptions, do not appear in English before that period, and the final e is practically silent.

The romance tells of a poor squire who loves the daughter of the King of Hungary. His confession of love is betrayed to the King by an eaves-dropping steward; the squire is attacked as he comes at night to bid farewell to his lady; but instead of being killed, as she thinks, he is carried to the King and is presently sent on his way to achieve glory in far-off lands as the Princess has previously commanded him. Meanwhile for seven years [2] she keeps with her the embalmed body of the steward whose men had left it, so mutilated as to be unrecognizable, at her door. Just as she is about to become an anchoress, the Squire returns and their marriage is celebrated. In the extant texts, at least, the plot elements are awkwardly managed. The mésalliance theme is unconvincing, for the King has no real feeling about his daughter's marriage to the Squire; the Princess makes no delay about loving her lowly suitor, but pauses before undoing her door [3] for a discourse of unconscionable length while he waits in peril of his life; her father, who is supposed to be kindly, nevertheless permits her to suffer seven years of needless anguish. But it is not by the structural flaws in the poem that the poet should be judged (Mead, p. lxxvii ff.). The spirit in which he wrote was delicate if naïve, and his art vividly and charmingly pictorial. All the glamour of the mediaeval pageant of life is there, in descriptions rich in details concerning lovely fabrics and armour, the stately course of mediaeval banquets, the sports and diversions of fifteenth-century lords and ladies. The Princess's anaphoric farewell to the glad things of the world (vv. 940–55) [4] and her

[2] On seven as a conventional number, see Mead, p. 48; Child, Ballads, Index.

[3] The plea, "Undo Your Dore," seems to have been the popular title for the poem before this was displaced by the present one (Mead, p. 71, n. 534).

[4] This has the tone of some of the moral lyrics of the fifteenth century. Cf. Chambers and Sedgwick, Early Eng. Lyrics. The entire seriousness of this passage, as indeed of the whole romance in setting, or incident, shows how mistaken was Brandl's idea (Paul's Grundriss d. germ. Phil. II, 1, 657) that it was a burlesque on romances of the exile-and-return type (cf. Mead, p. lxxix).

father's enumeration of the delights with which he would tempt her from her sorrow (vv. 738–852) give a vision of what was to the poet a kind of ideality. Its potent appeal for a later age is aptly set forth in the appreciative criticism of James Russell Lowell (*Literary Essays*).

ORIGIN. The author's familiarity with a certain number of Middle English romances is indicated by his references to such heroes as Libeaus, Arthur, Guy of Warwick (vv. 73; 614), by his stereotyped diction, and, as already suggested, by the conventional nature of his characters and the incidents in which they take part. In other words it seems improbable that in the *Squyr* there is any single basic fact or legend. As Mead (pp. xxvii ff.) pointed out, the supposedly lowly suitor who loves a king's daughter appears in *Apollonius,* in *William of Palerne,* in *Horn,* in *Roswall and Lillian.* Closest of all, perhaps, among the romances is the opening situation in *Guy of Warwick* [5] in which the heroine likewise imposes a quest for glory on her humble suitor. The Treacherous Steward who betrays the lovers is a purely stock character (Mead, p. xxx), even as absence as a Test of Fidelity is a stock situation.

The two most distinctive *motifs* in the *Squyr of Lowe Degre* are the substitution of the steward's body for that of a lover supposed to be dead, and the preservation of that body by a heart-broken lady. The nearest parallel to the first is the episode in *Florence of Rome* [6] in which the false brother-in-law, Miles, presents to Florence the mutilated body of a vassal as that of her husband. He does it in hope of winning her himself. In the *Squyr of Lowe Degre* the lady's father permits the deception in the hope of breaking her attachment for the Squire. The narrative setting for the two episodes is different, and this similar detail in the *Squyr* may well be an independent invention. But in view of the general uninventiveness of the author of the *Squyr* it seems improbable.

[5] Mead, p. xxxvii–xliv, believed in the strong probability that the author of the *Squyr* modelled his poem on that of *Guy*. He considered it proof that the author of the *Squyr* was not working from a French original because the *Squyr* has so many passages similar in phraseology to *Guy*.

[6] See *Florence of Rome,* n. 6. The parallel does not seem to have been noted before.

The ghastly notion of embalming the dead and keeping the relic of love or hatred in intimate fashion, is found, as Jefferson (p. 102) has pointed out, in a number of romantic narratives. In Boccaccio's story (*Decameron*, IV, 5) Isabella keeps the head of her lover in a pot of basil until she herself dies; in the fif-teenth-century romance of *Eger and Grime*, Lady Loospaine keeps the hand of her enemy Graysteel in a coffer; in the *Knight of Courtesy* a dying lover orders his heart to be carried to his lady.⁷ Other parallels between this story and that of the *Squyr* are to be found in the earlier scenes, in the secret love affair of the lady with a vassal, in their stolen interview in the garden, their betrayal by a spy, their separation. The known ancestry of the *Knight of Courtesy* makes it probable that it influenced and was not influenced by the *Squyr of Lowe Degre*, the author of which may even have known the French original of the former poem.⁸ In the *Châtelain de Couci* the combination of decorative and pictorial elements with frank mediaeval brutality corresponds closely with the descriptive richness and morbidity of the *Squyr*.

BIBLIOGRAPHY

TEXTS: (1) W. Wynkyn de Worde's edition, about 1520, under the title "Undo Youre Dore" (180 lines in two fragments), Britwell Court, Bucks. Eng.; (2) C. Copland's edition printed about 1555–60, Brit. Mus. (1132 lines), repr. by Ritson, III, 145–92, 1802; by W. C. Hazlitt, *Early Popular Poetry*, II, 21–64 (1866); (3) P. Percy Folio MS. (170 lines), ed. Hales and Furnivall, III, 263–68. The texts have been reprinted by W. E. Mead, *The Squyr of Lowe Degre, A Middle English Metrical Romance*, Boston, 1904. Trans. E. Rickert, *Romances of Love*, p. 153 ff.

STUDIES: Cf. Wells, *Manual*, p. 786.

Jefferson, B. L. "A Note on the Squyr of Lowe Degre," *MLN*. XXVIII, 102–103 (1913).

Mead, W. E. See Texts.

Rickert, E. See Texts.

Tunk, P. *Studien zur mittelengl. Romanze, the Squyr of Lowe Degre*. Diss. 68 pp. Breslau, 1900.

Weyrauch, M. "Zur Komposition, Entstehungszeit u. Beurteilung der *ME. Squyr of Lowe Degre*," *Eng. Stud.* XXXI, 177–82 (1902).

---

⁷ See the *Knight of Courtesy* here, note 18, where another instance of an embalmed head is noted in connection with *Gorlagon*.

⁸ The fact that the Squire is told to go to Rhodes implies that the author was here following the *Knight of Courtesy* and not its French original.

OCTAVIAN

VERSIONS. *Octavian* begins with the tale of a Calumniated Wife but passes swiftly to the amorous and militant adventures of her sons. Through the many texts into which it passed, the romance kept always something of the hearty humor and adventurous vigor of the *chansons de geste.*. Its earliest extant version (A) in French, seems to be the octosyllabic poem of 5371 lines copied by an Anglo-Norman scribe in an early fourteenth-century manuscript now in the Bodleian (Hatton 100, ed. K. Vollmöller, Heilbronn, 1883). In Vollmöller's opinion (p. iv) its author was a Picard poet familiar with Paris and its environs, who was writing between 1229–1244.[1] Foerster (*Aiol*, Heilbronn, 1876–82, p. xxvi) noted some borrowings from the two *chansons de geste, Aiol* and *Elie de Saint-Gille.* An inedited second French version (B) of *Octavian*, known as *Florent et Octavian de Rome*, is also in the form of a *chanson de geste.* Gautier (*Bibliographie*, p. 104) believed that the Anglo-Norman poem (A) is simply an abridgment of the 18,576 lines in mono-rimed laisses in *Florent. Florent* is known in three fifteenth-century manuscripts of the Bibliothèque Nationale, Paris, and through a fifteenth-century prose version which passed quickly into print.[2] A French *Octavian* printed in 1534 was translated and printed in German in 1535 and became one of the most popular of German Volksbücher (Weber, 1, p. lix). The story was the first in that famous collection of romances, *Das Buch der Liebe*, printed at Frankfurt in 1587. The Volksbuch was the basis of a play by Hans Sachs, 1555, a poem by Sebastian Wilde, 1566, and of popular versions in Danish, 1597, in Dutch, 1621, in Icelandic, 1733. Several of these books are known to have existed in earlier editions than those now extant. Streve

[1] The poet seems to think of Jerusalem as being in the possession of the Christians, as it actually was during these years. Paris (*Rom.* XI, 610) thought the reasons given by the editor for accepting this date unconvincing.

[2] Cf. Vollmöller, p. XVII; Paris, Rom. XI, 611; Gautier, *Bibliographie*, p. 103.

(cf. Stammtafel, p. 50) derived them all ultimately from the French A version.

In a third version similarly derived from the common source of the A and B versions, Streve placed both the French miracle play, *Le Roi Thierry et Osanne, sa femme* (ed. Paris et Robert, *SATF., Miracles,* v, No. xxxii),[3] and the original of the extant Italian versions of the story. These are found in the *Reali di Francia,* and in the early fourteenth-century Italian prose romance, *Libro di Fioravante* (ed. Rajna, *Collezione di Opere inedite,* 1872), which Rajna believed was the source of the first two books of the *Reali* (Paris, *Rom.* iii, 352). In chapters 17–60 of the *Fioravante* are set forth the adventures of Fioravante; in 61–77, those of Drugiolina, his innocent calumniated wife, and of her two sons; and in 78–81, the Eastern warfare of Octavian, one of those sons. The Italian stories are based on French originals, and the Drugiolina story is certainly connected with the French forms of *Octavian.*

In Middle English there are two versions of the *Octavian* story, a southern one now contained in a single fifteenth-century manuscript (A), and a northern one found in two manuscripts (C L) of the same period.[4] As all the manuscripts contain references to florins, which were not coined in England until 1343,[5] Sarrazin (pp. xviii and xxxviii) believed that the two versions were composed after that date, but, because of certain archaisms in the text, considerably before the end of the century. The southern version of 1962 lines is written in six-line stanzas riming aaabab, the *a* lines in iambic tetrameter and the *b* lines in iambic dimeter, the form subsequently so well known in Burns's *To a Mountain Daisy.* The northern version uses the popular twelve-line, tail-rime stanza, and frequent alliteration.

The notable differences between these two versions in dialect, verse form, and to a minor degree in context, led Sarrazin (p. xxxix) to believe that they were entirely independent of each

---

[3] Cf. Petit de Julleville, *Les Mystères,* ii, 306 ff. In the South-English version, the supernatural and religious element appears in the nightly visions which Florentyn has of the Virgin who bids him undertake the battle with the giant.

[4] Eule (p. 16) found that both MSS. were from the same source.

[5] Cf. A. Dodd, *History of Money,* 1911, p. 22. Campbell, *Squyr of Lowe Degre,* i, 243, note, gives the date 1337.

other, but in his later study Eule (p. 16) argued that both were derived from the same Middle English source. This poem Sarrazin (pp. xviii, xxxviii) and Streve thought to be a more or less close translation of the Anglo-Norman *Octavian*. Undoubtedly the general course of the story is the same, but Eule's list (pp. 8–11) of traits peculiar to the English versions made him favor the theory of a lost French source.[6] In both versions the characters and tone and temper of the story are Anglicized, but the northern version keeps on the whole closer to the extant French poem and in Sarrazin's opinion is fully its equal in quality. He was inclined (p. xliv) in fact to find in this version with its piety, pathos, and feeling, one of the best pre-Chaucerian poems, and to attribute it to the clerical author who wrote *Isumbras*. The two poems are in the same dialect, are found in the same Thornton manuscript, have a certain similarity of theme, and are associated in the condemnation expressed in the *Speculum Vitae*. On the whole this ascription seems as probable as Sarrazin's attribution (p. xxv–xxxi) of the Southern version to Thomas Chestre, the author of *Sir Launfal,* and also, according to the critic, of *Libeaus Desconus* (cf. Billings, *Guide,* p. 142). In Kaluza's opinion this Southern *Octavian* was Chestre's best and latest work (*Eng. Stud.*, XVIII, 185–7).

ORIGIN. After an account of the long childlessness of the rulers of Rome, *Octavian* tells that at length the Empress bears twins and is accused by her Cruel Mother-in-law of adultery.[7] The accusation, the stratagem [8] by which a Pretended Lover is found in the bed of the Empress, her condemnation and exposure [9] with her children in a forest, follow traditional lines of

[6] Sarrazin (p. xliv) also admitted the possibility. He could not otherwise explain such a reference as that in the northern version to Borogh Larayne (Bourg la Reine), outside of Paris, which an English minstrel was not likely to know. Eule found confirmation of his theory in the fact that the heroine's confidant, unnamed in the French versions, was called in the English Olyue, Olyuayne, as if from a French nominative and accusative case. Streve (p. 27), noting that the two English versions alone make the Empress daughter of King Dagobert of France, found in this detail an evidence of their French source.

[7] See *Lay le Freine* and *Knight of the Swan,* note 5.

[8] See *Erle of Tolous,* note 8.

[9] See *Emare,* p. 23.

the story of the Innocent Persecuted Wife. In the forest she loses her children, one being carried away by an ape, the other by a lion. The theft of the children by robber beasts, an episode first told in European story in connection with the Eustache legend,[10] and its combination with the story of the Persecuted Wife is characteristic of *Octavian*. The remaining part of the romance tells, with details varying in the different versions, the adventures of the mother and her two sons. The boys grow up, one in Paris, and one in the East. The outstanding features of this last part of the story are romantic and militant with some admixture of farce. The two sets of stories are best considered separately.

In the story of Florent, the boy is rescued by a knight from the ape that had carried him off, he is captured by robbers and sold by them to Clement, a butcher of Paris. The boy's noble lineage is revealed by his impracticality; he exchanges good oxen for a falcon and gives an absurd price for a young colt. He finally proves his knightly worth by the prowess with which, despite the handicap of Clement's wretched armour, he overthrows a great giant, the champion of the heathen Sultan who comes to besiege Paris. By this battle Florent wins the love of the Sultan's daughter, and, presently, with her own connivance, he carries her off and marries her.[11] Throughout this part of the story, in the French and English versions at least, comedy is introduced by way of the good-hearted, typical bourgeois Clement, who lustily beats Florent for his lordly extravagance, swells with pride over his victory, and in canny peasant fashion (C 1285; L 1070) carries off the mantles of the French nobles till they have paid for the feast.[12] In one comic adventure Clement rides off with the wondrous horned horse

10 See *Isumbras*, p. 7.

11 Florent's prowess in battle and his love affair with the Sultan's daughter were possibly drawn from the French *chanson de geste*, *Floovent*. Cf. Gautier, *Bibliographie*, p. 102; Rajna, *Reali*, I, 77. The extant MS. of *Floovent* is of the fourteenth century, but Darmsteter (*De Floovante*, Paris, 1877) proved that the original version was of the twelfth century. The earliest extant foreign redaction is a thirteenth-century Dutch version. Cf. Voretzsch, *Einführung*, p. 207; G. Brockstedt, *Floovent Studien*, Kiel, 1907, p. 6.

12 This scene offers a comic contrast to that in *Auberi*, where the nobles not only pay magnificently for their expenses, but disdain even to pick up their costly mantles. See *Richard Coeur de Lion* here.

of the Sultan from before the very eyes of the Saracen (C 1440). The contrast between knight and peasant which all this develops is in the typical manner of the *chansons de geste*.

Octavian, the son who is carried away by a lion, is rescued by his own mother. The lion, which had been carried by a griffin to an island, there kills the griffin and henceforth cares for the child as for its own whelp. On a pilgrimage Octavian's mother, hearing from sailors of the child in the lion's den, goes to it, finds it to be her own son, and takes it up. The lion follows her, to the consternation of the sailors, even on board ship. From this time on he serves as the boy's constant companion until years later he is killed, fighting in battle by the young knight's side. The curious story of the Faithful Lion was borrowed in the original version of *Octavian* either from one of the early saint legends, or from some Crusader's story, or, as seems most probable, from contemporary romances in which the episode of a knight to whom a faithful lion was attached, had achieved increasing popularity.[18] It is the most characteristic feature of the story of Octavian, whose subsequent history is, in all the versions except the French *chanson de geste*, briefly passed over. When he hears of the great defeat in which the King of France, his visitor, Octavian, the Emperor of Rome, and hosts of Christians, among them, the young hero Florent, have been captured, the young Octavian leads forth the armies of the King of Jerusalem, his own kindly protector. His victory over the Saracens, his release of the prisoners, the final defeat of the Sultan, the reunion of the long-separated family of the Emperor Octavian, make the inevitable sequel. In the French forms all this is a matter of some five thousand lines; in Middle English it is reduced to about five hundred lines.

The comparative insignificance of the part played by the two Octavians, father and son, in the romance of *Octavian*, is the best answer to any attempt to find there the romantic transformation of historical characters or events. Settegast's argument (pp. 52–57) that the wars of Octavian in the East, as set

[18] Cf. Brown. *Iwain*, p. 132 (Harvard Studies, VIII), who referred for the saint legend to Maury, *Croyances et Légendes du Môyen-Age*, Paris, 1897, p. 247. See also the *Erle of Tolous*, note 10; *Guy of Warwick*, note 17. In the main these are stories of Grateful Beasts, but in *Octavian* the lion's devotion is not thus motived.

forth in the *Fioravante,* were based on remembrances of the eastern wars of the Emperor Julian, rested on no stronger evidence than that history and romance alike describe the getting of foreign troops and the holding of a council of war, and on the dubious identification of Marzadonia (*Fioravante,* ch. 78) as Marcianopolis, which was besieged by the Romans in 376–77. His belief (pp. 58–64) that the chief personages of the *Octavian* story are to be identified as the Emperor Octavian Augustus and his family involved such peculiar combinations of historic names and personalities as to be wholly unconvincing. *Octavian* is made up of pure romance themes, the very use of which implies a long previous development of romantic material.

The source references in the various versions of *Octavian* offer room for conjectures rather than conclusions. The A version in Old French refers to "merueilles . . . de latin en romanz traites" concerning the reign of Dagobert, and to an "estoire" (l. 85) concerning his contemporary, Octavian, the Emperor of Rome. Similarly the South English version twice (l. 935; l. 1359) refers to a Latin source, "as seyd the Latyn," perhaps by way of reference to the allusion in the French text, perhaps because of the convenience of "Latyn" as a rime word. The author may, however, have believed sincerely enough that originally the story was told in Latin, in those "Bukes of Rome" to which the North-English version (l. 10) makes reference. The parallelism between the episode of the Loss of the Children in the romance and in the Latin legend of St. Eustache may have lent some color to this supposition.

BIBLIOGRAPHY

TEXTS: (1) A, Southern version (1962 ll.), Brit. Mus., Cott. Cal. A, II, ed. by Weber, III, 157–239 (1810); cf. Ward, *Cat. of Romances,* I, 762; (2) C, Cambridge Univ. Lib. Ff. II, 38 (1731 lines), ed. by Halliwell, *The Romance of the Emperor Octavian,* Lond., 1848; (3) L, Thornton MS., Lincoln Cathedral, A, 5 (1629 lines). All three manuscripts edited by G. Sarrazin, *Altenglische Bibliothek,* III, Heilbronn, 1885.

STUDIES, etc.   Cf. Gautier, *Bibliog. des chansons de geste,* pp. 103–4; Wells, *Manual,* p. 782.

Eule, R. *Untersuchungen über die nordengl. Version des Octavian.*
Diss. 40 pp. Halle, 1889.

Sarrazen, G. (See Texts) Introd.

Settegast, F. "*Floovent* u. Julian nebst einem anhang über die *Oktavien-sage*" (pp. 52–64), *Beihefte z. Zts. f. rom. Phil.* IX (1906).

Siefken, O. *Das gedüldige Weib*, pp. 48–61. Dresden, 1904.

Streve, P. *Die Octaviansage.* Halle, 1884.

SIR EGLAMOUR

VERSIONS. The Middle English Eglamour makes many references to an original book or written source and in two passages (vv. 712, 859) calls this the " Buke of Rome," [1] — by an apocryphal reference probably borrowed along with much else from *Octavian*. The imitation of French names, such as the hero's actual or assumed name, Eglamour or Auntour, that of his lord, Pryncesamour, or of the Emperor's daughter, Dyatour (v. 771), is too naïvely like Chaucer's humorous Pleyndamour (*Sir Thopas*, 2088) to make necessary the assumption of a French source. In short, *Eglamour,* compounded of incidents familiarized in Middle English romance before the middle of the fourteenth century, is best considered as the original work of some unknown Englishman. His stereoptyped phrases, his frank commendation of gift-giving to minstrels " Dat ðey myght ðe better bee," suggest for author the minstrel rather than the monk or clerk (Adam, p. xxvii). A certain homely flavor is occasionally given to his style by his liking for proverbial phrases such as, " De man, Dat hewes over-hey, — The chyppes falles in his eye," or by such touches of rough humour as come in the giant's lament for the great bear that was his " littill spotted hogelyn."

A single leaf of a manuscript (S) written late in the fourteenth century is the oldest extant text of *Eglamour*. We have also three fifteenth-century manuscripts (LCF), five sixteenth-century editions (ebwad), and the transcript of a sixth in the Percy Folio. Of all these the Thornton manuscript (L) has the best and fullest text. It contains 1335 lines in 113 twelve-line stanzas and was written about 1440. From a detailed study of this text Schleich concluded that L was an independent version of the source which also gave rise to M, the conjectured original of all the other texts. The source of the two primary versions, M and L, was, it is believed, a poem ascribed by Zielke (p. 47)

---

[1] See *Emare,* ed. Rickert, p. xlviii, n. 2, for conjectures about the " Buke of Rome." Cf. *Torrent of Partyngale* here, note 4.

to the border of the north-west Midland district, and written between 1380 and 1400. The date might be more exactly determined if it could be decided whether the author in lines 1273–74, " It es sothe sayd — That ofte metis men at unsett stevyn," was quoting Chaucer's lines (663, 667) in the *Knight's Tale*, " But sooth is seyd, gon sithen many yeres, — For al-day meteth men at unset steuene." But it is hardly more safe to assert that this proves *Eglamour* to have been written after Chaucer's poem than to be sure with Skeat that the phrase was used independently by the two writers.[2]

In addition to the narrative versions of *Eglamour* already noted, the history of the romance may be traced in various dramatic forms. The play of *Eglamour and Degrebelle* was given at St. Albans in 1444, and in 1580 Sidney's satirical formula for a popular play so strikingly parallels the plot of *Eglamour* that it is not improbable that he was familiar with some dramatization of the romance (Baskervill, pp. 467, 491). The play was certainly known in Germany in the seventeenth century though generally under the name of the heroine, Christabella. In these dramatic versions for the fairy tale motives of the first half of the romance was substituted a story of love and knightly adventure (Baskervill, p. 760).

ORIGIN. The first half of the romance tells of the three great tasks imposed on the Love-Sick Eglamour, a knight " of lytill lande," before he can win Christabelle, daughter of Pryncesamour, Earl of Artois. The hero kills a giant near Artois, goes a seven weeks' journey into " Sedoyne," kills a wild bear and its gigantic master, Marasse, goes home like Bevis with his victims' heads on his spear; then after twelve weeks' stay, his " bonys for to reste," he slays a fiery serpent near Rome. Triumphal processions are made; bells are rung for his sake; the Princess Organata of Sidon is offered to him and is refused; he receives from her a safety-ensuring ring; he is healed of a deadly wound by the Princess Dyatoure of Rome. As the tasks and these associated details are the veriest commonplaces of folk-tales, the

[2] Cf. Haeckle, *Das Sprichwort bei Chaucer*, Leipzig, 1890, p. 22. The *New Eng. Dict.* (Steven) has a number of instances showing the ME. use of " to set a steven," or " at unset steven," but there is no other example of such close parallelism as that between Chaucer's lines and *Eglamour*.

resemblance between this part of *Eglamour* and the ballad of *Sir Cawline* (Child, No. 61) is to be accounted for on the basis of popular common sources rather than by any consideration of the ballad as a version of the romance.[3]

The second part of *Eglamour* concerns the adventures of Christabelle, who bears a child in Eglamour's absence, is set adrift on the sea by her Cruel Father, and is rescued only after she has seen a griffin carry away the child she has wrapped in her red mantle. Exhausted and speechless she comes at length to her uncle, the King of Egypt. With him she lives for fifteen years until she is won in a tournament and is married to her own son, Degrebelle, who has been nobly reared by the " King of Iraelle." When through his arms, which bear the picture of a griffin carrying a child, she recognizes her son, he refuses to give her up except to a man who can overthrow him; a tournament is proclaimed, and thither comes Eglamour, who has been fighting for fifteen years in the Holy Land. He overthrows his son and is recognized by Christabelle when he explains why his shield bears the device of a lady and child in a boat. The wedding of the long-lost lovers is celebrated, and young Degrebelle receives the very maiden Organata who was offered to his father so many years before. Here, as always in mediaeval romance, ladies are immortally young.

The " patchwork " character of this part of the story is evident (Gerould, p. 440). The exposure of the heroine and her child, her seven days' woe on the sea, her kindly reception in a foreign land, come clearly from the exposure of the Calumniated Wife in the Constance-Emare type of story. The loss of the child [4] wrapped in the red mantle and golden girdle, is an

---

[3] *Cawline* also begins with the episode of the Love-Sick Knight visited by his lady who comes at her father's command. She reproaches her lover and bids him rise and fight with the Eldridge knight. The description of the combat in *Cawline* seems to be connected with that in the romance of *Eger;* it is followed by a combat with a giant whom Cawline kills with his " Eldridge " sword, even as Eglamour kills his giant with a sword brought from " the Grekes " sea and given him by Christabelle. The successive fights of a hero with a wild beast and its gigantic master are found in *Sir Lionel* (Child, No. 18, vol. 1, 209), another ballad which has much in common with *Eglamour*. In the C version of *Lionel*, the giant's place is taken by a " wild woman " whose lament for her " pretty spotted pig " may be compared with that of the giant in Eglamour (l. 545).

[4] Gerould (p. 441) rightly insisted on the incidental nature of the epi-

episode which represents the unification, so to speak, of two episodes, one, the Loss of the Children, a regularly recurrent incident in the Eustache legend and its romantic derivatives, and the other, the occasional Treasure theme of the same set of stories. But one need go no further back than the Middle English romance of *Isumbras* to find in close sequence the episodes of the treasure wrapped in a red mantle carried away by an eagle, and of the child stolen by a wild animal. The incident also occurs in *Octavian*, and from this, perhaps, the *Eglamour* poet derived the idea of making the robber beast a griffin.[5] Like *Octavian*, *Eglamour* similarly combines the story of a persecuted lady and her children with heroic exploits of a type far more romantic than the Crusading adventures of *Isumbras* or his prototype, St. Eustache. In *Octavian* these exploits are accomplished by the sons of the heroine; in *Eglamour* by her husband, but they are sufficiently alike to suggest direct relationship between the two romances. Between Eglamour's combat with the giant Marasse, for instance, and that of Florent with the gigantic champion of the Sultan, there is some correspondence not only of incident but even of phrase, at least in the versions contained in the Thornton manuscript.[6]

The feebler poet of *Eglamour* seems also to have been influenced by the Middle English romance of *Sir Degare* from which he drew the Œdipus-like episode of the marriage of a mother and son. In both cases the discovery of the relationship prevents the tragic sequel of the classic story. From *Degare*, too, it seems probable, came the hint for the Father and Son combat which in *Eglamour* follows the son's proclamation of a tourna-ment for the awarding of his mother's hand.[7] Another instance

---

sode of the Lost Child in both *Eglamour* and the romance of *Sir Torrent*. Neither romance has any direct connection with the Eustache legend, though both have often been said to be derived from it. Cf. Adam, *Torrent*, p. xxiv; Holland, *Chretien de Troyes*, Tübingen, 1854, who held that *Octavian*, *Eglamour*, and *Torrent*, were all derived from the legend.

[5] Gerould, *ibid.*, noted that the griffin appears only in *Octavian*, in *Uggieri il Danese* (*Rom.* IV, 401–2), which has borrowed the episode from *Fioravante*, in the Italian version of *Octavian*, and in *Torrent*.

[6] In both romances the Single Combat takes place before the walls of a city, and much is said of the terror of the townspeople when the giant comes. Cf. *Eglamour*, 547, " the giant on the wallis dange "; *Octavian*, v. 740, " the walles doune gan he dynge."

[7] Cf. Murray, *Sohrab and Rustum*, p. 53, for *Eglamour*.

of the *Eglamour* poet's lack of inventive faculty [8] is his repetition of the scene in which the heroine recognizes her husband as she has recognized her son, by his curious symbolic arms.

BIBLIOGRAPHY

TEXTS: (1) S, Duke of Sutherland's MS. (lines 1–160) now Egerton 2862, cf. Kölbing, *Eng. Stud.*, VII, 193; Schleich (see below) p. 91; *Brit. Mus. Cat. of Add. MSS.* 1910, p. 239; (2) L, Lincoln Cathedral, A, I, 17, extracts printed by Halliwell, *Thornton Romances*, pp. 273–87; A. S. Cook, *Sir Eglamour*, N. Y. 1911; (3) F, Camb. Univ. Lib. Ff. II. 38, pr. by Halliwell, *ibid.*, pp. 121–76; (4) C, Cott. Cal. A, II. (1311 lines); cf. Ward, *Cat. of Romances*, I, 766; 820; (5) P, Percy Folio, ed. Hales and Furnivall, II, 341–89. Early Editions: (6) e, Advocates Library, Edin., edition printed by W. Chepman and A. Myllar, Edin., 1508; repr. Laing, *The Knightly Tale of Golagros and Gawane*, Edin., 1827; (7) b, fragments of a book printed by R. Bankes, Lond. cir. 1530, repr. Hall, *Archiv.* XCV, 308–11; (8) w, Brit. Mus., edition pr. by J. Walley, cir. 1540, extracts pr. by Laing (see under e), and summarized by Ellis, *Specimens*, pp. 527–38; (9) a, Brit. Mus., edition by Wm. Copland, 1548–61; (10) d, Oxford, Douce 261, edition pr. in 1564; (11) p, Percy Folio MS. ed. Hales and Furnivall, II, 338. A critical edition of the poem based on L was published by G. Schleich, in *Palaestra*, LIII, Berlin, 1906. Rev. *Archiv.* CXVIII, 441; *Eng. Stud.*, XXXIX, 433.

STUDIES: Wells, *Manual*, p. 781.
Adam, E.   (See *Torrent*) Introd. pp. xxiv–xxxii.
Baskervill, C. R.   (1) "Some Evidence for Early Romantic Plays in England," *Mod. Phil.* XIV, 229 ff. (1916). (2) "An Elizabethan *Eglamour* Play," *ibid.*, p. 759 ff.
Gerould, G. H.   "The Eustace Legend," *PMLA.* XIX, 439–41 (1904).
Schleich, G.   See Texts. See also "Ueber die Beziehungen von *Eglamour* u. *Torrent*." *Archiv.* XCII, 343–66 (1894).
Siefken, O.   *Das geduldige Weib*, pp. 52–6 (1904).
Zielke, A.   *Untersuchungen zu Sir Eglamour*. Diss. 60 pp. Kiel, 1889.

---

[8] The *Eglamour* poet repeats somewhat helplessly such hackneyed phrases as "white as foam," ll. 25, 638; "white as flour," ll. 184, 920, 1210; "white as whalesbone," ll. 680, 780, 1053; "white as swan," l. 1284, etc.

TORRENT OF PORTYNGALE

Versions. A single fifteenth-century manuscript and a few fragments of a sixteenth-century edition contain the only known version of the long-winded romance, *Torrent of Portyngale*. It is a poem of 2669 lines written in the tail-rime, twelve-line stanza form, but with so many imperfections of rime, metre, and stanzaic structure, that it was possible for Halliwell, who first edited the text, so to misunderstand its nature, as to print it throughout in six-line stanzas. In a second edition of the poem Adam restored the basic stanza structure and many of the original rimes which the scribe who wrote the Chetham text had often misplaced. The scribe was either superlatively careless and more to be cursed than Chaucer's Adam; or else, as Halliwell conjectured (Preface, p. v), he was writing the poem down from oral recitation. It has innumerable small variations from the better text preserved in the fragments of the early edition, but unquestionably scribe and printer worked from the same original version of the poem. Adam (p. xvi) ascribed the original to the eastern border of the East-Midland district. The text contains a number of fairly archaic words, but the style and content of the romance, and especially its connection with *Sir Eglamour,* make it probable that *Torrent* was a rather late fifteenth-century composition. As it is so full of references to the saints, of pious invocations and prayers, the hero never beginning an exploit without prefacing it with a proper petition, as it makes rather frequent mention of the rites of the church,[1] and tells, not of gift-giving to minstrels but of thank offerings to churches, Adam (p. xx) thought it may have been composed by a monk or some other pious cleric.

Origin. The presence of a few French names and phrases in *Torrent* is inadequate evidence that there was ever a French

[1] Masses, Confession, Baptism, etc. Few scenes in the poem are more absurd than the one in which the princess grieves for her lost children because she does not know how they will be baptized (l. 1892).

original, especially in view of the extraordinary likeness between *Torrent* and *Eglamour*. In large outline the plots are
identical; [2] Torrent loves Desonelle, Princess of Portugal, and
her Cruel Father imposes five tasks, the killing of far-off giants,
upon his vassal knight. Incidentally, the hero kills dragons and
is offered the hands of numerous princesses. In his absence
Desonelle is delivered of twins, is exposed on the sea, loses the
children to robber beasts, and is ultimately, after the boys have
grown to young manhood, reunited to them and to Torrent.
Despite entire change of names and setting, and the intrusion
of many superfluous details, such as the description in every instance of the giant's castle which Torrent wins and of the prisoners whom he releases, *Torrent* is so close to *Eglamour* in
incident, in the principal characters, even in phraseology,[3] that
it must be either from the same source as *Eglamour* [4] or simply
an amplified redaction of the romance itself. This last possibility was accepted by Halliwell (*Thornton Romances*, p. xxii),
disputed by Adam (p. xxvii) in favor of the first hypothesis,
and again and, it would seem, authoritatively, accepted by
Schleich. In the matter of phraseology Schleich made the important point that *Torrent* is closer to the later versions of
Eglamour than to the more vigorous version preserved in the
Thornton manuscript, the oldest of the complete texts of that
romance. The verbal correspondences are, he thought, too many
to justify the belief that the *Torrent* poet was working merely
from memory either of *Eglamour* or of its source.

In the second part of *Torrent* there is greater divergence from
Eglamour, chiefly because the *Torrent* poet apparently wished
to omit the episode of the marriage of the mother and son. In

---

[2] The minor differences (changes of name, setting, order of incidents,
nature of presents, etc.) which Adam (p. xxviii) noted, are insignificant in
comparison with the fundamental likeness of the two romances. Certain
additions in *Torrent* can be fully paralleled elsewhere. The scene in which
a virgin princess leads the hero safely between two lions (v. 286), records
a bit of folk-lore found also in *Beves*, 2392. The consternation caused by
Torrent's appearance with these lions (v. 387) is like that in *Octavian* when
the mother and child and robber lion appear together. For Torrent's Island
Combat see *Guy of Warwick*, note 11. For the supposed connection
of *Torrent* with the *Eustache* legend see *Eglamour*, note 4.

[3] See Adam, p. xxxi; Schleich, p. 364.

[4] Like *Eglamour* and *Octavian*, *Torrent* likewise refers to its source as
the " Buke of Rome."

Eglamour, it will be remembered, this leads directly to the tournament in which the hero, overthrowing his own son, regains his lost lady. In *Torrent* one battle and two tournaments are needed to accomplish the same result. In each of them Torrent tilts with his own son, and this triple use of the modified Father and Son Combat is simply a final instance of the constant tendency of the *Torrent* poet to double or triple whatever he conceived to be a good point in his original. It is surely in reminiscence of *Eglamour* that he describes the symbolic devices borne by Torrent and his sons, although he forgets to make these arms the means, as they are in *Eglamour,* of the heroine's partial recognition of her relatives.

The *Torrent* poet's zest for trivial and unrelated detail, a characteristic woefully true of the later romancers, is probably the explanation for the surprising number of proper names which come into his story. Giants, swords, forests, as well as cities and kingdoms, alike have their names in greater number proportionally than occur elsewhere. Most interesting among them are the references to Saint Anthony, who rescues Torrent's child, to Saint Nicholas de Barr (Bari, Italy), to whom Torrent makes offerings, and to Weland,[5] as the maker of Torrent's sword, Adolake (Hathloke).

BIBLIOGRAPHY

Texts: (1) C, Chetham Libr. Manchester, ed. J. O. Halliwell, Lond., 1842; by E. Adam, *EETSES.* li, 1887; cf. E. Kölbing, *Eng. Stud.,* vii, 195; 344; *ibid.,* xii, 432; notes, Zupitza, *ibid.,* xv, 1–12; (2) Fragments of an early printed edition, Douce, Bodl., repr. Halliwell, Appendix.

---

[5] Cf. Halliwell, *Torrent,* p. vii, and Zupitza, " Ein Zeugnis f. die Wielandsage," *Zts. f. deut. Alterthum,* xix, 129. Other references to Weland in Middle English literature are found in Layamon's *Brut* (ed. Madden, 1847, 11. 463, 21129) and in *Horn Childe.* See for full study of the Weland legend in mediaeval and modern literature P. Maurus, " Die Wielandsage in der Literatur," *Münchener Beiträge z. rom. u. engl. Philologie,* xxv, 1–224 (1902), and *Die Wielandsage, Weitere neuzeitliche Bearbeitungen,* Munich, 1910; also G. B. Depping and F. Michel, *Wayland Smith, A Dissertation on a Tradition of the Middle Ages,* Lond., 1847; and Schofield, *PMLA.* xv, 172 (1900).

STUDIES: Wells, *Manual*, p. 782; Körting, *Grundriss*, § 113.

Adam, E.   See Texts.

Gerould, G. H.   See *Isumbras* here.

Holthausen, F.   "Zu mittelengl. Romanzen, *Torrent of Portyngale*," *Anglia* XLII, 429–49 (1918).

Schleich, G.   See *Eglamour* here.

Spence, L.   *Dictionary of Mediaeval Romance and Romance Writers.* (Full outline of *Torrent*).   London, 1913.

SIR TRIAMOUR

VERSIONS. The first part of *Sir Triamour* (to l. 612) is of special interest as it preserves the only Middle English version of the well-known French story of Sebilla, the persecuted wife of Charlemagne, and of the Dog of Montargis. The original version of this tale of the Chaste Queen and the False Steward seems to have been one of the best productions of the trouvères who at the end of the twelfth century were writing of what may have been ancient epic stories. One version in French alexandrines survives in fragments of two manuscripts, one edited by Scheler (*Bull. de l'Académie royale de Belgique*, 2nd Ser. 1875), and the other, which was not discovered until 1915–1917, by Baker. A résumé "a cantoribus gallicis" was given in the early thirteenth-century chronicle of Alberic de Trois Fontaines (quoted by Guessard, p. xii), who thought it a beautiful story which could move those who heard it to laughter and to tears. Another poem on the same subject, but so greatly inferior that Paris (p. 395) called it "d'une secheresse incroyable, d'une grossièrté qui indique l'extrême décadence de l'art," is the Franco-Italian poem known as *Macaire*[1] extant in the thirteenth century Venetian manuscript[2] which has from time to time engaged so much laborious study.[3] In this the queen bears the name Blanciflor. A version in French prose is preserved in MS. 3351 of the Arsenal and in Spanish prose in a fourteenth

[1] For further references in regard to this and other versions see, Paris, *Charlemagne*, pp. 389–95, and Baker, *Rom.* XLIV, p. 7.

[2] Edited by Mussafia, *Altfrz. Gedichte*, Vienna, 1864, who thought (p. 4) that the author of *Macaire* had shortened his French original to suit himself; and again edited by Guessard, *Les Anciens Poètes de la France*, 1866, who believed (p. xiii) that the author used a very old short poem to which the author of the story known to Alberic must have added extensively. The Anglo-Norman fragments published by Baker correspond to vv. 912–920 and 1007–66 of *Macaire*.

[3] Reinhold, *Litteraturblatt*, XXXIII, col. 150, announced a critical edition of the whole MS. Cf. Guessard, *Macaire*, p. ciii; Reinhold, *Zts. f. rom. Phil.* XXXV, XXXVI.

century manuscript of the Escurial, and in the printed editions of 1532 and 1551 (Gautier, III, 686–87; Köhler, II, 273 ff.). To the same prose version belongs a Dutch *Volksbuch* printed at Antwerp in the first part of the sixteenth century. To these texts Child (*Ballads*, II, p. 40) added two in German: a metrical tale of uncertain date, *Diu Künigun von Frankreich und der ungetriuwe Marschalk* (von der Hagen, *Gesammtabenteuer*, I, 169) found in many manuscripts; a meisterlied, *Die Kunigun von Frankreich, dy der marschalk gegen dem Kunig versagen wart*, which was printed in the fifteenth century (Wolff's *Halle der Völker*, II, 255). Later Hans Sachs dramatized the story of the false marshall (Keller, VIII, 54). In the nineteenth century, it may be noted, appeared various plays in French, Spanish, and English which made melodramatic use of the Dog of Montargis story (Guessard, pp. lxv, lxxiv).

In fourteenth-century England the story was certainly known, as an entry shows in the catalogue of the books of Peterborough (Guessard, p. lxxi). " Macharie and Queen Sible and the Dog of Montargis " makes the seventy-eighth tale in the fifteenth-century manuscript of the Anglo-Latin *Gesta Romanorum*, now known as Additional MS. 9066 (Herbert, *Catalogue*, III, 259). From some such abbreviated version as this it is probable the English poet of *Sir Triamour* got the idea for the first part of his story, though in it none of the characters bear their original names. The first English metrical version seems to have been written about 1400 in a twelve-line tail-rime stanza. Three manuscripts of it are extant, the earliest (C) belonging to the early part of the fifteenth century, and the other two (RP) to the sixteenth and the seventeenth centuries. Copland in the sixteenth century twice printed the romance (LB). In his study of the relationship of these texts, Bauszus decided that C, through some lost intermediary version (y), was from the same source (x) as that which gave rise to the source (z) of LBP. Bauszus (p. 50) thought the dialect of the poem more nearly that of the North Midland than other, but he found in the text both northern and southern forms.

The style of the first part at least of *Triamour* is neither dull nor prolix, though the author uses the undistinguished diction of *Octavian* and *Eglamour* and many other equally commonplace romances (Bauszus, p. 42).[4] The second part of the poem is perhaps best described in the words of G. W. Hales as a " fair specimen of the old romances with all their vices and virtues, prolixity, improbabilities, exaggeration, with their wild graces also, their chivalrousness, their pageantry." It is chiefly interesting for its reminiscent use of *motifs* familiar in much older texts.

ORIGIN. The Sebilla story opens with an incident but slightly indicated in *Triamour*. The queen is accused, because Charlemagne finds a dwarf in her bed.[5] In order to incriminate her the dwarf has placed himself there at the instigation either of his own revengeful passion which the queen has scornfully rejected, or because of the bribes of Macaire, the treacherous father of Ganelon, whose guilty passion has been similarly scorned. This scene is omitted by the English poet, who tells briefly of the accusation brought by the false steward Marrok against the wife of King Ardus of Aragon, although she was " true as the turtle on tree." The king has confided to Marrok the care of his queen and kingdom while he himself goes on a pilgrimage in the hope that God will hear his prayer for a child. The False Seneschal, who has wooed the lady in earnest, but, finding her true, pretends to have but tested her loyalty, accuses her on her husband's return of having sinned with a knight. On Marrok's advice Ardus banishes the queen with a single old knight, Sir Roger, for escort. The older versions

---

[4] Such lines as those in *Octavian*, v. 283,
> " They riden forth to a wylde forest
> There was many a wylde best,"

and those in *Triamour*, v. 1033,
> " He saw many a wylde beest
> Both in heth and in wylde forest,"

suggest Chaucer's derisive lines in *Sir Thopas*,
> " He pricketh thurgh a fair forest
> Ther-inne is many a wilde best."

[5] The episode of the Pretended Lover is found also in the various versions of the *Erle of Tolous* (cf. note 8), in those of *Octavian*, and, as Child (II, No. 59) pointed out in connection with *Sir Aldingar*, also in *Doon Alemanz*, and in the versions of the *Macaire* story. In the Didriks *Saga*, cc. 156–59, the queen Sisibe is entrusted to two nobles, one of whom, Hartvin, tries to win her favor and is threatened, as Margaret threatens Marrok, with the gallows. The king is then told that his wife has had a thrall for lover (Child, II, 41).

are full of epic traditions concerning the constant hostility to Charlemagne's royal house of Ganelon's treacherous family. Much is made therefore of the part his relatives play in bribing the dwarf, in urging the instant execution of the queen, and of the difficulties which Naime, one of Charlemagne's wisest counsellors, has in restraining them. It is at his advice that Auberi de Montdidier, one of the Emperor's best vassals, is sent to take the queen to the frontier. The sorrowful, suffering lady, who is about to give birth to a child, and this young knight are attacked in the forest by Macaire, and Auberi is killed, but not before his valiant efforts have given the queen a chance to escape into the woods. The English version [6] at this point seems merely to condense its French original to which reference is made in l. 316, — " as it is in the romans tolde."

The episode that follows in the French story sets forth the story of an animal faithful even unto death. Auberi's dog, which has vainly attempted to aid his master, does his best for the dead body, covers it with dirt, and guards the grave until, sent back by hunger to the royal palace, he arouses suspicion by a violent attack on Macaire. The dog leads the courtiers to Auberi's grave, and again on the advice of Naime, the suspected Macaire is forced to fight in a judicial combat with the dog. The fight ends with the man's defeat and confession. The English poet, by stupidly deferring the dog's attack on Macaire for seven years, by making it fatal, and having in consequence to omit the famous combat between the man and dog, has done but scant justice to his original.

The earliest literary treatment of an analogous story is Plutarch's tale of the dog which King Pyrrhus found guarding the dead body of its master. He took it away, and later at a review of the King's soldiers the dog identified and attacked the murderer of his master. In the *Hexameron* of St. Ambrose, written in the fourth century, there is a very similar tale localized in Antioch. It was this version, presumably, which Giraldus Cambrensis knew and introduced into the *Itinerarium Cambriae*, c. 1188 (Lond., 1585, I, 124). Giraldus's is the first extant text

---

[6] The account in *Triamour* of the king's resolve to exile the queen, and of how she is provided with a horse and a few florins, and of the grief of the people, is obviously close to that in the ME. *Octavian* (Weber, III, 265 ff.).

which introduces the typically mediaeval idea of the Judicial Combat, but it is believed (*Historical Litt.*, xxvi, 373) that he did not know the French story of Auberi's dog. This was, however, evidently known to Albéric not more than sixty years later. Albéric states that the reason for Charlemagne's dismissal of his wife, the daughter of Dedier, the Lombard king, was unknown, but that he sent her off in company with Auberi, that Auberi was killed by Macaire and avenged by his faithful dog in a judicial combat. The dog episode appeared not only in the versions of the Sebilla story already noted but in French art at least as early as the fourteenth century.[7] The title " dog of Montargis " comes from the painting in the hall of the château of that name (Paris, p. 392, n. 2).

In the Sebilla story the fleeing queen, after her escape from Macaire, encounters Varocher, a poor, kindly giant of a fellow who acts henceforth as her protector. Her child is born at an inn in Hungary. Her royal father presently receives her and decides on a war with Charlemagne in order to avenge her injuries. The subsequent attack, the grotesque, gallant deeds of Varocher, and the reconciliation of the king and his wife, contain those comic parts of the story to which Albéric referred. Of all this there is nothing in the second part of *Triamour*. The queen gives birth in the forest to Triamour;[8] she is found and taken home by a kindly knight, Sir Bernard Messengere. The birth in the wood recalls that of Tristan and of Josian's children in *Beves*. Triamour, like many another poor and un-

---

[7] Guessard, *Macaire*, p. xxix, enumerated various references to the story in French literature. In the fourteenth century *Deduits de la Chase* by Gui de la Buigne, there is a reference to painted scenes of the story. Guessard repudiated the theory that there was ever at Montargis a Celtic dog cult which might have given rise to a story thus lauding a dog. The etymology of the name was thus explained, *Mont;* Celtic *ar*, French *du*, Celtic *ki*, French *chien*. Of general interest is Baugert's, *Die Tiere im altfrz. Epos*, Marburg, 1885.

[8] *Bauszus*, p. 32, compared with this name various similar ones in ME. romance, Triamour, the name of the fée in Chestre's *Launfal*, Pryncesamour in *Eglamour*, Segramour in *Emare*, Pleyndamour in the lost romance mentioned by Chaucer in *Sir Thopas*, and the lady in *Libeaus Desconus* " that highte la dame d'amour." In the first part of *Triamour* the original French names were changed. Macaire became Marrok; Auberi, Roger; and Joseran, the protector who cares for the heroine after the birth of her child, Bernard Messengere (Mowswinge).

known knight, wins a princess " fresshe and amerous " at his first tournament but, being wounded, rides away, leaving his reward unclaimed for a year and a day. A mild version of the Father and Son Combat appears in this tournament, for the young hero strikes down his own father, whom he knows no more than Degare knows his father in the forest combat. Triamour, with his father's aid, attacks and kills the cowardly son of the German Emperor. The young hero kills cowardly foresters out of hand and also a great hart that has harmed his greyhounds. Later Triamour becomes the champion of his unknown father in the fight to be waged against the Emperor's challenger, Marradas. In the description of this battle occurs an episode strongly reminiscent of Florent's fight with the Saracen giant (*Octavian*, Weber, III, 1095), — when Triamour kills his opponent's horse and is taunted by him for the accident. The mighty champion Burlond, of whom we are told that, when his legs were cut off at the knee, he then " on his stumpes stood," suggests the famous squire in Chevy Chase (st. 50): when " his leggis were smitten off, / He fought upon his stumpes." At the end of the romance, when he marries the princess, Triamour, like Degare, has the satisfaction of uniting his long separated parents.

BIBLIOGRAPHY

TEXTS: (1) C, Cbg. Univ. Libr. Ff. II, 38, ed. J. O. Halliwell, Percy Soc. XVI, 1846; (2) R. Rawlinson, a fragment of 75 verses; (3) Additional MS. 27879, Br. Mus., a 17th c. MS. containing 10 articles of the Percy Folio MS. ed. Furnivall and Hales, 1868, II, 78–135; (4) L, Copland's edition, 1593, reprinted by Utterson, 1816, I; (5) B, Copland's edition, undated, Bodl. Abstract, Ellis, *Spec.* 491; Ashton p. 171 ff.

STUDIES: Cf. Edwardes, *Summary*, p. 171; 404; Gautier, *Bibliog. des Chansons de Geste* (Macaire, p. 143), Paris, 1897; Wells, 120, 782. Baker, A. T. "Fragments de la Chanson de la Reine Sibile," *Romania* XLIV, 1–13 (1915–1917).
Bauszus, H. *Die mitteleng. Romanze Sir Triamour.* Diss. 58 pp. Königsberg, 1902. (Critical text, ll. 1–132.)
Bonilla y San Martin, A. *Libros de Caballerias*, Madrid, 1907, I, 503 ff.
Gautier, L. *Les Epopées Françaises*, Paris, 1880. See *Macaire*, III, 684–719.

Köhler, R. " Zu der altspan. Erzählung von Karl u. Sibille," *Kleinere Schriften*, Berlin, 1900, II, 273–304, repr. from *Jahr. f. rom. u. eng. Lit.* XII, 286 ff. (1871).

Paris, G. *Historie Poétique de Charlemagne.* Paris, 1905.

Siefkin. *Das geduldige Weib*, pp. 62–66.

Spence, L. *Dictionary of Romance*, pp. 358–362. (Outline of Triamour.)

ROSWALL AND LILLIAN

VERSIONS. In 1804 Sir Walter Scott (*Works*, 1868, v, 407) remarked: "Within the memory of man an old person used to perambulate the streets of Edinburgh singing in a monotonous cadence, the tale of *Rosswal and Lilian.*" It is probable that this tale was some such abbreviated version of the romance as that in the extant stall copies and prints of the eighteenth century, — texts which contain about four hundred lines. The earlier and longer version from which these must have been derived is now represented by the edition printed at Edinburgh in 1663 (A), by a later edition of 1679, by that printed at Newcastle, and by various later reprints such as David Laing's in 1822. The first text (A), written in the dialect of southern Scotland, contained 846 lines in short riming couplets (Lengert, *Eng. Stud.*, XVII, 360). The rimes and the style of this version, its many allusions to earlier heroes and heroines of romance, show that it could not be dated before the fifteenth century.[1] On the other hand, the story must have been fairly well known early in the sixteenth century and possibly before that date since it had then passed into ballad form. In 1580 it was entered as "The Lord of Lorne and the False Steward" in the Stationers' Registers (Arber, II, 379), and a few years later was referred to as an old ballad "of king Harrie's' day." The oldest extant text of this ballad version is in the Percy Folio (ed. Hales and Furnivall, I, 180–98). It contains some traditional material not found in the romance version, but the general similarity of the two texts and their identical use of the

---

[1] There are three catalogue lists: verses 15–24 say that Roswall surpasses Ulisses, Gandifer, Achilles, Troyalus, Priamus, Clariadus, the fair Philmox, Florentine of Almanie, Lancelot du Lake; verses 343–45 that Lillian was fairer than the lady Pelicane, than Helen or the true Philippie, or the lady Christian; and in verses 391–401 the hero is besought to take the name of Hector or Oliver, or Sir Porteusor, of the worthy Amedus, or the noble Predicase, Sir Lion-dale, Florent of Albanie, or Lancelot du Lake. See Rickert, Notes, for tentative identifications.

name Dissawar,[2] which in each version the hero assumes, persuaded Child (*Ballads*, v, 47) that the ballad was, at least in part, derived from the romance.

ORIGIN. Despite the lateness of its versions and its conventionalized style, *Roswall and Lillian* is far closer to primitive folk-tales than many a romance of much earlier date. Its primary theme is that of the Male Cinderella, i.e., of the royal youth who is forced to become a menial servant; but this is combined with various distinctive, popular *motifs*. To begin with, Roswall is exiled from his home because he imprudently releases three of his royal father's prisoners. Despite an attempt to rationalize these characters, they have the same function as the supernatural Helpful Companions who appear so often in folk-tales. In the group of tales analyzed by Lengert (p. 347 ff.) and by Child (v, 45–7) for the sake of their likeness in this incident to *Roswall,* only one grateful being appears; he is a wild man (Bosnian), a peri (Tartar), an iron man (Der Eisenhans, Grimm, *Kinder-Märchen,* No. 136; cf. Bolte-Polivka, *Anmerkungen,* III, 94–114), a robber of fabulous strength (Russian), an invisible knight (Polish). In the ballad version of *Roswall* this episode of the Released Prisoners is omitted and the boy's absence from home is accounted for in remarkably non-popular fashion by saying that he was sent from Scotland " to learne the speeches of strange londs."

In the romance Roswall is accompanied into exile by a False Steward, who takes advantage of the boy when he is drinking from a brook, threatens him with death, and robs him of his gold and letters. The romance offers no explanation for this villainy, but it can, perhaps, be found in five of the twenty analogues cited by Lengert. These begin with a charge laid on the hero not to travel with a beardless man or one deformed, and the boy's disobedience brings his troubles upon him. The forbidden person appears and gets control over the lad in precisely the same fashion as that used by Roswall's faithless

---

[2] The name has not been satisfactorily explained. Does it mean Unaware (cf. *Percy Folio,* Disaware)? Is it from Dis-avoir, *i.e.,* without possessions (Child, Glossary), from disavow (Rickert), or formed by analogy with such a name as that of Libeaus Desconus? For the somewhat similar use of such a cognomen see *Degare* and *Emare.*

servant. In other words it seems possible that the episode originally developed from the currency of certain superstitions concerning types of people whom it was considered unlucky to
encounter.[3] But in both *Roswall* and the *Lord of Lorne* any
distinctive attribute in the villain's appearance has been lost
and the mother's warnings to her son are couched in the most
general terms (*Roswall*, ll. 166–72).

The remaining portion of *Roswall* follows in general the formula of stories of the False Princess, a type well represented
by Grimm's *Die Gänsemagd* (*Kinder-Märchen*, No. 89; cf.
Bolte-Polivka, II, 273–85). In this the true princess is forced
to become a goose-girl, her ugly maid marries the king, and only
when the princess is overheard telling her sad story, first to
her horse's head, and then to a stove, is the truth discovered.[4]
Arfert's study (*op. cit.*) of the Substituted Bride *motif* in folk-
tale and romance, established the fact of its wide diffusion and
pointed out that within this story-type it is no unusual variation to have a royal youth in the part of the princess. In the
Goldenmärchen studied by Panzer (*Hilde-Gudrun*, p. 251), the
gold hair of the boy, accidentally revealed, brings him the
notice, then the love, of a true princess. In *Roswall* the hero,
who is serving humbly at court, is chosen by the Princess Lillian
because of his "wonder fair bodie." The romance omits the
traditional detail which in the ballad tells how the hero evaded

[3] The influence of popular superstitions on the evolution of character
types is a subject much in need of further investigation. Köhler commented
on "Der jungling u. der bartlose," *Archiv f. litteratugesch.* XII, 137; *Germania*, XI, 398. P. Arfert, *Das Motiv von der untergeschobenen Braut*, Diss.,
Rostock, 1878, p. 32, mentioned tales involving warnings against beardless
or deformed men. In many folk-tales red is the villain's color. Jones, *Folk
Tales of the Magyars*, Folk Lore Soc. 1886, p. 329, quoted the Magyar
jingle: "A red dog; a red nag; a red man; none is good." Cf. *Argyllshire
Hero Tales*, Folk Lore Soc. 1889, p. 475. In the Three Counsels type of
story studied by Greenlaw, *PMLA*. XXI, 589, 596, the prohibition against
trusting to or travelling with a red-bearded man is not infrequent. Cf. Baum,
JEGP. XXI, 520–29 (1922), " Judas's Red Hair."

[4] Child, v, 48, noted as genuine traditional material this confession to a
horse's head or to some other inanimate object. Cf. the story of Midas's
wife telling his secret to the reeds, or the dwarf in Beroul's *Tristan* who tells
Mark's secret to a hawthorn. Cf. Schoepperle, *Tristan*, II, 269–70. For the
theme of the Substituted Bride see P. Arfert, *op. cit.*, pp, 50–71; Bolte-
Polivka, II, 284; Schoepperle, I, 206. See also under *Emare*, note 14, for
references to the *Berte* legend into which this theme enters largely.

his oath of secrecy to the False Servant by bewailing his fate to his horse. The princess overhears him and ultimately brings about his restoration to proper place and fortune.

In the romance the restoration of· Roswall follows a traditional pattern but of more elaborated kind. A tournament is proclaimed, and Lillian begs him to joust for his lady; Roswall pretends that he would rather hunt than joust, and each day rides away. Unquestionably at this point *Roswall* shows the influence of *Ipomédon,* in which the hero similarly chooses to deceive his lady and to win incognito the Three Days' Tournament. Roswall is provided with different suits of armour, white, red, and gold, by the Grateful Prisoners whom he had formerly released. In this reference to these helpful beings the episode reverts somewhat from its romanticized character to its original folk-tale type. The actual phraseology of *Roswall* is full of reminiscences not only of *Ipomédon,* but, as Lengert's notes show, of other romances such as *Eger and Grime.* Definite ballad imitation is suggested by such lines as:

> "He looked east and looked west,
> He looked over the bents brown." (ll. 478–9)

BIBLIOGRAPHY

TEXTS: (1) A, Black Letter (846 lines), Edin., 1663, Advocates Libr., ed. O. Lengert, *Eng. Stud.,* XVI, 321–56 (1891); (2) M, another early print, cir. 1679; (3) B, an undated print, Newcastle; (4) D, an Edinburgh print, cir. 1775, Douce Collection, Bodleian; summarized by Ellis, *Specimens,* 1848, pp. 578–84; (5) C, an Edinburgh stall copy, 1785; (6) L, an edition based on A and other prints, by David Laing, *Early Metrical Tales,* Edin., 1826. Trans. E. Rickert, *Romances of Love,* pp. 116–37.

STUDIES.

Bolte, J. G. Polívka, *Anmerkungen zu den Kinder-u. Hausmärchen der Brüder Grimm,* Leipzig, 1913–18. 3 vols.

Child, F. *Ballads,* v, 43–48 (1898).

Lengert, O. "Die schottische romanze *Roswall and Lillian,*" *Eng. Stud.,* XVII, 341–88 (1892).

Rickert. See Texts.

LAY LE FREINE

VERSIONS. *Le Lai del Fraisne* (ed. Warnke, 1901) is one of the most engaging stories told by Marie de France.[1] She wrote it presumably about 1165 when her other *lais* were composed, and certainly before 1190, for the poem contains a reference to the Archbishopric of Dol which was suppressed in that year (Rickert, p. 180). The direct statement that the adventure took place "en Bretaigne" might be held to localize the story and to indicate that by those who made and named the *lai* "pur la dame" (v. 536) Marie meant the Bretons, were these expressions of a less conventional character than they have been long recognized to be (Lot, *Rom.* XXIV, 1895, 527). Her poem contains 536 lines in octosyllabic couplets. In the thirteenth century it was greatly amplified and changed in the *Roman de Galeran de Bretagne* (ed. Boucherie, Montpellier, 1888; Langlois, *La Soc. frç. au XIIIᵉ Siècle*, 1904, pp. 1–39), and in the early years of the fourteenth century it was rather closely translated and somewhat condensed in a Middle English version. This poem of 340 lines, in the same metre as the original, is now preserved in the early fourteenth-century Auchinleck manuscript. It is as charmingly distinctive in style as is *Orfeo* and may, indeed, have been by the same author. The two poems have the same freshness of touch and are linked to each other by evident verbal borrowings (Guillaume, p. 463). Though the evidence at best is slight, it seems probable that the Middle

[1] Comparatively little is known of Marie de France beyond the facts which she herself gives in her various works, the *Lais* (c. 1160–70), the *Ysopet*, a collection of over one hundred fables (c. 1170–80), the *Espurgatoire Seint Patriz* (after 1190). See Miss Rickert, *Lais of Marie*, pp. 137–64; Warnke, *Lais*. Fox, *Eng. Hist. Review*, XXV, 303–06 (1910), XXVI, 317, found evidence for believing that Marie was in her later years, during the reigns of Richard I and John, the Abbess of Shaftesbury. E. Kinkler, *Marie de France, Sitzungsberichte*, Vienna Acad. Ph. Hist. Kl. Band 188 (1918), attempted to identify her with Marie de Champagne. This theory was soundly rejected by Bertoni, *Nuova Antologia*, Sept. 1920, pp. 18 ff. Cf. Bruce, *Evolution of Arthurian Romance*, Göttingen, 1923, p. 56.

English poet, a devoted reader of Marie's lays, which he happily characterizes in a little Prologue to the *Lay le Freine*, first made his translation of Marie's *Fraisne* and later, in even more independent mood and with even more mature grace, fashioned the *Lay of Orfeo,* to which he or a scribe transferred the Prologue originally written for the *Lay le Freine.*[2]

Marie's *Lai* offers a peculiarly interesting example of the transference of popular themes and beliefs to the setting of twelfth-century life and literature. The scene of the story shifts from the rich home of the parents of the heroine to the convent where she spends her girlhood and then to the castle where she lives as the lovely and respected mistress of the young lord, Gurun. Her liaison is regarded with serene unconcern by an author accustomed to the doctrines of courtly love. Marie even pauses for a bit of amused jesting over the young lord's gifts to the convent, gifts not given for the sake of his soul's good but for a chance to see the maiden. Deft bits of characterization and delightful realistic touches distinguish Marie's version, but beneath this artistry of expression certain primitive themes may be recognized.

The opening episode of the story depends on the widespread superstition that no virtuous wife could give birth at one time to more than one child. The same theme appears in the many versions of the *Octavian* story, wherein the birth of twin children provides a cruel mother-in-law with excuse for charging her son's wife with adultery. In a large number of stories, indeed in a majority of those cited by Köhler (p. lxxxvi ff.), not family but class prejudice expresses itself. A noblewoman taunts with a similar accusation a poor woman who is the mother of twins. Ultimately the proud lady herself gives birth to two or more children and to save her own repute attempts to destroy all but one. In these tales the poor woman's curse is fulfilled with a literalness which evinces popular satisfaction in that justice of fate or providence which, in story at least, so commonly surpasses that of men. In a few tales, as in Marie's *Lai* and in the account of the Countess Margareta of Holland (Eccard's *Corpus historicum medii aevi,* ii, 955), the two women are of equal rank. In pseudo-historical legends into which the theme

2 See *Orfeo* here, note 3.

passed, the story sometimes serves to explain a family name such as that of the Guelphs (Welpen).[3] In pure fiction the theme was to greater or less extent, as in the versions of the Swan-Children story, joined to that of the Swan-Maiden and the motive belief that a woman whose children are abnormal in form or number must necessarily be of demoniac or fairy origin.[4]

The disposal of the unwelcome children in stories of this general type presents all possible varieties of the Exposure *motif*. In Marie's *Lai* we are told that the proud, humiliated mother, having given birth to twin daughters, lets her maiden carry one away. The maiden leaves the child in an ash tree near a convent, and after it is found the child is henceforth known as Le Fraisne. Marie does not explain the reason for giving the name La Coldre to the child kept by the mother, but later when the question is raised by Gurun's vassals concerning his discarding of Freine and his marriage to La Coldre, they cleverly contrast the fruitless ash with the "*noiz e deduiz*" (l. 349) of the hazel. It is possible, as Miss Rickert and others have suggested, that the legend originally belonged to the village of La Coudre, which was not far from Dol, but in that case it seems difficult to explain the secondary place of La Coldre in the story. The choice of this particular name was probably due merely to Marie's fertile instinct for effective contrast.[5]

The second part of the *Lai* tells of the heroine's life in the convent, of her elopement with the nephew of the Abbess, of her self-abnegation when her lover is forced to discard her and

---

[3] Cf. Köhler, p. lxxxvii ff. Gibbs, *Chevelere Assigne*, p. xi, quoted the Guelph story. In this a noblewoman is punished for her pride and false accusation of a poor woman by becoming herself the mother of twelve children. She sends her maid to drown all but one in the river. The father of the children, meeting the woman, inquires what she carries and is told that she carries whelps. Insisting on seeing them, he forces a confession from the woman, has the children reared in seclusion, and ultimately brought home. On account of this episode the race of the Guelphs received and kept this name.

[4] See *Emare* here, note 11.

[5] It is, also, as Miss Rickert pointed out, *Lais*, p. 179, a mark of popular origin when names are thus derived from some physical peculiarity or from some circumstance connected with the early history of the child. Cf. Cinderella, Snow-White, Gold-Tree, Tom Thumb, Little One-Eye, etc. Cf. A. Nutt, "*Eliduc* and *Snow-White*," *Folklore*, III, 26 (1892), Matzke, p. 230.

wed another, and of her reunion with him and her kindred when she finds that the new bride is her own sister. Practically the same story is found in a ballad widely known in at least eight versions in English, also in German, Dutch, Danish, and Swedish texts (Child, II, 63–69). The ballad accounts for the maiden's separation from her kindred by the bald statement that she was stolen away as a child by pirates or by the future lover. Ultimately, though in some versions she has borne him seven sons, he decides to discard her, either because she is a " waif woman " or because he can get great wealth with a new bride. Like the little abandoned Fraisne, with whom in the ash tree a rich robe and ring were left, in several of the ballad versions the stolen maiden has with her certain tokens the recognition of which, on the part of her mother or sister, brings about the identification of herself. In a few versions her sister overhears the plaintive lament in which the girl names her parents, and in others it is Fair Annie's resemblance to herself that first arouses the bride's interest. In this detail may be preserved a trait more primitive than that found in Marie's version. Although her *Lai* antedates by four centuries the earliest known ballad version and the two stories are obviously the same, it has generally been felt that the ballad is not a derivative of the *Lai*, but that the two " have a common source which lies further back and too far for us to find " (Child, II, 67).

The idea in the ballads of the physical resemblance of the two maidens appears also in the romance of *Galeran de Bretagne*. Galeran is so moved by the resemblance of Florie to her sister Freine, whom he has loved and lost in youth, that he is about to marry Florie. To the physical likeness of the two sisters is likewise added the resemblance in name, a feature more clearly recognizable here than in Marie's *Lai* (Matzke, p. 226). So also in other romances the maiden offered to the hero in place of the one to whom he has been married or betrothed, frequently bears a name like that of his lost love. In the English *Horn* [6] the maidens are Rimenhild and Reynild; in Marie's *Eliduc* they are Guildeluëc and Guilliadun; in *Ille et*

[6] See *Horn* here, note 7, and Schofield, *PMLA*. XVIII, 35; Matzke, pp. 216–17, 225–26.

Galeron [7] by Gautier d'Arras they are Galeron and Ganor; in the various versions of *Tristan* the hero is drawn to Isolt of Brittany because her name is that of the lovelier Isolt of Ireland.[8] To this group of stories, which he made (pp. 227 ff.) also to include parts of the story of *Guy of Warwick* and of *Beves of Hampton*, Matzke gave the name of the Legend of the Husband with Two Wives. It was unquestionably popular in the twelfth and thirteenth centuries, but it seems necessary to distinguish between romances such as *Horn, Bevis,* and *Guy,* in which the second lady is simply an embarrassing reward and the hero's relation with her entirely devoid of emotional interest, and those in which it involves him in a psychological conflict and is introduced for precisely that purpose. It is difficult therefore to accept Matzke's belief (p. 234) that this whole group of stories not only " belong to a region in which the Celtic substratum could exert decisive influence," but that they " rest upon a more primitive habit of society in which a wife could be pushed aside for a new and more favorite rival." Rather do such romances as *Eliduc* or *Ille et Galeron* present a special twelfth-century adaptation of a test of loyalty in a lover or a husband. To *amour courtois* the rights of love were even more sacred than those of marriage, and for this reason an episode setting forth the emotional conflict of a man who was both husband and lover made an especial appeal to such writers as Thomas in his *Tristan,* or to Marie de France in *Eliduc.* In her *Lai del Fraisne,* however, there is no real conflict, for the lover gives way with complete docility to his vassals' demand that he marry a proper wife and beget a proper heir. However delicately revealed in this version or brutally in the ballads, the essential situation, the discarding of a mistress for a wealthy and legitimate wife, is not to be referred to any one race or time or creed.

The gentle service rendered by Fraisne or by Fair Annie at her lover's wedding-feast recalls the self-sacrifice of that mediaeval synonym for all patience, Griselda.[9] Whatever the origin

[7] Cf. Matzke, " The Source and Composition of *Ille et Galeron*," *Mod. Phil.*, 1907, IV, 471–88; Cowper, " The Sources of *Ille et Galeron*," *Mod. Phil.* 1922, XX, 35–44.

[8] Cf. Schoepperle, I, 158–77; II, 524–28.

[9] For references concerning Chaucer's version of her story in the *Clerk's*

of her legend, it seems impossible to connect it directly with Marie's *Lai*. The story of Griselda is essentially an exemplum on patience; it tells of the cruel succession of marital trials endured by a peasant girl married to a great lord. His apparent marriage to another is in reality her supreme test, and when she has endured that too with the patience that only a Chaucer in the Middle Ages seems to have suspected was " importable," she was properly rewarded. Her trials and her reward make a definite structural sequence. Fraisne's story, on the contrary, is pure romance; it tells of a girl losing birthright, home, family, friends, love itself, yet marvellously regaining them all. It is a love adventure only saved from tragedy by the law in popular fiction, mediaeval or otherwise, of the " happy ending."

BIBLIOGRAPHY

TEXTS: (1) Auchinleck MS. ed. Weber, 1810, I, 357–71; H. Varnhagen, *Anglia*, III, 415–23 (1880); Trans. E. Rickert, *Romances of Love*, 1907, p. 47 ff.

STUDIES: Cf. Wells, *Manual*, p. 783.
Child, F. *English and Scottish Ballads*, II, 63–83 (1886).
Foulet, L. "Marie de France et les Lais Bretons," *Zts. f. rom. Phil.* XXIX, 19–56, 292–322 (1905).
Guillaume, G. "The *Lay le Freine*," *MLN*. XXXVI, 458–64 (1921).
Holthausen, F. *Lay le Freine*, v. 91, *Anglia*, XIII, 360 (1890–91).
Köhler, R. See Warnke. *Vergleichende Anmerkungen*, pp. lxi–xcviii (1901).
Laurin, A. *Essay on Language of Lay le Freine*. Diss. Upsala, 1869.
Matzke, J. "The Legend of the Husband with Two Wives," *Mod. Phil.* V, 211–39 (1907).
Marie de France, *Lai del Fraisne*, ed. Warnke, *Die Lais der Marie*, Bibl.

Tale see Hammond, *Chaucer Manual*, p. 304; Wells, *Manual*, pp. 726–28. In the main Chaucer derived his story from the Latin version made by Petrarch in 1373 from Boccaccio's *Decameron*, Tenth Day, Tenth Tale. A. C. Lee, *The Decameron, Its Sources and Analogues*, 1909, pp. 348–56, mentioned among other early versions that by Sercambi (*Novelle*, ed. Renier, 1889, No. 108, p. 401) and the anonymous French *Mystère de Griseldis, Marquise de Saluces, par personnages*, 1395 (restauré par Ch. Gailly de Taurines et Léonel de la Tourasse, Paris, 1910). Cf. Monacis, *La Novella di Griselda secundo la lezione de un manuscritto non ancora illustrato del Decamerone*, Perugia, 1902; *Literaturblatt*, XXIV, 117–19; R. Schuster, *Griseldis in der frz. Literature*. Diss. Tübingen, 1909.

Norman, III, 1885, 1901, pp. 56–67; trans. F. Luquiens, *Four Lays of Marie*, N. Y., 1903; E. Mason, *French Mediaeval Romances*, Everymans Library, 1911.

Rickert, E. *Seven Lais of Marie de France.* Lond., 1901.

Schoepperle, G. *Tristan and Isolt*, 1913, vol. I, 158–77, *The Second Isolt;* vol. II, 525–28, *The Problem of the Second Isolt.*

Warnke. See Marie de France.

Zupitza, J. "Zum Lay le Freine," *Eng. Stud.* X, 41–48 (1886).

SIR DEGARE

VERSIONS. The romance of *Sir Degare* is preserved in five manuscripts and in three sixteenth-century editions, the relationship of which has not been determined. The earliest, the Auchinleck manuscript, contains the most complete version of the story and represents an original probably composed early in the fourteenth century in the South Midland dialect. The name of the hero, carefully explained (l. 229) to mean something that " almost lost it is " (v. 214), suggests the French word *esgare* and the possibility of a French source. Whether the Middle English version is a translation of this lost *Lai d'Esgare* or merely a clever imitation of the *Lai* style, the incidents are certainly those typical " aventures Whereof Britouns made her layes." The style is simple, brief, yet picturesque; the rime the familiar short-riming couplet. In date, form, and context, *Degare* belongs with the other Middle English versions of such lays as *Orfeo* or the translations of Marie de France's *Lanval* [1] and her *Lai del Fraisne*. From the Middle English redaction of this last poem, the *Degare* poet even borrowed definite ideas and phrases. But *Degare, Freine,* and *Orfeo,* must all have been of approximately the same date since in not one does the language antedate the fourteenth century and since they were all copied in the Auchinleck manuscript by the same scribe,[2] probably between 1330 and 1340.

ORIGIN. Within the comparatively brief compass of nine hundred and ninety-three lines the story of *Degare* manages to

[1] The long ME. version of *Sir Launfal* was preceded, according to Kittredge (*American Jour. of Phil.* 1889, x, 5) by an earlier version in Middle English. From this original, x, was derived the extant short version now represented by a poem of 535 verses in MS. Rawlinson C 86 (sixteenth century). This text is much nearer to Marie's *Lanval* than is the long version, and must represent rather closely the lost original version in Middle English. This must have been made at about the same time, in the same style and verse, as the other translations of " Breton " lays.

[2] See Muriel Carr, " Notes on a Middle English Scribe's Methods," *Univ. of Wisconsin, Studies in Language and Lit.,* II. p. 152 (1918).

combine an astonishing number of folk-lore and romance *motifs*. The name of the hero, like that of the maiden Freine, signifies the ultimately popular character of the tale. The taste for such cognomens reappears even in the later more composite romances of the type of *Emare* or *Degrevant*.

The first part of the story is devoted to an account of the hero's parents. His mother is long kept from marriage with the kings and princes who seek her hand by an over-devoted father who overthrows every suitor in a royal tournament. The tournament is said to be held on the anniversary of the death of the king's wife. Though shortened and rationalized, the situation evidently comes from the large group of stories in which a king seeks to marry his own daughter. In the folk-tales the desire generally rises because she alone can fulfill some special condition which the dead wife had made the king swear to observe. In English romances such as *Apollonius* or *Emare* the character of the Incestuous Father is more frankly recognized.[3] The Princess in *Degare* is made at last to meet a lover when she goes wandering in the forest. He is a magnificent-looking stranger who asserts that he has long loved her, ravishes her, and on leaving her, prophesies the birth of a child for whom he leaves his own pointless sword. Whether the Fairy Wooer was originally, as has been argued,[4] the Angel in Joachim's garden, or whether he belonged to the lineage of splendid Otherworld beings who appear in Celtic legend, there is little question that in this particular instance he was inspired by the account of Tydorel's father in the " Breton lay " of that name.

The description of the secret birth of this love-child, of the Maiden Messenger who at the princess's command carries him through a moonlit night to the door of a hermitage, the poet of *Degare* borrowed definitely from the English version of Marie's *Lai del Fraisne*. In the French version nothing was said of the moonlight, but the English translator added this effective touch which in turn the *Degare* poet was to borrow.[5] The latter tells

---

[3] That the poet had this in mind is shown by the Princess's uncalled for comment concerning her child: " Every man wolde it in euery stede/That my father on me it wan." See *Emare* here, note 6.

[4] See *Gowther* here, note 3.

[5] There are likewise passages of verbal imitation: cf. *Freine,* lines 85, 145, 149, 189, 197, with those in *Degare,* lines 179, 217 ff., 239, 245.

in detail of the gifts left with the child but in this makes a curious departure. In addition to the usual gold and silver, a pair of fairy gloves, which his mother has received from her unknown lover, is left with Degare and a written command to the effect that he is to wed no lady whose hands the gloves will not fit. A parallel to this is hard to find, since gloves are a somewhat too sophisticated article of dress for folk-lore to make common use of, but there is at least one parallel in the fifteenth-century Catalan version of *La Fille sans Mains* (*Rom.* xxx, 520), in which the dying wife of the Emperor Contasti begs him to marry no one less beautiful than she, nor one whom her gloves will not fit. This request motivates the episode of the father's insistence on marriage with his own daughter. Stories of this type were, however, so widely diffused [6] and the Catalan text itself is so late a composite, that there is no improbability in supposing that some much earlier version, using this particular feature, may have caught the attention of the original author of the *Lai d'Esgare*. In the Middle English version the gloves having been thus introduced, serve the purpose of Recognition Tokens when years later, the young Degare overthrows his grandfather in the suitors' tournament, receives his Mother, untouched of course by Time, as his prize, and only remembers, after the marriage ceremony has been performed, to try on her white hands the gloves of fate. The happy solution of this Œdipus-like situation in *Degare* or in *Eglamour*, where similarly a mother recognizes her son in her new-made husband, is typical of the care-free naïveté of romance when untouched by ecclesiastical influence.

Degare's own history, before this reunion with his mother, is briefly told. His bringing up in the woodland hermitage and his setting forth armed only with a rough oak sapling, suggest the beginning of the Perceval story of the Forest-Reared Youth. Degare's rescue of an old knight from a dragon, his refusal of the knight's wealth and daughter are mere commonplaces of knightly adventure. Equally well-known are Degare's combats with his relatives: he fights with his grandfather and, overthrowing him, wins his own mother; later he fights with his

[6] Miss Cox, *Cinderella, Folk-Lore Society*, pp. 52–79, enumerated sixty-six tales.

father, who appears as a wandering knight-errant and recognizes his own sword in the hands of his son. In Degare's quest for his father occurs an adventure which, unlike these others, suggests a definite literary source.

Accompanied by one follower, Degare goes through the forest until he comes to a lonely castle. The drawbridge is down, the gate open, but no living being appears. Degare enters the hall of the castle, in which a great hearth fire is burning, seats himself on a dais, and is presently served, first by three maidens in hunting guise who bring him venison, then by a yellow-faced dwarf clad in a furred green surcoat, who spreads the table and lights many torches. A lady and fifteen maidens, clad in red and green, enter and eat with the hero in silence. Later the lady plays sweet music [7] to him, and despite his amorous desires he falls into a deep slumber on which, next day, she gently rallies him. When he questions why she has so many women and no men, she tells him of the furious suitor who has ravaged her land and killed all her men except the dwarf. Needless to say, Degare promptly kills this giant, and when the lady offers herself and her possessions to the youth, he promises to return and accept her bounty within a twelvemonth.

All this seems to have some definite connection with Giglain, Gawain's son, about whom, near the beginning of the thirteenth century, Renaud de Beaujeu wove the elaborate romance, *Le Bel Inconnu* (ed. Hippeau, 1860). Renaud's source seems also to have provided material for the Middle English poem sometimes ascribed to Thomas Chestre, *Libeaus Desconus* (ed. Kaluza, 1890).[8] In both versions the hero similarly comes to the castle of a lady possessed or persecuted by a militant suitor. In Renaud's courtly version she is described as skilled in the Seven Arts, " la pucele as blances mains " (l. 1925), and is recognizable, despite Renaud's rationalizing tendencies, as the Fairy Mistress of a Bower of Bliss.[9] Her magic powers are described

[7] A parallel to this exists in the ancient Irish tale of the *inram Maelduin*. On the Island of Women, magic, sleep-inducing music prevents the companions from entering the fairy island. Cf. *Revue Celt*. IX, 489; Brown, *Harvard Studies*, VIII, 75.

[8] For the history of the conflicting views on the relationship of Renaud's poem and that in Middle English see Schofield, *Harvard Studies*, 1895, IV, 59 ff. Schofield believed the two poems had a common source.

[9] Cf. Schofield, *ibid.*, pp. 36, 129, 197, for indications of Renaud's borrowings from Chrétien's *Erec*, especially in the description of the *Ile d'Or*.

by Renaud as amusing illusory arts [10] which she practices upon
her lover in teasing punishment for seeming lack of devotion.
He is made to think himself in dire peril and later has to endure the laughing jests of the lady over his previous terror. In
Sir Degare the lady's fairy music enchants and inhibits the
hero, and her words, though more sedate and brief, have the
same jocose quality. Of this there is nothing in the *Libeaus
Desconus,* for here the lady is a sorceress, an evil *dame d'amour,*
ungraced by jest in her relations with Gingelein. But if in
these respects *Degare* is closer to the French poem, the more
prosaic description of the castle and the special reference to the
great fire burning in the hall, seem closer to the text of *Libeaus.*
The explanation may lie in the knowledge possessed by the
author of the French *Lai d'Esgare* of the lost common source
of *Le Bel Inconnu* and of *Libeaus,* or in the knowledge possessed by the author of the Middle English *Degare* of these two
extant texts.

BIBLIOGRAPHY

TEXTS: (1) Advocates Library, Edin., Auchinleck MS. W 41, ed.
Laing, Abbotsford Club, 1849; desc. Kölbing, *Eng. Stud.* VII, 178–91;
(2) Cambridge Univ. Libr. Ff II, 38 (about 602 verses); (3) Bodleian,
Selden C 39 (about 352 verses), printed by John King, 1560; (4) Percy
Folio MS., ed. Hales and Furnivall, 1867–69, III, 16 ff.; (5) Duke of
Sutherland's MS., now Egerton 2862, desc. *Eng. Stud.* VII, 192–93; (6)
undated edition by Copland, reprinted by Utterson, *Early Popular
Poetry,* 1817, I, 113.

STUDIES: Cf. Wells, *Manual,* p. 784.
Furnivall, F. See Texts, III.
Kaluza, M. *Libeaus Desconus,* Leipzig, 1890, p. cliv.
Schofield, W. *English Literature — to Chaucer,* pp. 186–87.

---

[10] The magician in Chaucer's *Franklin's Tale* practices similar illusory
arts. See *Parténopeus* here, note 9.

SIR DEGREVANT

VERSIONS. Two slightly imperfect Middle English manuscripts contain the only known version of *Degrevant*. Both manuscripts were written in the fifteenth century, and were derived from the same source, though this, according to Finsterbuch (p. 74), was not the original text of the poem. The Thornton manuscript, the earlier of the two, was written before 1430, probably not long after the composition of the poem. The lateness of its date and the thoroughly English character of the setting make it unlikely that there was ever an antecedent French version of the tale. The author seems to have been a minstrel; he prays for special blessing on those who love " gamen and glee " ; he praises his hero who loves to have " mynstralles in haulle," who of " gyfte was never gnede;" and he takes pains to point out that Degrevant's secret tryst is betrayed by a forester, not a minstrel, for " mynstrals are ay curtayse." His allusions show that he was familiar with romance stories. From the phrase, " me were lever than al ꝩe golde in Ryne " (v. 541), it would appear that he knew something of the *Nibelungenlied*. His hero, he says, was a " Knyghte of ꝩe Table Rownde,/As it es made in Mappamonde," [1] and was well known to King Arthur, dame Gaynore, Perceval, and Gawayne. The connection with Arthurian romance is, however, purely artificial, and aside from the similarity of name there is no reason to regard Degrevant as the villainous Agravain of Arthurian legend.

The dialect of the poem is northern and contains a number

---

[1] Halliwell suggested that the English writer, translating from an Anglo-Norman text, might have mistaken d'Ægrivauns for the entire name. Rickert, p. xlix, noted that in the list of Arthur's knights given by the chronicler, John Harding (1368–1460), is the name Degrevant. Harding was describing the great Round Table which still hangs in the palace hall at Winchester. (See description by Smirke, " The Hall and the Round Table at Winchester," *Proceedings of Archaeol. Institute of Great Britain*, 1846.) The romancer must have had some such chart in mind, an Arthurian " Mappamonde."

of curious North Country words. Like *Sir Perceval of Galles* the poem is fashioned in sixteen-line stanzas riming aaabcccb-dddefffe. The structure of the triplet and the tail-rime verses is explained by Luick and Finsterbuch by reference to that in the half lines of older alliterative poetry.[2] The devices in *Degrevant* for linking stanzas together by repetition of important words or by repetition of the whole or part of the last line or last two lines of one stanza in the introductory lines of the next appear in *Sir Percyvelle*, in the *Aunters of Arthur*, and the *Avowynge of Arthur* (Medary, p. 255). In these last two romances, as also in *Degrevant*, the end of the poem is linked to the beginning by the repetition of the introductory four lines. Brown (*Rom. Rev.* VII, 275) suggested that Welsh alliterative poetry of the thirteenth and fourteenth centuries may have influenced the authors of these romances in this matter of stanza linking. In his opinion the poem originated in or near counties which were a part of the old Welsh border. There is additional confirmation for this theory in the Welsh form Gaynor for the name of Arthur's Queen, in the allusions to Westwale (Thornton MS., v. 1511) and to Degrevant and his friends as "wylde men of the west" (l. 1367), and finally to a possible Welsh betrothal custom.[3] The only English place name in the romance is in v. 1401 to "towelles of Alsame" (Eylyssham), the town of Alysham in Norfolk, where the linen industry was established in the fourteenth century.

The value of the romance has been variously estimated. Halliwell (p. xxiii) thought its descriptive notices of early cos-

---

[2] Bülbring, "Avowynge," *Morsbach's Studien*, Bd. L (1913), argued that the triplet verses should be read with four, the tail-rime verses with three beats (Hebungen); Luick, *Anglia*, XXXIX, 269, believed that all the verses should be read with two beats. He thought that the triplet verses had the structure of the first half line of the alliterative long line, and that the tail-rime verses had that of the second half line. With this Finsterbuch, after his elaborate study of *Perceval* and *Degrevant*, in general agreed.

[3] The reference is to the habit of night courtship, or courting on a bed, which is called *cnocio* or *streicio* in Wales, *fenstern* in Germany, *kilt* in Switzerland, *questing* in Holland, and *bundling* in old and New England. Cf. Halliwell, note to l. 1544; Douce, Illus. of Shakespeare, I, 113; C. Masson, *Journeys in Balochistan*, Lond., 1842, III, 287, tells of the custom among the Afghan tribes. Cf. J. Rhys and D. B. Jones, *The Welsh People*, Lond., 1906, pp. 583; Rhys, *Arthurian Legend*, p. 175; Baskerville, "English Songs on the Night Visit," *PMLA*. XXXVI (1921).

tume and architecture of peculiar interest; Luick (p. v) found
its literary quality negligible; William Morris and his painter
friends, when they were adorning the House Beautiful at Upton,
Kent, chose to paint on its walls scenes from this picturesque
tale (Mackail, *Life of Morris*, I, 158). As a story of hunting
raids and swift reprisals, of gallant tournament and moonlit
wooing, it has indubitable variety. To a degree unusual in
Middle English poetry the author lingers over the description
of beautiful and luxurious things. Like the *Pearl* poet, he pauses
to describe the dress of the maiden, her pearl-fretted violet robe,
her gleaming ribbons, as she comes in the early morning by
the rose bushes where her lover waits. Like an early Keats, he
pictures a midnight feast where on ivory boards and in golden
cups, is " na dayntese to dere/Na spyces to spare," whilst the
lady harps " notes ful swet " to the lover beside her. The poet
makes rich and lovely the chamber of love; the roof is inlaid
with " besauntes " and painted with scenes from the Apocalypse
of St. John, the Epistles of Paul, and the " Parabylles " of
Solomon. The corbels are golden archangels, " ffyfthy made of
o molde "; the four " gospellers," Austin, Gregory, Jerome, and
Ambrose, stand on four pillars, and the walls are painted with
knights of many lands and kings enthroned, Charlemagne and
Godfrey of Bouillon and " Arthure de Bretayne." [4] The azure-
colored bed is embroidered with gay jewel work and popinjays
of green; it has sendal covered pillows " wroght in Westwale ";
its curtain run on red-golden rings. In all this there is certainly elaboration enough, but it is far too zestful to hint of

---

[4] Cf. J. C. Wall, *Mediaeval Wall Paintings*, Lond., 1914, p. 109. Wall's
description, pp. 44–8, of the twelfth century painting of saints, apostles, and
the Apocalypse in Kempley Church, Gloucestershire, is of special interest in
connection with the *Degrevant* passage. Many romances refer to painted
walls. Cf. O. Söhring, " Werke bildender Kunst in alt. frz. Epen." *Rom. Forsch.*
XII (1900); also the *Roman de La Rose*, the *Lady of the Fountain* in
the *Mabingion*, the French prose *Lancelot*, where Morgan shows Arthur the
paintings of Lancelot's adventures, etc. In addition to the peculiarly detailed
account of the painted walls, the reference in *Degrevant* to Alysham in
Norfolk leads one to suspect the poet of familiarity with a region which
was famous in the fourteenth century for the painted roofs and screens
produced by its native craftsmen. Cf. C. E. Keyser, *A List of Buildings in
Great Britain having Mural Decoration*, Lond., 1883 (Index, Norfolk). Cf.
W. O. Sypherd, *Studies in Chaucer's Hous of Fame*, Chaucer Soc., 1907,
pp. 83–86.

decadence. The author's description is as graphic in kind as is his power of characterization. Conventional as that is in some ways, it escapes again and again into piquancy. Degrevant may be love-vanquished at first sight of Melydore, but he keeps his wits and his vigor; and the maiden herself, though a "pervenke of pryse," is also a bit of a shrew who can bid her maid entertain her guest in " twenty deuelle way." Her father, indeed, she makes sweat with rage when he is chased by Degrevant within his own castle doors and is bullied there by his lively daughter. He agrees perforce to her marriage with his foe: " Hit is as ðou wylle;/I cane say na more."

ORIGIN. The opening episodes of the romance tell of the attack made on the hunting preserves of Degrevant by his powerful neighbor, of Degrevant's hasty return from the Holy Land, of his challenge, of his foe's second attack, and the battle in which Degrevant and his men hunt their opponents like deer through the fen. All this has been likened by Dr. Rickert (p. xlvii) to the hunting raid and the battle of Otterburn (1388), celebrated in the two famous ballads of the Battle of Otterburn and the Hunting of the Cheviot. Realistic as are the ballads and the romance, the latter has nothing of the race feud of the Percy and the Douglas. It is altogether local and personal in tone. The author seems to have a definite region in mind, a countryside of forest and fen, of glades and stream, of fell and " ling," yet near the sea, for the tide fills the moat of the castle of Degrevant's enemy, and Degrevant's rival comes by sea from France. These details might suggest portions of the sea coast of Cumberland or Westmoreland, if the reference to Degrevant as riding overnight out of Westwale is not to be taken literally. As for the defiant hunting and subsequent battle, — Nessler (*Geschichte der Ballade Chevy Chase*, Berlin, 1911), has pointed out that similar episodes are to be found in Geoffrey of Monmouth's *Historia* (1, c. 12), in *Guy of Warwick* (v. 6714), in *Degare, Triamore*, — in other words, that this bit of typical narrative antedated the ballads and presumably also the battle of Otterburn itself.

Degrevant has the closest analogies in plot to two Middle English romances, *Eger and Grime* and the *Erle of Tolous*.

Like the first, Degrevant presents a vivid and unusual setting, a wild country where the dun deer run in dales neighbored by the sea. Certain scenes, such as the first meeting of the lovers in the garden, the lavish richness of the lady's room where the hero is cared for, and the breaking of the parks [5] and the killing of his enemy's deer by the angry hero, suggest some actual relationship between the two stories. In both may be noticed likewise the tendency toward elaborate description.

With the *Erle of Tolous, Degrevant* has even more evident contacts. Both poems are found in the Thornton manuscript and begin with very similar prayers to the Trinity. In each the hero is attacked, in *Degrevant* in a hunting raid, in the *Erle* through invasion of his land by a foe whom presently he is to put utterly to rout. Becoming interested in the daughter (*Degrevant*), in the wife (*Erle*) of his foe, the hero makes a secret journey to her home, accompanied by only one man, his faithful squire (*Degrevant*), a treacherous captive (*Erle*). The wife of the hero's enemy reproaches him for his cruelty to the young man. The hero makes shift to see the lady in a garden (*Degrevant*), in a chapel (*Erle*). On departing from her home the hero is treacherously ambushed, but after a terrific combat fights his way clear. The ambush is planned by a forester (*Degrevant*), by the captive (*Erle*). Later on the hero enters his enemy's land in order to participate in a great tournament (*Degrevant*), in an ordeal by battle (*Erle*). After his victory peace is made and the hero marries the daughter (*Degrevant*), the widow (*Erle*) of his former foe. From these resemblances it is hardly possible to doubt that the author of *Degrevant* made use of the extant Middle English version of the *Erle of Tolous*.

---

[5] In *Degrevant* the word *park* is used in the legal sense of a land enclosure which was expressly intended for deer. Cf. Turner, *Select Pleas of the Forest*, Selden Soc., Lond., 1901, p. cxv, who noted that the word is still often found as a field name in the west of England. *Degrevant*, l. 107, refers to the breaking of the parks; l. 143, to making them " commoune "; l. 145, to re-enclosing them. *Chase* meant a private forest and warren (*Degrevant*, l. 1771), the land over which the exclusive right of hunting extended (Turner, pp. cix, cxxiii).

BIBLIOGRAPHY

TEXTS: (1) C, Camb. Univ. Libr. Ff 1, 6, ed. Halliwell, *Thornton Romances*, pp. 177–256; (2) L, Thornton MS. Lincoln Cath. A, 1, 17, excerpts by Halliwell, *ibid.* notes; stanzas 1–6, both MSS. by Schleich, *Eng. Stud.* XII, 140–2 (1888–9). Both MSS. entire, ed. K. Luick, *Sir Degrevant, Wiener Beit. z. eng. Phil. Bd.* XLVII (1917). Trans. Rickert, *Romances of Love*, p. 107.

STUDIES: Cf. Wells, *Manual*, p. 785.

Finsterbuch, F. "Der Versbau der mitteleng. Dichtungen *Sir Perceval of Galles* (pp. 1–174) und *Sir Degrevant.*" *Wiener Beit. z. eng. Phil.* XLIX. *Wien*, 1920. rev. *Literaturbl.*

Luick. See Texts.

Medary, M. P. "Stanza-Linking in Middle English Verse," *Rom. Rev.* VII, 243–70 (1916), *Degrevant*, pp. 255–6.

Brown, L. "On the Origin of Stanza-Linking in English Alliterative Verse," *Rom. Rev.* VII, 271–283 (1916).

Rickert. See Texts.

THE HISTORY OF SIR EGER, SIR GRIME, AND SIR GRAYSTEELE

VERSIONS. The history of *Sir Eger* can be retraced in England only to the end of the fifteenth century. Of the copies[1] once current only two have thus far been found. The best and oldest, a poem of 1474 lines, roughly written in short riming couplets, and divided, as it almost certainly was not in earlier versions, into six parts or cantos, is in Bishop Percy's Folio manuscript (P). The second text, a rambling, somewhat incoherent version of double the length and half the effectiveness of P, is known only in the Aberdeen print (L) of 1711 and its modern reprints. In vocabulary and orthography, however, Reichel (p. 4 and n. to v. 1006) thought this older than the Folio version. In each version the language is so modernized and corrupted that it is doubtful if even a much more careful study than has yet been given to it could determine the home of the original poem[2] or indicate with exactness the period of its composition. The extant versions seem to be independent derivatives of this lost original, but removed from it by a number of lost intermediary texts (Reichel, p. 15).

The earliest known allusion to the romance comes in 1497, when the Treasurer's Accounts of James IV of Scotland state that "twa fithelaris sang Gray Steil" to the king at Stirling (Hales, 1, 342). It was not even then a new song, to judge from the affiliations of the story with older romance. From the sixteenth century numerous references to *Eger* are recorded by both Laing and Hales (p. 343); in the *Complaynt of Scotland*, 1549, it is listed with other known romances; the name Graysteele was used at least three times as a sobriquet for well-

---

[1] Bishop Percy described a copy of the romance which he possessed in 1800. Cf. Furnivall, p. 342; *Complaynt of Scotland, EETSES.* XVII, p. LXXIX.
[2] Hales remarked (p. 342): "The language is unquestionably Scottish"; Reichel, p. 10, referred to the "mittelscottischen" original text. Beyond these mere assertions no one seems to have gone.

known personages in the sixteenth century; and several writers of note allude to the romance, — John Taylor, the Water Poet (1623), especially comments on its popularity in Scotland, and couples it in this connection with *Sir Degare*. Editions of the romance were printed in 1599, 1602, 1606, 1687 (Rickert, p. 182).

The romance tells of the sworn-brotherhood between two noble knights, Eger and Grime; of the defeat that Eger endures at the hands of Graysteele, a champion who challenges all comers in his land; of the pride of Winglayne, beloved of Eger, who will have none for husband but an unconquered knight; of Eger's fear to lose her when he has been defeated by Graysteele, of Grime's battle in the guise of Eger with Graysteele, and of Graysteele's death; of the fame of the exploit; of the humility of Winglayne before the supposed champion and of her marriage with Eger. Grime himself, more truly the hero of the story than Eger, meanwhile wins for himself the lovely Lady Loospaine (v. 1407; L version, Lillias), who has cared for Eger after his defeat, and later nobly welcomed and aided Grime. The plot has no special distinction, but no one who has commented on the romance has failed to feel the notable charm of its style, vividly pictorial as it is, quaintly humorous, terse or tender at will, and with a power of characterization which justifies Bishop Percy's verdict that this is one of the best of the ancient epic tales in the Folio (Hales, p. 353). A single passage, interesting, too, from the point of origins, may serve as illustration.

Eger returns from his conflict with Graysteele, battered in body but still more battered in spirit. He sits on his bed and tells his trouble to Grime; he is boyish, petulant, plaintive, and most frankly bewildered at his own discomfiture. He has had the best of weapons, the best steed, the utmost confidence in himself, the best possible spirit for the adventure. But Graysteele has defeated him, and for a final mark of ignominy, has cut off his little finger. The account most happily characterizes the impetuous youth and brings out the contrast between him and the silent stronger Grime, in truth " a dogged, canny Scot," who vainly tries to comfort him. Besides this the passage is especially rich in the pictorial detail which characterizes the

romance. Aptly it describes the " Forbidden Land " kept by
Graysteele, his " fresh iland " with its towered castles, and the
mighty knight himself in all his red magnificence. It tells of
the castle to which on his homeward journey the suffering Eger
comes one moonlight night, of the little arbor he enters, of the
lovely Lady Loospaine, " red as rose in rain " who cares for his
wounds and later comforts him with her sweet singing as he lies
in her rich chamber. The luxury of her abode, here and elsewhere in the romance, is repeatedly emphasized.

ORIGIN. The passage just summarized indicates the basic
type to which part at least of the story of *Eger* belongs. However much it has been rationalized by a story-teller more interested in personality and in scenes of fact rather than of fancy,
it belongs with the group of Fairy Mistress stories. Loospaine's
beautiful Otherworld abode lies beyond a river in the " Forbidden Land "; its entrance is guarded by the gigantic Graysteele;
the lady herself, of superlative beauty and healing powers,[3] is
recognizable as *fée,* and the main business of the tale is with
the combat through which she is won by a mortal knight. Schofield's brief comment (p. 232) that " at bottom this seems to
be a story of the *Iwain* type," is more than confirmed by a
closer comparison. *Iwain,* written about 1170 by Chrétien de
Troyes, was translated in the fourteenth century into Middle
English, and from this version (vv. 425–26) the *Eger* poet borrowed at least one couplet (vv. 119–20) and many incidents of
his narrative. The ill-fame of Graysteele, the secretly undertaken exploit of Eger to find him, Eger's overthrow, his account
of it to Grime, Grime's present departure, also in secret, to attempt the same adventure, his victory, and marriage with the
widowed Lady Loospaine, all closely parallel the first part of
Iwain.[4] Thus Colgrevance in Arthur's court tells of his wan-

---

[3] Loospaine gives to Eger a magic potion which at once restores his
strength, but the effect of it is lost when he returns to his own domain.
In the Old Irish *Serglige Conculaind* and the Old French *Iwain* the fairy
heroine gives the hero a potion which restores his lost wits. Cf. A. C. L.
Brown, *Iwain, Harvard Studies* VIII, 34–40.

[4] Ed. by W. Foerster, 3rd ed. Halle, 1906. For the Middle English version, cf. Schleich's ed. Oppeln, 1887; Billings, *Guide,* pp. 156–60; Wells,
Manual, 65–67, 771.

derings in the strange forest (Chrétien's Broceliande), of his
fair welcome at a castle, of his encounter with a Giant Herds-
man who directs him to a Perilous Well, of his defeat there at
the hands of a knight (Chrétien's Esclados the Red). Thus
Iwain, having heard the tale, goes secretly away to try his
fate, meets and kills Esclados, and ultimately weds Laudine,
the Red Knight's widow. Although *Eger* is much condensed,
these structural likenesses in the narrative indicate an essential
dependence on the older story. The important change in *Eger*
which makes Graysteele the enemy of Loospaine, the murderer
of her brother and her one-day husband, instead of her husband
and protector as was Esclados in Chrétien's tale, may be accounted for, at least according to Brown's theory in connection
with *Iwain,* as representing a tendency by which in primitive
tales the servant of a *fée,* " originally only a creature of the
fée, sent out by her to test the hero's valor," takes on the guise
of a suitor or a husband whom it becomes necessary to overthrow before she can be won by a mortal lover.[5] Brown (*Iwain,*
p. 50) has indicated the probable confusion that took place even
in Chrétien's Celtic sources between the *fée* story proper, and
the story of a giant and his unwilling captive. There is ancient
enough authority, therefore, for the hostility between Loospaine
and Graysteele.

In addition to the structural similarity to *Iwain, Eger* has
still some other possibly Celtic connections. One of these is
the strange attribute ascribed to Graysteele. In preparing
Grime for his combat Loospaine tells him, as " no woman alive
knoweth so well " as she, that Graysteele's power increases by
a man's strength with every hour from midnight until noon,
and wanes correspondingly in the afternoon. There is obvious

[5] Cf. Brown, *ibid.,* ch. IV, The Combat Motive. As regards *Eger,* the L
version, which ends with the marriage of Eger to Loospaine after the
death of Grime, represents, perhaps, the influence of a more primitive version than P. In the simple form of the story there would be but one hero
and one heroine, as in the ballads of *Sir Cawline* or *Sir Lionel,* and it would
be he who won the lady by his own exploit. In this case Eger would
originally have won Loospaine for himself, as in L he ultimately does. His
present unsatisfactory part in the romance may, therefore, be due to the
introduction of the Sworn-Brotherhood *motif,* and the consequent doubling
of the hero's rôle. On the other hand the two heroes may both have belonged to the original story, if that were, as is suggested below, a variant
of the *Nibelungenlied*.

analogy here with Gawain's increase of strength from morn to noon, a trait which has been held to connect Gawain with a Celtic solar myth.[6] Of less primitive character, though in entire accord with traditional descriptions of the magnificent beings of the Celtic Otherworld as they are rationalized in mediaeval romances, is the emphasis on Graysteele's splendor and might. Like Esclados in Chrétien's *Iwain*, like Valerin, Guinevere's Otherworld lover in Ulrich von Zatzikhoven's *Lanzelet* (ed. K. Halm, Frankfurt, 1845, 1. 4972 ff.), or Gasozein in Heinrich von dem Türlîn's *Diu Crône*,[7] Graysteele is a warrior of sumptuous appearance,[8] a noble and heroic figure, yet a foe to the lady of the story. Like the mysterious knight, who in the Old French *Lai de l'Espine* kept the ford on the vigil of St. John, Graysteele defends a " riding place " across his river, and fights with the true hero of the story. Of their adventure a *lai* might well have been made, even as the French poet says the " Bretons " made one concerning the fight at the Ford of the Thorn. Finally, in the *Eger* poet's description of Loospaine herself, there is a detail for which there seems no antecedent save in Celtic tradition. The lady is said (vv. 619–21) to have between her eyes a curious pin spot of white and red, and, when he looks upon it, poor Grime forgets all other things. For Loospaine's lovely blemish the only notable parallel is the famous and fatal " love spot " which made the Irish hero Diarmaid's beauty irresistible to the women who beheld it.[9]

These traditional Celtic elements, if such they be, offer an interesting contrast to the affiliations of the *Eger* story with so complete a product of Anglo-Saxon and Teutonic imagination as *Beowulf*. Grendel's strength of thirty men, his character as a demon of the fens, the arm which Beowulf tears from him, and

---

[6] Cf. J. Weston, *The Legend of Sir Gawain*, Lond., 1897, pp. 12; G. Paris, *Hist. Lit.* xxx.

[7] Ed. by G. H. Scholl, Tübingen, 1852, vv. 3699; cf. K. G. T. Webster, " Arthur and Charlemagne," *Eng. Stud.* xxxvi, 341; Schoepperle, *Tristan*, ii, 535.

[8] See *Orfeo* here, note 7. Hale's idea (p. 351) that " the brilliant opulence of Graysteele's appearance points to an Oriental origin," is unsupported by any evidence.

[9] For full bibliography concerning the ancient texts of the Diarmaid story and of the modern Irish and Scotch oral versions, see Miss Schoepperle's *Tristan*, ii, 399, n. 2, 401–2.

exhibits as a trophy in Hrothgar's hall, are dimly recalled in the mighty stature and prowess of Graysteele, in the detailed account of his great hand which Grime cuts off, and gives, in token of her enemy's death, to Loospaine, and of her exhibition of it in her father's hall before all the nobles. So also in the ballad of *Sir Cawline* (Child, No. 61), which in its first adventure seems derived from the same source as *Eger,* the Eldrige King who haunts the moors at night, seeking whom he may destroy, who is wounded and flees away, leaving his hand to Cawline, is to some degree reminiscent of Grendel.[10] Perhaps the transition from the epic monster to the strange warrior of the ballad may be dimly traced through that story of Gervase of Tilbury to which Scott (*Minstrelsy of the Scottish Border,* ed. Henderson, Edin., 1902, II, 319) first called attention. It told of a ghostly warrior at Ely who could be summoned on moonlit nights at a certain entrenchment by any challenger. In this and in the current folk-tale, also referred to by Scott (*Marmion,* n. 4), concerning the bloody spirit who haunted a forest in the northern Highlands, insisting on battle with all whom he met, the Warrior tale has no hint of any romantic interest. In comparison with *Eger,* therefore, it is of interest only as showing the distribution and continuance of a story from which certain primitive details might have been absorbed by the romance.

The possible mixture of Celtic and Teutonic elements in the account of Graysteele and Grendel, is further suggested by the presence in *Eger* of certain ideas that have been held to be characteristically Teutonic. Among these Dr. Rickert (p. xxiii) mentioned: the sworn-brotherhood of the heroes, the defence of a ford or pass, the use of the cut-off fingers as evidence of death, the naming of the mysterious sword Erkyin or Edgeking, brought from beyond "the Greekes sea," and so terrible that "no man durst abyde the winde" of it before his face.[11] To

[10] Sir Cawline is perishing with love for a Princess; she bids him kill "the eldridge king"; the strange champion comes. "By an aukeward stroke" (v. 1029) Cawline cuts off his hand and brings it back to the Princess. So also "with an arkward stroke" (v. 1029) Grime strikes Graysteele on the knee.

[11] It should be noted that although these features do appear in Teutonic story, they appear also in Irish, Norse, and French epic. The Defense of a

these may be added the important episode of the ruse which is practiced on the proud Winglayne.[12] Grime wins her for his friend Eger no less surely than Sigurd won Brunhilde for Gunther, although the details of the story differ widely. In the P version of *Eger* the ruse is never revealed, but in L, Winglayne, who has gone with Eger to visit his newly wedded friend, leaves her husband in furious anger when she discovers the truth. One may admit with entire justice the stupidity of L; but in the unmotivated death of Grahame (Grime), who falls sick and dies shortly after his marriage, in the separation of Winglayne and Eger, is it not possible to catch some faint remembrance, more clearly preserved than in P, of that most famous story in which the hero who had won the Valkyrie only to give her up, and himself to wed another, ultimately paid for his deceit with his life? English romance [13] elsewhere shows the influence of the famous legend, and late though the L version is, it is not impossible that its lost original owed to the older romance not only the ruse of Grime, but its tragic sequel.

Eger, as it stands, seems then to show the combination of a simple folk-tale in which a hero wins his bride by killing a superhuman creature with a Celtic Fairy Mistress story modified by French romancers, plus the story of a Valkyrie-like heroine and the ruse by which she is married to a conquered man. Besides this mixture of racial stories, of human and supernatural elements, certain historic and realistic features claim attention. Investigation along these lines has been carried no further than the brief pioneer suggestions of Dr. Rickert (p. xxiii). The exact description (v. 101) in the poem of Graysteele's land, a tract lying along a river which soon empties into

---

Ford is an especially frequent theme in Old Irish epic. Cf. *Die altirische Heldensage Táin bó Cualnge, ed. Windisch,* Leipzig, 1908, *passim.* For the Friendship and Sworn-Brotherhood themes see note 7 under *Amis* here and note 3 under *Athelston.*

[12] On the Valkyrie nature of Brunhilde see V. Gildersleeve, *Mod. Phil.* VI, 343–75 (1908–09). It is the ruse practised on Winglayne which connects her with Brunhilde and which differentiates her from the many heroines of folk story who are in love with a giant or a monster and who set their mortal lovers apparently impossible tasks in order to be rid of them. Cf. Gerould, *The Grateful Dead,* ch. II, " The Lady and the Monster."

[13] See *Sir Degrevant* here; also under the bibliography of *Beves of Hampton* the articles by Hibbard and Brockstedt.

the sea, of the seven cities by the sea (v. 935), of the two fords that cross the river, of the island on which all comers have to encounter Graysteele, suggested to her that strip of "Debatable Land" along the Solway, between the Esk and the Sark, which was the scene of so many conflicts between the English and Scottish borderers in the fifteenth and sixteenth centuries. In this district one of the principal clans was the Grahams, and to their name the hero Grime (Grahame in the L version) seems to owe his own. Grime is said (v. 21) to be of Garwicke, which Scott identified with Carrick in Ayrshire. In the sixteenth century Grime's fight with Graysteele was localized, according to the reference in Sir David Lyndsay's *Interlude of the Auld Man and his Wife*, "necht half a myle beyond Kinneill," a name Dr. Rickert identified with that of a stream in Dumfriesshire. The fact that the ballad *Sir Lionel* (Child, No. 18), which is at least slightly related to *Eger*, is localized by the Esk, is again an indication of the presence in some form of the Graysteele legend in the Solway district. Further investigation of these tempting clues is greatly to be desired, even though they lead but into a "Land of Doubt,"—a name that in the 1711 edition of the poem was piously substituted for the "Forbidden Country" of old romance.

BIBLIOGRAPHY

TEXTS: (1) Percy Folio MS. (1474 lines), ed. Hales and Furnivall, I, 340–400, Lond., 1868; (2) *Eger and Grime* (2861 lines), Aberdeen, 1711, repr. D. Laing, *Early Metrical Tales*, pp. 1–96, Edin., 1826; 1899: abstract with quotations, Ellis, *Specimens*, pp. 546–567 (1848). Trans. from the *Folio* E. Rickert, *Romances of Friendship*, pp. 137 ff.

STUDIES:
Hales and Furnivall. See Texts, pp. 341–54.
Reichel, G. "Studien zu der schottischen Romanze: *The History of Sir Eger, Sir Grime, and Sir Graysteele*." *Eng. Stud.* XIX, 1–66 (1894). A comparison of the versions, notes on the text, glossary.

TABLE OF ABBREVIATIONS AND REFERENCES

Italics here indicate the abbreviated form of reference used throughout this book. This list of references is supplementary to the special bibliographies for each romance. It includes all general collections of Middle English romance texts of whatsoever date; also the general histories of mediæval literature printed between 1900–1923 and the special studies which cover several romances or deal with themes recurrent in Continental and Middle English romance. See Index for classification by subject.

Amer. Jour. of Phil. American Journal of Philology. Baltimore, 1880–
Anglia. Zeitschrift für englische Philologie. Halle, 1877–
Anglia Bbl. Beiblatt zur Anglia. Halle, 1890–
Archiv für das Studium der neueren Sprachen und Literaturen, ed. Herrig. Braunschweig, 1849–
Arnold, F. C. Das Kind in der deutschen Litteratur des XI–XV Jahrhunderts. Diss. Greifswald, 1905
Aron, A. Traces of Matriarchy in Germanic Hero Lore. Univ. of Wisconsin Studies in Language and Literature, IX. 1920
Ashton, J. Romances of Chivalry. London, 1890
Ausgaben und Abhandlungen aus dem Gebiete der romanischen Philologie. Marburg, 1881–

Baake, W. Die Verwendung des Traummotivs in der englischen Dichtung bis auf Chaucer. Diss. Halle, 1906
Baldwin, C. An Introduction to English Mediæval Literature. New York, 1914.
Baskerville, C. R. Early Romantic Plays in England. *Mod. Phil.*, 1916, XIV, 229–51; 467–512
Becker, P. A. Grundriss der altfrz. Literatur. Heidelberg, 1907
Bédier, J. Les Légendes Épiques. Paris, 1908–13, 1914–21
Beszard, L. Les larmes dans l'épopée jusqu'à la fin du XIIe siècle. Zeitschrift für rom. Philologie, 1903, XXVII
Billings, A. H. A *Guide* to Middle English Metrical Romances. N. Y., 1901, 1905
Bolte, J. and G. Polívka. *Anmerkungen* zu den Kinder- und Hausmärchen der Brüder Grimm. Leipzig, 1913–18
Bonilla y San Martín, A. Libros de Caballerias. Madrid, 1907
Booker, J. M. A Middle English Bibliography to 1907. Heidelberg, 1912
Brandl, A. Spielmannsverhältnisse in frühmittelengl. Zeit. Kön.-preuss. Akad. der Wissenschaft Sitzungsbericht. Berlin, 1910, XL, 873–92
British Museum Catalogue of Additional Manuscripts. London, 1906–10. *B. M. Catalogue of Romances*, H. L. D. Ward, vols. I, II, 1883–93; J. Herbert, vol. III, London, 1910
Brown, C. A. A *Register* of Middle English Religious Verse. Oxford, 1916–20

Cambridge History of English Literature, vols. I, II. Cambridge, 1907–08
CCCbg. Corpus Christi College, Cambridge

Chambers, E. K. The Medieval Stage. Oxford, 1902
Chauvin, V. *Bibliographie* des Ouvrages Arabes. Leipzig, Liége, 1892–1909
Child, F. J. The English and Scottish *Ballads*. 5 vols. Boston, 1898
Clephan, R. C. The Tournament. London, 1919
Comfort, W. W. Character Types in the Old French Chansons de Geste. Publications Modern Language Association, 1906, XXI, 279–434
Crane, R. The Vogue of Mediæval Chivalric Romance during the English Renaissance. Diss. Menasha, 1919
Creek, H. Character in the "Matter of England" Romances. Diss. Urbana, 1911. Cf. *JEGP*. x, 429–53 (1911)
Cripps-Day, F. H. The History of the Tournament in England and in France. London, 1918
Critchlow, F. On the Forms of Betrothal and Wedding Ceremonies in the Old French Romans d'Aventure. Diss. Chicago, 1906
Curry, W. C. The Middle English Ideal of Personal Beauty in the Metrical Romances, Legends, Chronicles. Diss. Baltimore, 1916

Deutschbein, M. *Studien* zur Sagengeschichte Englands. Cothen, 1906

Easter, B. De la Warr. A Study of Magic Elements in the Romans d'Aventure. Diss. Baltimore, 1906
EETS. Early English Text Society, Original Series. London, 1864–
EETSES. Early English Text Society, Extra Series, 1867–
Edwardes, M. *Summary* of the Literatures of Modern Europe to 1400. London, 1907
Ellis, G. *Specimens* of Early English Metrical Romances. London, 1805; revised by Halliwell, 1848
Eng. Stud. Englische Studien. Heilbronn, Leipzig, 1877–
Esdaile, A. J. A List of English Tales and Prose Romances printed before 1740. London, 1912

Faral, E. Les Jongleurs en France au Moyen Age. Paris, 1910; Sources Latines des Contes et Romans Courtois du Moyen Age. Paris, 1913
Farnsworth, W. O. Uncle and Nephew in the Old French Chansons de Geste. N. Y., 1913
Fellinger, F. Schwangerschaft und Geburt in der altfrz. Literatur. Göttingen, 1907; Das Kind in der altfrz. Literatur. Göttingen, 1908
Foerster, W. Der Feuertod als Strafe in der altfrz. erzählenden Dichtung. Studien zur engl. Phil. L. Halle, 1913
Folk Lore Society Publications. London, 1868–
Frahm, W. Das Meer und die Seefahrt in der altfrz. Literatur. Diss. Göttingen, 1914
Fundenberg, G. Feudal France in the French Epic. Princeton, 1918

Galpin, S. "Cortois" and "Vilain," A Study of the Distinctions Made by French and Provençal Poets of the 12th, 13th, and 14th Centuries. New Haven, 1905
Garnett, R., and E. Gosse. An Illustrated History of English Literature. London, 1903–04
Gautier, L. Les Épopées Françaises. 2 ed. Paris, 1878–97; *Bibliographie* des Chansons de Geste. Paris, 1897
Geissler, O. Religion und Aberglaube in den mittelengl. Versromanzen. Diss. Halle, 1908

Gerould, G. H. Saints Legends. Boston, 1916
Germania. Stuttgart, 1856–58; Wien, 1859–92
Goerke, G. Ueber Tierverwandlungen in franz. Dichtung und Sage. Diss. Königsberg, 1904
Groeber, H. Grundriss der romanischen Literatur. Strassburg, 1902
Gross, C. *Sources* and Literature of English History. N. Y., 1915
Grossmann, W. Frühmittelengl. Zeugnisse über Minstrels. Diss. Brandenburg, 1906
Grundtvig, S. Danmarks Gamle Folkeviser. Copenhagen, 1853–90
Gummere, F. The Sister's Son. An English Miscellany. Oxford, 1901
Guyer, F. The Influence of Ovid on Crestien de Troyes. Romanic. Review, 1921, XII, 97–134; 216–47

Hagen, F. H. von der, *Gesammtabenteuer.* 3 vols. Stuttgart u. Tübingen, 1850
Hallauer, M. Das wunderbare Elemente in den Chansons de Geste. Diss. Basle, 1918
Halliwell-Philipps, J. O. The Thornton Romances. Camden Society. London, 1844
Halpersohn, R. Über die Einleitung im altfrz. Kunstepos. Diss. Heidelberg, 1911
Hammond, E. *Chaucer,* A Bibliographical Manual. N. Y., 1908
Hartland, E. S. Primitive Paternity: Myth of Supernatural Birth. London, 1909–10
Hartshorne, C. H. Ancient Metrical Tales. London, 1829
Hazlitt, W. C. *Remains* of Early Popular Poetry of England. London, 1864–66
Herbert, J. See British Museum Catalogue
Heyl, K. Die Theorie der Minne in den ältesten Minneromanen Frankreichs. Diss. Kiel, 1911. Marburger Beiträge z. rom. Phil. IV.
Huebner, W. Die Frage in einigen mittelengl. Versromanen. Diss. Kiel, 1910

Jacobius, H. Die Erziehung des Edelfräuleins im alten Frankreich nach Dichtungen des XII, XIII, und XIV Jahrhunderts. Beihft. Zts. für roman. Philologie, XVI. Halle, 1908
Jahresbericht über die Erscheinungen auf dem Gebiete der germanischen Philologie. Berlin, 1879, Leipzig, 1883–
JEGP. Journal of English and Germanic Philology. Illinois, 1905–

Kahle, R. Der Klerus im mittelengl. Versroman. Diss. Strassburg, 1906
Ker, W. Mediæval English Literature. London, 1912
Koehler, R. Kleinere Schriften. Berlin, 1898–1900
Koerting, G. Grundriss der Geschichte der engl. Literatur von ihren Anfängen bis zur Gegenwart. 5th ed. Münster, 1910
Krämer, P. Das Meer in der altfrz. Literatur. Diss. Giessen, 1919
Kuehn, O. Erwähnung u. Schulderung von körperlichen Krankheiten in altfrz. Dichtung. Diss. Breslau, 1902; Medizinisches aus der altfrz. Dichtung. Abhandlungen z. Gesch. der Medizin, Hft. VIII, Breslau, 1904
Kurtz, B. Studies in the Marvelous. Univ. of California, Berkeley, 1910

Lalande de Calan, C. de. La Bretagne dans les Romans d'Aventures, Revue de Bretagne, 1903, XXX, XXXI; L'Element Celtique dans les Romans d'Aventures. Saint-Brieuc, 1911

Landau, L.   Hebrew-German Romances and Tales and Their Relation to the Romantic Literature of the Middle Ages.   Leipzig, 1912

Lane, F.   Ueber Krankenbehandlung und Heilkunde in der alten Liter. des alten Frankreich.   Diss.   Göttingen, 1904

Langlois, C.   La Société française au XIIIe Siècle d'après dix Romans d'Aventure.   3e ed.   Paris, 1911

Lawrence, W. W.   Mediæval Story and the Beginnings of the Social Ideals of English-Speaking People.   N. Y., 1911

Leach, H. G.   Angevin Britain and Scandinavia.   Cambridge, 1922

Leibecke, O.   Der verabrete Zweikampf in der altfrz. Litteratur.   Diss.   Göttingen, 1905

Lot-Borodine, M.   La Femme et l'Amour au XIIe Siècle d'après les poèmes de Chrétien de Troyes.   Paris, 1909;   Le Roman Idyllique au Moyen Age.   Paris, 1913

Luetjens, A.   Der Zwerg in der deutschen Heldendichtung des Mittelalters.   Breslau, 1911.   Germanistische Abhandlungen, 38

Luft, F.   Über die Verletzbarkeit der Ehre in der altfrz. Chansons de Geste.   Berlin, 1907–08

Literaturblatt für germanische u. romanische Philologie.   Leipzig, 1880–

Magnus, H.   Der Aberglauben in der Medicin.   Abhandlungen zur Geschichte der Medicin, VI.   Breslau, 1903

Mason, E.   French Mediæval Romances.   Everyman Library.   N. Y., 1911

Massing, E.   Die Geistlichkeit im altfrz. Volksepos.   Darmstadt, 1904

Menendez y Pelayo, M.   Origenes de la Novela Nueva.   Biblioteca de Autores españoles.   Madrid, 1907

Merk, C. J.   Anschauungen über die Lehre und das Leben der Kirche im altfrz. Heldenepos.   Halle, 1914

Meyer, F.   Jugendziehung im mittelalter — nach den altfrz. Artus- und Abenteuerromanen.   Solingen, 1896

MLN.   Modern Language Notes.   Baltimore, 1886–

MLR.   Modern Language Review.   Cambridge, England, 1905–

Morris, R.   *Specimens* of Early English.   Part I, Oxford, 1887;   Part II, Morris and Skeat, 4th ed., Oxford, 1898

Mod. Phil.   Modern Philology.   Chicago, 1903–

Mott, L.   The System of Courtly Love.   London, 1904

Mueller, O.   Turnier und Kampf in den altfrz. Artusromanen.   Erfurt, 1907

Mueller, R.   Die Zahl 3 in Sage, Dichtung, u. Kunst.   Teschen, 1903

Neumann, E.   Der Söldner (soudoyer) im mittelalter nach den frz. u. provenzalischen Heldenepen.   Diss.   Marburg, 1905

Noack, G.   Sagenhistorische Untersuchungen zu den Gesta Herwardi.   Diss.   Halle, 1914

Nutt, A.   The Influence of Celtic upon Mediæval Romance.   London, 1904

Ogle, M.   Classical Literary Tradition in Early German and Romance Literature.   *MLN.*   1912, XXVII, 233–42;   *Amer. Jour. of Phil.*, 1913, XXIV, 125 ff.

Oschinsky, H.   Der Ritter unterwegs u. die Pflege der Gastfreundschaft im alten Frankreich.   Halle, 1900

Palaestra, Untersuchungen und Texte.   Leipzig, Berlin, 1898–

Panzer, F.   Hilde-Gudrun.   Halle, 1901

Paris, Gaston. Poèmes et Légendes du Moyen Age. Paris, 1900
Paul, H. *Grundriss* der germanischen philologie, 3 vols. Strassburg, 1891–1900
Paul und Braune. *Beiträge* zur Geschichte der deutschen Sprache und Literatur. Halle, 1874–
Percy Society. Publications of the Percy Society. London, 1840–52
Petit de Julleville, L. Les Mystères. Paris, 1880
PFMS. The Percy Folio Manuscript, ed. Furnivall and Hales, 4 vols. London, 1867–69
PMLA. Publications of the Modern Language Association of America, Baltimore, 1884–1901, Cambridge, 1902–
Potter, M. Four Essays. The Horse as an Epic Character. London, 1917
Prelle de la Nieppe, E. Les Costumes chevaleresques et les armes offensives des XII, XIII, XIV siècles. Annales de la Soc. Archéol. de Bruxelles, 1900
Puckett, H. W. The Fay, Particularly The Fairy Mistress, In Middle High German. Modern Philology, 1918, XVI, 297–313

Quellen und Forschungen zur Sprach- und Culturgeschichte der germanischen Völker. Strassburg, 1874–

Reich, O. Beiträge zur Kenntnis des Bauernlebens im alten Frankreich auf Grund der Zeitgenössischen Literatur. Diss. Göttingen, 1909
Remmpis, M. Die Vorstellungen von Deutschland im altfrz. Heldenepos und Romanen und ihren Quellen. Zeitsch. fur roman. Phil. 1911, XXXIV
Revue Celt. Revue Celtique. Paris, 1870–
Rickert, E. Romances of Friendship, vol. I; Romances of Love, vol. II. London, 1908
Ritson, J. *AEMR.* Ancient English Metrical Romances. 3rd ed. London, 1802
Robson, J. Three Early English Metrical Romances. Camden Soc. Lond. 1842
Rom. Romania. Paris, 1872–
Rom. Rev. Romanic Review. New York, 1910–
Rom. Forsch. Romanische Forschungen. Erlangen, 1883–

Sallentien, V. Handel u. Verkehr in der altfrz. Literatur. *Roman. Forsch.* 1912, XXXI, 1–154
Savage, E. Old English Libraries. London, 1911
SATF. Société des anciens textes français. Paris, 1875–
Schepp, F. Altfrz. Sprichwörter und Sentenzen aus den höfischen Kunstepen. Diss. Greifswald, 1905
Schevill, R. Ovid and the Renascence in Spain. Univ. of California; Berkeley, Publications in Modern Philology, 1913, IV, 1–268
Schmidt, Fr. Das Reiten und Fahren in der altfrz. Litteratur. Diss. Göttingen, 1914
Schoepperle, G. Tristan and Isolt, A Study of the Sources of the Romance. Frankfurt a. M., London, 1913
Schofield, W. English Literature from the Norman Conquest to Chaucer. N. Y., 1906; Chivalry in English Literature. London, 1912
Schroetter, W. Ovid und die Troubadours. Halle, 1908
Schubert, C. Der Pflegesohn (Nourri) im frz. Heldenepos. Diss. Marburg, 1906
Siefkin, O. Das geduldige Weib. in der englischen Literatur bis auf Shakspere. I, Der Konstanzetypus. Diss. Leipzig, 1903

Soechtig, O.   Zur Technik altengl. Spielsmannsepen.   Leipzig, 1903
Soehring, O.   Werke bildender Kunst in altfrz. Epen.   Erlangen, 1900
Spence, L.   A Dictionary of Mediæval Romance and Romance Writers.   Lond.
    1913
Studies in Philology, University of North Carolina, N. C., 1906–
Studien zur Vergleichenden Literaturgeschichte.   Berlin, 1901–09
Suchier, H. und Birsch-Hirschfeld.   Geschichte der frz. Litteratur von den altesten
    Zeiten.   Leipzig. 1900–13

Thoms, W. J.   A Collection of Early Prose Romances.   Revised ed.   London,
    1907
Tilley, A.   Medieval France.   Cambridge, 1922

Voltmer, B.   Die mittelenglische Terminologie der ritterlichen Verwandtschafts
    u. Standesverhältnisse nach den höfischen Epen u. Romanzen des 13 u. 14
    Jahrhunderts.   Diss.   Kiel, 1911
Voretzsch, C.   Einführung in das Studium der altfrz. Literatur.   Halle, 1905, 13

Walker, T.   Die altfrz. Dichtungen vom Helden im Kloster.   Tübingen, 1910
Ward, H.   See British Museum Catalogue
Weber, H.   Metrical Romances of the XIII, XIV, and XV Centuries.   3 vols.
    Edinburgh, 1810
Webster, K. G.   The Twelfth Century Tourney.   Kittredge Anniversary Papers.
    Boston, 1913
Wells, J. E.   A *Manual* of Writings in Middle English.   1050–1400.   New Haven,
    1916; Supplement, 1919
Weston, J.   Chief Middle English Poets.   Boston, 1914; Three Days' Tourna-
    ment.   London, 1902
Wilmotte, M.   L'Evolution du Roman français aux Environs de 1150.   Acad.
    Royale de Belgique, Bulletin, 1903; De l'origine du roman en France la
    traduction antique et les éléments chrétiens du roman.   Paris, 1923
Witter, E.   Das bürgerliche Leben im mittelenglischen Versroman.   Diss.   Kiel,
    1912
Wöhlgemuth, F.   Riesen und Zwerge in den altfrz. erzählenden Dichtung.   Diss.
    Tübingen, 1906
Wood, M. M.   The Spirit of Protest in Old French Literature.   N. Y., 1917
Wülker, R.   Geschichte der englischen Literatur.   Leipzig, 1906–07

Zadi, E.   Der Trobadour Jaufre Rudel und das Motiv der Fernliebe in der Welt-
    literatur.   Diss.   Greifswald, 1920
Zeitschrift für deutsches Altertum und deutsche Litteratur.   Berlin, 1841–
Zeitschrift für französische Sprache und Litteratur. Oppeln, Leipzig, 1879–91,
    1891–
Zeitschrift für romanische Philologie   Halle, 1877–
Zeitschrift für vergleichende Literaturgeschichte.   Berlin, 1887–

INDEX OF MATTERS AND LITERATURE

The Index lists alphabetically all the references in this book to classical and mediaeval authors, to *motifs* and themes in mediaeval literature, to historical English personages, and to Middle English romances. All anonymous foreign literature or literature of doubtful attribution is indexed under the language in which it is written. For modern references here cited by the author's name only, see the preceding Table of Abbreviations and References.

I. AUTHOR'S NOTE

Thirty-five years have elapsed since the publication of *Medieval Romance in England*, a work now long out of print but still, according to the present publisher, in frequent demand. It is regularly cited in current bibliographies.

Scholars who reviewed the work, some of whose reviews are listed below, agreed in affirming its special value for the study of the sources and development of the thirty-nine non-cyclic romances discussed in it. With some minor exceptions, these discussions have stood the test of time.

Since 1924, however, the bibliography of the scholarship in this field has greatly increased. It was planned at first that full bibliographical lists of publications concerned with these particular romances should form a supplement to the new edition. These lists would employ the same form as that used in the first edition, and, being added to them, would constitute a complete guide to the literature of the subject up to the year 1959.

Reasons of health obliged the author to modify this plan, but she has sought to accomplish the same purpose by a somewhat novel method, that is, by giving specific references to the five standard bibliographies of medieval literature listed below. (See III). This method results in a comprehensive and co-ordinated bibliographical index for each romance. For the invaluable nine supplements to Wells' *Manual of Writings in Middle English*, which up to now have lacked a general index for additions to material originally included in the *Manual*, the new edition of *Medieval Romance* provides one for the non-cyclic romances with which it is concerned. It performs the same function for the same group in the annual bibliographies of Middle English in the *Publications of the Modern Language Association*.

The references noted *infra* for each romance indicate the

precise *volume* and/or *page* of the general bibliographies indexed. This mode of reference is followed invariably and so avoids the many variant systems of numbering, systems that at times are both cumbersome and confusing. Though the general bibliographies (III) inevitably repeat information, they often add to it by critical notes, by mention of book reviews, by cross references, and by corrections of earlier citations.

The romances themselves, grouped in other works under diverse headings, are here arranged in simple alphabetical order according to the personal name of the hero or heroine. Titles of rank, such as *King* or *Sir*, which appear so inconsistently in romance titles before the names of some heroes (*King Horn, Sir Orfeo*), and not of others, here follow the personal name. So, likewise, do such descriptive terms as *Le Bone* for *Florence of Rome*, or Lai (Lay) for such poems as *Lai le Freine* or the *Lay of Havelok*.

The system of bibliographical reference here employed does, it is true, leave the actual compilation of bibliographical information for any one of these romances to the reader, but he can be assured that if he follows up all the sources here indicated, his final citations will rest on five of the most widely used, expert, and persistent bibliographical efforts of our time.

II. REVIEWS OF *MEDIEVAL ROMANCE IN ENGLAND*

Modern Language Notes, XLI (1926), 406f., by Kemp Malone.

Journal of English and Germanic Philology, XXV (1926), 105-114, by Howard Patch.

Modern Philology, XXIV (1926-27), 122-24, by John M. Manly.

Folk-Lore, XXXVI (1925), 291-93, by M. Gaster.

Zeitschrift für romanische Philologie, XLVI (1926), 500, by Alfons Hilka.

Beiblatt zur Anglia, XXXVI (1925), 332-336, by Gustav Binz.

Saturday Review of Literature, Dec. 27, 1924, 1, 419. Anon.

Year's Work in English Studies, V (1926), 91f., by E. V. Gordon.

Modern Language Review, XX (1925), 339, by Cyril Brett.

III. GENERAL BIBLIOGRAPHIES

CBEL. *Cambridge Bibliography of English Literature*, I (600-1660 A.D.), ed. by F. W. Bateson, New York, Cambridge (England), 1941 (data to 1936); CBEL, V, Supplement, A.D. 600-1900 (data to 1955), ed. by George Watson, Cambridge (England).

MAN. *Manual of Writings in Middle English*, 1050-1400, by John E. Wells, New Haven, London, Oxford, 1916; Sixth Printing, 1937; Supplement (S) I (1919); II (1923); III (1926); IV (1929); V (1932); VI (1935); VII (1938); VIII (1941), cf. p. 1657 for issues of the *Manual* and its Supplements; IX (1951), with data to 1945, ed. by Beatrice Daw Brown, Eleanor K. Heningham, Francis Lee Utley. A thorough revision of the Manual and its Supplements is to be published. All issues have been published at New Haven, Conn. for the Connecticut Academy of Arts and Sciences, by the Yale University Press.

PMLA. *Publications of the Modern Language Association of America.* Its "American Bibliography" or "Annual Bibliography" under the heading "English Language and Literature" has annually devoted a section to Middle English. This began with vol. XLII (No. 1. 1927). "Bibliography for 1958" appears in vol. LXXIV (No. 2, 1959).

R & O Renwick, W. L. and Harold Orton, *The Beginnings of English Literature to Skelton, 1509*. Revised 2nd edition, London, 1952. Selective bibliographies and notes on the Middle English romances.

Bossuat Robert Bossuat, *Manuel Bibliographique de la Littérature Française du Moyen Age*, Melun, 1951; Supplement (S) for 1949-53. Paris, 1955.

346

IV. INDEX OF NON-CYCLIC ROMANCES AND BIBLIOGRAPHICAL REFERENCES (1926-1959)

Amadace (das), Sir. CBEL, I, 154-55; V, 116. *MAN*, p. 787; S, I, 1006; S, II, 1107; S, III, 1210; S, IV, 1302; S, V, 1390; S, VI, 1491; S, VII, 1608; S, VIII, 1706. R & O, pp. 387-88.

Amis and Amiloun. CBEL, I, 154; S, V, 116. *MAN*, p, 787; S, II, 1107; S, III, 1210; S, VI, 1491; S, VII, 1608; S, VIII, 1706; S, IX, 1899. *PMLA*, LII (I), 1234. R & O, p. 387. Bossuat, pp. 22-24; S, p. 22.

Apollonius of Tyre. CBEL, I, 94f. *MAN*, p. 784; S, I, 1006; S, II, 1106; S, III, 1209; S, V, 1389; S, VI, 1491; S, VIII, 1705; S, IX, 1898. R & O, pp. 383f. Bossuat, pp. 119f. *PMLA*, LXXIII (2), 150.

Athelston. CBEL, I, 150f; V, 115f. *MAN*, p. 766; S, II, 1101; S, III, 1205; S, IV, 1296; S, V, 1383; S, VI, 1485; S, VII, 1601. R & O, p. 358. *PMLA*, XLV (1), 21.

Beues of Hamtoun. CBEL, I, 150. *MAN*, p. 765f; S, I, 1003; S, II, 1101; S, III, 1205; S, V, 1382; S, VIII, 1700; S, IX, 1892. R & O, p. 357f. Bossuat, pp. 30-32; S, p. 23. *PMLA*, XLIV (1), 13 (under Dickson).

Breton Lais. CBEL, I, 151; V, 116. *MAN*, p. 783; S, I, 1006; S, II, 1106; S, III, 1209; S, IV, 1301; S, VI, 1490; S, VII, 1607; S, VIII, 1704. R & O, p. 381. Bossuat, pp. 144-46.

Chevalere Assigne. CBEL, I, 146; V, 115. *MAN*, p. 777; S, II, 1104; S, III, 1208; S, IV, 1299; S, V, 1387; S, VI, 1489; S, VII, 1605; S, VIII, 1703. R & O, p. 374. Bossuat, pp. 86-88; S, p. 34 (*Chevalier au Cygne* et de Godfrey de Bouillon).

Cleges (Sir). CBEL, I, 158; V, 116. *MAN*, p. 787; S, III, 1210; IV, 1302; V, 1390; VI, 1492; VIII, 1706. R & O, p. 388. *PMLA*, LIII, (S) 1233.

Degare (Sir). CBEL, I, 153; V, 116. *MAN*, p. 784; S, II, 1106; S, III, 1209; S, IV, 1302; S, V, 1389; S, VI, 1490; S, VII, 1607;

347

S, VIII, 1705. R & O, p. 382f. *PMLA*, XLVI (S), 1347; L (S), 1250; LXXI (2), 132.

Degrevant (Sir). *CBEL*, I, 158; V, 116. *MAN*, p. 785; S, I, 1006; S, II, 1107; S, III, 1209; S, VI, 1491. R & O, p. 384.

Earl of Toulous. *CBEL*, I, 153. *MAN*, p. 784; S, I, 1006; S, II, 1107; S, III, 1209; S, VI, 1490. R & O, p. 383.

Eger (Sir), Sir Grime and Greysteel. *CBEL*, I, 160; V, 117. *MAN*, S, V, 1382 (No. 762); S, VI, 1484; S, VII, 1600. *PMLA*, XLVI (1), 1346; XLVIII (S), 1311; LII (S), 1237.

Eglamour of Artois (Sir). *CBEL*, I, 157. *MAN*, p. 781; S, I, 1005; S, III, 1208; S, IV, 1301; S, VI, 1490. R & O, p. 379.

Emare. *CBEL*, I, 152. *MAN*, p. 783; S, III, 1209; S, V, 1389; S, VI, 1490; S, VIII, 1705. R & O, p. 382.

Florence of Rome (Le Bone). *CBEL*, I, 158; *MAN*, p. 782; S, II, 1106; S, III, 1209; S, IV, 1301; S, VI, 1490. R & O, p. 380. Bossuat, p. 127.

Floris and Blauncheflur. *CBEL*, I, 153f. *MAN*, p. 785; S, I, 1006; S, II, 1106; S, III, 1209; S, IV, 1302; S, V, 1389; S, VIII, 607; S, IX, 1898. R & O, p. 384. Bossuat, pp. 125-27; S, p. 39.

Freine, Lai le. *CBEL*, I, 151f. *MAN*, p. 783; S, II, 1106; S, III, 1209; S, IV, 1301; S, V, 1389; S, VIII, 1705. R & O, p. 381. Bossuat, p. 143; S, p. 37.

Gamelyn, Tale of. *CBEL*, I, 151; V, 116. *MAN*, p. 766; S, III, 1205; S, IV, 1296; S, V, 1383; S, VI, 1485; S, VIII, 1700; S, IX, 1892. R & O, p. 359. *PMLA*, LXVII (3), 25.

Generydes. *CBEL*, I, 159. *MAN*, p. 785; S, III, 1209; S, VI, 1491. 1392-95.
R & O, p. 384f.

Gowther (Sir). *CBEL*, I, 153; V, 116. *MAN*, p. 784; S, I, 1006; S, II, 1106; III, 1209; S, V, 1389; S, VI, 1490; S, VII, 1607; S, VIII, 1705; S, IX, 1898. R & O, p. 383. Bossuat, pp. 131f; p. 145 (No. 1542).

Guy of Warwick. *CBEL*, I, 149; V, 115. *MAN*, p. 764f.; S, I, 1003; S, II, 1101; S, III, 1204; S, IV, 1296; S, V, 1382; S, VI, 1484; S, VII, 1601; S, VIII, 1699; S, IX, 1892. R & O, p. 355f. Bossuat, p. 128f. *PMLA*, XLVI (S), 1346.

348

Havelok, Lay of. CBEL, I, 148f.; V, 115. *MAN,* p. 763; S, I, 1003; S, II, 1100; S, III, 1204; S, IV, 1296; S, V, 1382; S, VI, 1484; S, VII, 1600; S, VIII, 1699; S, IX, 1892. R & O, p. 354f. Bossuat, p. 53 (Cf. No. 523); S, p. 145 (No. 1544). *PMLA,* LXXII (2), 194.

Horn (King). CBEL, I, 147; V, 115. *MAN,* p. 762f; S, I, 1003; S, II, 1100; S, III, 1204; S, IV, 1295; S, V, 1382; S, VI, 1484; S, VII, 1600; S, VIII, 1699; S, IX, 1892. R & O, p. 352f. Bossuat, p. 53. *PMLA,* XLV (1), 24; XLVI (S), 1346; LXXIII (2), 152.

Horn Childe and Maiden Rimnild. CBEL, I, 148. *MAN,* p. 763; S, II, 1100; S, III, 1204; S, IV, 1296; S, VI, 1484. R & O, p. 353. Bossuat, p. 53 (No. 524).

Ipomadon. CBEL, I, 155. *MAN,* p. 785; S, I, 1006; S, II, 1107; S, III, 1210; S, IV, 1302; S, V, 1389; S, VI, 1491; S, VII, 1607; S, VIII, 1705; S. IX, 1898. R & O, p. 385. Bossuat, p. 110f.

Isumbras (Sir). CBEL, I, 156f. *MAN,* p. 781; S, I, 1005; S, III, 1208; S, IV, 1301; S, VIII, 1704, R & O, p. 379. *PMLA,* XLVIII, (S), 1311.

King of Tars. CBEL, I, 154; V, 116. *MAN,* p. 782; S, II, 1106; S, III, 1209; S, VIII, 1704. IX, 1898. R & O, p. 380. *PMLA,* LVI (S), 1226; LVIII, (S, Pt. 2), 1205; LXIV (2), 21.

Knight of Curtesy. CBEL, I, 160. *MAN,* p. 787; S, I, 1006; S, III, 1210; S, V, 1390. R & O, p. 387. Bossuat, p. 111f. (No. 1161-76).

Lai or Lay. See *Freine, Havelok.*

Miscellaneous Romances. *CBEL,* I, 153-160; V, 116f. *MAN,* 784-788.

Non-Cyclic Romances. *CBEL,* I, 147-160; V, 115-16.

Octovian. CBEL, I, 156. *MAN,* p. 782; S, II, 1106; S, III, 1208; S, IV, 1301; S, V, 1388; S, VI, 1490; S, VII, 1607. R & O, p. 379f.; Bossuat, p. 39. *PMLA,* LXX (2), 128.

Orfeo (Sir). CBEL, I, 151f; V, 116. *MAN,* p. 783; S, I, 1006; S, II, 1106; S, III, 1209; S, IV, 1301; S, V, 1389, S, VII, 1607; S, VIII, 1705. R & O, p. 381. *PMLA,* LI, (S), 1225; LXXIV (2), 121.

Parthenope of Blois. CBEL, I, 159; V, 116f. *MAN,* p. 785; S, II, 1107; S, III, 1209; S, IV, 1302; S, VI, 1491; S, VIII, 1705. R & O, p. 385. Bossuat, p. 130f; S, p. 39. *PMLA,* XLIII (1), 14; LX (S, 2), 1206; LXI (S), 1289; LXIII (S, 2), 34.

Reinbrun. MAN, S, IX, 1782, 1892 (under *Guy of Warwick*)

Richard Coer de Lyon. CBEL, I, 150; V, 115. *MAN*, p. 786; S, I, 1006; S, II, 1107; S, III, 1210; S, IV, 1302; S, V, 1389; S, VI, 1491; S, VII, 1608; S, VIII, 1706; S, IX, 1898. R & O, p. 386. *PMLA*, LXI (S), 1237; LXXI (2), 132.

Roberd of Cisyle. CBEL, I, 157; V, 116. *MAN*, p. 788; S, I, 1006; S, III, 1210; S, V, 1390; S, VI, 1492; S, IX, 1899. R & O, p. 388.

Roswall and Lillian. CBEL, I, 160.

Seven Sages of Rome. CBEL, I, 155; V, 116. *MAN*, p. 792: S, I, 1007; S,II, 1109; S, III, 1211; S, IV, 1302; S, V, 1391; S, VI, 1492; S, VII, 1609; S, VIII, 1707. R & O, p. 399f. Bossuat, p. 132f.; S, p. 40 (*Sept Sages de Rome*). *PMLA*, LII (S), 1238.

Sir. See*Amadace, Beues, Cleges, Degare, Degrevant, Eger, Eglamour, Gowther, Isumbras, Orfeo, Torrent, Triamour.*

Squyr of Lowe Degre. CBEL, I, 159f. *MAN*, p. 786; S, III, 1210; S, V, 1389; S, VI, 1491. R & O, p. 385.

Torrent of Portyngale (Sir). CBEL, I, 159. *MAN*, p. 782; S, II, 1105; S, III, 1208; S, VI, 1490. R & O, p. 379.

Triamour (Sir). CBEL, I, 159. *MAN*, p. 782; S, III, 1208; S, V, 1389; S, VI, 1490; S, VIII, 1704. R & O, p. 380.

William of Palerne. CBEL, I, 156. *MAN*, p. 765; S, I, 1003; S, II, 1101; S, III, 1204f.; S, IV, 1296; S, V, 1382; S, VI, 1484; S, VII, 1601; S, VIII, 1699; S, IX, 1783. *PMLA*, XLII (1), 16; XLIII, 16. Bossuat, p. 129f. S, p. 39.